THE END

FROM GLORY TO A WHOLE NEW BALL GAME, EVERTON 1985-1994

GAVIN BUCKLAND

First published by Toffeeopolis in 2024.

First Edition

Toffeeopolis, Mount Vernon Publishing Group,
71-75 Shelton Street, Covent Garden, London, WC2H 9JQ.
www.toffeeopolis.com

Toffeeopolis is a collective of Evertonians that operates as an imprint of
Mount Vernon Publishing Group.

ISBN: 978-1-917064-02-6 | ISBN: 978-1-917064-07-1 (Softback)

A CIP catalogue record for this book is available from the British Library.

Cover design and typeset by Thomas Regan at Milkyone Creative.

Photos: Alamy

CONTENTS

PREFACE

THE END WAS NOT SUPPOSED TO BE LIKE THIS. MORE THAN THIRTY years after John Moores walked into Goodison Park with the avowed intention of making Everton the most powerful and successful club in the land, they were within minutes of suffering relegation after forty years in the top flight. The Mersey Millionaires were now the Mersey Mediocrities.

The End, the third and final book on Moores' time in L4, traces the final years of his dynasty as the club moves from huge success to skirting dangerously with the drop, while boardroom lethargy and indecision leave Everton falling behind their so-called peers as a new vision for domestic football takes shape.

Such an eventuality had seemed remote in May 1985. Crowned champions of England and, in the eyes of many – and not just their supporters – unofficial kings of Europe, Howard Kendall was intent on making that title official twelve months later. But the club ended up as collateral damage in the crossfire between the English football authorities and UEFA during the fallout from the Heysel disaster. Shorn of European football, the Toffees continued to trade punches with Liverpool as the two clubs rubber-stamped their supremacy in the most intense and dominant rivalry seen in this country up until that point.

But then the equilibrium was disturbed when the club's most successful manager swapped the Goodison dugout for northern Spain in a shock move to Athletic Bilbao. The first cracks in the edifice appeared and then quickly widened as Colin Harvey added more evidence to one of football's oldest axioms: that all managers can coach, but not all coaches can manage. With increasing amounts of money in the game only adding to the pressures of the job, one of the club's greatest sons ultimately fell short.

What happened next stretched the boundaries of belief. With expectations that Joe Royle would be striding into the executive lounges at Goodison, a former team-mate renewed marriage vows accompanied by his predecessor in the job. But in his second coming Kendall found a club losing its way on and off the pitch. As the old guard had all but disappeared, he was not alone in finding the latest generation of players were cut from a different cloth and management methods so effective a decade before were now all but obsolete. With Kendall and the club running out of both options and money, like Harvey he proved the wisdom of one of the game's adages, in his case that you should never go back. Although there was far more to his departure than met the eye.

While Kendall's second spell ended in disappointment, the departure of chairman Philip Carter reduced both boardroom business acumen and the club's influence on the wider game. Everton had been one of the initiators of the Premier League, yet by the time of its take-off the Big Five had arguably lost a member. Meanwhile the death of Moores in September 1993, plus a family largely ambivalent towards the club, set the ball rolling for a damaging and long-running battle for ownership between a consortium headed by Bill Kenwright and former Liverpool season-ticket holder Peter Johnson.

But off-the-pitch issues were merely an executive sideshow to a battle for survival overseen by Mike Walker, parachuted in at not-inconsiderable cost from Norwich City. The 'Silver Fox' watched on as a group of players lost confidence and games in equal measure while the threat of the drop reached the footballing equivalent of DEFCON 2.

Consequently, by the time the 1993/94 season concluded, Evertonians were saying farewell to not only one of the most demanding campaigns in memory but to the Moores era itself. One of the most influential individuals in post-war football passed away when the English game was on the cusp of previously untold riches. As this volume will show, the irony was the club were in no position to reap the benefits. That said, because of his approach to the game documented in *Money Can't Buy Us Love*, *Boys from the Blue Stuff* and now *The End*, the great man would still have watched the corporate powerplay and largesse on show with approval.

1

AND THE BANNED
PLAYED ON

BY THE END OF MAY 1985 HOWARD KENDALL'S EVERTON WERE NOT only the best team in England, but the finest in Europe. Following one of the most dominant campaigns in domestic history, the Toffees had romped to the First Division title with five games to spare, eventually finishing thirteen points ahead of their closest rivals. Although Manchester United thwarted the quest for a rare domestic double in the FA Cup final, Everton had showed potential for true greatness in the European Cup Winners' Cup. After a memorable aggregate victory over German giants Bayern Munich in the semi-final, the magnificent performance during a 3-1 triumph over Rapid Vienna in the final drew comparison with the finest post-war English teams. 'Everton under Mr Kendall seem capable of winning all the competitions they are in,' Bayern boss Udo Lattek said later. 'They are super fit and almost superhuman in their search for success.'

The individual strengths of Kendall's well-oiled machine were manifest. Neville Southall was one of the best goalkeepers on the planet; the resolute defence, led by skipper Kevin Ratcliffe, contained pace, power, and endurance. The Scottish striking duo of Graeme Sharp and Andy Gray may have been physical but possessed enough cunning and goalscoring prowess to trouble the best defenders. Prior to his unfortunate injury in December 1984, Adrian Heath was their antithesis, a diminutive and nimble forward who scored goals and made things happen for others. Nevertheless, the middle of the park transformed Kendall's side from a very good team to a potentially great one. Peter Reid and Paul Bracewell's relentless pressing denied the opposition oxygen and, in possession, the former's constant probing was complemented perfectly by his partner's flawless passing. On the left Kevin Sheedy opened out the pitch, his left foot a thing of wonder: the source of perfectly delivered crosses and beautifully crafted goals. On the opposite flank Trevor Steven combined balletic balance and rare individual skill with an eye for goal. Few quartets have contained more of the special mix of ingredients required for the perfect midfield. Beneath the team's exterior was a resilience and competitive desire possessed by only the finest.

With Kendall and Colin Harvey providing the right combination of leadership, man-management and top-class coaching off the pitch, those Everton fans returning from the Netherlands looked upon the mauling of Rapid Vienna as merely a dress rehearsal for the main act – an assault on the European Cup and the long-awaited chance to establish the club as a continental power. Brian Clough was commentating on the final in Rotterdam and asked at the end, 'On that performance, how long is this team going to rule Europe?' The answer was a fortnight. Events across the Dutch border meant Howard Kendall's Everton were the best European champions English football never had.

Heysel horror

The deaths of 39 spectators ensured that the 1985 European Cup final, between Liverpool and Juventus at the Heysel Stadium, Brussels remains one football's darkest days. The catastrophe was the latest in a long list of violent incidents involving English clubs and

FA chairman Bert Millichip (right) and FA secretary Ted Croker at Bradford City's Valley Parade ground, where 56 people died following a fire in early May 1985. By the end of the month things were to get even worse.

the national team over the previous decade-and-a-half, blighting both the reputation of the sport and the country.

The list of shame is too long to cover in full. Lowlights include, in 1974, Tottenham Hotspur fans fighting with police and Feyenoord supporters in the same De Kuip stadium where Everton lifted the Cup Winners' Cup eleven years later. Upwards of 200 people were injured. In September 1983 the fans of both clubs renewed hostilities in the UEFA Cup and later that season a Tottenham supporter was shot dead in Brussels. Leeds United were banned from Europe after their followers laid waste to the Parc de Princes after the 1975 European Cup final. Two years later Manchester United were lucky not to suffer the same fate when their fans rioted in Saint-Étienne, with the second leg of their Cup Winners' Cup tie moved to Home Park, Plymouth. West Ham United were forced to play the second leg of their 1980 Cup Winners' Cup tie against Castilla behind closed doors after trouble in their away end at the Bernabéu. In chaotic scenes more than fifty fans were ejected and, during fighting after the game, one was killed by a bus outside the ground.

Two years later Aston Villa fans rioted at Anderlecht in their European Cup semi-final, resulting in forty arrests and 26 injured. During the aftermath, with fans of the national team having wreaked havoc in places like Luxembourg, Copenhagen, Turin, Paris and Basel, UEFA spokesman René Eberle warned: 'There is a feeling in Europe that enough is enough. There are lots of options open to us, from cautions and fines to the exclusion of clubs.' Not for nothing was hooliganism known at the 'English disease' on the continent. Although other countries like West Germany and the Netherlands possessed troublemakers, nobody else exported violence. It was against that backdrop of more than a decade of trouble – and the fact hooliganism held a regular place on the front and back pages – that the English authorities and their international counterparts were operating in the aftermath of Heysel.

30 May 1985

Within 24 hours of the final, FA chairman Bert Millichip and secretary Ted Croker were flying home from Mexico, where England were playing an end-of-season tour, on the orders of the Prime Minister, Margaret Thatcher. After arriving at the association's Lancaster Gate headquarters, the pair spoke with Arthur McMullen, vice-chairman of the FA, and Jack Dunnett, president of the Football League. Croker had been on the UEFA disciplinary committee for a decade and knew exactly how European colleagues would react, so he and Millichip provisionally agreed a plan to withdraw English clubs from

UEFA competitions for the following campaign. Dunnett rejected the proposal as prejudging the UEFA response. 'I felt that if we didn't announce we were withdrawing, the punishment meted out by UEFA later would be much more severe,' Croker revealed in his memoir, *The First Voice You Will Hear Is*.

31 May 1985

'Quarantine our sad, sick game,' proclaimed a *Guardian* editorial two days after Heysel, reflecting the view of most of the population who were disgusted by the scenes in Belgium and over previous years. During the morning, Liverpool announced their withdrawal from the following season's UEFA Cup. After talks with Thatcher, Millichip and Croker told the press on the doorstep of 10 Downing Street that all English clubs would be withdrawn from European competition. Croker added: 'It is now up to English football to put its house in order.' Although there was general support from clubs, the Football League claimed the decision was unnecessary and taken 'in an emotional atmosphere'. But as David Miller pithily responded in *The Times*, 'How many dead, it had to be asked, are needed to make it necessary?'

At Goodison there was understandable frustration. 'I just hope there is a change of heart within the next few weeks,' remarked Kendall, 'We worked hard all season to finish top of the League with the reward of a European Cup place. We were looking forward to it after a successful campaign on and off the field in the Cup-Winners' Cup.' Secretary Jim Greenwood attacked the timing of the ruling, commenting: 'We feel it would have been sensible for our FA to follow the same course as UEFA rather than be pressurised into what could prove to be an irrational decision at a time when emotions are running high.'

2 June 1985

With the ball now in their court, UEFA were expected to wait until July to pass judgement, but president Jacques Georges called an executive meeting at a day's notice. Unsurprisingly, Europe's governing body banished English clubs from their competitions 'for an indefinite period of time'. Three years earlier UEFA warned that, if hooliganism continued 'the punishments will get stiffer and stiffer, until the only solution is to kick out British clubs.' Now they were as good as their word. English football could not say it had not been warned. 'English clubs are having to pay the price of so-called supporters who come simply to plunder and kill,' Georges admitted. 'We are not talking just about the odd rocket or firework, but about those people who will end up setting fire to the entire stadium and burning the spectators alive.' As an additional sanction, Liverpool were subsequently banned for a further three years. Already considering legal action, Everton chairman Philip Carter responded: 'I think it is a bit premature for me to be saying anything about this announcement. I would rather wait and let the dust settle for a few days.'

The open-ended nature of the ban was not helpful, but the consensus was it could mean anything from two to five years. Meanwhile, the press, from red-top tabloid to stuffy broadsheet, were supportive of UEFA's actions. 'Europe is in no mood to play host to guests who can always guarantee to get drunk, break up homes, rob innocent citizens, insult everyone in sight and who have now shown that they can kill people,' Frank McGhee wrote in the *Daily Mirror*. Within hours, talks started between banned clubs over hosting a tournament in Saudi Arabia to generate alternative revenue.

6 June 1985

Those plans stalled because four days later FIFA announced a worldwide ban on English clubs. Largely derided as disproportionate because matches outside of Europe attracted few domestic fans, were very lucrative and trouble-free, the decision was reversed five weeks later. As another concession, English clubs remained free to play friendlies in Europe.

28 June 1985

With Liverpool having already withdrawn and Tottenham accepting the ban, the remaining four English clubs affected – Everton, Manchester United, Southampton and Norwich – took their case against the FA, UEFA, and FIFA to the High Court. They argued the ban was a restraint of trade which would have 'extremely serious consequences for football clubs and professional footballers in England'.

They were hardly reading the room. In a political and public climate demanding English football should serve an extended period of penance, the move was widely vilified. 'They [the four clubs] should accept it without squealing,' cried a *Daily Mirror* editorial 24 hours later, before adding, 'It is sometimes said clubs get the fans they deserve. If the four go ahead with their legal action tomorrow, it will look as if they have got the chairmen they deserve too.' Croker himself admitted, 'I was surprised to receive this request from the clubs. I thought most people, in and out of football, had agreed the time had come for a year out of Europe.'

Unsurprisingly, Mr Justice Vinecott threw out their case, arguing the FA had the right to not nominate teams and it was 'fanciful' that UEFA and FIFA would accept an English court order in any case. He also observed that escalating the challenge to the Swiss courts may have a damaging effect on rehabilitation. The judge's summing up is the definitive view on the subject. 'I need hardly add that the feelings of shame Mr Croker referred to must have been felt by every Englishman who viewed on the TV screen or read later about these events,' Vinecott remarked, before concluding 'that everything should be done and plainly seen to be done to ensure events as dreadful as this should never occur again.'

Out

Vinecott's closing statement is the crux of the immediate post-Heysel world. Zero tolerance towards English clubs in Europe was the only way such scenes could be avoided in the immediate future. As David Miller wrote, 'Football has come to the end of its credibility as a public event...Britain is viewed worldwide as little more than a zoo of dangerous animals, which are released upon innocent foreign cities.'

Furthermore, a key issue was the involvement of Liverpool supporters, after two decades of relatively good conduct. Rightly or wrongly, this convinced authorities that any English club's followers were a potential source of trouble. Previous unblemished behaviour did not guarantee the same in future. Yes, those who felt like innocent scapegoats – such as Everton – could feel aggrieved, but UEFA were not punishing English clubs as individual entities, the organisation was placing a strait-jacket on them to force authorities into finding a solution whilst eliminating the possibility of another Heysel. Everton supporters may have argued that good behaviour in Rotterdam earned the club an exemption, but earlier in the season UEFA security experts warned of the risk of trouble if the final was against Celtic, who were later knocked out by the beaten finalists, but only after crowd trouble at Parkhead necessitated a third game at Old Trafford. Unhappiness was still the prevailing mood at Goodison. 'We feel we've been robbed of an opportunity our players had earned and deserved,' Kendall admitted. To make matters worse, clubs abroad regretted Everton's absence. A Juventus spokesman said, 'Without the English, it will be a hollow triumph for whoever wins it this time.' Terry Venables, who had just taken Barcelona to the Spanish title, was equally apologetic. 'It's crazy that Howard and his team should be excluded for something that was not their fault,' he said.

However, the main problem was the diktat was open-ended. The unofficial deal with the English authorities was 'show us your fans can be trusted and we will reconsider the ban.' Yet the following years showed very few lessons had been learned. One of the many inconsistencies of the whole process was the edict did not cover the England national team, even though their followers had been the source of some of the worst violence. Not uncoincidentally, the original self-imposed twelve-month ban by the FA would not have affected the national side if extended to them, as they had played all their away qualifying games for the 1986 World Cup. Therefore, one of the more unedifying aspects of the whole affair was Ted Croker schmoozing the UEFA executives in Paris during August 1985 to ensure England could take part in the qualifying matches for the next European Championship, three months after placing a ban on clubs playing in competitions abroad. Given the national team was the FA's greatest asset, there was an element of hypocrisy and self-interest at play.

Predictably the continuing loutish behaviour of England fans largely ensured UEFA were in no rush to reintroduce their clubs to European competition. There were thirty arrests at the away game against West Germany in September 1987. Violence erupted during the England-Scotland encounter at Wembley in the following spring when there were 99 arrests inside the ground. Ninety fans received treatment for injuries with trouble continuing in the London Underground and West End afterwards. At that year's European Championship in West Germany it was even worse. Over five nights of violence the arrest tally amongst England supporters reached 400 but that told only half the story. 'The damage the English have done is measurable not by a head count of injuries,' Ed Vuillamy noted in the *Guardian,* 'but by the sheer hostility and exhaustion caused among those who encountered the bellowing mobs.' The forlorn campaign by the FA to return English clubs to Europe was doomed to failure. Tellingly, the organisation turned down an opportunity to host the 1992 European Championship because, significantly, they could not guarantee the safety of spectators. The European ban was only lifted, of course, after Italia '90.

However, there have been many misleading narratives about the five-year exclusion. One being that it was government-led and somehow seen, with no little imagination, as an attack on the city and working class, which is completely wide of the mark. Margaret Thatcher could no more ban clubs from playing in Europe as she could stop British athletes going to the 1980 Olympics in Moscow, a much higher profile event, which they eventually attended against the wishes of the government. FA secretary Ted Croker was a politically adept and authoritative figure, who was more than capable of fighting his corner. Indeed, Croker's robust opposition to some government-led initiatives – such as identity cards for fans – probably deprived him of the knighthood awarded to his predecessors. 'Mrs Thatcher behaved…in a bullish, almost hectoring fashion, giving the impression she thought football was responsible for these tragic events through negligence,' he wrote in his 1987 memoir about the post-Heysel meetings. 'She seemed to have no feeling for the game whatsoever...I was left with the feeling that she would not have thought it a loss to the social scene if football was stopped altogether.'

The absence affected all the major cities in the country, not just Liverpool, and some of those clubs who suffered, like Oxford United and Norwich City, were hardly bastions of working-class culture. If the ban was a government attack on the lower classes then it was a spectacularly ineffective plan to put millions in their place by stopping, in most cases, a few thousand travelling abroad a couple of times a year while at the same time any troublemakers among them were free to go on foreign holidays or wreak havoc with the national team, which is what happened. The irony being that a significant number of hooligans were of middle-class background. However, the government's rationale for intervention – that English hooligans running amok damaged the country's reputation – was completely understandable.

Ultimately then, there were only two parties who could influence any decision: UEFA and English football supporters. The problem with the carrot-and-stick approach – the ban could be lifted if fans of the national team behaved – was the assumption that the majority held allegiance to affected clubs and therefore had an incentive to keep the peace. That was not the case. Given the large number of names of lower-division clubs on flags abroad over the years, the fans involved in violence faced few consequences for their behaviour. Indeed, as the domestic game sped towards generating an unpopular and self-serving wealthy elite, extending the ban was an unexpected benefit for the hooligan element who brought so much shame to the sport and country.

2

GARY'S GOODISON LINKS

AWAY FROM THE FALLOUT OVER HEYSEL, THERE WAS STILL A footballing business to manage. In early summer 1985, Gary Lineker was out of contract at Leicester City yet, curiously for a player with 77 goals during the previous three campaigns, there was ambivalence among England's top clubs towards the forward. Tottenham were rumoured to be interested but elsewhere there was silence, so much so that Jon Holmes, Lineker's agent, ended up contacting Ron Atkinson, as Manchester United was the striker's preference. But the United manager was going on holiday and chairman Martin Edwards later phoned Holmes to say that as Frank Stapleton had turned down a move to Bordeaux, they could not take a deal forward.[1] During the previous season, Gordon Milne, Leicester manager and a former Liverpool player, had tipped off Bob Paisley, his counterpart at Anfield. Yet Liverpool, despite scouting Lineker several times and holding brief talks, did not come in.

So why was there an element of doubt? Lineker was a 24-year-old late developer. There were weaknesses: he was poor with his back to goal and tended to go to ground too easily. Lineker's attitude towards training was notoriously casual. 'You could look at Gary in those days and think, "Well you know, maybe he scores goals, but he hasn't got much more to go with it,"' Milne later admitted. Manchester United, with all their wealth, could easily afford Lineker and the Stapleton aspect was probably a smokescreen. Liverpool's failure to bid was probably because Ian Rush and Lineker had similar attributes. With Tottenham silent – 'I've seen him play 17 games for you and he's scored 14 goals, but I can't see what's in him,' their manager Peter Shreeves told Milne – and Arsenal showing no interest, only one club remained as a viable option.

During Everton's turgid performance in the FA Cup final, Manchester United played a high line, knowing full well that with Andy Gray and Graeme Sharp there was no option

---

[1] This was the second time Manchester United had missed an opportunity to sign Lineker. In 1978 legendary coach Jimmy Murphy strongly recommended him to Dave Sexton but the United boss took no further action.

of knocking the ball over the top. The squad lacked somebody with sustained speed and Kendall was attracted to Lineker's pace over distance. After Adrian Heath was injured the previous December, the Everton boss watched Lineker several times and, although he always denied a move was in the offing, Kendall had a bid turned down before the March transfer deadline. Three months later, with United and Liverpool prevaricating, Kendall spoke with the England international[2] and after a second meeting, at the Coventry Post House hotel on Saturday, 22 June, a deal was struck.

At his welcoming press conference, Lineker showed a flair for public relations which would assist him later in his own media career. 'Everton have always been my number one club,' he told the attending press, which was not strictly true. 'After last season's success, I was tempted to leave things as they were,' Kendall admitted, 'but it's not every day that a player of Lineker's class becomes available. He is a proven scorer at every level, right up to the international scene.' The only outstanding issue was the fee: Lineker was out of contract and the case went to a tribunal. With Everton offering £400,000 and Leicester wanting £1 million, its verdict was £800,000. 'You don't know how good he is,' Milne informed Kendall afterwards. 'It wasn't just him, it's the reminder he'll give to the rest,' the Everton boss warned.

Nevertheless, by not leaving things as they were, the Everton manager was creating a problem, with five strikers effectively chasing two starting places. Heath was expected to return from injury for the start of the season, while recent arrival Paul Wilkinson had scored two goals, including a derby winner at Goodison. Consequently, the two threatened by Lineker were Gray and Sharp. The latter always believed Kendall did not rate him and on the day of the FA Cup final against Manchester United the *Daily Mirror* reported that the March deadline bid for Lineker had failed over possible complications involving Sharp in exchange. Even though the Scot had scored thirty goals during the campaign, his future was uncertain. With a reported price tag of £700,000, within 48 hours of Lineker's transfer both Arsenal and Spurs made inquiries.

That said, Gray was ultimately sacrificed. The striker went to see Kendall at Bellefield before the summer break over his future, with the manager telling him: 'I think you underestimate yourself Andy, there's always a place for good players at Everton.'[3] Yet four days later Kendall turned up at Gray's new home to tell him that Aston Villa had

---

[2]   Only after Leicester manager Gordon Milne had tracked Lineker down to snooker player Willie Thorne's club in Leicester.

[3]   Perhaps the Everton manager was being economical with the truth. Jon Holmes told the journalist Colin Malam for his 1993 biography of the England player, *Strikingly Different*, that Kendall had informed him, 'Andy Gray's going to go because he's not actually doing it away from home. It's the right time for him to make a move.'

the indications are that she appreciates that the problem is too big to be left to football,' Kelly said. 'The dreadful events at Luton, Birmingham[4] and Brussels have shown that something had to be done. How terrible that it should have come about this way.' The other initiative on the government's agenda was more controversial: identity cards for supporters. The widely-held viewpoint at the time was that the initiative was too bureaucratic and, in more primitive technological times, impracticable. Police also felt it had little relevance to the fight against hooliganism.

Yet some did not welcome the intervention. 'I'm sick and tired of reading about European bans, proclamations from governments and statements from people who don't understand the feeling in our game,' Howard Kendall argued in the *Sunday Mirror* before the season's start, 'For goodness' sake, let's get on with our football, I have a team bursting to play now.' After a pre-season tour to Canada, his side kicked off the new campaign at a sun-drenched Wembley against Manchester United in the Charity Shield. For the first time supporters could see the champions wearing their new blue and white kit – literally those two colours as the shirt-front was notoriously half-white, half-blue. To say there was a mixed response would be an understatement. 'I echo the thoughts of many Everton supporters as I protest at yet another new Everton kit,' the legendary local radio presenter Billy Butler commented in the *Liverpool Echo*, 'It's on two points that the fans are angry. After 100 years of being the Blues, we are now the Blues and Whites! The famous all royal blue shirt which has graced so many famous players has gone – all that tradition thrown away for financial gain.' The fiscal benefit Butler referred to was from the shirt parading the name of the new club sponsors, Japanese electronics giants NEC. The deal was worth £500,000 over three years.

At Wembley the release of 2,000 red and blue balloons created an almost carnival atmosphere and thankfully, with the sport on trial – 'The most important season in the history of the Football League,' according to Jimmy Hill – the 82,000 spectators were well-behaved. On the pitch the title favourites quickly found their groove during a 2-0 victory through goals from Trevor Steven and, as a bonus, returning substitute Adrian Heath, whose mullet haircut and blond highlights would not have looked out of place at the Live Aid concert in the stadium the previous month. 'Everton seem more than ever the team for the second half of the '80s, as their neighbours dominated the last ten years,' Steve Curry wrote in the *Daily Express*.

---

[4]   Referring to the Millwall supporters' riot at Luton in March 1985 and the death of a Leeds fan at Birmingham City on the same day as the fire at Bradford two months later.

The two-sided triangle

Amazingly, given their imperious performance at Wembley, the Toffees were only joint-favourites, at 3-1, with Liverpool and Manchester United, for the title. Seven days later, though, the opening day showed why only Liverpool in the previous 25 years had been able to defend the crown. Fate decreed that the champions were sent to Lineker's former club but his successor stole the show. Mark Bright had netted 28 goals in 27 reserve games during the previous campaign and, after Derek Mountfield fired the dominant visitors ahead, the youngster scored twice in the second period as the home side triumphed 3-1.

Lineker – serenaded by chants of 'what a waste of money' by the home support – enjoyed a quiet game and force of habit dictated the striker accidentally walked into the Leicester dressing room at half-time. Remarkably it was the first occasion Everton had lost an away league game after leading during Kendall's four-year tenure. The only bright spot on a chastening afternoon was that, with supporters' behaviour under scrutiny, there were no arrests among the 3,000 travelling fans.

Three days later, with Graeme Sharp failing a fitness test, Heath was back in the starting XI for the home game against West Brom and struck twice in a 2-0 victory. The crowd favourite's return only complicated Kendall's thinking about his best front pairing, which was the main talking point throughout the opening months. When Sharp was dropped for Heath before the away game at Spurs on August Bank Holiday Monday, a flashpoint was inevitable, especially as Lineker's first Everton goal in a 1-0 victory cemented his own first-team place. Meanwhile Sharp was banished to the reserves at Hull City. 'I'm very upset at being left out as I don't think I deserved it,' he declared, 'The boss made it clear he thinks Gary and Adrian are the best partnership and it doesn't look good at all, so I may have to move.' But the claim was ignored by his manager. 'There is no way it is cut and dried, as Graeme has put out,' Kendall remarked, 'Players react sometimes, saying things on the spur of the moment which possibly is not in keeping with what happens in the long term.' The manager, though, did show some understanding: 'It was a very hard decision. It is not a pleasant task having to tell a player who always gives his very best that he is being omitted.'

Sharp remained on the substitute's bench for the visit of Birmingham City five days later, when Lineker netted a hat-trick in a 4-1 victory. But when the Scot was recalled for the trip to a physically challenging Sheffield Wednesday outfit, it was Heath's turn to be both substitute and upset. 'I don't feel I should have been left out,' he said, 'I felt good and I want to play. I can't afford to be sitting waiting.' With both players out of contract at the end of the campaign, warming the bench hardly improved their bargaining position. At Hillsborough, the visitors were irresistible, pummelling the home side 5-1 after conceding an early penalty before striding off to a standing ovation. 'Everton proved they were true champions last night, producing a memorable performance dripping with style and class,' was Tim Taylor's view in the *Daily Express*.

Although not on the scoresheet, Sharp played selflessly and was a perfect foil for Lineker, yet Kendall dropped the striker again for the home match against Luton. 'The Heath-Lineker partnership has still to be fully proved,' Kendall observed beforehand, 'We have to find out more about it.' It was a strange comment in many ways, indicating that the Everton manager had spent £800,000 on a player with no real thought on how the team should set up. But in Kendall's defence he told James Mossop of the *Sunday Express* that the original belief was Heath would be out until Christmas. 'He has amazed me. He is such a determined little fellow,' Kendall told Mossop. 'Now we have a selection problem...I know it may be impossible to keep everyone happy.'

His Scottish forward remained unhappy. 'The boss has had enough time to sort out who and what his strike force should be,' Sharp said. 'I don't want to hear any ballyhoo from Graeme,' Kendall responded, 'What I would like to hear him say is that he is going to fight for his place back.' When Sharp went to see his manager, Kendall turned the screw. 'You don't even look like scoring,' he informed him. The disgruntled substitute only muddied the waters by netting from the bench in a 2-0 victory against the Hatters. With Lineker and Heath both performing poorly, Sharp's frustration after the game was understandable: 'I don't think the goal will make any difference. The last time I scored I was dropped. You've got to remember the 75 minutes I was on the bench. That's no good to me...a transfer request is one of the options I've got.' An angry Kendall hit back. 'Graeme has no chance of a move and would be wasting his time asking for one,' he asserted. 'It looks as though the players want to pick the team but I shall decide it and nobody goes.' Unsurprisingly, with Andy Gray now at Aston Villa, manager Graham Turner was rumoured to be taking more than a passing interest in events at Goodison. With a poor performance during a 3-0 defeat at Queens Park Rangers raising questions over the team's ability to retain the title – 'That's the worst we have defended for a very long time,' Kendall remarked – Roy Hayes pulled no punches in the *Liverpool Daily Post*: 'Certain members of the crew which many pundits said would carry off additional bounty for years to come are now talking of mutiny...but discontent in whatever form can never be allowed to fester.'

Kendall eventually recalled Sharp for the Screen Sport Super Cup encounter at Old

Trafford in midweek where the striker netted in an impressive performance. While that was enough to make the number nine shirt his own, former strike partner Heath was seeking showdown talks with an unsympathetic manager. 'I shouldn't have to justify my team selection to anyone and Adrian will leave this club only when I say so. He's under contract,' Kendall stated firmly, 'I'm looking for a balance up front and at present I think I have it.'

Some supporters, who flooded the letters page of the *Football Echo* with complaints, did not share that view. 'Can't manager Howard Kendall see for himself that the present strike-force of Lineker and Sharp has so far failed to live up to expectations,' wrote one correspondent, 'You don't have to be a genius to see the way in which the team is having to adjust to Lineker's requirements and the championship is already rapidly running away from us.' Meanwhile others wanted a return to the tried and trusted. 'Mr. Kendall seems to forget it was the Heath-Sharp partnership which got us to the top of the table,' one fan pointed out, 'What a waste of money "on the ground again" Lineker was. He even seems to have trouble keeping his balance.' But Kendall defended his corner. 'We have to forget about last season and look to the future,' was his response. 'I've never been one for looking back. We signed Gary Lineker and what I am saying is that his goal sense up to now has been tremendous. He's always a threat, always has chances in a game and puts most of them away.'

However, in contrast, Heath had clearly lost that extra zip in and around the box that made him such a dangerous opponent. The nasty edge possessed by all great players had largely diminished, probably due to the psychological effect of injury. By leaving him out, the Everton manager was also inferring that Heath was not the same player as before the cruciate ligament injury – the 1984 version was probably the first outfield name on the team sheet rather than third-choice striker now. After watching his team struggle to a 2-0 home win over Oxford, a furious Heath told the press he would be confronting his manager. 'I am not going to listen, I am going to do the talking,' he warned, 'Today is the beginning of the end for me…My contract ends this season, but I believe they will let me go before then.' However, in an injury crisis, the one-time record signing would not be sidelined for long.

4

EMERGENCY WARD GOODISON

FOLLOWING A GOALLESS OPENING THREE GAMES, GARY LINEKER'S time at Goodison exploded with six goals in three matches, enough for him to win the first *Daily Mirror* Player of the Month prize. Although the narrative since is that Everton changed their style to accommodate the England international, that was not obvious in the opening six weeks of the season. Five of Lineker's first six goals were not the result of balls played over the top but were headers, a pattern that continued throughout the campaign.

Getting the treatment

While Lineker was finding his feet, others were relocating to the treatment room. The first casualty of the campaign was Peter Reid, who damaged an Achilles tendon playing for England in mid-September. Initially expected to be out for four weeks, after two operations and several false starts the midfielder was sidelined for five months. The other major casualty was Derek Mountfield who needed a cartilage operation. Expected to be out for six weeks, due to complications the centre-half was sidelined until March. Although Reid's influence was huge, Kendall possessed experienced midfield options in Alan Harper, Kevin Richardson and Heath himself. At the back there were no such luxuries and the Everton boss initially selected FA Youth Cup winner Ian Marshall to replace the former Tranmere defender.

Marshall's first league game was at Goodison for the Merseyside derby and he was a bemused onlooker, like the majority of the 51,509 spectators, during a shocking opening half from the champions who found themselves three goals down at the break. Even during the previous season there were some who felt the defence was suspect and those suspicions, even allowing for Mountfield's absence, gained credence when player-manager

Kenny Dalglish – 'I invited him in for a pre-match drink but he refused,' Kendall joked afterwards – opened the scoring with a powerful drive just twenty seconds into the contest. The home team, without Reid to offer protection and bemused by Liverpool deploying Mark Lawrenson as a sweeper, played a suicidal high line, left the visitors too much space and conceded further goals from Ian Rush and, painfully, the recently signed Steve McMahon. Kendall brought on Heath for the hapless Marshall at the break and the temperature of the game immediately rocketed. Sharp struck one in off the bar on the restart and when Lineker finished off a brilliant one-touch move with eight minutes left, the scene was set for a dramatic finish. But it was Dalglish who missed the best opportunities, incredibly twice firing wide with only Southall to beat. Although there was much to admire, the brave fightback was too little, too late, and only masked the champions' shortcomings. 'The Evertonian sound and fury could not disguise the fact that Liverpool, when the chips were down and things really mattered, were enormously the better team,' Brian Glanville concluded in *The Sunday Times*.

The pulsating encounter was one of the best derbies of the modern era, leading the watching Bobby Robson to claim: 'I have been in football for thirty-five years, and I don't recall seeing a better game in my life…It was glorious – a match no other country in the world could produce.' The irony was a global audience could watch the compelling encounter on television, a privilege denied to the host country. But that presented an opportunity. 'At least the wider world will have noticed that our football can reach heights of commitment and passion, on the field and off, without losing its temper,' Patrick Barclay pointed out in the *Guardian*.

Chelsea challenge

By the middle of October, there was a renewed sense of optimism in the domestic game. 'A football season which began in a state of gloom and trauma, under the deep shadow of the Brussels disaster, the Bradford City fire, the ban from Europe, the withdrawal of television, is showing vigorous signs of life,' Brian Glanville wrote. 'The word, unfashionably, is entertainment… in only a couple of weeks football has thrown up so many vibrant games that Gordon Taylor, secretary of the players' union, is pleading for television to return forthwith so that the people may see such splendours.'

The main reason for the *joie de vivre* was Manchester United. Only a draw against Luton on the first Saturday in October stopped Ron Atkinson's side from equalling Spurs' top-flight record of winning their first eleven league games, set 25 years before. Their lead at the top stood at an enormous ten points over Liverpool and Chelsea, with the champions a further point behind. 'Only Rambo can stop United taking the championship,' John Wragg claimed in the *Daily Express*. Seven days after the derby loss Everton travelled to Stamford Bridge, where just over twelve months before the Toffees had belatedly kick-started their title challenge. Even at such an early stage, with United looking invincible and holding such an enormous lead at the top, on a beautifully sunny afternoon an eventful game looked to have severely dented any chances of retaining their crown. With Pat Van Dan Hauwe partnering Kevin Ratcliffe, the untried rearguard was punished as early as the third minute, when an unmarked Kerry Dixon headed home. After Nigel Spackman fired wide from the penalty spot for the home team, three minutes before the break Pat Nevin took advantage of John Bailey's uncertainty on the left to deliver a cross which David Speedie nodded in. Within sixty seconds Kevin Sheedy pulled a goal back.

In the *Guardian,* David Lacey's claim that 'events were conspiring against the League champions' gained traction when, twelve minutes into the second period, Sharp became the second player to miss the target from the spot. Nevertheless, the incident that makes this game (in)famous followed shortly after. Cautioned for dissent by referee Vic Callow after Chelsea's penalty award, only the still frustrated Southall understood why he travelled fifteen yards outside his box to thwart Dixon by handling the ball, leaving the referee with no option but to send him from the pitch. What little sympathy there may have been towards the Welshman – described as 'quiet and undemonstrative' in the matchday programme – disappeared when the goalkeeper angrily flung his jersey to the floor before throwing his gloves at the referee and shoving a member of the coaching team out of the way. Kevin Ratcliffe took over[5] – 'I kept goal a few times as a kid' was his reasoning – but the Welsh skipper only had to make two saves as the ten-man visitors threw everything at their hosts in an ultimately fruitless effort to salvage a point. 'The manful way in which the champions coped with the handicap,' Lacey concluded, 'diverted attention away from the shortcomings in their game, which are threatening to weaken their challenge.' Those included the movement of Van Den Hauwe to centre-half, which damaged the left-hand side and, most significantly, Reid's absence. The harmful defeat left the champions fourteen points behind leaders United after just twelve matches. Afterwards, Kendall knew who was to blame. 'The referee was 100 per cent right,' he claimed about the sensational dismissal. 'Southall was upset about the penalty incident, but the game went on long enough after that for him to get over it. He made two bad decisions in the game

---

[5]   The last occasion an Everton outfielder has worn the goalkeeper's gloves, meaning the game featured three Welsh internationals between the sticks, with Southall's childhood contemporary Eddie Niedzwiecki in goal for Chelsea.

and regrets them. I certainly do.'

The two teams reconvened at Stamford Bridge a month later in an equally frantic game in the League Cup. There have been few more dramatic starts to an Everton match. Dixon again put the home side ahead after just 53 seconds yet within a minute the visitors levelled, through a superb Sheedy free-kick. Unbelievably Bracewell put them 2-1 ahead after fourteen minutes but, with an epic on the cards, fortunes changed. Referee Dennis Hedges was a notorious nit-picker and on the previous Saturday had booked four players and awarded 58 free-kicks in a fixture at Plymouth. Before the game, the match official had warned players against using bad language so when Sheedy muttered something offensive to the referee after he failed to award a free-kick, the Ireland international was in trouble. Even though Sheedy did not continue the discussion, Hedges promptly sent the midfielder from the pitch. To rub salt into the wounds, the referee later failed to dismiss David Speedie, after the Scot had kicked Kevin Ratcliffe in plain sight before Pat Nevin equalised. Afterwards, with Lineker moved to midfield, the visitors held Chelsea at arm's length for a well-earned draw. 'If I were to say anything now I would blow my top,' Kendall angrily said afterwards. 'The incident completely ruined the game but the lads showed tremendous spirit and we must have a good chance in the replay.'

The sequel was equally fractious. A feature of the campaign was Everton's unfortunate habit of conceding early goals. On the Saturday after the Stamford Bridge draw, they went behind after a minute against Southampton at the Dell. This followed recent opposition strikes by Kenny Dalglish (20 seconds), Bournemouth's Colin Clarke (13 seconds) and Dixon's 53-second effort. Before the September goalless draw at Aston Villa,[6] Kendall had joked: 'If we kick off we'll put the ball straight back to our goalkeeper Neville Southall and let him take his time.' The frustrated manager consequently bemoaned the bad habit in the matchday programme for the replay against Chelsea and told the players beforehand: 'Whatever you do tonight, don't concede another early goal.' But Kendall and the disbelieving 26,373 spectators witnessed Dixon race away from the halfway line to put Chelsea ahead after just 61 seconds. Although Lineker equalised on nine minutes and the visitors had Darren Wood sent off, a header from defender Joe McLaughlin sealed the victory. 'It was a quality finish by Dixon, a great goal, but it emphasised that we are not right in the middle,' Kendall remarked, 'We know that, but the situation demands that we cope with it. It certainly doesn't help your cause when you go down early on.'

---

[6] When Kevin Ratcliffe and Andy Gray exchanged elbows in the face during the game before leaving the pitch arm-in-arm.

Mac knives the Toffees

Apart from Chelsea, West Ham United were another London club on the rise. Though they were tipped for relegation at the start of the campaign, manager John Lyall made two significant signings in the summer: Mark Ward – released by Everton four years before – joined from Oldham Athletic and striker Frank McAvennie from St Mirren for £340,000. After a slow start, the Hammers were purring when the champions arrived at Upton Park on the first Saturday in November. Unbeaten in ten league matches, the home team stood seventh in the table, with their new blond-bombshell forward having scored twelve goals in fourteen matches. Everton had regrouped after the Chelsea defeat, taking four points from two games, Kendall shuffling the pack as Alan Harper took over the left-back berth with Adrian Heath moving into midfield.

The first half was a strange one, the visitors appearing to be in control but with the home side having all the chances. Southall, who displayed top form throughout, blocked McAvennie when clean through. In the second period Everton moved through the gears and deservedly went ahead when Sharp cleverly dummied Lineker's cross and Steven finished easily. Twelve months earlier the visitors would have killed the game, but that loss of steely determination allowed McAvennie in twice during the final quarter-of-an-hour and he left a peak Southall powerless with two smart finishes. The defeat raised serious questions about the team's capacity to retain their title – on the Saturday evening they stood seventeen points behind unbeaten leaders Manchester United, who had won thirteen of their first fifteen games, and seven behind Liverpool. 'Choked, I've left a sick dressing room, I'll tell you,' Kendall sadly admitted.

The main issue continued to be the defence. The fledgling partnership of Ratcliffe and Van Den Hauwe was struggling to find an understanding which allowed opposition strikers too much space, something McAvennie had brilliantly taken advantage of. Reid's absence was equally important. The Footballer of the Year's ability to sense danger and break up play protected the back four and he was always there as an option when team-mates were in possession. The side missed his tactical direction and calming influence. 'Nobody else has his capacity for chugging around the field like a busy tank-engine in a marshalling yard,' David Lacey once memorably wrote about the midfielder, 'picking up a stray truck here, a goods wagon there and generally helping everybody over the hump.' One of Reid's strengths was getting the team up the pitch by driving through the middle but in his absence the balance was missing. Trevor Steven, for one, was having a difficult time. The wide man would feed Reid and then move forward, but now both the former Burnley player and colleagues sat deeper. Consequently, the team did not press as effectively as in the previous campaign.

Seven days later there were further problems when Van Den Hauwe missed the home game against Arsenal through injury, forcing the deployment of Gary Stevens as centre-half with Neil Pointon making his debut at left-back, following a £50,000 move from Scunthorpe. However, any worries proved groundless as the tepid visitors put in a dreadful performance and were routed 6-1. The other piece of good news on the day was Manchester United losing their unbeaten record in a 1-0 defeat at Hillsborough. 'We must maintain our form and not concern ourselves with the points gap or how other sides are doing,' Kendall said.

With Stevens still at centre-half, the defensive problems continued at Ipswich Town with the visitors two goals down on the half-hour, before fighting back to lead 3-2. After Terry Butcher equalised, it took a Trevor Steven penalty twelve minutes from time to wrap up the points. The Everton boss uncharacteristically stepped onto the pitch at the end of the game to shake hands with his victorious players: 'That's not something I normally do, but it was a tremendous show of character, they were really determined.' But the goodwill ended there. 'We can't afford to give away as many as we have been doing if we intend to keep our title,' Kendall grumbled afterwards. 'It's no use complaining about the absence of Derek Mountfield because he's been away nine weeks and we have to manage without him. We looked terribly vulnerable during the first half.' The Everton manager had hardly helped by offloading utility defender Ian Atkins for £100,000 to Ipswich and then, having recalled John Bailey to the team, he promptly sold the full-back to Newcastle United. Squad depth was therefore limited and the youth and reserve teams, so strong under Colin Harvey, had become threadbare.

With United drawing at home to Spurs, the gap to the top had reduced by five points in a week, although defensive problems continued to hamper Everton. Kendall's team twice came from behind to emerge victorious 3-2 at Southampton at the end of November, thanks to a rasping left-footed drive from Trevor Steven five minutes from the end. 'I think people have come to expect us to make a poor start, but they also expect us to fight back and win,' the Everton boss admitted afterwards. With Heath – nine goals in eighteen games – Steven and Sheedy all in midfield and the free-scoring Lineker up top, the team possessed enormous attacking potential and looked far more effective when forced to chase games with the shackles off. But 4-3 and 3-2 away victories are not sustainable for a championship-chasing side and, although only Liverpool had scored more than Everton's 41 goals after nineteen games, the 25 conceded was the third-highest total among the top twelve clubs. At that time, the best teams were rarely involved in the games producing the most goals and tellingly the 66 shared in Everton's matches up to that stage was the joint-highest in the top flight.

Nevertheless, thanks to a last-minute Colin West equaliser for Watford at Old Trafford on the same afternoon, sixth-placed Everton stood nine points behind Manchester United when Leicester City visited Goodison on 14 December. Playing either Gary Stevens or Pat Van Den Hauwe in central defence had weakened the full-back positions so Ian Marshall returned to the team on a disastrous afternoon for the champions. Kevin Richardson put the hosts in front after 26 minutes, but Marshall's inexperience was on show when he clumsily felled Alan Smith in the box, with Gary McAllister equalising from the spot. A quarter-of-an-hour from the end Kevin Ratcliffe inexplicably pushed forward in search of an offside decision and Smith strode forward to slot the winner past Southall. Coming four days after the home League Cup defeat to Chelsea, Kendall was understandably furious. 'It's no good talking about injuries because we had seven internationals in our side and I'm not making excuses for them,' he said, 'He [Ratcliffe] stepped forward trying to play offside – something you don't do when you have a youngster like Ian Marshall behind you.' With United disappearing over the horizon, Ian Ross candidly remarked in the *Liverpool Daily Post*: 'I suppose Everton's chances of actually retaining their League title could at best now be described as remote.'

The calamitous defeat to a side with one win in ten away games reopened the old wounds around the club-record signing. 'I feel it is now time for Mr Kendall to make changes,' wrote one correspondent in the *Football Echo*. 'He must admit he was wrong to buy Lineker and sell Gray.' Another was just as forthright. 'Gary Lineker does not fit in at Goodison…his style of play is more suitable to a kick-and-rush game such as at Forest, Wednesday and Liverpool,' he wrote. 'The team are trying to suit Lineker, are failing and suffering in their game. Howard Kendall should accept he had made an error and unload Lineker, who does not battle for the team.'

Although Lineker had scored nineteen goals, the fans' scepticism was understandable. As a newcomer to a title-winning team and the replacement for a truly heroic figure who had enjoyed a unique rapport with the fans, he was always going to have to earn their confidence. The team he joined was full of players willing to fight for their colleagues, get their hands dirty and battle to the very end. On the surface, Lineker's seemingly apathetic attitude and unwillingness to engage in physical combat marked him out as the opposite. 'He is a remarkable player, able to cloak himself in anonymity for perhaps 75 minutes,' Derek Hodgson once wrote in the *Observer*, 'then scoring twice.' Consequently, unlike the man he had replaced, there was no immediate affinity with fans. He was not *one of them* in a similar manner to Romelu Lukaku thirty years later. However, that opinion was way off the mark, Lineker possessed an inner steel and had the intelligence to work out the best way to hurt the opposition was to play to his strengths. As Kendall told Lineker's biographer Colin Malam when he heard from the player's agent Jon Holmes that his client had never been booked:

> Then, since there weren't many stitches in Gary's face and his nose was still straight, I began to wonder whether he wanted to show aggression, wanted to win badly enough. He does, but he doesn't show it like other players by aggression or by mouthing. He finds space in the area, that's what he does; and his timing is perfect.

'We are battling again'

On Christmas Day, Everton stood sixth in the table, with forty points from 22 matches, nine behind Ron Atkinson's side. 'You don't win trophies in the first half of the season,' Kendall told the *Liverpool Echo*, 'If we can get everyone fully fit, then we will remain a match for anyone.' Twenty-four hours later that claim was tested when an injury-hit Manchester United, with no Bryan Robson, travelled to Goodison. The opening fifteen minutes were an illusion with the visitors, both physical and competitive in the middle, going ahead when Frank Stapleton slid in Colin Gibson's cross at the near post. The lead lasted less than five minutes, with Sharp scrappily equalising from a Sheedy corner. Thereafter the forward duo probably had their best game of the season as a partnership, Lineker's pace constantly pulling the United central defenders out of position, while Sharp's physical presence and ability to hold up the ball produced one of the performances of his career. Probably for the first time during the campaign, the team played with the passion and intensity of the season before as the visitors withstood a tremendous siege of their goal, until just before half-time when United failed to clear a corner and Lineker headed home Sheedy's cross. Three minutes after the break, Lineker's cross sped across the six-yard box to Sheedy and this time Sharp converted his cross to complete a dominant 3-1 victory. 'Their superiority was so marked that a match which began with passionate intensity ended almost in tranquillity,' was Peter Ball's view in *The Times*. 'Their performance yesterday suggested that the threat from Merseyside is gathering pace.' The departing home fans, among the 42,000 crowd, were already aware of the news from the other end of the M62, where earlier Liverpool had been surprisingly beaten 1-0 at Maine Road. Everton now stood fifth, just two victories off the top. 'Manchester United's one-horse title race is developing into a cavalry chase,' Derek Potter wrote in the *Daily Express*.

On Boxing Day twelve months earlier, a vital 2-1 win at Sunderland, plus dropped points by all their title rivals, had acted as a springboard for the rest of the campaign and Kendall was hoping history would repeat itself. His belief gained further traction when Sheffield Wednesday were pushed aside 3-1 at Goodison two days later, the result flattering the hosts who had to withstand a fierce barrage in the second period, the Owls striking the woodwork twice and having one effort cleared off the line. With United's game postponed, the third-placed Toffees moved within three points of the leaders and one behind a threatening Chelsea. For all the doubts about the defence, in 24 games they had conceded thirty goals, only one more than at the same stage in the title season. 'We are battling again,' said Kevin Ratcliffe of an inspired league run which had brought 22 points from a possible 27.

Afterwards, Kendall used Lineker's two-goal performance to defend his striker from critics. 'When a new man comes into the club he first has to win over the other players and then the fans. Gary has now done that,' the Everton boss argued. 'He is a quality player and he removed any doubts on Boxing Day in the win over United.' Contrary to popular belief, the classic Lineker goal was not following a ball over the top, but one from the Gray textbook. No fewer than eleven of his first 21 goals were headers, but whereas the Scot's came from traditional crosses, with Lineker it was different. 'He's always on the move to get in front of defenders and we try to exploit that,' Kendall explained. 'We don't put looping centres in but cross the ball with pace...Gary is not a giant who towers above defenders, but he's produced some real flying headers and we are all delighted with his goal return.' Lineker later felt that the two Christmas games were hugely important in developing his relationship with supporters. 'There was a faction who didn't take to me in the first half of the season,' he explained. 'That changed over Christmas when we played Manchester United and Sheffield Wednesday and I scored three goals. That was the turning point for me, and I was lifted by having the fans solidly behind me.'

On New Year's Day the Toffees travelled to Newcastle aiming to keep up the pressure on leaders United, but what appeared to be an easy victory ended in near catastrophe. The confident visitors were initially at their aristocratic best, moving the ball smoothly around a difficult, icy surface. 'They bewildered Newcastle with their unremitting support play,' Patrick Barclay wrote in the *Guardian* as Everton took the lead when Lineker's delightful back-heel set up Trevor Steven to score. But on 58 minutes came a series of incidents that possessed long-term ramifications. Paul Gascoigne broke through the middle and was fouled by Bracewell. Following an off-the-ball tussle between the two, referee Colin Seel penalised Bracewell and cautioned him for verbal abuse. Sharp waded in and followed the

Graeme Sharp scores in the Boxing Day victory over Manchester United. After a difficult start to the campaign the champions were firmly back in the leading pack at the end of the year.

midfielder into the book. Suddenly the passive home crowd were energised and the temperature became red-hot when Gascoigne equalised from the resulting free-kick. Before the restart Heath entered Seel's notebook for arguing. With St James' Park now in ferment, the champions were unusually rattled and within sixty seconds Bracewell and Newcastle's Billy Whitehurst were involved in a full-blooded challenge which resulted in the Toffees midfielder being carried off on a stretcher.[7] Ironically then, Bracewell had been the source of a sequence of events that ultimately became career-threatening.

With Harper on as a substitute, seven minutes later Kevin Sheedy left the fray with a groin injury and shortly afterwards Peter Beardsley put the Geordies ahead with a typically brilliant solo goal. An increasingly calamitous afternoon became worse when Steven limped off, leaving Everton with nine men on the pitch before the hobbling midfielder returned for the closing minutes. Yet somehow, amid the mayhem, they dragged out an equaliser, and a point, via a Sharp penalty. Nevertheless, some uncharacteristic ill-discipline had been costly. 'We talked ourselves out of two points,' a frustrated Kendall said, 'One of the most difficult things for players to do is not to react to decisions which they think are wrong. But they have to learn to keep their mouths shut.'

---

[7]   In fact there was a sense of relief 24 hours later when an X-ray revealed there was not a broken leg, as first feared, but a badly bruised shin. Given Bracewell's subsequent long-term absence, the former may have been preferable.

Reid returns

Everton were in the midst of an injury crisis in early January – 'We're thinking of entering all the five-a-side tournaments,' joked Kendall – with remarkably none of the title-winning midfield quartet appearing in the FA Cup third-round victory over Exeter City. During the following home league game against QPR there was a midfield of Heath, Harper, Richardson and Paul Wilkinson for the second half. Two goals down following strikes by the excellent partnership of Gary Bannister and John Byrne, the home side got one back via a penalty before the unlikely quartet forged a terrific second-half fightback which produced a memorable 4-3 victory. 'Winning football is as much about character and team work as about individual ability,' Ian Hargraves pointed out in the *Liverpool Echo*. 'Everton have both qualities in abundance and even when some of their stars are missing.' Seven days later there was good news for Kendall on no less than three fronts: two goals for Lineker secured an easy 2-0 victory at Birmingham on a day when Manchester United contrived to lose 3-2 at home to Nottingham Forest after leading with ten minutes remaining. The gap at the top was now down to two points. Equally significantly Peter Reid made his comeback for the reserve team at Goodison and played a full ninety minutes. With a creaking squad, the midfielder's return was more than welcome. Not only was Bracewell sidelined but Sheedy had been struggling with a series of niggling injuries and had hardly trained properly all season. The number of matches where the Ireland international had needed late fitness tests was already into double figures.

Reid's path back to full fitness was documented in his diary of the 1985/86 season, produced in collaboration with journalist Peter Ball. In the book he faithfully recorded the events 24 hours before the encounter against Spurs on the first Saturday in February, giving an insight into his manager's people skills:

> *Anyway I got to Bellefield and the boss called me in and said, "Do you feel all right?" So I said "Yes" and he told me I was playing tomorrow, which is typical of his style. He doesn't mess about. I think he hadn't said anything to me yesterday, because he didn't want me to have too long to think about it, as it is my first game for five months. He is very good at that. He protects you very well. When I had to have my second operation he kept that out of the press, and he let me start my come-back quietly.*

Kendall's faith was well-placed in a dour game played in a freezing, swirling wind. Peter Shreeves' side came for a point and showed little attacking intent but, with eight minutes remaining, the champions had nothing to show for their domination and Kendall was preparing to take his returning midfielder off. Then the footballing fates dramatically intervened. Lineker's cross was touched back by Steven to the prowling Reid, at the edge of the box, and he chested the ball down and fired home off the underside of the bar to the delight – and relief – of the 33,000 crowd.

But celebrations were very nearly premature. 'I had the number six card ready because he was shattered,' Kendall said afterwards and the Everton boss really should have taken the scorer off after the goal, as the five-month absence caught up with the returning hero. Receiving the ball near the centre-circle with only seconds remaining, the rusty Reid left his back-pass to Southall both short and straight into the path of John Chiedozie. Fortunately, the Everton keeper rushed out and the speedy winger – never a natural finisher – ran it past him and out of play. After Reid, and to be fair the crowd, caught their breath they were able to celebrate a vital victory: with United not playing until the Sunday, Kendall's team now stood top, albeit having played two games more. To complete a satisfying afternoon, Liverpool lost 2-1 at Ipswich after leading and were now three points off the pace. As David Lacey memorably put it in the *Guardian* at the time, the most critical period for any bridgehead is the first 24 hours and to complete a perfect weekend, United suffered the same fate as Liverpool at West Ham. Seemingly out of the race only eight weeks into the campaign, Kendall's team were now 6-4 favourites for the title, with Man United at 3-1, Chelsea 7-2 and Liverpool 5-1.

Graeme and Gary's goals

After a stop-start opening to the season – and probably contrary to the views of some supporters – Graeme Sharp had developed into the ideal partner for the club's record signing, Lineker. Sharp's often underrated strength was getting the best out of a variety of companions. The link-up with Adrian Heath was most effective when the two were in and around the opposition box with the ball on the ground: with Lineker it was outside the area and when the ball was played from deep.

That said, Sharp was modest enough to admit their potency was two-pronged. 'He was a joy to play with,' he told Lineker's biographer Colin Malam, 'The understanding wasn't something we set out to work on: it just happened. Gary had great awareness and was definitely the best finisher I've ever played with. In fact, he was the best attacking partner of the 13 or 14 I had in my time with Everton.' Sharp was showing a wider armoury than previously, with better link-ups and greater awareness of colleagues, as well as avoiding the off-the-ball squabbles and distractions which could affect his play. 'The main reason for his emergence as an outstanding centre-forward at the age of 25 is that he has learned to play with his head rather than his heart,' Jason Thomas argued in *The Sunday Times*. Howard Kendall added: 'This explains why Graeme has scored more goals in the last year or two. He is no longer missing out on the scruffy goals, the close-range tap-ins.'

Opponents had also taken note of Sharp's more cerebral approach. 'When we played at Everton recently, I couldn't help noticing the intelligence of his runs,' QPR's Terry Fenwick revealed. 'It was quite obvious that a lot of work has gone into this aspect of his game. Once, he would often go for balls he had no chance of winning but now, because of the timing of his runs and his positioning, he is finding that he can unsettle defenders without getting that close to them. He caused our centre-half Steve Wicks a lot of problems just by getting him on certain angles.'

The front pairing was at its potent best when Manchester City turned up at a freezing Goodison, on the second Tuesday in February, in front of some welcome guests: the television cameras. Three months earlier talks had broken down again – 'This is the end. There will be no league football on television this season,' John Bromley claimed – and there appeared to be no chance of a reconciliation between the two parties. However, following peace talks between the BBC's Jonathan Martin and Philip Carter at the BBC Sports Review of The Year in December, the Football League and television companies ended their stand-off and signed a £1.3m deal for the rest of the campaign for twelve live games – six league and six cup – or £1.8m less than what they could have had in the previous summer. 'The money we got was peanuts but it was a question of getting back into the swing,' Carter later said. 'It was a stupid situation, if I can say so now. I think it actually brought home to people that there was something wrong with not having our national sport on television.' One of the options of the deal was the rights for highlights of midweek league games, something prohibited previously. So when the ITV cameras pitched up at Goodison for *Midweek Sports Special* the game was making domestic football history.

With Everton's game at Watford postponed on the previous weekend, the home team were hoping to take advantage of a couple of favourable results. On the Saturday, Chelsea, needing to defeat Oxford United at Stamford Bridge to go top, contrived to lose 4-1 while 24 hours later the big game at Anfield produced the desired outcome as Liverpool and Manchester United drew 1-1. Beat City and remarkably the Toffees would be five points clear of the field. Even against a team on a run of five successive league victories, with Lineker and Sharp working perfectly in tandem that eventuality was never in doubt. The Englishman showcased his predatory talents to perfection, confirming that one of the strengths of all great strikers is not being afraid to gamble even if, more often or not, there is no pay out. After just nine minutes Lineker anticipated Paul Power's misdirected back-pass to fire past goalkeeper Eric Nixon. The striker's uncanny knack of sensing a defender in danger was again on display a minute after the break. There appeared to be little risk as Nicky Reid dribbled out of the area but Lineker, who had hovered around the City player, took full advantage when the defender unexpectedly trod on the ball to score past the stranded Nixon. Ten minutes later Sharp's beautifully weighted, clipped first-time pass over the City defence fell perfectly for his partner, who lobbed the onrushing Nixon for his second hat-trick of a prolific campaign. Sharp took advantage of poor defending to complete the rout near the end. 'I felt Sharp was outstanding against City in terms of leading the line,' Kendall said afterwards, 'holding things up and putting himself about. He was getting on the end of crosses and winning headers and got the goal he deserved in the end.' With 46 goals between them – more than the vaunted McAvennie-Cottee and Dixon-Speedie partnerships – the pair were firing the champions towards retaining the title. 'I've been delighted with their goal return,' a delighted Kendall added, 'They always look a threat and if they keep it going it will be tremendous for the club.'

5

FACE-OFF

ON THE FINAL SATURDAY OF FEBRUARY CAME ONE OF THE MOST
significant fixtures of the entire campaign, when Everton took their eleven-game unbeaten
run to a frosty Anfield. Five points ahead of their rivals, a victory would surely put Kenny
Dalglish's side out of the picture, or so it was thought.

Advantage at Anfield

Like their rivals, Liverpool had suffered a series of injuries and had taken just ten points
from the previous nine league games, against the champions' impressive tally of 25. With
Paul Walsh and Dalglish injured, Jan Molby was incongruously deployed as an auxiliary
striker whereas only Mountfield and Sheedy were out for the champions. Nevertheless,
the key injury was to a player on the team sheet: goalkeeper Bruce Grobbelaar was
rumoured to have failed a fitness test on a damaged elbow before the game.

   Those absences meant Dalglish abandoned the sweeper system which had nonplussed
Everton at Goodison. 'Liverpool change their tactical formation as often as Miss Jan
Leeming, the television news reader, changes her hair style,' Brian Glanville commented
in the *Sunday Times*. The opening half was standard derby fare: crunching tackles laced
with gelignite but all the meaningful action came in front of the Everton supporters
populated at the Anfield Road end as the visitors dominated, with Richardson, Steven and
Sharp all having good chances. But the major talking point was an extraordinary incident
on eighteen minutes. Alan Hansen rolled an awkward ball across his own penalty area to
Mark Lawrenson, whose short back pass to Grobbelaar from ten yards out went beyond
the keeper. The onrushing Richardson was felled by Lawrenson and as the ball trickled
towards the goal-line, the Liverpool defender was forced into a desperate clearance.

   There was more of the same in the second period – the away team winning the corner
count 7-0 – with Grobbelaar producing a stupendous save when he tipped Steven's shot
round the post. With a first derby goalless draw for three years in the offing, fifteen

minutes from time there was another surreal moment. Picking up the ball thirty yards out, Kevin Ratcliffe's shot appeared to take the mildest of deflections but should have been a straightforward take for Grobbelaar who, perhaps conscious of his injury, inexplicably allowed the ball to squirm under his body and over the line. 'My shot took a deflection and I was jumping up and down to see if it had gone in and somehow it had,' the scorer said afterwards, 'but they all count.'

With the celebratory roars of the mass of Evertonians still circulating around the ground, the home team generated their only real opportunity of the game. Steve McMahon's through ball pierced the Everton defence, Rush rounded Southall but, with the home supporters expecting a familiar outcome, in came the immaculate Pat Van Den Hauwe to clear the Welshman's goal-bound strike. Within seconds, Harper's clever pass released the possibly-offside Lineker who chipped the ball over the advancing Grobbelaar.[8] As the striker celebrated his thirtieth goal of the season with joyous away fans by the corner flag at the Kop end, there was a feeling that the visitors had not only clinched the game – but quite possibly the title. 'Only the most compulsive backers of outsiders can now want to bet against their chances of keeping this First Division Championship,' Hugh McIlvanney announced in the *Observer*.

Afterwards the Everton skipper was, perhaps unwisely, critical of the vanquished. 'That wasn't the Liverpool you expect to see out there,' Ratcliffe said, 'I don't know what they were trying to do and, in the end, I don't think they knew either.' Meanwhile, Dalglish was in typically tetchy mood after a first home defeat of the season. 'Just when we started to play a bit in the second half we gave them a poxy goal,' he complained, 'and then Van Den Hauwe kicks one off the line from Rushie and they go up the park and score a goal that was five yards offside.' Such a deluded assessment failed to impress McIlvanney, who commented, 'Whether or not Lineker's goal was questionable, such a simplistic analysis ignores the evidence that Everton these days are intrinsically superior to their old rivals.'

Reined in

The great journalist's opinion appeared sound as the clock ticked towards 4 p.m. on Sunday, 2 March. Twenty-four hours earlier Everton had struggled to defeat Aston Villa 2-0 at Goodison, with a goal apiece for the striking partnership. Sharp had signed a new four-year deal before the game and Villa centre-half Allan Evans was full of praise for the

---

[8]   Ted Macauley of the *Daily Mirror* detailed a statistical analysis of Lineker and Ian Rush over the game. The Welshman enjoyed 45 touches of the ball and made 34 passes of which twenty went to a team-mate. Lineker was far less busy: just 24 touches and making only *four* passes to an Everton player over ninety minutes. Yet the England international was the only one of the pair to find the net, leading Macauley to (prematurely) proclaim: 'LINEKER IS KING.'

duo afterwards. 'With those two together Everton are going to be winning things for four years,' he said, 'They've got to be the best in the business.'

The victors moved six points ahead of Manchester United and eleven ahead of Dalglish's side, having played one game more. On the Sunday afternoon, in a match broadcast live by the BBC, Liverpool travelled to Tottenham desperately needing a victory. After conceding an early goal to Chris Waddle, the visitors dominated but with the score 1-1 in the closing seconds those Everton fans watching nervously at home knew a ten-point gap over their rivals, with eleven games left, was probably insurmountable. But then came one of those inexplicable moments that can shape seasons. Tottenham's experienced skipper Steve Perryman jumped under a harmless, bouncing loose ball on the halfway line, Ronnie Whelan strode forward and fed Ian Rush, who netted a priceless winner. 'Ian Rush scores the goal that keeps Kenny Dalglish's team in the championship,' the watching John Motson proclaimed afterwards. Although Everton had matters very much in their own hands, the Welshman's goal left a nagging doubt.

The importance of that last-gasp strike was magnified when Everton next played in the league a fortnight later, a tough-looking home fixture against Chelsea.[9] With Liverpool defeating QPR and Southampton during the interim, the gap at the top had narrowed to just two points. Meanwhile, with freezing weather having played havoc with the fixture list over the previous two months, Chelsea stood fourth in the table, eight points behind the champions but with three games in hand. Kerry Dixon, David Speedie and Pat Nevin gave the Stamford Bridge outfit no little quality and, in previous meetings, the Toffees had repeatedly failed to get to grips with their combative approach.

It was the same story at Goodison. With plenty of grudges still simmering after three dismissals in the three games the teams had already played so far that season, the contest was another abrasive encounter with Pat Van Den Hauwe an early candidate for the fourth red card when a blatant elbow caught Speedie flush in the face. Everton also reverted to earlier type when conceding the first goal, as the defence failed to clear Eddie Niedzwiecki's long punt and Jerry Murphy fired home. At the break, an object thrown by the crowd felled the visitors' left-back Doug Rougvie, who had just been booked for fouling Steven. 'There was too much bad blood for this to be an encounter for the purists,' Stephen Bierley wrote in the *Guardian* about a game with 41 fouls. 'Feuds simmered.' Despite a corner count of 14-2 in their favour, only when Adrian Heath came from the bench did an equaliser seem likely – duly arriving four minutes from time, via a

---

[9] For the first time ever Goodison hosted a live league game, the match broadcast by ITV.

Kevin Sheedy header, after the substitute had ferreted his way down the left flank. The result – one that frankly helped neither team – left Everton just three points ahead of their local rivals, but with a game in hand.

Twelve months earlier Kendall's team carried all before them but now they increasingly looked tired and, with no Reid to provide direction, short on imagination. Sheedy was nowhere near full fitness while Gary Stevens and Trevor Steven – without a league goal from open play at Goodison all season – were out of touch. There was too much reliance on the long ball to Sharp's head. Having said that, injuries were taking their toll. At Luton six days later, the defence had a distinctly makeshift look: the returning Derek Mountfield partnered Van Dan Hauwe in the middle with Harper and Pointon at full-back. The balance was further disturbed when Sheedy limped off with a hamstring strain before the break and was replaced by centre-half Ian Marshall. However, there was still no doubting the side's competitiveness. After the formidable Mick Harford twice saw headers strike the woodwork, in the opening minute of the second half the visitors went ahead in freakish circumstances when Kevin Richardson's shot from the edge of the area squirmed over the line via two deflections. With nine minutes left, an unlikely and very fortunate three points was within grasp before Luton skipper Steve Foster crucially intervened. The head-banded marauder nodded home Ricky Hill's free-kick before, four minutes later, a similar effort was flicked on by Liverpool-supporting Mike Newell for a deserved victory. 'If my goal has helped Liverpool win the League championship this season, then I'm absolutely delighted,' the match-winner said afterwards, a quote that thankfully remained under wraps three years later when Newell arrived at Goodison.

In his first four campaigns, Kendall's Everton had lost after leading on only three occasions, yet this was the fourth defeat from a winning position over seven months. Although there had been injuries, this was not all down to missing personnel. The resilience and capacity for closing down games that characterised the title-winning campaign was not as prominent. As champions they were naturally the hunted and not the hunter. 'Winning the title is one thing, defending it is a different matter altogether,' Kendall had warned at the start of the season. To make a freezing, miserable day even worse, the news arrived from Anfield that Liverpool had overwhelmed Oxford 6-0, a result that took them top for the first time in two years.

'If I look back it was the one game which disappointed me the most,' Kendall later reflected, 'We were a goal up and looking very comfortable. We slipped, allowed Luton to score two goals from set-pieces and lost valuable ground.' If March had already seen an eight-point lead at the top disappear, then the month was about to get much worse for the Everton boss.

That sinking feeling

After England's disastrous 3-2 defeat by West Germany in Leon at the 1970 World Cup, the journalist Ken Jones recalled joining vanquished manager Sir Alf Ramsey at the side of his hotel swimming pool. 'Of all the players it had to be him,' Ramsey continually muttered into his drink as he drowned his sorrows. 'Of all the players it had to be him.' 'Him' of course was Gordon Banks, the great goalkeeper who had missed the game through stomach problems. Replacement Peter Bonetti was more than competent but clearly at fault for two goals. Not only was Banks peerless as a goalkeeper but the security he provided due to his very presence on the pitch imbued the team with unlimited confidence.

Had journalists encountered Howard Kendall on the evening of Wednesday, 26 March, they would probably have heard something similar. 'Him' on this occasion was another goalkeeper who, like Banks, was world-class and utterly irreplaceable. During that afternoon's friendly in Dublin between the Republic of Ireland and Wales at a muddy Lansdowne Road, Neville Southall jumped to catch a harmless cross but, on landing, his foot disappeared into the sodden turf. The eventual diagnosis was catastrophic: dislocated ankle and badly damaged ligaments. Peter Reid later reflected the concerns of all Evertonians in his autobiography: 'I went into training the next day praying that the news would be better than I feared. As it turned out, it was worse – much worse.' The Welshman was out for the rest of the season and beyond.

Like Banks, Southall was the player his team could least afford to lose. 'If any one player has been responsible for Everton's successes over the last two years then it is surely Southall,' David Lacey argued in the *Guardian*. The big keeper's understudy was a virtual unknown: Bobby Mimms, a £150,000 signing from Rotherham twelve months before.[10] 'It's a big responsibility for the lad, but this is why we bought him,' Kendall told the press, before adding some reassurance. 'He is an excellent keeper, and I have no fears about him letting us down.' The 22-year-old had made one appearance already, in a 1-1 draw at Manchester City following Southall's suspension for his Chelsea dismissal. That was always going to be a one-off, but a prolonged run at the business end of the campaign brought different pressures.

Within 72 hours, on Easter Saturday, Mimms made his home debut in what turned

---

[10]   Mimms arrived at Goodison after Tommy Docherty at Wolves had turned down Kendall's £160,000 offer for an 18-year-old Tim Flowers.

out to be a testing encounter against an improving Newcastle. There may have been a new face in goal, but the defence thankfully had a familiar look as for the first time in more than six months the championship-winning rearguard all started. Yet though up at the break thanks to Kevin Richardson's snap-shot on the half-hour, during the second period Peter Beardsley and Paul Gascoigne tormented the rusty backline. 'I was very impressed [he] has good feet and is not afraid to play,' Peter Reid said of Gascoigne who struck a post before shooting wastefully over from six yards out, while Beardsley's trickery led to John Anderson finding the net with an effort which was unluckily disallowed. Then, with six minutes left, came what appeared to be a crucial moment in the title race. Ratcliffe clumsily fouled Glenn Roeder in the Gwladys Street penalty area but, with a 41,116 crowd holding their collective breath, Beardsley shot wastefully over. The victory – combined with Liverpool's goalless draw at Sheffield Wednesday – took the title-holders two points ahead with a game in hand. 'If Everton do hang on to their League crown – and it's looking increasingly likely – then they will look back on the visit of Newcastle as a major turning point,' Roger Kent wrote in the *Liverpool Daily Post*.

Manchester United remained five points behind in third but at a wintry Old Trafford on Easter Monday, the champions put in a disciplined performance for a goalless draw. Injuries meant Mark Higgins incongruously appeared for the home team and ironically it was the former Everton skipper's goal-line block from Graeme Sharp's header that provided the only major talking point of a desperately poor game. Liverpool defeated Manchester City 2-0 at Anfield on the same afternoon to go top again on goal difference from their rivals, who now had seven matches to play, their game in hand worn like some sort of warm comfort blanket. If both clubs had designs on the league title, on the following weekend they also continued their pursuit of the most coveted trophy in English football.

6
TWO FOR A DOUBLE

'FOR THE THIRD SEASON IN SUCCESSION, EASTER HAS TURNED THE English professional football programme into a contest between Merseyside and the rest,' Ian Hargraves wrote in the *Liverpool Echo*. Hargraves was not only referring to the title chase, as once again the two giants were in the later stages of the FA Cup. For the fourth time in the decade, they had been kept apart in the semi-finals of the two major domestic cups – Liverpool facing Southampton with the Toffees up against Sheffield Wednesday at Villa Park.

Towards the Twin Towers

Kendall's quest for a third successive FA Cup final appearance had started with home defeats of Exeter City and former-club Blackburn Rovers, before a tricky tie at Spurs, which due to the inclement weather was delayed for three weeks until early March. The fifth-round game was a classic Everton away performance at the time: keep it tight in the first period before opening out. On this occasion the home team's uncharacteristically robust approach tried to unsettle the visitors – 'There were a few incidents,' a diplomatic Kendall remarked – including a dreadful tackle from behind by Mark Falco on Kevin Ratcliffe which resulted in the skipper being out for a month. Five minutes after the break the visitors went ahead when a stretching Ray Clemence failed to grasp Reid's cross, which fell to substitute Adrian Heath who hooked the ball home. On 73 minutes the visitors doubled their advantage when Trevor Steven's cross was converted by the menacing Lineker from a similar position. Although Falco finally did manage to beat Southall with a header in the final minutes, afterwards it was Pat Van Den Hauwe's turn to perform heroics, an acrobatic goal-line clearance preventing an equaliser.

Three days later Kendall's team journeyed to Kenilworth Road for a rematch of the previous year's semi-final. Luton's revenge looked secured when Mick Harford and Mark Stein put them two goals ahead just after the hour, against the run of play somewhat. But

Sharp responded straightaway with a header[11] and thirteen minutes from time Heath – now holding the unenviable tag of super-sub – took advantage of Steve Foster's hesitancy in the six-yard box to snatch a richly-deserved equaliser in front of the travelling fans. 'Going a couple of goals behind, somewhat illogically, Everton proved for the second time in a week what a resourceful, resilient Cup team they are,' Brian Glanville wrote in *The Sunday Times*. Four days later what supporters remember as the archetypal Lineker goal – a long ball from deep with searing pace taking him clear of the defence – was the difference in a hard-fought replay at Goodison. The match-winner was typically modest after the fact. 'I was not conscious of any pressure from the Luton defenders, but I was lucky because the ball bounced just right,' he revealed. Nevertheless, his manager held nothing back about the striker's 33rd goal of the season. 'It was a fantastic goal; you could hear the crowd buzzing for minutes afterwards,' Kendall proclaimed, 'It was something very special.'

Gary Lineker's winning goal against Luton, although remembered as a typical strike from the England international when at Goodison, that was not the case.

---

[11] Producing one of the most unjust attributions of a goal in history. All newspaper reports state Sharp beat Steve Foster to the ball and cleanly headed home. Most gave the goal to Sharp but the Sunday tabloids mysteriously credited it as an own goal by defender Mal Donaghy, standing several yards away. The tabloid source was used in future record books but access to the match archive in recent years shows Sharp should have been credited.

The semi-final against Sheffield Wednesday was originally scheduled for Old Trafford but, given the deteriorating relations between Merseyside and Manchester supporters, the Football Association wisely moved the tie to Villa Park. By then Gary Lineker had joined the absentees. With doubts over the striker's fitness, Kendall had asked Bobby Robson not to pick him for a friendly in the Soviet Union on the same day as Southall's injury, but the England boss played Lineker for a full ninety minutes. The Everton manager was furious and his mood hardly improved when the top scorer limped off at Old Trafford on Easter Monday with a hamstring strain.

Lineker was conspicuously absent at Villa Park, as was Kevin Sheedy. On a sunny, blustery spring day Howard Wilkinson's side, backed by a magnificent support, stormed out of the traps and had much the better of the first half, their hard running and physical style making the favourites uncomfortable. But the most significant moment was on the half-hour when Trevor Steven limped off with a thigh strain and was replaced by Alan Harper. The substitute crucially intervened four minutes after the break. Derek Mountfield's forward header caught out the onrushing Wednesday defence and Harper was onto the ball immediately to lob Martin Hodge.

Within three minutes Wednesday deservedly levelled when Carl Shutt headed in from close range but, near the end, Sharp missed a golden chance to settle the game when he poked the ball agonisingly wide from inside the six-yard box. Kendall held his head in his hands but seven minutes into extra time the Everton boss was out of the dugout as the Scottish striker more than made amends. Everton's only other real performer on the day, Paul Bracewell, produced an inviting cross from the left which sailed over the heads of the Wednesday defence and Sharp met the ball with a trademark, crunching volley into the roof of the net. The goal was worthy to win any semi-final and it did just that, Everton becoming only the second team to reach three successive FA Cup finals at Wembley. Kendall played tribute to his match-winner after the game: 'From the second 45 minutes onwards he was tremendous. He fully deserved his winner and you will have to go a long way to see a better exhibition of centre-forward play.' With three first-team players injured and a fourth off in the opening period, the victory once again brought into focus the psychological strength of Kendall's side, as Ian Ross reflected in the *Liverpool Daily Post*:

> *They should have been over-powered, over-run and beaten but they weren't – and there, in a nutshell, you have the Goodison secret. They have been called resilient, professional, uncompromising and brilliant. They are that and much more. The strength in depth is staggering; the self-belief and will to win totally unbelievable.*

A key contributor over the previous month had been semi-final scorer Alan Harper. At White Hart Lane in the fifth round, he had started the game at right-back before moving effortlessly to central defence after Kevin Ratcliffe had gone off injured. Such versatility was priceless. With Liverpool also victorious against Southampton, the first all-Merseyside FA Cup final on 10 May was now a reality. In the interim the two best teams in England also had a league title to contest.

The secret diary of Adrian Heath, aged 25

Since Kendall had gone with the Sharp-Lineker axis, the bubbly former Stoke City player filled the many midfield gaps but was now marginalised following Reid's return. Heath had still not signed a new contract and, although there were crucial goals off the bench against Spurs and Luton, he remained frustrated over the lack of game time. 'I can't afford another season like this one,' he admitted after the semi-final. 'I've got a lot of self-belief and I'm sure that if I was playing regularly then I could get well into the twenties in terms of goals. I still hope something develops at Everton. Looking back, it seems that the bad injury I received against Sheffield Wednesday last year might have cost me my Everton career, but that is football.'

Adrian Heath about to come on and make a crucial impact in the FA Cup sixth-round tie at Luton in March. However, bench-warming was not to the striker's liking.

Although Heath had clearly lost the edge (and some confidence) that, eighteen months before, enabled him reach standards seldom seen by any Everton player during the post-war era, there was plenty of rumoured interest from big clubs. 'Heath,' Barry Flatman wrote in the *Daily Express*, 'would walk into nearly every other First Division attack.' Arsenal and Spurs had been linked earlier in the season – as had Liverpool. The striker was not necessarily in the shop window when Everton travelled to Highbury but, with a tepid game goalless, after a clearly unfit Lineker went off with 25 minutes left Heath had another opportunity to prove his worth. And he did just that. Six minutes later Stevens flicked on Steven's corner and up popped the substitute to volley home at the North Bank, where he had struck so memorably against Southampton. 'What do you do when you need every point you can get to win the League Championship, and your opponent's goalie is having such a blinder that he won't be beaten in the next ten years,' asked Julie Welch in the *Observer*, 'Answer – send on Adrian Heath.' The striker's intervention proved, once again, that Heath was a far more effective finisher when coming off the bench. 'He hates being called Super-sub,' said Kendall afterwards, 'Look, we'll call him anything he wants provided he keeps scoring goals like that.' Any hope of the Toffees returning to top spot were extinguished with the news that Liverpool had pulverised Coventry City 5-0, leaving both teams locked together at the top with the Anfield side's superior goal difference now effectively giving them an extra point.

The defending champions travelled to a glue-pot Vicarage Road three days later, where Heath again found himself on the bench.[12] On this occasion only until half-time when Lineker went off with a recurrence of his hamstring injury, but not before putting the visitors ahead with his final touch. An injury-ravaged home team put Everton under significant pressure in the second half, with Paul Bracewell clearing off the line before a late Graeme Sharp header clinched a hard-earned victory. 'Everton demonstrated once again last night,' Ken Rogers wrote in the *Liverpool Echo*, 'that when it comes to nerve, courage and commitment, they have got few equals.' For the first time in six weeks, the main combatants had played the same number of league games and Kendall's team were now three points ahead with just five matches left. The lead lasted 24 hours, when Liverpool's hard-earned 1-0 victory at Luton Town took them back to the summit. Heath was in for Lineker when relegation-threatened Ipswich Town visited Goodison on the

[12] On that evening the move to sell Gary Lineker gained momentum. Lineker's agent Jon Holmes was talking to England manager Bobby Robson in the boardroom after the game and Kendall walked in. When Robson left, the Everton boss said to Holmes, 'I'm glad you're here. How do you fancy going abroad? I've got to tell you Barcelona have been in. We've put them off, but they've come back. It's a lot of money and I feel I ought to offer Gary the chance to go or not. I'll put it to him tomorrow.'

Saturday when, in rain-sodden conditions, the home team struggled to break down the East Anglian side. The crucial moment arrived halfway through the second period when Kevin Richardson crossed from the left and Sharp glanced a header over Paul Cooper for a hard-fought victory. To a degree, the performance was unimpressive from a team who appeared to be playing from memory. Yet Liverpool were equally uninspiring on the same afternoon, grinding out a 2-1 victory at West Brom thanks to an Ian Rush winner.

Lost in the Forest

As the league season reached the final Saturday of April, Everton had four games left, one more than their rivals, with both level on 79 points. Ten more would guarantee retention of the title. The two Merseyside clubs were also looking over their shoulders at West Ham United, who had enjoyed a terrific run and stood on 72 points from 37 matches. The Toffees travelled to Nottingham Forest – ten games unbeaten – for a tricky fixture in front of a sun-kissed crowd of 30,171, the highest for a league game at the City Ground for six years. Throughout the first half the visitors showed their 'customary, crustacean attitude they adopt for their away games' according to Brian Glanville in *The Sunday Times*. However, with news that Liverpool were 3-0 ahead against Birmingham City, the second period was an altogether more attractive affair. Young Forest winger Franz Carr had struck a post early on and was unlucky when Neil Webb converted his cross but the linesman incorrectly flagged that the ball had gone out of play. Van Den Hauwe then cleared off the line. In almost unbearable tension, an increasingly frantic Everton had plenty of possession but created only one real opportunity, when Sharp arrived at the far post from Stevens' cross but agonisingly the ball struck his knee and came back off the woodwork. Kendall bafflingly left Heath on the bench until four minutes from time – 'too little, too late' David Lacey claimed in the *Guardian* – and, despite the efforts of both teams, the match ended goalless.

Brian Clough was a huge admirer and afterwards he heaped praise on Kendall's side: 'Without the steel in their side they would have lost. They will be unable to play in Europe next season, and they don't know what they're missing abroad. Everton would grace any football field.' For all Clough's admiring glances, with Liverpool easing to a 5-0 victory, Dalglish's side were now two points clear. Even worse Peter Reid left the game on crutches and was out of the Wednesday trip to Oxford.

The visitors' largely safety-first attitude raised questions over both Kendall and his malfunctioning attack. 'Before the Forest match we knew that three wins and a draw would enable us to keep the title,' the manager said afterwards, 'Well, that's the draw, now we need the three wins. It's in our own hands. It's as simple as that.' That was true but the Blues' boss was playing a high-stakes game, regarding the match in hand – against West Ham two days after the final Saturday of the campaign – 'Like an IOU from Fort Knox' according to Lacey. There was a danger if they failed to gain maximum points from Oxford and Southampton that the West Ham game could become an irrelevance. Meanwhile the attack, so potent earlier in the season, was floundering. Lineker had netted only one league goal in two months, but was clearly not 100% fit, his greyhound pace thwarted by a hamstring injury. At Forest, although the build-up play was good, there was a lack of variety. 'At the moment we're a little bit apprehensive in front of goal though we're still getting plenty of crosses into the penalty area,' Kendall said.

And so to Manor Ground on the Wednesday, scene of Heath's dramatic intervention nearly two-and-a-half years before. As on that occasion the home team, desperate for points themselves during a relegation battle, could be dangerous opponents and had just destroyed the highly-fancied QPR 3-0 in the League Cup final. In an unusual development, the two title favourites were both playing away from home simultaneously, although Liverpool kicked off at Leicester fifteen minutes later. Intriguingly, West Ham had defeated Manchester City 48 hours before, to go within two points of the champions and a victory at Upton Park over Ipswich on the same night would keep their remote title hopes alive.

On a cool spring evening, the visitors were without Reid, with Kevin Richardson stepping in. As expected, the first half was nerve-wracking, with barely a shot fired in anger. 'This was a game in which both sides were deeply immersed in their own objectives,' Clive White said in *The Times*. 'Both sides refused to give ground as they clashed with the regularity of stags in the mating season.' Consequently, the foul count averaged well over one per minute in the opening half-hour as tempers flared. Sharp (in the opening minute) and Ratcliffe were both booked after squaring up to opponents while even Colin Harvey entered the referee's notebook. It was that sort of evening but as the players trooped off at the break, they heard that Liverpool were leading 2-0 after thirty minutes.

With both sides knowing a draw was probably of little use to either, the second half was more expansive. However, there are several myths attached to this game worth exploring. The first is that Everton deserved to win. They did not. Most chances went to the home team, who showed more energy and imagination throughout. Big striker Billy Hamilton struck the woodwork with a header and saw another miraculously cleared off the line by Gary Stevens, with the ball ricocheting off the underside of the bar. Mimms pulled off a brilliant save from a Ray Houghton header on the goal-line. The second is that Gary Lineker missed 'four or five' big opportunities. Yes, there were three openings for the England striker but, apart from one, they were half-chances at best. The big moment occurred midway through the half when Sheedy's long ball left him clear of the Oxford defence but, in attempting to move the ball to his right side, the striker's mis-control took it in the opposite direction and Alan Judge in the Oxford goal comfortably blocked his left-footed chip. 'I've had a few embarrassing misses in my career...but if I had to nominate one, it would be the one at Oxford because it was so important,' Lineker later admitted. The final myth, of course, is that the striker's performance was affected by the absence of his 'lucky boots', thought at the time to have been left in Liverpool. But as Colin Harvey revealed to author Simon Hart in *Here We Go: Everton in the 1980s* the boots were later found under a radiator in the dressing room.

For all that, with ten minutes left the game was still goalless, so Kendall brought on Heath, again too late in the contest. But with 120 seconds left the mortal blow arrived. Hamilton picked up a long ball inside the Everton box, set up Les Phillips and the midfielder beat Bobby Mimms from the edge of the box. It was a goal the home team thoroughly deserved and, when the cameras cut to Kendall with his head in hands in the dugout, the gathering gloom at the Manor Ground was now engulfing Everton's league season as well. With no way back the players sat in the dressing room knowing that Liverpool's comfortable 2-0 victory at Filbert Street had left them five points ahead, needing a victory at Stamford Bridge on the final day to clinch the title. After the game Kendall initially cut an uncharacteristically glum figure. 'The title was in our hands, now it's not and that's the most disappointing thing,' he admitted, before adding, 'The league isn't over yet. We'll all be there fighting on Saturday. I have suddenly become a Chelsea fan!'

To rub salt into the wounds, West Ham had now emerged as Liverpool's closest challengers, a 2-1 victory against Ipswich taking them a point ahead of the Toffees. Should the leaders fail to win on the Saturday, there was a possibility of Everton and West Ham engaging in a title shoot-out on the May Day Bank Holiday.

Title inquest

Sadly that did not happen. Although Everton crushed Southampton 6-1 at Goodison in a rather surreal atmosphere and West Ham won 3-2 at West Brom, a Kenny Dalglish goal in the opening half clinched the title for the Anfield side. Two days later the Hammers were beaten 3-1 at Goodison as Kendall's side clinched second place, two points behind the champions – their total of 86 four less than in the previous campaign but sufficient to have lifted the title in nine of the previous twenty seasons, using three points for a win. 'We have had another great season and the lads made a tremendous attempt at retaining the title. It is to their immense credit that they went so close,' a disappointed Kendall revealed afterwards. 'I said that the side which finished above Liverpool would win the Championship and I was proved right. That still applies.'

When seen in the context of a 42-game league campaign, there is an argument that Everton overachieved given their appalling luck with injuries. Just four weeks into the campaign they lost Reid and Mountfield for five and six months respectively. Kevin Sheedy was barely 100 per cent fit and Paul Bracewell was in constant pain due to the injury picked up by Newcastle. The goalless draw at Nottingham Forest in late April was only the sixth time that the championship-winning midfield quartet had played together all season. Although Bobby Mimms was more than adequate cover for Neville Southall, there is no doubting the absence of the Welshman affected the confidence of the team. By early May it was obvious that Lineker was nowhere near fully fit too. 'I thought Peter Reid and Gary Lineker both looked jaded,' Sir Alf Ramsey claimed in his *Daily Mirror* column after the away win at Arsenal. To be fair, Liverpool had also suffered injuries but, at the business end of the league campaign, their squad was largely fit.

The thoughts since are, of course, that Lineker's arrival disturbed the equilibrium of the championship-winning team. The general feeling is that the team utilised the striker's pace and eschewed some of the qualities of twelve months before. Kendall himself told Lineker's biographer, Colin Malam:

> *When Gary came into the side, we became more direct, played a long ball. He used to exploit the space we have in English football between a square back-four and the goalkeeper. He was absolutely brilliant with that – the ball played over the top, the pace on to it and the deadly finish. Nobody could catch him. So it was a case of Gary's goals, and not many from the other players who'd scored previously…With Sheedy's vision and Gary's pace, it was often the case of the two-pass goal: the goalkeeper to Sheedy, Sheedy over the top to Lineker, Lineker goal.*

Nearly forty years later they are probably the recollections of most supporters – yet the facts do not really support that thesis. Only a handful of Lineker's forty goals came from the long ball over the top, most were either poacher's efforts or via headers – the type more commonly associated with the 1984/85 season. The striker himself later rejected Kendall's claims. 'I don't think my presence changed the style of the team at all,' he said. 'Most of my goals came from crosses anyway, or one on ones, a bit like Michael

Owen goals. I don't ever remember a team talk saying we had to use more long balls to take advantage of my pace.' Peter Reid, for one, agreed with Lineker's assessment.

Contributing to that perception is for long periods of the season the team sat deeper and did not squeeze the play as effectively. Reid's lengthy absence undoubtedly contributed but so did the lack of fitness of Bracewell and Sheedy. Steven had failed to hit previous heights until the final few months when Reid returned. Consequently, the constant mixing and matching in the middle of the park meant the team did not press with the same intensity. In the crucial away victories at Southampton and Spurs in the early spring of 1985 all four goals came from opposition defensive errors while sitting deeper produced fewer opportunities to spread the goals around. The potency from set-pieces that characterised the latter stages of the previous campaign had also diminished.

There was another reason for the goals not being spread. Kendall told Malam that Lineker's team-mates became lazy. With the former Leicester player and Sharp forming such a formidable partnership the tendency was to look for the pair when in possession, so they were left with the goalscoring burden. Getting the ball forward swiftly to the front pair became the easy option. If the strikers were on form, that was an acceptable tactic but when both suffered a goal drought later in the campaign – the defeat at Oxford signalled the end of a sequence of just seven goals in nine league games – the goalscoring capacity of the team was limited. Watching the goalless draw at Forest, Everton had forgotten how to create.

Although it sounds churlish, Kendall's management style also played a part in ceding the title. As discussed in *Boys from the Blue Stuff*, the Everton boss rarely played on the offensive away from home. His initial aim was to close space and opponents before opening out where possible. Despite being the best team in the country, there were only two away league wins in 1984/85 by more than a single goal. Brian Glanville, for one, always felt that Kendall's side rarely made their dominance count away from home. 'Everton have not in the past charmed the birds from the trees,' he wrote in *The Sunday Times* in September 1985. 'Successful they may have been, but the word one would most readily apply to their football was functional. Lots of busy up-and-downing, a midfield which worked like beavers but was seldom touched by the grace of flair, a back four which had frequent recourse to the offside game.'

Although harsh, there was an element of truth in that analysis. After the hard-fought 1-0 win at Arsenal in April, the Everton manager queried why neutrals wanted West Ham to win the title 'for the good of football', making the point that 'People talk about West Ham playing entertaining football and yet they've scored 20 goals less than us. This proves that we are just as entertaining and scoring more goals.' Yet in the *Guardian*, David Lacey claimed that West Ham were popular because, by allowing their opponents to play, they were naturally involved in more entertaining games. In contrast, Everton prioritised stopping opponents. Lacey pointed to Kendall's post-match comments after the Highbury game as confirmation: 'It became a game where we were attacking and they were attacking. I don't like those games. You like having chances yourself, but you also like denying them to the opposition.' This approach worked over a campaign as, by the law of averages, the quality of Kendall's team ensured they would win far more than they lost. However, by the spring of 1986, when Everton needed victories on the road, they required something more imaginative and proactive. The champions garnered just four goals and eight points from the last six away league games as, although they denied the opposition chances, barely any were created. Heath had proved a potent substitute but bafflingly played only a total of fifteen minutes when goals were needed at Forest and Oxford. Also, some of the hesitancy was undoubtedly due to a need to protect Bobby Mimms in goal, but a more positive approach was still required. However, it was never Kendall's style to go on the offensive from the off.

Paradoxically, such a risk-averse approach only added further jeopardy. Everton's insistence that the title was always in their gift, because of the game in hand, left little margin for error but the dropping of five points at Forest and Oxford meant the West Ham match was meaningless. The draw at Forest was only a good result if they had won at Oxford. 'Everton feel they could have and should have pulled out that little extra which would have given even Liverpool too much to do,' Clive White said in *The Times*. White likened the title chase to the famous 800m Olympic final in Moscow six years before, when Sebastian Coe became distracted and was slow to counter Steve Ovett's burst late in the race. By the time the favourite responded, it was too late. 'Everton remain convinced that they lost their title by default,' White wrote. 'They were caught ball-watching instead of watching the opposition...so Everton were taken by surprise by the famous Liverpool kick finish which gathered 34 points from the last 36.' Kevin Ratcliffe later claimed that the 2-0 victory at Anfield may have lulled the squad into a false sense of security: 'It was a good performance and we got what we deserved; but in the end it did us more harm than good. That victory may have made us too comfortable, taking that vital edge off our play.'

A fair assessment. They may have been runners-up, but Kendall's side had the chance for the ultimate revenge within a week. However his earlier statement seemed dangerously apposite: 'The problem for one of the teams is they will be heading to Wembley having just lost the title to their rivals.'

Wembley woe

It took nearly a century for the first all-Merseyside domestic cup final to happen, but the second arrived just two years later. The second Saturday in May witnessed an estimated 60,000 fans pouring out of the city for the historic event, with 26,000 on 400 coaches and a further 8,000 on sixteen trains. The bookmakers' odds reflected the narrow margins: LFC 6-4 and Everton 15-8[13] over ninety minutes but curiously both 10-11 to lift the trophy.

Twenty-four hours earlier Kendall had presented Dalglish with the Manager of the Year award but the Everton boss was in confident mood beforehand. 'I don't think the fact that we were pipped for the championship by Liverpool will have any bearing on the outcome. You don't need to motivate players for a game like this,' he claimed. Twelve months before the press were split over the winner, but this time they were unanimous regarding the outcome. 'It will be close, perhaps desperately so,' said Stuart Jones in *The Times*. 'It will be crunchingly competitive, too, but as Merseyside's finest hour and a half looms one name suggests that Liverpool are about to achieve the double by winning the FA Cup final at Wembley. That name is Kenny Dalglish.'

On face value, both teams entered the contest in great form: Everton two defeats in 29 league and cup games, Liverpool unbeaten in seventeen. Yet trajectories were heading in opposite directions: Kendall's outfit had started the year at their best before tailing off with their rivals doing the opposite. 'We have seen the best of Everton,' Jimmy Hill said on the BBC before kick-off. Of some solace for the league runners-up was they had won four of the previous five derbies.

Although both finalists could select their first-choice XI, Everton had fitness issues with the usual suspects plus Mountfield had also broken down in training on the Friday but passed a fitness test beforehand. Elsewhere, for some, the star strikers would decide the contest. 'You can mention the names of Ian Rush[14] and Gary Lineker in the same

---

[13]   Curiously the same odds as for the 1981 FA Cup fourth round at Goodison.

[14]   One of the great Everton fallacies is Rush could have joined the club, with Gordon Lee claiming he was in for the Welshman in 1980 but did not have the money. That latter bit may have been true but Liverpool always held first refusal on the striker, having made an agreement at Anfield on Boxing Day, 1979. Manchester City – through their former player Alan Oakes, who was Chester manager – were second-in-line. Rush's later claim that Everton were his only club is debatable to say the least, as there was another candidate. Interviewed by the *Daily Mirror* in his Chester days, Rush said, 'If I could choose it would be Manchester – Manchester United. Everton were the first club I watched as a kid but when I first went to see Manchester United it hit me straight away that this was a place where I wanted to score my goals… there's nothing quite like the atmosphere at Old Trafford.'

breath as the likes of George Best and Denis Law,' Jimmy Greaves said in his *Daily Mirror* column. Referee was Alan Robinson, who had taken charge of the League Cup final two years before.

Nevertheless, in front of a 98,000 crowd paying record receipts of £1.2 million, the pair of deadly marksmen were bystanders during the opening quarter-of-an-hour in a repeat of the incoherent and sluggish play that characterised the previous year's final. Then after seventeen minutes of assorted fouls and stoppages came one of the game's major talking points. Sharp was all set for a clean header from Stevens' angled cross but Steve Nicol's clumsy lunge took away his legs and the striker was left in heap. It was a clear penalty to even the most biased of observers. Two years before Robinson had controversially failed to award a spot-kick when Alan Hansen handled on the line from Adrian Heath and the Portsmouth-born official was in no mood to apply redress. Incredibly he waved away Evertonian claims. It was a baffling decision and the only explanation for the referee's inertia is that the incident – like in 1984 – came too early in the contest. 'Everton are entitled to feel that someone somewhere had loaded the dice against them,' Hugh McIlvanney wrote in the *Observer*. With the industrious Reid and Bracewell beginning to gain a stranglehold in the middle, twelve minutes later supporters were entitled to believe no luck was needed. Lineker fastened onto Reid's long ball and, although Bruce Grobbelaar parried his first mishit effort, the striker reacted swiftly to plant the rebound into the net.

A goal ahead at the break, Everton effectively lost the contest in the opening ten minutes of the second period. With Liverpool uncharacteristically losing both composure and organisation, the Toffees dominated and Kevin Sheedy – otherwise quiet – forced Grobbelaar into a fine save from a free-kick before his right-footed shot arced agonisingly wide. Then came a strange moment which people have claimed since was the turning point. The Liverpool goalkeeper dropped Sheedy's cross and full-back Jim Beglin impeded him before he gathered the ball safely. The goalkeeper then screamed at his team-mate, squaring up before shoving him in the chest. In total command, Kendall's team seemingly had Liverpool exactly where they wanted them, but within three minutes conceded a costly equaliser. Stevens' poorly directed pass down the touchline was picked up by Ronnie Whelan, who fed Jan Molby and the Dane's through ball to Rush was followed by a clinical finish. Within seven minutes the champions were 2-1 ahead. On the BBC afterwards Terry Venables queried Derek Mountfield's fitness and the centre-half really should have picked up a long ball to the right wing but Rush got there first, and Molby's cross was finished off by Craig Johnston at the far post.

Kendall then took a decision that still baffles. Adrian Heath had twice scored from the bench during the earlier rounds, and it was no surprise to see the striker stripped off and ready for action. To the amazement of everyone present he replaced Gary Stevens, when the obvious substitution was for Trevor Steven, whose disappointing performance was in keeping with a moderate campaign. Although the attacking threat was increased, with three at the back and Bracewell filling in when required, the team lost all shape and left big gaps in the middle of the park for Molby to exploit. There was no surprise when an unmarked Rush made it 3-1 near the end, a goal that surely would not have been scored had there been a more effective substitution. When the final whistle sounded distraught Everton fans and players watched on in agony as their rivals celebrated becoming only the third club to record a league and cup double in the twentieth century. 'They had blown it and they knew it,' Ian Ross wrote in the *Liverpool Daily Post*, 'They had let Liverpool off the hook and they knew it. They had foolishly provided the spark to light a fire which was to totally envelope them. And they knew it.' Kendall's gripe afterwards was that referee Robinson had got a key decision wrong when Sharp was sent spiralling in the first half. 'To me it was a blatant penalty,' he claimed, 'I know it sounds like sour grapes but there are turning points in matches and we could have gone 2-0 up at half time.'

In truth, it sounded like a bit of sour grapes and did not address why Everton lost a final that seemed theirs for the taking after an hour. Firstly, there was a sense of destiny on Liverpool's behalf. As Hugh McIlvanney commented: 'How else can the losers rationalise a match in which they went a goal ahead and achieved an almost disdainful superiority for nearly an hour and yet finished the day comprehensively beaten and all but demoralised?' The psychological impact of losing the title to their rivals seven days before also came into play: when Liverpool equalised there seemed a sense of inevitability about the result so familiar in later years. Peter Reid was critical of the back four and in his diary of the campaign submitted a withering assessment:

> I am angry, because I though some of the lads bottled it. At 1-0, when we just needed to be strong in certain areas, I thought we bottled it a wee bit. It doesn't need me to name names, I think the lads know who they are. The elementary mistakes we made were scandalous. I think it was all about character at the time, and we just didn't show enough as a team. And that is what wins you games.

Notwithstanding long-standing fitness issues with several players, they were fair points. The performance in the final thirty minutes was deeply disappointing, not helped by the substitution. There were occasions in the final month or so that the team desperately missed Andy Gray's drive and personality, so vital the year before, and this was one of them. In contrast, the accumulated experience, expertise and winning mentality garnered by the Liverpool backroom staff (and players) over their two decades or more of success massively contributed to the remarkable transformation after half-time. In contrast, Kendall (and Harvey) had far less experience in truly big games and that probably showed, particularly regarding the panicky substitution.

About the controversial replacement, Kendall was defiant after the game, rejecting any accusations that it was punishment for Stevens' lapse. In *Only the Best is Good Enough* he claimed the substitution 'suggested that I was annoyed by his basic error of judgement but it wasn't that, I was simply shuffling things around.'[15] The move was possibly influenced by Heath's game-changing entrance at Goodison in September, when he replaced defender Ian Marshall at the break. But that was a gamble worth taking as the team was 3-0 down with nothing to lose and carried insignificant risk in the context of the early stages of a 42-game league campaign. But at Wembley, in a season-defining encounter, the match was still delicately balanced at 2-1 with eighteen minutes left when Kendall risked everything with three at the back. A bad decision that backfired completely was arguably in keeping with the way the Everton boss had managed the final month when the domestic double was effectively gifted to their rivals.

Kendall did not see it that way at Wembley. 'We haven't finished the season with nothing. It's a marvellous season we've had. We've finished second in the League and been to Wembley. Most clubs would settle for that,' he said, before ruefully adding, 'but it's a shattering end to the season when you think of who won the Double.'

---

[15]   The Everton boss had previous for this. At Portman Road in September 1983, he angrily substituted John Bailey immediately after the full-back's suicidal back-pass had gifted the home side a first goal. Everton lost 3-0.

7

BLUEPRINT FOR THE SUPER LEAGUE

AS THE TWO MERSEYSIDE GIANTS CONTINUED TO CARVE UP THE domestic game's major prizes, the so-called 'Big Five'[16] continued in their mission to take more of the financial cake, following the 1983 Chester Report. As discussed in *Boys from the Blue Stuff*, the document made three major proposals: reduce the top flight to twenty teams with regionalised lower leagues; redistribute television income towards the biggest clubs and remove the sharing of revenue from home games with the away team. However, due to the archaic voting structure in the league – each club in the top two divisions got a vote each and the bottom two leagues four each in total, with an overall three-quarters majority required – those outside the Big Five largely voted against them[17] with the only concession being the home team keeping all the gate receipts. 'The First Division are becoming increasingly intolerant of a situation where they are required to subsidise clubs in the lower divisions when they have financial problems of far greater magnitude than the clubs in receipt of those subsidies,' Philip Carter told the report's author, Sir Norman Chester.

Big Five, big ambitions

The origins of a super league of big clubs go all the way back to 1980 when Carter met his Manchester United and Tottenham counterparts at Goodison to discuss ways of improving their commercial prospects. There were other clandestine gatherings. In the same year Celtic and Rangers representatives met with leading English clubs at Goodison, with the Scottish clubs keen on joining a super league. Within eighteen months Carter

---

[16]   A term first used in stories over the new television deal in early 1985 to describe Everton, Liverpool, Manchester United, Arsenal and Spurs. It was not the first time the description had been used: at the turn of the decade the Big Five was Liverpool, Manchester United, Arsenal, Ipswich Town and Nottingham Forest.

[17]   The key group being the so-called 'Bates-Noades' axis, named after Chelsea chairman, Ken Bates, and his Crystal Palace counterpart, Ron Noades. They were a cabal of potential trophy-winning clubs outside of the Big Five who inhabited the top two divisions.

was hosting six club chairmen and then the group expanded to ten and then all his counterparts. 'We were exploring every avenue so we had these meetings, after which we talked to the FA about our ideas,' Carter told Joe Lovejoy for his book *Glory, Goals and Greed: Twenty Years of the Premier League*. 'They said, "No chance, we'll block it. Legally, you can't do it." So our plans were put on hold, but with talks continuing behind the scenes.'

Consequently, by the autumn of 1985, with plummeting gates, no European football or television income, the Big Five's frustrations over the failure to implement the Chester Report in full started to boil over. 'We cannot continue forever and a day to divide our money among 92 clubs,' Carter angrily remarked, 'Under the new format we must concentrate on the senior clubs. The third and fourth divisions will be concerned about the situation. We are starting on a long road of change and there will be financial problems for some clubs.' In early October, there were reports that eighteen clubs would be breaking away from the Football League to play in a separate league under the jurisdiction of the FA.

A month later, after the Big Five continued to push for structural and financial changes, a meeting of chairmen agreed in principle to reform the organisation of the Football League. But there were differences of opinion over the approach and consequently a sub-committee of ten leading football figures – led by Carter – were billeted in a hotel at Heathrow airport and tasked with pulling a blueprint together for ratification by the clubs. 'There is no way we want to see any of the third and fourth division clubs going out of business or any of their players being put out on the dole,' Carter warned, 'But we have got to look at ourselves as in the entertainment business of the 80s and 90s. If we don't, then some of us are going to die. But I stress nothing will be to the detriment of the smaller clubs.'

The outcome was a ten-point plan – the so-called Heathrow Agreement. The major features were that the top flight should be reduced to twenty clubs by 1988 with a play-off for the final promotion place in the lower divisions. The First Division should receive fifty per cent of the rewards from television and sponsorship with the levy on gate receipts – intended to help the smaller clubs – reduced from 4% to 3%. The archaic voting structure required revision. The threat of a breakaway by the top clubs, if their plan were not accepted, acted as a grim backdrop to the meeting. However, Carter said: 'This is very exciting and important. We feel it will capture the imagination of the public.'

Nevertheless, by March 1986, with no agreement with league chairmen reached, Carter reaffirmed the previous threat. 'If we [the Big Five] do not get the support then the First Division clubs will have to look at their future again,' he said. 'We hate bringing out the idea of a Super League or a breakaway. But if things stay the same there is no way the

major clubs will allow themselves to be dragged down into obscurity.' After meeting at
Villa Park that month, the First Division chairmen warned that they were prepared to go
it alone unless the plans for reform got support at the forthcoming April summit. Carter
also confirmed that a feasibility study for a breakaway league had been drawn up by a
select committee under David Dein, the vice-chairman of Arsenal, and added a further
warning: 'We have said all along that we want these changes to be implemented within the
present league structure…we reserve the right to take whatever action we deem necessary.
We are not happy with the way football is going and we will not be happy if the ten-point
plan is rejected.' The consensus was any super league would immediately become a closed
shop, leaving clubs seeking promotion out in the cold.

With English football standing on the precipice, league chairmen accepted all the
proposals of the Heathrow Agreement at April's extraordinary general meeting. For once,
it seemed that, after years of self-interest, club leaders were united in looking at the bigger
picture and the health of the game. Yet they were given little choice. Browbeaten by the
most powerful clubs in the land, they had no other option. Accept either the proposals
publicly unveiled in December, or the certainty of a so-called super league being formed.
After nine months of secret negotiations, the chairmen of Arsenal, Everton, Liverpool,
Manchester United and Tottenham Hotspur had got what they wanted. But if the 92
English clubs thought the agreement ended their financial problems, or any talk of a
super league, they were wrong.

The Superfluous Cup

During the 1985/86 campaign, the European ban forced leading clubs to find new and
imaginative ways of generating income. The coffers were also adversely impacted by the
absence of television cameras before Christmas: not only the missing income from BBC/
ITV but also no coverage significantly devalued ground sponsorship deals, by anything
up to £40,000 a game for matches that would have otherwise been televised.

With the UEFA ban only extending to competitive games, Everton attempted to play
lucrative fixtures abroad. The most startling development was an agreement for two
games in Baghdad against the Iraq national team in January 1986, which was eventually
cancelled over security concerns relating to the ongoing border dispute with Iran.[18] The

---

[18]　Chelsea were one team who did take up the offer, playing a game against the Iraqi national team in March 1986. The
squad also met their infamous leader Saddam Hussein after the game. The match ended 1-1 although the following day's
newspapers recorded it as a 2-1 victory for the home side. 'And they say fake news is a modern phenomenon,' Pat Nevin
recalled on the official Chelsea website.

ban also made the 1985 UEFA Super Cup – a one-off fixture between the European Cup and Cup Winners' Cup holders – defunct. There had been talks between Juventus and Everton over an ersatz version of the fixture later that year and, after the Baghdad trip was cancelled, Philip Carter, Kendall and secretary Jim Greenwood travelled to Zurich to meet officials of the Italian club – the outcome was a provisional agreement to play two fixtures, home and away. UEFA placed certain conditions on the games: they must be of an essentially friendly character; no extra time or penalties and no trophy award. Also the authorities would not support any matches until April at the earliest, feeling any meeting beforehand was too close in proximity to the Brussels disaster. With both clubs facing pressure fulfilling competitive fixtures, they could find no convenient dates and, with the European club finals and World Cup looming, the idea was quietly dropped.

One initiative that filled the gap in the fixture list was a new competition created by the Football League, for those six clubs who had been banned from Europe. 'For want of a better name, since they are yet to find a sponsor, they are calling it the Football League Super Cup,' wrote David Lacey in the *Guardian*. 'A sponsorship agreement with a leading brewer fell through this week which was perhaps just as well. No doubt the brewers were acting in good faith but would they really have wanted to be associated with a competition born out of a disaster which had followed a heavy day of drinking in Brussels?' The fact that the Super Cup was announced three weeks into the new season hardly added to its lustre, as did the general apathy towards a sport carrying no television coverage. The six teams were divided into two groups of three, with the top two qualifying for the two-legged semi-final stage before a showdown at Wembley in May. Eventually the Super Cup found a sponsor in ScreenSport, a fledgling cable television company, who broadcast all the games live.

Ironically, in early September the much-derided competition produced one of the games of the season. When Everton travelled to Old Trafford for their opening group encounter, there was little cause for optimism. Manchester United had won their opening eight matches but, with home attendances exceeding 50,000, there was just 33,859 people present to watch the champions, with chairman Martin Edwards recording in his programme notes that he hoped the cup would 'only last for a year', on the basis that UEFA may lift the ban on English clubs. Everton temporarily halted United's early season charge in its tracks, following a game the *Guardian* called 'a breathtaking spectacle replete with dramatic incident, subtle skills and half-a-dozen excellent goals.' After United dominated the opening stages, both Sheedy and Lineker scored with headers before the home team pulled one back with a penalty before the break. In the second half the Ireland international scored one of his finest goals, a 25-yard daisy-cutter of ferocious power that sizzled into the corner of Gary Bailey's net in front of the travelling fans at the Scoreboard End. Sharp's late header wrapped up a superb 4-2 victory. 'That should have reminded people that we are the champions,' Kendall said afterwards. The Everton boss was less enthusiastic two weeks later when Norwich City came to Goodison, his pre-match team-talk in many ways acting as a coda for the Super Cup. 'What a waste of time this is – out you go,' was the extent of his famous instruction. Everton won 1-0 in front of just 10,329 hardy spectators at Goodison – with a repeat result against Manchester United in December securing top spot.

In the other group – featuring Liverpool, Southampton and Tottenham – all six games witnessed attendances of less than 15,000 fans. Everton's trip to Spurs for the first leg of their semi-final in wintry conditions saw a goalless draw and only 7,548 spectators lumbering through the turnstiles, the lowest gate at White Hart Lane for forty years. 'When the decision was made by the six clubs that qualified for Europe it seemed a sensible idea but on reflection it's a competition the public don't want,' Tottenham boss Peter Shreeves admitted afterwards. He was not wrong and Shreeves was probably relieved when six weeks later Everton, without eight first-team regulars, won the return leg 3-1. The European ban hit home at that point: instead of playing a European Cup tie in mid-March against say, Barcelona or Juventus, Everton were featuring in the semi-final of a competition that nobody really wanted, least of all the paltry 12,008 supporters. The other semi-final was equally farcical, with three months between the two legs of the Liverpool-Norwich clash, Dalglish's side going through at Anfield only four days before the FA Cup final. In keeping with this derided cup competition, due to fixture congestion the two-legged final was delayed until the following season, with Liverpool victorious over an injury-ravaged Everton 7-2 on aggregate, watched in total by 47,000 spectators – the usual attendance for a single derby game, which spoke volumes for a tournament which now thankfully sits in the shadows.

Gary's gone

With supplementary games hardly money-spinners, club finances for the campaign spelled out the damage caused by the European ban. Despite a similar domestic season, there was a small profit of £13,000 compared to one of £700,000 in 1984/85, with income alone down by £500,000. Although Everton remained one of the richest clubs in the country, in a financially stricken sport they, like every other club, had to sell to buy.

As the 1985/86 season reached a climax, Gary Lineker's scoring exploits had obviously made him a potential target for continental giants. After Kendall had informed Lineker's agent, Jon Holmes, of Barcelona's interest after the away game at Watford during April, 24 hours later the Everton boss told the player, who immediately expressed a desire to speak to the Catalan club. Kendall subsequently told Holmes that Juan Gaspart, their vice-president, would call, except he did not. 'It was all on and off, on and off,' Holmes told Lineker's biographer Colin Malam, 'Gaspart was ringing and we were supposed to have a meeting, then nothing happened – typical Barcelona scenario.' Further complications arose because Lineker had flown out for the Mexico World Cup and when Gaspart eventually contacted Holmes on Friday, 6 June, England were playing Morocco. After productive talks, Holmes kept Lineker updated and flew out to Barcelona the day after England defeated Poland 3-0 in their final group match, with Lineker scoring a famous hat-trick. 'So it wasn't really true to say it was that game that made the transfer, because it was already on,' Holmes later said. 'The only thing Gaspart said after it was, "Oh, it'll cost us more money now!"' Except it did not. Although publicly quoted at anything between £2.5m and £2.8m, the fee agreed before the World Cup of £2.2m remained unchanged.

The variance is possibly due to complications around a clause stipulated by the original tribunal twelve months before, which was that Leicester were entitled to a third of any profit on a sale in the next two years. With Barcelona reportedly unwilling to go beyond their £2.2 million offer, once Leicester took their cut of just under £500,000 then Everton were making a disappointing profit of less than £1 million on the deal. However, with the tribunal clause not entirely binding, Everton negotiated the Foxes' share down to £250,000, on the basis any deal would not otherwise go ahead and in twelve months they would not get a penny. This upped their profit to a more palatable £1.15m – or what they would have received on a deal worth £2.5 million had Leicester taken their full share. However, the actual cash value was less, as Holmes confirmed in Lineker's biography, 'I saw the contract and the fee was £2.2 million…it was cash up front.'[19] This is confirmed by the fact the club blocked Lineker's Barcelona debut in a friendly against Andorra in early August as the fee had not been paid in full.

[19]   Everton's accounts for 1986/87 confirm that £2.9m transfer income was received from June 1986 to May 1987. Given four other players left during the campaign, for total fees nearing £800,000, the balance in the accounts is the £2.2m for Lineker, confirming Holmes' account that it was a cash up-front deal. Everton have been subsequently criticised for not including a provision to review the fee after the striker's successful World Cup, when they would have got more. Yet that is with the benefit of hindsight. Had there been a clause to do that, Barcelona would undoubtedly have agreed to a starting amount of considerably less than £2.2m before the World Cup – say £1.8m. If Lineker had failed in Mexico then Everton would have received a smaller fee than eventually agreed. Probably correctly, they went with the safest option.

Despite complexities over the deal and tabloid stories that several clubs were chasing his signature, Holmes made the above-mentioned visit to Barcelona the day after the Poland game to agree personal terms. But with Lineker still in Mexico there were problems: the Catalan club told Holmes they were happy for him to sign on his client's behalf as they could not wait. But the agent, following discussions with the player and his family, kept the Spanish club on hold until the England striker returned from the World Cup, when the contract was signed.[20] It was worth waiting for: an annual salary of £250,000 over eight years.[21] Apart from money, Lineker had another reason for leaving: 'I have a desire to play in European football. It is a shame English clubs are banned from Europe – I believe they need each other.'

Gary Lineker with Kendall after being voted PFA Footballer of the Year. Also voted Football Writers' Association Footballer of the Year, the striker was a wanted figure.

---

[20]   By the time Lineker and Terry Venables played a straight bat to Des Lynam's questions on the BBC after the World Cup final, in all likelihood the player's contract had already been signed, with the deal announced 24 hours later.

[21]   Spanish clubs already had a Bosman-like rule that players at the end of their contract could leave on a free, so were handed long deals.

Kendall was surprisingly sanguine in the aftermath. 'I did not recommend to the board that we should sell Gary so that we had that amount of money to spend on someone else,' he revealed, 'It is very difficult to stand in someone's way when a contract of that kind is put in front of him. I suppose that for the second season in succession I shall be criticised for selling a striker.' Kendall also confirmed that terms were agreed with the Catalan club before the start of the World Cup, leaving Lineker to agree his own contract when he returned home.

Subsequently Lineker holds a curious place in the Everton annals. Like Fred Pickering before him and Tony Cottee afterwards, his Goodison career is seen as emblematic of a relatively fallow period in the club's history after championship success. Somebody who put personal gain before the wider needs of his team-mates. For a long time, he was also regarded as some sort of pariah for rarely referencing the club, even though the twelve months at Goodison witnessed his most prolific scoring spell. Both are enormously unfair. 'There has been a bit of revisionism about what Gary brought in the short time he was at Everton and a lot of people question whether the team suffered because it was built too much around him as an individual,' Peter Reid later claimed. 'I can see that argument, but it's straightforward - if we had kept things tighter at times we would have won more games because we had one of world football's best goalscorers up front.' As for not talking about his time at Goodison, Lineker argued, not unreasonably, that it was because nobody ever asked him about it – perhaps a reflection of the club's falling stature in the years following his departure. 'Why don't I talk about them more often?' he told the *Liverpool Echo* in 2008, 'I do my best, but I'm a presenter rather than a pundit so I have to try and be more objective than some other people.' When he did speak he was always honest in his opinions. 'There's no doubt at all that Everton was the best team I ever played in,' the striker said in the same interview. Only time would tell whether Lineker's departure weakened or strengthened that side.

Welcome Waggy
Elsewhere there was little major transfer activity. However, there were a couple of surprising deals, one of which was the acquisition of 32-year-old former England 'B' international Paul Power from Manchester City for £65,000. 'Paul is a very fit lad who can operate at left-back or in midfield,' was hardly a ringing endorsement of the Mancunian's qualities but in many ways the deal made sense. Neil Pointon was injured and would miss the start of the season while Kevin Richardson was out-of-contract with an uncertain future.

However, the Everton boss was keen on strengthening central defence. Injuries had plagued Derek Mountfield throughout the previous campaign and, in retrospect, it was possibly a mistake to include the local-born player in the cup final starting line-up. Kendall made an inquiry to Dundee United about Richard Gough and included Hearts' Craig Levein, Chelsea's Joe McLaughlin plus, optimistically, Mark Lawrenson on his shortlist. Kendall made no move for Terry Butcher, who went to Rangers from Ipswich, because he was very much left-sided and could not play with Kevin Ratcliffe. Norwich City's defensive bulwark Dave Watson then emerged as the leading candidate. Born in the Scotland Road area of the city, the centre-half had joined Liverpool as a teenager and, after only six weeks as a professional, plus fifteen reserve games, moved to Norwich City in November 1980 for a fee that eventually rose to £100,000.[22] Although the Anfield side had significant cover at the back, Bob Paisley later confessed, 'I knew I'd regret it.'

Within a month the 19-year-old was in the first-team and making an immediate impression on somebody with whom he would form a close association. 'I had never heard of him until he signed,' team-mate Joe Royle admitted, 'but having seen what he has done in a short time I think he can go all the way to the top.' Watson's time in East Anglia was feast or famine: two relegations from the top flight plus two promotions, including one as Second Division champions in 1986. However, twelve months earlier Watson – now installed as skipper – had surprisingly lifted the League Cup trophy at Wembley following a 1-0 victory over Sunderland. It would not be the last time the defender would climb the 39 steps to collect silverware.

By August 1986, with doubts over Mountfield's long-term fitness following further knee surgery and Van Den Hauwe also injured, Kendall contacted the East Anglian club. After Philip Carter held talks with his Norwich City counterpart, Robert Chase, the asking price was £1 million with Everton offering just £600,000 in return. Even after the Goodison club upped their offer to £750,000 for somebody who had just signed a new three-year deal, Chase stood firm to the player's frustrations. An unhappy Watson was determined to move on. 'Norwich are asking ridiculous money for me,' he protested, 'Being realistic, they have just gone totally overboard.' With Kendall backing off, claiming £1 million deals between English clubs were a thing of the past, and now checking on his back-up list of centre-halves – which resulted in a £600,000 offer for McLaughlin – the deadlock was broken when an eye-watering fee of £900,000 was agreed ahead of the

---

[22]   Plus a startling contractual condition that Liverpool would receive £100,000 should Watson ever be capped by England. It took just three-and-a-half years for the Carrow Road outfit to pay up: the defender making his international debut in the famous 2-0 victory at the Maracana in June 1984.

player putting pen to paper at Villa Park. [23] It was the highest domestic deal for five years and more than Kendall had wanted to pay but, given the club's parlous injury position, the manager had little choice. 'I needed the best – and Watson is the best,' Kendall proclaimed, 'I have read all the stuff about it being ridiculous to pay so much for a defender and it leaves me cold. To win trophies you have to have quality – and Everton are in the business of winning trophies.' However, the likelihood of picking up the major prizes in the forthcoming campaign was threatened by an injury list which was not so much a list but a small pamphlet.

---

[23]   The venue selected as it was midway between the two parties and curiously a key ground in Watson's early playing career. It was there in 1980 that Norwich City manager Ken Brown was first alerted to his potential after watching him play for Liverpool reserves.

8
MIXING AND MATCHING

THE INJURY LIST CONFRONTING KENDALL AT THE START OF THE 1986/87 campaign was largely carried forward from the previous season. Neville Southall was progressing but still some months away from returning. Gary Stevens was suffering from a stomach muscle strain and ordered to rest, while Derek Mountfield had only just returned to training. Neil Pointon had ruptured knee ligaments in March and was not expected to return until November. Pat Van Den Hauwe was said to be suffering from a 'blood disorder', a condition subject to much speculation and idle gossip among the local population for most of the season.

The two biggest worries were in the centre of midfield. After his injury-ravaged 1985/86 season, Peter Reid picked up a stress fracture of the shin during the World Cup and started the campaign in plaster with no obvious return date. The biggest concern, though, was his partner, Paul Bracewell. Originally diagnosed with a shin problem after the infamous tangle with Billy Whitehurst on New Year's Day, he was still able to feature in nineteen of the final 26 games of the season, although suffering continuous pain. Kendall hoped that a summer of rest would resolve the issue but eventually the former Stoke and Sunderland player needed an ankle operation, leaving him too in plaster by August.

Charity begins at Wembley
Apart from Dave Watson and Paul Power, Kendall had added other players to the squad during the summer. The Everton boss returned to his old stomping ground at Stoke to pay £150,000 for promising right winger Neil Adams. With doubts over his midfield duo, Kendall laid out £100,000 for 22-year-old Kevin Langley from Wigan Athletic, having spent £100,000 for striker Warren Aspinall from the Latics at the end of the previous campaign.

There was good news elsewhere with Adrian Heath unsurprisingly signing a new four-year deal when Lineker departed. Peter Reid's future had looked cloudy during the summer, with the England international out of contract. Spurs were one interested party – they wanted Reid in exchange when Kendall had tried to bring Gary Mabbutt to Goodison the previous winter – but the London club's hopes were extinguished when the midfielder signed a two-year deal. Kevin Richardson was another player out of contract and, after featuring in the opening two games of the campaign, the Geordie left for Watford for £250,000 during early September. Graham Taylor, Watford's manager, had made several approaches since first casting eyes on the midfielder in an FA Youth Cup tie between the clubs in 1981 and Richardson would go on to have a long and successful career, particularly at Arsenal and Aston Villa, and ended up winning an England cap eight years after leaving Goodison. Several times during this period supporters wished he was still at the club: also, the likelihood is Richardson would have succeeded Kevin Ratcliffe as skipper. Kendall wanted to use the money to buy Manchester United's Mike Duxbury but saw his bid rejected.

Two players who had largely unfulfilled Goodison careers for different reasons. Paul Bracewell and Andy King challenge for the ball at Kenilworth Road in March 1986.

Consequently, a patchwork squad travelled to Wembley for the Charity Shield against Liverpool in mid-August. With television showing the game live for the first time, there was little sign that Merseyside derbies under the Twin Towers were losing their novelty value, as a full house of 98,000 watched a Toffees scratch XI featuring only five recognised first-teamers. However, showing the resilience and versatility that characterised the entire campaign to follow, the underdogs ground out a 1-1 draw, with an Ian Rush equaliser 100 seconds from time cancelling out Adrian Heath's 81st minute strike. Alan Harper moved seamlessly into Gary Stevens' right-back position while Kevin Langley also impressed, although the midfielder fired wide when put straight through at 1-0. However, the way Liverpool continually opened up the defence only reinforced the need for a new centre-half, which was rectified during the following week. Encouragingly the man of the match was Trevor Steven, who showed a welcome return to the form of two seasons before, after a disappointing campaign last time out. 'At the end of the day, we have fielded a young and inexperienced team against possibly Liverpool's strongest side,' the wideman claimed after what was largely seen as a moral victory. 'We can hold our heads up high and take credit from our overall performance.'

Marshalling resources

A total of 16.5 million spectators passed through the turnstiles during the 1985/86 league season, a reduction of 1.4 million from the previous campaign and the lowest in the post-war era. Over six years gates had dropped by a third. Even allowing for strengthening the top flight's powerbase after the Heathrow Agreement, English football remained in a parlous state. Leading players like Gary Lineker and Mark Hughes had gone to Barcelona, while Ian Rush's had agreed to join Juventus, in a move deferred for twelve months. In the *Guardian* David Lacey described the domestic product as 'a dying entertainment eking out an existence in squalid surroundings,' while, on the first league Saturday of the campaign, a searing editorial in the same paper opened with a requiem for the game:

> *As the lads line up this afternoon, they must already be sick of hearing that 1986-7 is English football's make or break season. The claim is rubbish. Every season for years has been the make or break season and, in case anyone missed it, English football broke years ago. It is only because non-violent football supporters are all such incorrigible sentimentalists that it is still possible to pretend otherwise.*

Yet there was still room for optimism amid the gloom. The previous campaign had witnessed the most entertaining and enterprising fare seen on English grounds for several years, resulting in an open title race which, although ultimately unpalatable for Everton supporters, put football on the back pages for all the right reasons. The all-Merseyside FA Cup final was the de facto European Cup final when set against the supposed real thing:

a truly rotten goalless draw between Barcelona and Steaua Bucharest in Seville four days later, settled by probably the worst shoot-out in tournament history. The forthcoming campaign was also expected to produce a strong challenge from north London, where George Graham and David Pleat had taken over Arsenal and Tottenham. Elsewhere Manchester United were looking to regroup under Ron Atkinson while hopes were that West Ham and Chelsea would continue to progress. That said, after winning six of the nine domestic trophies over the three previous seasons, with five further runners-up spots, the two Merseyside clubs were still the benchmark. 'None [of the challengers], in my view, have the durability that seems to mark this latest phase of domination of our League,' was Steve Curry's view in the *Daily Express* after the Mersey powerplay at Wembley in the Charity Shield.

Unsurprisingly, the bookmakers saw the title race in the same way: Liverpool 9-4, Everton 3-1, Manchester United 4-1, Tottenham 10-1, Chelsea 15-1. Emlyn Hughes has a certain reputation among Everton supporters but his comment in the *Daily Mirror* that 'I wouldn't bet tuppence on any other team except Liverpool or Everton winning the League title this season,' echoed the feelings of many. The opening day of the campaign did little to dampen that prediction: while Liverpool were easing to a 2-0 victory over Newcastle, at Goodison Park a 35,198 crowd watched on as the home team overcame Nottingham Forest by the same scoreline. Kevin Sheedy's display showed that he was probably fitter than at any time over the previous twelve months, the Ireland international producing two sumptuous strikes to wrap up the points on an afternoon filled with narratives from the previous campaign. 'I scored nine goals last season but I'm looking for fifteen to twenty this time,' the match-winner revealed, 'Now that Gary has gone the onus is on everyone to try and score and hopefully this is just the start for me.' Thankfully it was, as Sheedy would go on to have the finest season of his Everton career. Elsewhere, previous defensive frailties allowed speedy winger Franz Carr the freedom of Goodison as Forest struck the woodwork twice. Understandably fingers were pointed at the new signing. 'Certain aspects of our defensive play were not what they should have been,' Kendall said, before adding, 'That is not down to Watson or any individual but overall we should have been better defensively.'

Two days later, on Bank Holiday Monday, the Toffees travelled across the Pennines and came away from Hillsborough with a 2-2 draw, following goals from Graeme Sharp and Kevin Langley. The relatively unknown foot soldier – St Helens-born and a Liverpool fan – had been a star of the opening weekend and, at 6ft 2in, added a muscular presence to the Blues' engine room, tackling hard while being a threat in the opposition box.

'Howard Kendall's £110,000 investment in Kevin Langley seems small change compared to the near £1 million transfer fee forked out for Dave Watson,' Ken Rogers claimed in the *Liverpool Echo*, 'But the former Wigan midfielder could prove to be one of the shrewdest buys of the season if he continues to progress at his present rate.' Understandably, having plied his trade in the lower divisions, the midfielder failed to maintain that early-season form and was out of the team by late autumn, before moving to Manchester City, but his combative efforts over sixteen league games were vital.

Ian Marshall was another forgotten – or soon-to-be-forgotten, at least at Goodison – player. Previously deployed unsuccessfully as a centre-half, the last remaining member of the 1984 FA Youth Cup-winning team found himself named as a substitute at Coventry City five days later. Despite largely dominating proceedings, the visitors were a goal down with ten minutes left when Marshall came on as a replacement for Langley. The impact was immediate. David Phillips' clearance from a corner went straight to the substitute, who smashed the ball home for a deserved equaliser in front of the away supporters. Marshall's only league strike for the club preserved the unbeaten start.[24] After four points from the next two games, a fortnight later Kendall's outfit travelled to the unlikely surroundings of a dilapidated old stadium in south-west London for a meeting with one of the decade's great success stories.

Wombling free

Plough Lane, Wimbledon's home ground in the 1980s, was an unforgiving place for visiting players and supporters. The stories of sabotage are legion: dirty changing facilities with no electricity, cold water only in the showers, plus the omnipresent ghetto blaster from the home dressing room. For away fans the amenities were equally austere, notably toilets that were contained within a portacabin at the front of the terraces, stood on stilts for hygiene reasons. The Dons had only joined the league in 1977, but had moved briskly through the pyramid and just nine years into their tenure they were promoted to the top flight. There was snobbery about both their size – four-figure home attendances were the rule, not the exception – and a long-ball, physical style of play best described as primitive. 'There are those who claim that what Wimbledon play isn't really football,' Ted Croker

---

[24] Arguably not his most important goal for the club – that was at the end of the previous season. Played as an emergency striker for the reserves at Huddersfield, Marshall's goal secured a 1-0 victory which ensured the ignominy of relegation from the Central League was avoided. After leaving Goodison in 1988, Marshall had one of the more interesting post-Goodison careers, being part of the Joe Royle revolution at Oldham Athletic before flourishing at Martin O'Neill's Leicester City at the end of the 1990s – one significant achievement, for Evertonians at least, was an injury-time winning goal for the Foxes at the Kop end in April 1999.

once said. He also controversially argued that the club should have no place in the First Division. Gary Lineker famously said the best way to watch them was on Ceefax. Even more famously their nickname, 'The Crazy Gang',[25] seemed apt.

Nonetheless, that does the supposed imposters a disservice. Within their ranks during the latter half of the decade were some players who would enjoy long and successful careers at bigger clubs. They were one of the first to use extensive video analysis and player data. Unsurprisingly, the upstarts had shown the top flight no respect and, in fairy-tale style, stood top when Kendall's men visited a very wet and windy SW17 where the best and driest view in the ground was from the packed away-end toilets.

In front of a league-record crowd at Plough Lane of 11,708 – with the game shown live in 33 countries around the world, from Iceland to Jamaica, the Everton boss paid the home team the compliment of fielding three central defenders to counter the challenging long clearances of goalkeeper Dave Beasant, with Ratcliffe sweeping behind Watson and the returning Derek Mountfield. For all that, the visitors went ahead on just four minutes when a slip allowed in Trevor Steven whose pass was slid home by Sheedy. Everton remained in control for a further half-an-hour before Wimbledon surprisingly equalised, when Wise's skimming cross fooled the unsteady Everton defence and Alan Cork finished at the far post. In the second period Mimms saved well from the scorer before Sharp netted the winner, heading home when unmarked from a Sheedy free-kick. The visitors held on for a fortunate victory after a frenzied, muscular contest where they had displayed all the durability required by champions.[26] 'Someone had to spoil football's fondest fairy story and, thankfully, Everton ended it with the grace and efficiency that makes them such an attractive power,' James Mossop noted in the *Sunday Express*. When Everton then vanquished a poor Manchester United side 3-1 at Goodison in a game broadcast live by the BBC, Kendall's makeshift side stood an unlikely second in the table. But that was about to change.

Waggy wobbles

Mixing and matching only has a limited shelf life – even the best managers can only survive without a corps of their best players for so long. To be fair the Everton boss rarely complained about the hand he had been dealt, but even Kendall must have wondered

---

[25] A description usually attributed to John Motson, after the 1988 FA Cup final, but a moniker first used by the *Daily Mirror's* Tony Stenson in 1985, who described Wimbledon thus: 'Rag-arse Rovers – soccer's Crazy Gang.'

[26] Up to the end of the 2023/24 season this remains the last occasion Everton have won away in the league against a team who were top of the table.

how many mirrors had been cracked when all four full-backs were injured for the visit to Spurs at the end of September. The absence of Harper showed how much the team missed his versatility – Mountfield played at right-back and Heath was forced into midfield. The visitors rarely threatened at a sunlit White Hart Lane, going down to a brace from the prolific Clive Allen. The second arrived after a moment of comedy: Kevin Ratcliffe uncharacteristically misjudged Ray Clemence's long kick, clumsily slipped and fell and allowed the Tottenham striker to fire past Mimms.

With the unbeaten run now over, talk naturally turned to the detrimental impact of those in absentia. However, when Kendall finally spoke about the injury list, creditably he did so from an unexpected angle. Even in the dark days of his early years, the Everton boss rarely fell into the trap of public self-pity and he was in no mood to change. Before Arsenal visited Goodison, the Everton boss laid down a challenge to his players: 'Make headlines for yourselves and not our absent stars,' he retorted, 'We have a lot of injuries but people weren't talking about them when we beat Manchester United less than a fortnight ago. Now the biggest compliment the players who take on Arsenal can get is to ensure people talk about them at the end of the match and not those who are injured.'

Sadly that was not the case. Newly installed as manager, George Graham was developing the main feature of his Highbury tenure: a miserly, but formidable, defence which gave no quarter. Eight league games had featured a miserable ten goals in total, the Gunners scoring just five with the same number of clean sheets. The only goal at Goodison was in keeping with that pattern. Steve Williams took their first corner and fired the ball towards a near post covered by Ratcliffe, Sharp and Sheedy. Sharp appeared to be pushed and a second later a bemused Sheedy looked round to find the ball, which had passed through his legs, nestling in the back of the net. With no Reid and Bracewell to set the tempo, or establish a foothold in opposition territory, chances were at a premium against a well-drilled backline as Everton lost at home in the league without scoring for the first time in three years.

Dave Watson was clearly struggling to adapt to life at Goodison and the club-record signing endured a nightmare afternoon in the early autumn sunshine at Selhurst Park when newly-promoted Charlton Athletic – on leave from The Valley – shocked the Mersey aristocrats. Their hero was Jim Melrose, a Scottish striker who had previous with the visitors. Twice in the opening period the journeyman took advantage of a slack Everton defence – and an out-of-position Watson in particular – to score, either side of a Kevin Sheedy free-kick. After the Ireland international equalised again from another free-kick just after the break, twelve minutes from time substitute John Pearson beat

Ratcliffe in the air and the header fell into an area where Watson was exposed against two players, one of whom was Melrose, who slammed home the winner. The Everton centre-half immediately punched the ground in anger. Remarkably, it was the second treble of Melrose's career against the Toffees, the first being for Coventry City at Highfield Road, four years before.[27] Even more curiously, for the first time Kendall had lost three successive league games during his time as Everton manager.

With Everton sliding to seventh in the table, there were recriminations over a surprising loss to a team who had started the day eighteenth. While '£900,000 centre half Dave Watson was left to reflect on one of the worst performances of his life,' according to the *Sunday Mirror's* Mark Irwin, Kendall was furious in the aftermath. 'It was too much of an end-to-end game from a manager's point of view,' he said, 'I was disappointed that we didn't score more goals and very, very disappointed with our defending.' Mihir Bose in *The Sunday Times* isolated the issue further: 'Kendall sees it as a collective defensive problem. Yesterday the problem consisted of two people: central defenders Ratcliffe and Watson. Ratcliffe has been strangely hesitant in recent matches but it was Watson who provided Kendall his headaches.' As a former Liverpool reserve replacing a home favourite in Derek Mountfield, the transition was always going to be difficult. However, that shift was further complicated by his struggle to adapt to Everton's high line – the first two goals came after Charlton broke the offside trap – and the fact that, unlike at Norwich, he was not the defensive leader. With no Reid and Bracewell to offer protection and problems at both full-back positions, in many ways Watson's early struggles were an accident waiting to happen and not necessarily all of his own making. Having said that, those mitigating circumstances cut no ice with supporters. 'The main problem is the number five position currently occupied by Watson', a frustrated fan wrote in the *Football Echo*, 'At Tottenham and Charlton I just could not believe what I was seeing from such an experienced player.'

Here comes the cavalry

Charged with returning the walking wounded to the first-team, physio John Clinkard[28] was another feeling the pressure. 'It's beginning to get to me, I'm desperate for a day off, or even just a lay-in,' he admitted, 'Just getting the organisation right is a major headache.

---

[27] Melrose is still the only player to score hat-tricks against Everton for different clubs and one of only four to record two trebles (or more) against the Toffees.

[28] Famously, Clinkard's nickname was 'Magnum', due to his uncanny likeness to the moustachioed American private detective played by Tom Selleck. So much so that when a new bar was opened in Wigan called Magnums, there was only man who was going to perform the opening ceremony.

For one thing there are not enough beds for everyone.' With house-full signs in the physio room at Bellefield, the trip to the Dell in mid-October summed up Kendall's powers of improvisation. The starting XI featured just four players who featured in Rotterdam, with Mountfield at right-back, a full-back in right midfield (Harper), a wide man in a central creative role (Steven) plus a central midfielder featuring wide left (Langley). With Heath also playing in midfield, the forward pairing was Sharp and Paul Wilkinson. To make a difficult position even worse, five minutes before half-time Watson left the pitch with a hamstring strain, which necessitated a further rearrangement of an already reshuffled line-up. With substitute Warren Aspinall moving into a striking role, Langley returned to his usual position and Sharp occupied unusual territory on the left wing.

The away fans camped behind Peter Shilton's goal, realising the team were up against it, provided some of their most vociferous backing of the season. Ironically, Aspinall's arrival changed the game, the substitute injecting some vigour into a dour encounter where the visitors' efficient offside trap had attracted chants of 'boring, boring' from home supporters. Everton took control and were rewarded twelve minutes from time. Sharp picked the ball up deep on the left-hand side, sent a perfect fifty-yard pass to Heath and when his cross was fired into the box, Kevin Bond tripped Wilkinson. Referee Alan Gunn pointed to the spot and Trevor Steven converted comfortably. Immediately afterwards Aspinall turned skilfully on the byline, crossed and Wilkinson's header beat Shilton. Kendall was in combative mood after the 2-0 victory. Asked by the press whether his team's offside tactics were ruining the game for spectators, the Everton boss trenchantly replied, 'If teams like Southampton can't produce the knowhow to time their attacking runs and beat such tactics, the blame is on them.'

Looking after number one

Off the pitch there was positive news regarding Neville Southall. After his appalling injury in Dublin the goalkeeper had the plaster removed in June but his rehabilitation was limited to the police swimming pool in Aigburth. 'If you were at that pool that summer you'd have seen me hopping up and down the swimming pool on my injured leg, trying to build up strength,' he recalled in *The Binman Chronicles*. After six months that had 'almost driven me crazy, through boredom and uncertainty' the Welshman returned to training in late September and three weeks later was in the reserve team, typically a month ahead of schedule. 'It is very pleasing to see him back,' was one of Kendall's great understatements.

To Southall's surprise, he was recalled for the home game against Watford at the end of October. Yet the Welsh international's return was overshadowed by a colleague who had shared the treatment room at Bellefield, one who dominated the game in a manner rarely seen at the ground. 'Derek Mountfield left Goodison last night still trying to decide whether or not his contribution to a bizarre afternoon came into the category of triumph or tragedy,' wrote Peter Welbourn in the *Sunday Express*. Following a goalless opening period, the centre-half opened the scoring after 53 minutes but joy was short-lived as, within sixty seconds, the scorer brought down John Barnes in the area and Kenny Jackett converted from the spot. Just after the hour David Bardsley tripped the rampaging Power and Trevor Steven restored the lead from a retake – Watford keeper Steve Sherwood being distracted by a photographer's groundsheet which blew in front of him when the Everton player converted the original.[29] Then twelve minutes from time, Mountfield was again on the scoresheet but this time at the wrong end, the centre-half misjudging Lee Sinnott's long throw in the windy conditions and his back-header shot past a defenceless Southall.

Remarkably the 24-year-old was still not finished. Within four minutes he was affecting the game again at the other end, on this occasion when Sherwood missed Harper's cross and Mountfield headed the winner. There were some heroics from the returning keeper, as five minutes from time Southall's marvellous save from Mark Falco's header brought back memories. Mountfield's double took his record to eighteen league goals in ninety appearances, a remarkable achievement for a centre-half. However, the unlikely 'hat-trick' left the centre-half quipping: 'I'm a bit peeved they won't give me the match ball.' Elsewhere though, it was Southall making the headlines and who better to pay tribute than a player with whom he is synonymous. 'He is a world-class keeper and that was a world-class save,' said Mark Falco, 'He has done it to me before when I was at Tottenham and he's obviously lost none of his ability through being out so long.'

Naturally the return of Southall opened the question of Bobby Mimms' future. The answer came within 48 hours, the former Rotherham keeper slapping in a transfer request. 'I don't think I deserved to be dropped,' he predictably complained, 'I was left out of the team after doing nothing.' With no chance of winning his place back, Mimms had several loan spells before leaving for Tottenham in February 1988. After an unhappy time at White Hart Lane, he spent six years at Blackburn, making three appearances in the title-winning 1994/95 campaign before ending his career in the lower divisions. Neville Southall later said that Mimms was too laidback and did not work hard enough in training,

---

[29]   The incident appearing in the famous 'What Happened Next' section on BBC's *Question of Sport* in March 1988.

which possibly explains why an initially promising career failed to develop.

Yet any thoughts that Southall's return would herald an immediate march back up to the top proved ill-founded. Following a televised 1-0 loss at West Ham – a fourth successive defeat to a London club – capital rivals Chelsea once again proved crudely effective opposition at Goodison in a 2-2 draw. 'Everton are rarely outfought, but Chelsea's muscular tactics and commitment have shaken them in recent seasons,' Peter Ball pointed out in the *Observer*. Four visiting players were given a yellow card – Pat Nevin one surprising entry in the referee's notebook – while Kevin McAllister saw red after punching Sheedy when he complained about a head-high challenge. Remarkably it was the fourth dismissal in just over twelve months during games between the two teams.[30]

Both Everton goals were in keeping with a messy, niggling contest. The opener came from a first-half Steven penalty and then, when Chelsea goalkeeper Tony Godden was penalised for time-wasting, Sheedy's free-kick from ten yards bypassed a nine-man wall on the goal-line. Typically, those strikes were not enough to clinch the points for the dominant home team, as Keith Jones undeservedly equalised a minute before the break and then Colin Pates snatched a late draw when Southall missed a Doug Rougvie cross. 'Everton had been mugged,' Peter Ball concluded but the Chelsea chairman disagreed. 'We had to try and beat the referee and linesman as well,' growled Ken Bates in the bowels of Goodison after the game, although that was not the majority view. The costly draw left the Toffees eighth, albeit in a logjam at the top and only four points behind new leaders Liverpool. A week later Sheedy's excellence plus an inspired Southall – 'He was incredible,' Adrian Heath said afterwards – kept Leicester at bay in a 2-0 win at Filbert Street, with the former scoring a magnificent goal from 25 yards to secure a hard-earned result. New leaders Arsenal, impressive 4-0 victors at Villa Park, were at the summit on 28 points with, in far more democratic times, no fewer than five clubs a single point behind.

A week later came what was now, by some distance, the most important fixture in English football: the Merseyside derby. Remarkably when the two sides locked horns at a windswept and wild Sunday afternoon at Goodison it was their fourteenth meeting in three years, with a further League Cup quarter-final tie scheduled for the new year. Sadly, but unsurprisingly given the conditions, the much-awaited encounter in front of the millions watching on BBC and a 48,247 crowd – the highest in England so far that season – was probably the most disappointing during that period.

---

[30] To put into context during an eighteen-month spell between September 1985 and March 1987 there were five players sent off in Everton games, of which four came against Chelsea.

The goalless draw was a by-product of two shocking decisions made by experienced referee George Courtney. The first came midway through an attritional opening period, when only a die-hard home supporter could have argued Ian Rush had used excessive force on Mountfield before turning in the area and firing past Southall. The Spennymoor official did though and controversially blew for a foul. Within minutes Courtney was dismissing more protests, this time from the home team. Heath quickly turned Mark Lawrenson in the penalty area and was left sprawling on the damp turf after being clearly caught by the defender's leg. It was an obvious penalty but Courtney provided the perfect example of a referee righting two wrongs. Following those incidents, apart from a Heath header that struck the bar and some skirmishes in the Everton box, there was little to warm the spectators at the final whistle, their initial passion and enthusiasm having long since morphed into an indifference which produced jeers, chants of 'boring' and then silence. That was most unfair on the combatants, who made the most of difficult conditions. As Stuart Jones pointed out in *The Times*, 'Less talented sides would have been reduced to a giant-sized version of blow football.' The draw left Everton fifth but on the cusp of a run of form the like of which has rarely been seen at Goodison.

9

UNLEASHING THE POWER

MANCHESTER UNITED 5-0. BAYERN MUNICH 3-1. THESE ARE PROBABLY regarded as the two best performances in Howard Kendall's first tenure as Goodison boss. Yet in pure footballing terms one game ranks above even those memorable occasions. Everton's 4-0 victory at Newcastle United on Boxing Day 1986 was the aesthetic high point of Kendall's reign. Under the headline 'Everton unleash a challenge too powerful', *The Times'* John Wardle wrote:

> *You will not find many among the 35,000 who marvelled at their brilliance yesterday who would bet against Everton's chances of coming out on top in May. They can rarely have played better in manager Howard Kendall's time at the club, giving an awesome display of running, precise passing and decisive finishing.*

The perfect display was at the heart of a wonderful run of form that, in quality terms, ranks as the finest in the club's post-war era. At its core was one of Goodison's most gifted players.

Sheedy shines

This largely unforeseen change in direction was rooted in November's Merseyside derby. Kendall had been playing Neil Adams and Sheedy out wide with Trevor Steven and Kevin Langley in the middle. The Ireland international was in great form, producing a majestic performance throughout a superb 4-1 triumph at Carrow Road in the League Cup four days before, when a goal displayed his quick thinking and talent for the unorthodox. Adams' cross from the right bounced awkwardly but, though off balance and with his weight on his right-hand side, the gifted midfielder merely let the ball pass across his body, altered his shape to the left and side-footed it, at chest height, past the keeper from twelve yards. It was a quite brilliant effort that took him into double figures for the campaign, already one more than the previous season. However, with Langley struggling for form and Steven in an unfamiliar role, the Toffees lacked a controlling presence in midfield which was a key part of Kendall's management. So when Langley was taken off with fifteen minutes left of the Goodison derby, the Everton boss moved Sheedy into that position for the first time.

The change proved pivotal. Sheedy stayed there for the trip to Maine Road on the final Saturday in November and it was immediately apparent that his vision, flair and passing range added an extra dimension which had not been there even with Peter Reid and Paul Bracewell. Following a scare when Paul Moulden equalised Adrian Heath's early strike, the visitors were frustratingly level at the break. 'We'd been sloppy. The game should have been over and done with then,' Kendall remarked after the game. With Sheedy dictating proceedings, Everton regained the ascendancy in the second period, going ahead when goalkeeper Perry Suckling was somehow beaten by Paul Power's relatively tame effort from the inside-left channel. The former City favourite immediately appeared bemused. 'I really didn't know what to do or how to react,' he said with some embarrassment after the game. 'If it had been a more vital situation I would probably have regretted scoring.' Howard Kendall thought it was a vital situation, famously admonishing the player for not celebrating. Six minutes from time, Sharp fed Heath for a third goal, the deserved 3-1 victory being Everton's first on the ground in fourteen years. Kendall may have been critical of Power over his goal, but he was effusive in his praise for the 32-year-old, who covered every blade of grass on his return to Maine Road. 'We just didn't have an oxygen tank ready for him,' Kendall joked, 'He had done a tremendous amount of work in midfield after playing at left-back all season.' However, for all Sheedy's technical excellence and a reinvigorated Trevor Steven's endeavour, man of the match was Heath, who rediscovered the form that made him such a dangerous opponent two years before. 'Nobody marked Heath because nobody could find him,' Cynthia Bateman said in the *Guardian*, 'He darted about like a cursor on a computer screen, with equally devastating effect.'

Four days later Newcastle were the visitors to Goodison for a Full Members Cup third-round tie – another tournament created to fill the gap arising from the European ban. The 7,530 privileged spectators at Goodison saw 'the Blues coast into the last eight of the competition with a superb display of controlled and often exhibition football,' according to the *Liverpool Echo's* Ric George. Sheedy opened the scoring as early as the fourth minute with a crunching half-volleyed drive from twenty yards out. By the break Sharp had his first club hat-trick, which included a beautifully crafted second when the Newcastle defence was unlocked by a series of crisp, first-time passes and the Scot chested home Sheedy's cross inside the six-yard box. More brilliant play by Sheedy set up Heath for a fifth near the end.

The magnificent 5-2 victory also marked the return to the first team of Dave Watson after his enforced lay-off, but Kendall was keen to stress it was not necessarily a permanent change. 'When you have got a quality squad, you are always going to have good competition for places,' he said, 'We happen to have two of the most outstanding number fives in the country.' The other good news was that, on the day of the City game, Peter Reid and Paul Bracewell successfully returned for the A team, as did Gary Stevens. The full-back was immediately promoted for the visit of Norwich City, who were put to the sword for the second time in eighteen days in another compelling four-goal display.

The crowning glory of a magnificent 4-0 victory – 'In today's performance you can just hand out the superlatives,' a jubilant Kendall said – was the final goal, a special strike unique in Goodison's long history. 'Even those masterful South Americans could not have bettered the magical climax to Everton's 4-0 triumph provided by Adrian Heath and Kevin Sheedy,' John Keith proclaimed in the *Daily Express*. With the visitors caught up the pitch, Heath signalled to Neville Southall to deliver his kick wide. After passing to Sheedy, Heath sprinted towards the area. Sheedy, now standing 25 yards out and with the bemused Norwich defence facing him, merely chipped the ball skywards and, such was the perfect judgement of the delivery, the striker did not have to break stride before making a difficult finish look easy by volleying into the net. 'It was a moment to cherish, a moment assured of its place in Merseyside's football folklore,' Keith remarked.

Meet the president

At half-time during the Merseyside derby at Goodison, the BBC's Bob Wilson spoke with Philip Carter. However, the interview was not about the Toffees' progress under Kendall, but because Carter was now president of the Football League. After impressing peers with his negotiating skills during the dispute over the proposed super league and television contract, Carter had been elected to the role six months before. His in-tray was stacked high, but right near the top was the League's response to the Government's demands for a compulsory membership scheme for supporters – which all 92 clubs opposed. There had been an ongoing battle between the two groups, with the League initially aiming for seventy per cent membership, on the grounds of cost and providing freedom for the casual fan to attend games.

As president of the Football League, Philip Carter signs a new sponsorship deal for the First Division with the 'Today' newspaper in 1986. The Everton chairman was now one of the most powerful figures in English football.

One club, however, pushed ahead with the full scheme. Luton Town had been one of the first clubs to introduce an artificial pitch and their compliance with the government diktat proved equally controversial. One of the by-products of the scheme was the exclusion of away supporters. Although the League was content with the ban for First Division games, on the basis they evened themselves out, the problem was in one-off cup games, with their specific rules on ticket allocations for travelling fans. Initially the League accepted Luton's proposal for cup ties but, within 48 hours of his appointment, Carter performed a *volte face*. In September, the League kicked them out of their own competition when Luton refused to lift their ban on away supporters for the League Cup tie against Cardiff City. Consequently, a fact-finding visit to the club by the management committee in late November, led by Carter, quickly turned sour. After Carter asked the club to return their £5,000 sponsorship pool money from the competition, Luton chairman David Evans accused the committee of containing 'vindictive' people.

Evans was obviously talking about the League president but, typically, the two combatants had only a fortnight to wait for their next meeting. The atmosphere in the

Kenilworth Road boardroom may have been a touch Arctic, therefore, when Everton – without any of their supporters, naturally – visited on the second Saturday in December. Like their Merseyside rivals – who had lost 4-1 there in October – Kendall's side struggled to adapt to the plastic surfaces of Luton and QPR and had never won at either venue, which given their natural passing style was strange. History repeated itself at Kenilworth Road, with a 1-0 defeat thanks to a fortuitous Mike Newell goal when the striker stuck out his head to redirect Mark Stein's mishit shot. But the major talking point of the game was one of the unintended and unfair consequences of having no away supporters. Early in the first half there was shouts from the home crowd following a push by an Everton player and the linesman immediately flagged for a foul. Conversely, in the dying seconds of a game the visitors largely dominated, there was stony silence when Steve Foster appeared to divert the ball to safety with his hand in the penalty area. 'A quite obvious handball,' said Steve Curry in the *Daily Express*. Yet, the only noise within the general hush came from the protests of the Everton players, who surrounded referee Darryl Reeves, but the Uxbridge official remarkably waved away their complaints.

The controversial decision highlighted an adverse effect of no away fans. Unusually, one player who was very vocal in the aftermath was Paul Power. 'The ball struck Foster's hand, no doubt about that, I had a full view of it,' the veteran claimed. 'He [the referee] was influenced by the home supporters, without a doubt. Even if we'd had only a handful of our own supporters here today to appeal and catch the attention of the referee I'm sure we would have got the penalty.' David Lacey agreed, pointing out in the *Guardian*: 'The officials would be less than human if they were not affected by a constant hubbub in favour of the home side which lacks any semblance of counterpoint.' After the game John Moore, the Luton manager, was certainly impressed with Everton's performance, declaring he would be putting money on the visitors lifting the title. 'With a name like John Moore he could hardly do otherwise,' Lacey added.

Reid returns, Sheedy shines

By December 1986, Peter Reid's most recent competitive game had been the legendary World Cup quarter-final against Argentina during the summer. The intervening period had been spent either in rehabilitation or on countless trips to specialists but, on the back of encouraging performances for the A team and reserves, the resolute midfielder was substitute for the home game against Wimbledon. Reid's twenty-minute cameo from the bench began with a standing ovation but even this was overshadowed by another dazzling performance from the home team, who treated the Goodison crowd to a virtuoso display.

'On Saturday they struggled for twenty minutes, then suddenly changed gear to overwhelm their opponents with vintage high-speed movements involving half a dozen players at a time,' Ian Hargraves wrote in the *Liverpool Echo*. 'Adrian Heath, Trevor Steven, Kevin Sheedy and Gary Stevens looked players of true international class as they tore Wimbledon's gallant defence to shreds.' The restoration of the Stevens-Steven axis on the right was a vital component of the impressive run with the latter, like Sheedy, producing the best form of his Goodison career, looking physically stronger than before. But their powerplay needed a strong element of central midfield discipline and, with Alan Harper seamlessly linking with Sheedy, they got just that. The result was a series of hugely impressive performances that brought praise from their vanquished rivals. 'That was some of the finest football I have seen,' Wimbledon chairman Stan Reed said after their mauling, 'It was a pleasure to watch even though we were well beaten.'

Nevertheless, the victory was merely the *hors d'oeuvres* to the main course at St James' Park on Boxing Day afternoon. Before the game Kendall, knowing he was returning to home territory, paid tribute to the travelling support. 'Everyone at the club appreciates it. We want to hear them on Friday,' he demanded. 'They won't let the Geordies outshout them.' In front of a season's best gate of 35,079, there was little chance of that happening as Everton – with only five outfielders from Rotterdam in the team – produced a performance of mesmeric beauty, with BBC radio's Bryon Butler speculating whether Kendall was controlling the game via a remote control in the dugout.

The dominant visitors went ahead on 22 minutes when Heath picked up a loose ball at the edge of his own box, moved swiftly up the pitch and fed the onrushing Harper, whose first-time delivery was met at the far post by a sliding Power, who had galloped fully sixty yards. Ten minutes after the break, Sheedy, who performed like a quarterback throughout, produced a brilliant pass for Power to run onto and his cross was converted by Steven. Five minutes later it was the same story. Sheedy's ball was played into the inside-left channel to Heath, who fed Power and the veteran midfielder's pass inside produced Steven's second of the afternoon. The crowning glory on a superlative display was a fourth goal of real pedigree. Steven moved like a thoroughbred down the right flank and his perfect cross was met by a well-placed Heath header in front of the ecstatic visiting supporters. 'It is absolutely simple but it is beautiful to watch,' said an admiring Clive Tyldesley on the local station Radio City. With Liverpool losing 1-0 at home to Manchester United in the morning and Arsenal only drawing at Leicester, the magnificent 4-0 victory took Everton second, four points behind the Gunners. The press praise after the game was fully deserved. 'A masterful display,' according to Ian Hargraves, 'Everton scaled new heights of excellence,' John Donoghue wrote in the *Daily Express*. 'For sheer consistency of standard right the way through the team, it was almost the complete performance.' For the manager it was a special day, both personally and professionally. 'I went into the dressing room after the game and told my players what a great pleasure it had been to watch them,' Kendall confirmed afterwards. 'It's always a thrill to come back to your home town and turn on a winning performance…I think it's the best we have played all season.'

After moving to the centre of midfield, Kevin Sheedy enjoyed the finest season of his Goodison career in 1986/87.

Two days later, the remarkable run of form continued as Leicester City were destroyed 5-1 in a dazzling demonstration of attacking football at Goodison. With Sharp suspended, deputy Paul Wilkinson scored twice but the highlight of the afternoon came, unsurprisingly, from Kevin Sheedy. Three minutes were left on the clock when he produced a perfect chip from twenty yards out that sailed over goalkeeper Ian Andrews. There was a brace also for Adrian Heath, who took his tally to ten goals in as many games. Given the striker and Sheedy always had great footballing empathy, there was no surprise that this run of form coincided with the latter's move into the centre of the park. The coruscating display also brought a glowing tribute from visiting manager and former Everton player, Bryan Hamilton. 'It was men and boys,' he proclaimed, 'Everton are a fantastic side, different class. They are the best team we've played and they have strength in depth.' On New Year's Day, there was another rout at Goodison and this time it was the turn of Aston Villa, beaten 3-0 after a goalless opening period. Fittingly, the three players who had contributed most to the brilliant sequence of results provided the highlight for the third goal. Steven found Heath on the right and his beautifully weighted cross was met with another Sheedy crunching volley from twelve yards out.

All the talk after the game was about the Ireland international, who now had fourteen goals for the campaign, many with a characteristic stamp of quality and innovation. Playing in the middle had afforded Sheedy more responsibility and opportunities to go and fetch the ball himself – when playing out wide he was completely reliant on others feeding him. Also, under Colin Harvey's tutelage, there had been a vast improvement from him in working harder when not in possession, but the combative streak and steely resolve shown in his central role was perhaps a surprise to some. One of his illustrious predecessors in the Ireland midfield was a big fan. 'I am a long-time admirer of Kevin Sheedy,' John Giles wrote in Dublin's *Sunday Tribune*. 'He is a natural player with beautiful control of the ball. Always well balanced, his distribution of the ball with his left foot is as good as I have ever seen.'

But even a player such as Sheedy had their talents neutralised on QPR's dreaded plastic pitch[31] when Everton were at Loftus Road two days later. The visitors' record there was abysmal: no goals scored in three games on the surface, with two damaging defeats. The psychological impact was obvious in the opening period. Having carried all before them for six weeks, the visitors reverted to the default Kendall away-game plan of containment in front of 19,287 frustrated spectators, including a huge away support. 'I asked my players to do certain things they haven't done in recent weeks, simply because of the surface,' the Everton boss said beforehand. With offsides and throw-ins aplenty as the ball constantly ran out to touch – 'the ball's out of play so much officials must be tired of putting their arms up,' Kendall remarked afterwards – Everton came for a point but ended up with all three thanks to the only moment of quality over ninety laborious minutes. The visitors broke up a Rangers attack, countered and after Steven fed Sharp,

---

[31]   The first goal scored on a plastic pitch was netted by Andy King, of all people, for QPR against ironically, Luton Town in September 1981.

the striker slalomed through three defenders before calmly sliding the ball past the onrushing David Seaman. Although victorious, the Everton manager cut loose about the surface after the game. 'We are in the entertainment business, but we found it very difficult to perform out there,' he declared, 'I don't like it, the players don't like it and I honestly believe the fans don't like it. The difference between our recent performances and today's was purely down to the pitch.' QPR boss Jim Smith notably did not disagree. Thankfully, four weeks later, the Football League banned any other clubs installing new surfaces and by 1991 the four in England using them – Luton, QPR, Oldham and Preston North End – had to reintroduce grass pitches. Very few complained.

Odds on Snods

Ian Snodin first played against Everton for Doncaster Rovers in the FA Cup at Goodison in January 1985. Moving to Leeds United that summer, the midfielder continued to progress under the watchful eye of Billy Bremner[32] and, with Kendall impressed, the Everton boss made an initial approach for the England Under-21 midfielder at the end of the year. Leeds rejected the offer, with the Elland Road club wanting more than £500,000. The informal contact between the clubs continued and, twelve months later, Leeds wanted a swap deal involving the unsettled Bobby Mimms plus cash, one that Kendall also turned down. With the club suffering an injury crisis and the Snodin situation drifting, Kendall also explored other options and Arsenal turned down a £800,000 bid for their England Under-21 midfielder, Stewart Robson.

Liverpool, West Ham and Tottenham were also interested in Snodin but by early January only the Merseyside giants were left in the race and, after both had previously offered £650,000 and then £750,000, when the ante was upped to £840,000 Leeds chairman Leslie Silver told the player it was time to go. Settled at Leeds and inspired by his manager, ironically Snodin was against any agreement. 'I didn't want to go to either club, to be honest,' he later told the *Yorkshire Post*. But with Leeds wanting to push through a deal, the sought-after starlet travelled across the Pennines to speak to the two clubs. With both offering similar wages, the choice ultimately came down to the player. After much thought, Snodin chose the blue side, which certainly contributed to one of the shortest medicals in history. 'I was literally there half-an-hour,' he told the *Yorkshire Post*, 'It was a case of "you have turned them [Liverpool] down and you are signing no matter what!" No matter if I'd walked in on one leg, I think he'd [Kendall] still have signed me!'

---

[32] Bremner getting the Leeds job in the summer of 1985 after Colin Harvey turned it down.

Ian Snodin signs after famously choosing Everton over their Merseyside rivals.

Eleven days after joining, the new signing made his home debut as a substitute against Sheffield Wednesday, who featured brother Glynn. Once again Sheedy proved inspirational at a freezing Goodison, engaging in a personal duel with the outstanding visiting goalkeeper Martin Hodge. 'It was worth donning the thermal underwear just to see Sheedy's glorious left foot at work,' Leslie Duxbury revealed in the *Observer*. The midfielder may not have scored but Everton eased to a 2-0 victory thanks to a Steven penalty and a first goal from Dave Watson, who headed home at the Gwladys Street End. The welcoming cheers were an indication that fans were warming to the defender, who had looked more at home since returning to the side in December. Although Watson was now more comfortable with Everton's high line than before his injury – 'Looking back that was the best thing that could have happened to him. It gave him the opportunity to sit in the stand and watch how Everton played,' Kevin Ratcliffe later said – the biggest difference was playing in a settled defence following the return of Southall and Stevens. Typically, the record signing suffered a further injury, twisting a knee when passing back to Southall, forcing another two-game absence. Afterwards former Goodison stopper Hodge was effusive in praising his former club. 'They are in line for more silverware,' he said. 'They create more chances in one game than any other teams do in seven or eight.' But there was particular praise reserved for Sheedy. 'The performance of the midfielder… was magical,' wrote John Keith in the *Express*. 'His passing, crossing and shooting were breathtaking to witness.'

10
SOME BAD BLOOD

WITH ARSENAL ONLY GRINDING OUT A DOUR LIVE TELEVISED goalless draw against Coventry City on the Sunday after Everton's victory, the gap at the top was down to two points in mid-January, with Liverpool a further five behind the Toffees. What appeared to be an open title chase in the autumn looked to have only three remaining horses. However, league commitments were set aside when the two Merseyside giants clashed at Goodison in the quarter-final of the League Cup.

Seeing red at Goodison

With Everton enjoying imperious form in the league and their close rivals having netted just four goals in seven games, the home side wore the unusual mantle of favourites for the League Cup tie. A situation that, for many reasons, has never been a comfortable one for Everton and beforehand – with no victories in five derbies – Kendall was not the first or last Goodison boss questioned over a psychological problem. 'We certainly don't have any complex about Liverpool,' he responded. 'Looking more closely at our recent games against them you'll find things aren't that bad. If you forget the Cup Final - which we do – we've drawn with them twice and lost to them twice. Both those defeats were in the Super Cup where we fielded a depleted side made up of young players.' On a misty and frenzied Wednesday evening, the crowd of 53,323 – the last Goodison gate of more than 50,000 – saw a contest carrying echoes of bruising encounters from two decades before. After a bright start from the home team, the major talking point occurred midway through the opening period. Stevens took a heavy touch in the opposition half and overstretched, with a sliding Jim Beglin taking the full brunt of his subsequent attempt to retrieve the ball. Incredibly, play continued until the referee was made aware of the extent of the problem. With the seriously injured full-back carried off, the rest of the opening period was subdued, as if players and crowd knew the severity of the situation. The home team appeared to be affected more as their fortified opponents gained the upper hand. With a replay on the cards, typically, the *coup de grâce* was administered by Rush six minutes from time, the Welshman firing home from inside the box.

All talk after the game was about the reaction to Stevens' tackle. 'WAR' screamed the *Daily Mirror* headline. Alan Hansen sarcastically remarked, 'Apart from the fact that it was high and an hour late, I'd say it was a fair tackle.' Manager Dalglish was equally cynical, claiming that 'Only one person knows whether it was deliberate and that was the person who committed it. Everyone else is guessing.' Apart from being off the mark – Stevens' leg was at ground level and he was not sanctioned – both comments, particularly Dalglish's, were inflammatory. Kendall was furious and, after expressing sympathy for Beglin, he exempted Stevens from blame. Nevertheless, the Everton boss reserved his anger for the opposition bench: 'I could not believe the reaction of the Liverpool side. People were pointing a finger at him and when people start gesturing on the field it upset the lad and it upset me too, because I know him.' England manager Bobby Robson also absolved the player of any wrongdoing. 'Beglin also thought it was his and you had two players converging on a fifty-fifty ball,' he explained, 'The Liverpool player got there a fraction before Stevens. And at the pace of today's game, you've only got to be that bit late that, instead of playing the ball, you catch the player.' Twenty-four hours later the mood was more conciliatory. Hansen insisted the tackle was late and clumsy but not deliberate, admitting, 'I have possibly seen worse tackles in which a player has got away with nothing more than a bruised shin.' Nevertheless, the *Liverpool Echo* pulled no punches in a special editorial piece: 'For just a few mad moments last night the traditional calm and sportsmanship for which Liverpool Football Club have been renowned appeared to have been missing... the sight of officials and players pointing accusing fingers – as if the tackle by Stevens was intentional – was wrong, and they should have known better.'

With Arsenal beaten 2-0 at Old Trafford on the following Saturday, to complete a miserable week the Toffees blew the chance to go top for the first time 24 hours later. In a game broadcast live at the City Ground, the die was cast as early as the fifth minute. Adrian Heath's curling shot cannoned back off the post, Paul Wilkinson's follow-up was miraculously stopped on the line by Forest's Chris Fairclough before Steven struck a third effort against goalkeeper Steve Sutton's legs. The wide man was then at fault for the only goal of the game when his poor clearance eventually ended up at Neil Webb's feet and the powerful midfielder drove home the only goal of the game. With Liverpool having beaten Newcastle 2-0 at Anfield on the same weekend, two points now separated the top three, with sixteen games remaining. 'We've had a bad few days,' Kendall said afterwards, 'We could have been in the semi-finals of the Littlewoods Cup and top of the First Division. But we'll pick ourselves up and get on with it.'

Back to the top

If Everton were to get on with it, they had to do so without Kevin Sheedy for six weeks. After a below-par performance on the banks of the Trent, the midfielder's previous knee problem worsened and, in a shock development, the only answer was a cartilage operation. It was a bitter blow for not only Everton's player of the season thus far, but one of the contenders for Footballer of the Year.

They may have blown their opportunity to go top in Nottingham but on the first Saturday in February, fate provided a further chance with Arsenal's League Cup semi-final causing the postponement of their home game against Liverpool. Yet, after forty minutes against Coventry City at Goodison, any chances of reaching the summit appeared remote. The imaginative visitors – revitalised under John Sillett and George Curtis and later to win the FA Cup – dominated the opening period with embarrassing ease, Cyrille Regis' thirteenth minute goal a poor reward for their complete supremacy. 'Were these the champions-elect we were watching, and if so, which team?' asked a puzzled Stephen Brierley in the *Guardian*. But in the dying embers of the half, Gary Stevens – unfairly vilified by some after the previous home game – was the deserved subject of some luck. Taking a wild left-footed swing at the ball outside the box, the full-back's shot took a wicked deflection off Nick Pickering and nestled in the far corner of Steve Ogrizovic's goal. 'We hardly deserved it,' Kendall said after the game. 'For "hardly" read "did not",' Brierley commented. Seven minutes into the second half there was further good fortune when Lloyd McGrath was harshly ruled to have handled in the box, and Steven converted the penalty. Adrian Heath's header completed a hard-earned victory and confirmed top spot. 'Somebody up there must wear a blue and white scarf,' Chris James claimed in the *Daily Mirror*.

Although Heath was in the goals, usual forward partner Graeme Sharp had been struggling, the striker injuring a knee against Liverpool before going off after an hour when returning against Coventry. The Scot was having a curious season. He had not played badly but at the same time had scored just one league goal – at QPR – in five months. The move of first Steven, and then Sheedy, to the middle of the park deprived him of the service from wide which had proved so profitable in the previous two campaigns. Meanwhile, the change in style perhaps was more suited to strike partner Heath – the ball played swiftly from the middle of the park into the edge of the penalty area, rather than from out wide, was more attuned to his strengths.

Sharp was out of the next game, a return to the scene of the crime at the Manor Ground, Oxford. It may have been Valentine's Day but there was no love lost between the teams, a grudge dating back to the game at Goodison sixteen months before that continued in the return fixture the following April. In their October 1985 defeat on Merseyside, referee George Tyson had deprived Oxford of a very late penalty after Ian Marshall clearly got both hands on the ball in the box. To make matters worse, after the protests subsided the home team went up the other end and Paul Bracewell sealed a 2-0 victory. At full time there were chaotic scenes, visiting manager Maurice Evans had to be restrained from confronting the referee by his own players while enraged goalkeeper Steve Hardwick stalked the touchline waiting to take on all-comers.

As it happens, Hardwick was the crucial figure in a key fixture for both teams, with Oxford in the mire following five defeats from six games. Unsurprisingly, the previous rancour reappeared in a bad-tempered encounter. Oxford went ahead with a controversial penalty awarded midway through the first half, when referee John Martin decreed that Gary Stevens had impeded David Leworthy when they went for David Langan's centre. John Trewick[33] made no mistake from both attempts, with the retake needed following encroachment. Strangely Leworthy, and not notorious strike partner Billy Whitehurst, was the main source of strong-arm tactics, although the latter's boot connected with Southall following a (surprising) legitimate challenge. That said, Whitehurst did get booked for a bad foul on Ratcliffe. With an off-form and clearly unfit Reid's frustrations over Oxford's bruising tactics threatening to boil over, the visitors laid siege to their opponents' goal in front of the packed away following in the second period. After Hardwick had made a string of fine saves and Dave Watson could have completed a hat-trick, with two minutes left the deep-lying Oxford defence failed to clear a loose ball and Sharp's replacement, Paul Wilkinson, volleyed into the net.

Although Everton's dominance should have secured a victory, the goal ensured there was no repeat of the damaging loss of ten months before and the hard-earned point would carry greater significance seven weeks later. At full time, as skipper Ratcliffe angrily confronted the referee and Oxford centre-half Tommy Caton left the field nursing a black eye, Leworthy and Southall – also with a swelling over his eye – engaged in an unseemly scuffle which was only ended by their team-mates and Kendall, with the referee

---

[33] Trewick may have had a largely forgotten career but he did contribute one of football's most infamous quotes. On West Brom's ground-breaking tour of China in 1978, the squad were visiting the Great Wall and Julian Pettifer from the BBC documentary team asked the player for his thoughts on one of the acknowledged wonders of the modern world. 'When you've seen one wall, you've seen 'em all, haven't you?' was his considered and cultured response.

booking the Oxford striker in the tunnel.

Afterwards a visibly angry Kendall broke off a radio interview to instruct Ratcliffe to give 'no comment' orders to the squad, although Southall did say that 'It's a man's game and I've no complaints.' When he returned, the Everton boss praised the 'tremendous courage and passion' of the players before defending them: 'When you've got any character you react to things – but it should be done nicely.' Meanwhile, the fire alarm that shrilled through the main stand and clubhouse after the game seemed wonderfully in tune with the red-hot temperatures generated by an encounter where 'Excessive will-to-win, lack of self control and indecisive refereeing all combined to spoil what could have been a highly entertaining match,' according to the *Liverpool Echo's* Ian Hargraves.

While Everton's courage at Oxford could not be questioned, there was more than a fair degree of finger-pointing eight days later, when a muscular Wimbledon team forced the Toffees into an uncharacteristic second-half submission at Plough Lane. The fifth-round FA Cup tie was finely balanced, 1-1 at the break, before the home team rampaged through the compliant Everton defence, adding two more goals. Not for the last time, striker John Fashanu was at the centre of attention. After clashing twice with Ratcliffe, who finished the game with a shirt covered in blood and two stitches above a cut eye, Fashanu was alleged to have struck an Everton fan following the final whistle. Kendall was critical of the side in the aftermath, implying that some had gone missing, although he did show his sense of humour was still there, quipping, 'I have had a statement ready for three and a half years and unfortunately I have to use it – we will now concentrate on the League!'

Off the perch

'Our year starts here,' Kendall also declared outside the Plough Lane dressing room. Although there was little sign of any momentum being recovered six days later, when Alex Ferguson fielded a five-man midfield at Old Trafford in his first managerial contest against Everton. Kendall, with few options up front, responded in kind and the result was a turgid goalless draw and ninety minutes of purgatory for 47,421 largely uninterested spectators. 'You don't plan to bore the fans,' Kendall remarked later, 'You do what you think you have to do when you're chasing something. I'm not saying we'll play like that for the next thirteen games.' However, in the *Daily Express*, James Lawton showed little sympathy and pulled no punches:

Does English football truly have the will to survive? The evidence was chillingly negative

*at Old Trafford this last weekend. There are 0-0 draws which teem with creative
tension. They swirl and splutter and if they leave you unfulfilled you do not question
that there has been intrigue about what might happen. This could not be said of the
exchange between United, a lost glory of the game, and potential champions Everton.
It was never a test of quality. WHAT IT WAS WAS AN EXAMINATION
OF BANKRUPTCY.*

Given injuries to key players, the Everton manager's caution was understandable,
especially after seeing his side overrun at Plough Lane on the previous Sunday. 'We saw
what happened at Wimbledon last week. It was hard for Everton to play against that
style,' Alex Ferguson said after the goalless draw. 'Strength, stamina, force, gives European
teams so much trouble.' And that was really the trend with English football at the time:
the emphasis on the physical not the technical, with long-ball teams like Watford,
Sheffield Wednesday and now Wimbledon flourishing after promotion. However, after
just four months in the job, the Manchester United manager had identified the main
problem. 'We're getting lads who've been shouted at by their coaches to mark and clear
their lines and nothing else,' he complained, 'and often it is just too late to change them…
there are problems playing creatively in the English game.' At Old Trafford the
workmanlike Everton midfield, shorn of Sheedy, offered little to counter that argument,
leading Lawton to conclude that one of the challenges facing English football was that
'Everton, talented, well organised but deeply unadventurous, threatened to steal the great
prize of the title this spring.'

The criticism was worryingly like that of Bingham's 'robots' more than a decade
before, but the current side had the pedigree of previously being champions and, at their
best, played with a quality that more than matched anybody else. To be fair, Lawton had
just returned to the country after living in Canada for several years, so had not had the
chance to view Everton through the prism of two seasons before. However, the
comments reopened the debate over Kendall's default position of containment when
playing away from home: Lawton was not the only experienced football writer to conclude
that on their travels Everton were less than the sum of their considerable parts and should
have been displaying more imagination as prospective champions. They were all fair
points. Even in his Blackburn days Kendall knew the value of a clean sheet, especially
away from home.[34] But the Everton boss was becoming increasingly adept at knowing the

---

[34]   In their 1979/80 Third Division promotion campaign, Blackburn won eight of their last twelve away games 1-0.
During the following season – the last to feature two points for a win – they just missed out on promotion despite goalless
draws in more than a quarter of their games (11/42).

time to go on the offensive and when to be pragmatic. At Old Trafford, shorn of key players, Kendall chose the latter but whether the goalless outcome was a point gained or two lost was debatable. With Liverpool defeating Oxford 1-0 at Anfield, the two Merseyside giants were now locked at the top with 55 points from 29 games, only Everton's superior goal difference keeping them in first position.

The tenure lasted until the following weekend, when the title chase tilted in Liverpool's favour. Dalglish's side moved to the summit after comfortably disposing of Luton Town 2-0, while 24 hours later Everton lost 2-1 at Watford, after leading at the break. When the reigning champions went to Highbury three days later and returned with a single-goal victory, they had accumulated 26 points from a possible thirty in a ten-match unbeaten sequence. A similar run twelve months before had turned the title race on its head. Now the blue half of Stanley Park hoped that history would not be repeated.

11

BACK IN BUSINESS

SOMETIMES SEASON-CHANGING EVENTS ARE NOT THOSE THAT COME easily to mind but are hidden away in the finer detail. One occurred in the Park End goalmouth on Saturday, 21 March 1987. Although the Toffees had beaten Southampton 3-0 on the ground seven days before, they went into the home fixture against Charlton nine points behind their city rivals, albeit with two games in hand. Everton supporters, fearing the same nightmare as the previous spring, were increasingly disgruntled over a poor run of form featuring removal from both cup competitions and the real possibility of Liverpool disappearing over the horizon in the league. 'There is definitely discontent running through the team,' said one correspondent to the *Football Echo*. 'They have gone from playing brilliantly to producing pathetic performances.'

There was a familiar target. Dave Watson was poor in the loss at Vicarage Road and again the record signing was a target for the fans' vitriol, with familiar calls for Mountfield's return. But the latter was equally unsettled and had asked for a move six weeks before, with Manchester United, Sheffield Wednesday and Chelsea all rumoured suitors. Kendall rejected both his request and fans' demands as Watson retained his place before scoring against Southampton. However, Kendall was so irked by criticism of the record signing that he used the programme notes before the game against Charlton to voice his displeasure:

> *After a couple of defeats, a section of the supporters seemed to pick on Dave and, quite honestly, there was an awful reaction when his name went up on the team-sheet last Saturday. I don't know what these people want… I thought it was terrible to see the letters column in The Echo last Saturday devoted almost entirely to the so called "great debate" about our centre-half position. I suppose the same people who voiced their dissatisfaction before the Southampton game were among those cheering when he scored.*

There was an interesting use of words in the column. The Everton boss referring to a section of support as 'these people' and his valid point about their fickleness over Watson's goal revealing scars still there from his own treatment three seasons before. Indeed, in some respects Kendall's support of Watson echoed his chairman's backing during the dark days of 1983. That said, to restore morale, the manager made a call to arms. 'The battle is on and it's up to us to start putting pressure on them quickly,' he promised, 'It's going to be as tight as it was last season and it's down to us to make sure it goes our way.' But seven minutes from the end of a hard-fought game against the London club events were not going Howard's way. A struggling Everton were locked at 1-1 and new signing Ian Snodin had just been sent off for the third time during the campaign, following a dust-up with Andy Peake, who also saw red. 'These things are normally handbags at five paces, but today it wasn't,' remarked an unhappy Kendall.

With a potential draw leaving Everton eight points behind with only one game in hand, the home team needed some inspiration or a lucky break. They got the latter in one of the season's pivotal moments. Kevin Ratcliffe's cross headed towards the far side of the box where Mark Read's attempted clearance struck Gary Stevens' outstretched right leg. The ball could have ballooned literally anywhere but, in a stroke of enormous good fortune, it ricocheted back towards the Charlton goal and past a startled Bob Bolder for a hardly-deserved winner. 'If Everton failed to play like potential champions they had the luck it takes to land titles,' John Keith wrote in the *Daily Express*. Peter Reid later commented about Stevens' 'tackle': 'I remember saying to my dad in the players' lounge after the game that things like that win you championships.'

Wayne chips in

Supporters dreaming the goal would have the same impact as Ian Rush's at White Hart Lane twelve months before had those hopes realised within 24 hours. Coincidentally at Tottenham on the Sunday afternoon Bruce Grobbelaar allowed Chris Waddle's long-range shot to bounce over him as Liverpool lost for the first time in the league since Boxing Day. Spurs' victory also took them to the periphery of the title race, fourteen points off the top but with a ridiculous five games in hand.

While Tottenham's chances were merely a hypothetical exercise, Kendall's side travelled to Highbury a week later when, instead of eight points behind with a game in hand, the gap was a manageable six with two spare. George Graham's young side had stalled since early January, with no league victories during that time, and were scoreless in the previous five matches. Although Everton had restored some lost confidence, Peter Reid was out of form and was unusually substituted at Old Trafford and then particularly poor in the cup defeat at Wimbledon where, by his own admission, he overdid 'the hair dye to such an extent that everybody in the country noticed!'. With Alan Harper breathing down his neck, Reid had a crucial meeting with Kendall before the Highbury contest. 'I need to see a bit from you, or I can't justify playing you,' the manager informed him, 'because you've had your eight or ten games now, and I'm not seeing anything.' The warning worked: with Ian Snodin having his best game since joining, Reid was a player reborn. 'The match at Highbury was the first time I felt any sharpness,' he revealed in *An Everton Diary*, 'I got in a few tackles and still felt strong at the whistle.'

Reid needed to work hard as the visitors resolutely defended a single-goal lead for more than an hour, the crucial strike coming from Wayne Clarke, bought for £300,000 from Birmingham City three weeks before.[35] For the second time in six days, Everton had a goalkeeper to thank for assisting their title aspirations. On this occasion, John Lukic fluffed a clearance from the edge of the box straight to Clarke who, from 35 yards out, chipped it back over the guilty party, the ball appearing to take an age before nestling in the net. But Lukic's opposite number was the game's star player, Neville Southall producing a peerless display. 'We relied on our goalkeeper,' Kendall stated, 'He had a marvellous game and he confirmed my belief that he is the best in the business.'

On the same afternoon events at Anfield provided a massive bonus. With their game against Wimbledon locked at 1-1 ten minutes from time, up popped substitute Alan Cork to head an unlikely but deserved winner at the Kop end for the new boys. When news of the goal reached those away fans with transistor radios at the Clock End at Highbury, it was the cue for massed celebrations, which puzzled at least one Everton player. 'Neil Pointon came over to the dugout to take a throw-in and asked why our fans were cheering,' Kendall told the ITV cameras after the game, 'But he'll learn, he'll learn!'

However those were merely side issues to the big question of the day posed by the *Guardian's* David Lacey. On an afternoon featuring several heavy squalls, he asked 'Would Reid's hair rinse, which has changed from pepper-and-salt to Marmite, stand the test?' Thankfully the dye, like his team-mates, passed the examination in north London with, literally in his case, flying colours. That victory at Highbury, plus Liverpool's surprise defeat, caused a shift in the title odds with Coral having both teams at 10-11, Spurs at 16-1 and Arsenal lengthening to 66-1. The Everton boss, though, was wary of the betting market. 'First we were favourites,' he pointed out, 'then it was Arsenal and just as suddenly it was Liverpool. Now we are back in business again.'

---

[35]   Clarke was not necessarily first choice. Kendall tried to buy Kerry Dixon from Chelsea but was put off by the £1 million asking price, or a lower cash payment and Adrian Heath in exchange.

That business took Everton back to London on the first Saturday of April for a tough fixture against a Chelsea team unbeaten at home since before Christmas. There was a further boost with a recall for Sheedy after nine weeks out following his cartilage operation, Kendall admitting his importance to the side 'is reflected in the way that I have tended to bring him back earlier than most after injury'. With Liverpool facing Arsenal in the League Cup final at Wembley 24 hours later, the opportunity of going top, on goal difference with a game in hand, was not lost on the travelling thousands who stood unsheltered from the driving rain at a sodden Stamford Bridge. It was not lost on their manager too: 'After being nine points adrift just a few weeks ago we now have a tremendous incentive.'

In many ways the exhilarating contest possessed an epic quality, not dissimilar to the famous victory at Spurs two years before, almost to the day. The parallels were largely due to the form of one man. 'Seldom has there been more irrefutable evidence than that on Saturday that Southall was the difference between victory and defeat,' Clive White wrote in *The Times*. The Welsh international's key intervention had come fourteen minutes from time when the score was level at 1-1, the away team fortuitously going ahead midway through the first half when Alan Harper's left-wing corner skidded off Joe McLaughlin's boot. On 73 minutes Kerry Dixon powered through for a deserved equaliser before Southall's heroics turned the clock back to White Hart Lane. The scorer appeared certain to put Chelsea ahead only for the Everton goalkeeper to produce a wondrous reflex stop from his point-blank header. 'I couldn't believe he got it,' Dixon said later, echoing Mark Falco's words after he too had been thwarted by Southall's genius. Whereas the save against Spurs secured a priceless three points, as White remarked on this occasion it was the difference between defeat and victory. Immediately the visitors broke upfield, Reid fed Harper some thirty yards out and the midfielder's brilliant shot – 'which bent and dipped and did everything' according to Reid – was too much for Tony Godden in the Chelsea goal. There were just thirty seconds between the dramatic save and goal.

The remainder of the game was memorable for two incidents. Within minutes Harper, imbued with confidence, produced an even better strike from Reid's pull-back which went into orbit after rattling Godden's crossbar. When the ball eventually returned to earth, after leaving a circle of mud on the woodwork, the Chelsea goalkeeper brilliantly palmed away Clarke's header. A moment of pure farce followed in the final minutes. Reid powered forward and was clearly tripped by Keith Dublin way inside the box. When the ball ran on Steven produced a clean finish into the bottom corner for 3-1. Or so it seemed. But then referee Terry Holbrook, somewhat after the fact, pulled play back for

Wayne Clarke in the crucial victory at Stamford Bridge.
The striker would prove to be an inspired acquisition for the end of the campaign.

the original offence and incredulously gave a free-kick outside the box to the bemusement of the angry visitors.

After the game, with Everton now back at the summit on goal difference and having a game in hand, the *Guardian's* David Lacey stated 'Championships are seldom won or lost with such suddenness' on a remarkable thirty seconds which seemed certain to have a profound influence on the campaign. With five of their last eight matches at home and only an Anfield visit in three weeks likely to pose a problem, a delighted Kendall said, 'You can say that it is entirely in our hands now…the way we have closed that nine-point gap on Liverpool is encouraging.' Those soaked Everton fans leaving Stamford Bridge may also have noted the huge symbolism of Harper's memorable winner. Kenny Dalglish's goal had secured Liverpool's title there at Everton's expense but eleven months later the midfielder's goal had gone someway to snatching it back – and at the very same end.

The sense of a momentum shift at the top was only reinforced 24 hours later when, rather than in driving rain, a sun-kissed Wembley crowd watched Arsenal defeat Liverpool 2-1 in the League Cup final. The damaging setback – the first time in four years Liverpool had lost three successive games – only added to the pressure on Dalglish's side when they travelled to Norwich six days later, with Everton facing an injury-hit West Ham at Goodison.

It was a very different occasion to their previous home game three weeks before when, while staring down the barrel, they chiselled out that lucky victory over Charlton. Confidence fully restored, against the Hammers the championship favourites reverted to their irresistible form of the festive period by rattling in four goals before the break – 'They just had players everywhere,' young defender Tommy McQueen commented – before easing off in the second half. To add to the feel-good factor amongst the 35,731 spectators, there were enormous cheers around the ground when news came through of Liverpool's capitulation at Carrow Road – leading 1-0 with twenty minutes left, the visitors lost 2-1 in echoes of Everton's damaging defeat at Luton a year before. 'They've hit form at the right time,' said admiring Hammers boss John Lyall, 'There is variety in attack, plenty of experience and a high quality of finishing.'

Perhaps Lyall was referring to Peter Reid's first-half goal. Twenty-four hours earlier the England international had spoken glowingly about the left-footed talents of Kevin Sheedy and West Ham's Liam Brady, now he produced his own extraordinary left-footed curler into the corner at the Park End. 'I had to show Sheedy and Brady what to do…I think my last left-footed goal was for Bolton in about 1975,' he quipped afterwards about a strike which reaffirmed the midfielder's re-emergence from the dark days of February and March, something the manager was willing to talk about. 'Recently he has not been the Peter Reid I know and I had thought about leaving him out. I had a very good player in Alan Harper to take his place,' he said, 'He got it back at Arsenal and has played better in each game. Now I am delighted with him.' The victory left Everton 11-4 on to regain the title, with Liverpool 9-4 and Tottenham 12-1.

Like the previous campaign, Everton's final league game, this time against Tottenham, had been rescheduled to the midweek after the final Saturday of the season. Consequently, in the event of the title being undecided on the last weekend, Liverpool secretary Peter Robinson asked the Football League to move their final game against Chelsea so it would be staged simultaneously with the Spurs clash. The logic was that Everton, and possibly the London club, may know exactly what was needed to clinch the title, with Liverpool powerless. The irony, of course, was the Football League chairman was Philip Carter, who agreed to their request in any case. It was up to Everton to ensure that eventuality was not required.

Easter Parade

In a much more egalitarian era of English football, Easter was always seen as a key time in the title race. Over the holiday period Everton faced a trip to Villa Park on Easter Saturday and Newcastle at home two days later, with Liverpool's corresponding fixtures against Nottingham Forest and Manchester United. On the following weekend there was a small matter of an Anfield derby. Villa's four previous home games had attracted an average of 13,000 fans and there was no surprise when, on a glorious Saturday afternoon, Evertonians accounted for probably half of the 31,218 crowd. Although always in control, the visitors had to wait until the second half to strike, Watson headed back Stevens' free-kick and Sheedy produced a thumping volley of technical brilliance from the edge of box for the only goal. 'Another important victory for Everton, but gained with professionalism rather than panache,' was Brian Glanville's typically trenchant view in *The Sunday Times*. The manager was more focused on the enormous travelling army. 'I've never seen away support like it – that was a cup semi-final atmosphere,' he said, 'It makes a difference, it gives the lads a lift, with a following like that you don't want to let them down.'

With Liverpool victorious for the first time in five games, the three-point gap remained when Newcastle, unbeaten in nine matches, arrived at Goodison on Easter Monday. With Paul Gascoigne in the ascendancy, the leaders were uncharacteristically nervous in the opening half and had Ian Snodin to thank for a goal-line clearance from Darren Jackson. Nevertheless, four minutes after the break the home team went ahead when Clarke headed in Power's far-post cross and the former Birmingham player added a second on 68 minutes. The striker's hat-trick, completed during injury time, was merely a sideshow, with most of the 43,576 spectators already in carnival mood having just heard the news of Peter Davenport's[36] late winner for Manchester United against Liverpool at Old Trafford.

After the game Kendall paid tribute to the hat-trick hero. 'His arrival was well-timed…apart from a good first touch, he is a cool and clinical finisher,' the manager said before speaking about his goal at Highbury. 'Few players would have had the nerve to take aim from 35 yards and, as it was the only goal of the game on the same afternoon

---

[36]   Davenport had ironically played for Everton's A team as an amateur before being released by Gordon Lee. In March 1987 Kendall made a second effort to buy Davenport, but United turned down the £170,000 offer and attention was turned to Wayne Clarke. Davenport's earlier aborted £500,000 transfer to Goodison in early 1985 is covered in *Boys from the Blue Stuff*.

that Liverpool lost at home to Wimbledon, you might say it was a hell of a good time to score for your new club.' Davenport's goal left Everton six points ahead, with a vastly superior goal difference and a game in hand. As Liverpool had only four remaining matches, Kenny Dalglish was forced to admit: 'If Everton beat us on Saturday they'll win the title.' His managerial rival was more circumspect. 'We're not claiming anything yet,' the Everton boss said, 'There is still fifteen points for us to go for and that is our target.'

On the final Saturday in April, Kendall's side therefore travelled to a gloriously sultry Anfield with a ninth title in their grasp and, just as importantly, a chance to banish for good the disappointment of twelve months before. However, there was an extraordinary development before the game, only revealed some time afterwards. The television companies had utilised their fourteen-match limit for the campaign under the extant agreement so, operating outside any contract and without the knowledge of the Football League, both clubs approached ITV to show the match live. The parties struck a deal: the channel would broadcast the showdown live at 7.30 p.m. on the Saturday evening. In return they would pay a £200,000 fee to the clubs, who would pocket £50,000 each, with the balance being paid over to the Football League. However, the authorities got wind of the agreement and, with a threat of legal action, the League blocked the transmission on the grounds they wanted the whole fee divided between all clubs. 'That broke new ground because it meant the [two] clubs were instantly getting more cash over and above the usual TV share-out,' revealed a League source, 'The League plan did not kill the Saturday plan. The greed of Merseyside's big clubs killed it.'

The Football League's stance was ludicrously short-sighted. For a sport crying out for both money and good publicity, a potential title-deciding clash between the two best teams in the country, broadcast on peak-time Saturday-night television, was an absolute godsend. With eighty of 92 clubs technically insolvent, the League were prepared to turn their back on bringing £100,000 into the game for the sake of undermining an archaic structure. There was also a fear within the League that clubs top-slicing their own income was setting a dangerous precedent which could jump-start a super league. 'We could then have had big clubs doing their own private deals all over the place,' the source said, 'It just wasn't on.' The twist being, of course, that the League's obstinacy led to the big clubs doing exactly that within five years. In a further irony, although Granada TV had shown recorded highlights of several league games in the north-west on a Saturday evening during the campaign, an electricians' dispute removed even that opportunity.

With no domestic coverage, more than forty countries around the globe took the game live and the electrifying opening showed what domestic television companies were missing. 'The soul of English football, and of this city, was laid bare,' said Rob Hughes in *The Sunday Times*, 'The passion comes from the people who, despite the unemployment of one in four, still produce £2 million for wage bills per club per season to ensure Merseyside is a cut above the rest.'

There was just ten minutes on the clock when Ian Rush fed Steve McMahon and the former Everton player's shot from just outside the box screamed past Southall and into the top corner. However, when Alan Hansen climbed over Wayne Clarke shortly after, a free-kick was awarded on the edge of the Liverpool area. Sheedy did not disappoint. Although the Liverpool wall was less than ten yards away, the Ireland international used Peter Reid as a screen and the arced run-up allowed him to hook the ball around and over the wall and his rocket flashed into Mike Hooper's net at the Kop end, to the delight of the massed away fans who had infiltrated large sections of the terracing.[37] The rest of the half was a frenzied display of frightening all-out warfare with the identity of the principal combatants not unexpected. Peter Reid was involved in a private battle with Jan Molby, plus Steve McMahon, and after catching the Dane high in the midriff, the Huyton-born player was sandwiched by simultaneous tackles from both men to the left and right. 'Where in the world would you match the physical spectacle, the unrelenting effort?' Hughes asked rhetorically. Ironically the home team restored their lead during time added on for constant stoppages. The goal was disappointing to concede: Ronnie Whelan's corner was flicked on by Craig Johnston into the six-yard box where Rush rose unopposed and headed past Southall.

During the second half Everton dominated proceedings at Anfield in a manner rarely seen, yet despite several skirmishes in the home goalmouth, the nearest the champions-elect came to parity was a Heath header which struck the post. In truth, the visitors fell into the trap of launching high and hopeful balls into the opposition box, with little success. Although Everton looked better with the ball out wide, both Steven and Sheedy – unfit but rarely at his best in derby games – were well marshalled. There was always a

---

[37]   The celebration of course has gone down in legend. As Sheedy wheeled away he appeared to a flick a V-sign to the Liverpool supporters in the Kop. With referee Neil Midgley failing to notice any potential wrong-doing, the matter would not have escalated but for a member of the public writing to the Football League. Their secretary Graham Kelly studied a TV recording and cleared Sheedy but he was obliged to notify the FA, who ultimately had powers of sanction. They subsequently charged both Sheedy and team-mate Adrian Heath of bringing the game into disrepute but, in typical bureaucratic style, took three months to hold the hearing. The subsequent claims that the disciplinary committee was full of ageing FA 'blazers' are not true, however. It featured Eric Dinnie, their hugely experienced and respected disciplinary secretary, plus vice-chairman Harold Smith, an Ipswich director who played a key role in reviving the club under Bobby Robson. They found both players guilty. However, largely due to previous good disciplinary records, there was no further punishment. The irony being that, even as a former player, Sheedy had enjoyed good relations with Liverpool fans. 'They were always fine with me,' he said later, 'I can honestly say now, that it was a spur-of-the-moment reaction and I was not being disrespectful. To this day, I still don't know what made me do it.'

chance that the dominant visitors could be knocked out with a sucker punch and that proved the case. Ratcliffe got caught under Gary Ablett's cross five minutes from time and the ball fell to Rush, who clipped it over Southall for a 3-1 victory. 'It's like a morgue in our dressing room,' Kendall admitted afterwards, 'But we're not relegated, we are top and it's entirely in our own hands.'

With their lead now three points but with a game still in hand, seven days later, on the Saturday of the May Day Bank Holiday weekend, the Toffees faced a relegation-threatened Manchester City, with Liverpool travelling to cup finalists Coventry City. With Kevin Sheedy's knee ruling him out, the largely inept leaders struggled at a damp Goodison, waiting more than half-an-hour to win their first corner and rarely troubling goalkeeper Eric Nixon. Meanwhile the visitors – without an away win in sixteen months – remarkably showed greater penetration. Paul Stewart gave the Everton defence a torrid afternoon and, on the hour, his rising shot crashed back off Southall's crossbar. [38] Consequently, the only highlight of an anti-climactic, goalless afternoon was news of a Coventry victory, which left Kendall's side effectively needing two points to lift the title, with three games to play. 'The reason we are where we are at the top is because we play as a team, but we were all over the place here,' Kendall said, 'But the important thing is we haven't lost. Now we need only two draws or a win to clinch the title.'

Carrow to the heart

And so for the second May Day Bank Holiday in three seasons the title beckoned for Everton. Whereas two years before there were more than 50,000 Toffees fans at a febrile Goodison Park, in the more genteel flatlands of Norfolk the travelling support mustered just several thousand, who serenaded the away team with a chant of 'bring on the champions' before kick-off. Norwich themselves were enjoying a fine campaign and had lost only twice at Carrow Road, once in the league and to the champions-elect in the League Cup.

There were seven players in the starting line-up who had faced QPR two years before, including Graeme Sharp who returned for the injured Clarke. However, in many ways, the game was over, and the championship clinched, during the first minute. Forcing a corner in the opening ten seconds, Steven's delivery eventually reached Van Den Hauwe and the full-back crashed the ball into the roof of the net from just outside the six-yard box. Off the pitch, Kendall's most awkward moment in the opening half was slipping to

---

[38] The City side featured Kevin Langley, who therefore played both for and against Everton during the campaign. As did Warren Aspinall, who had moved to Aston Villa and featured at Villa Park on Easter Saturday.

the floor in the directors' box when attempting to sit on a fold-up chair. (Incredibly the Everton boss did the same in the dugout after the break, this time in full view of the television cameras.)

Thereafter Everton showed why they had the best defence in the top flight – with Watson magnificent – by nullifying any sort of threat from the Canaries. At the other end Steve Bruce kicked off the line from Trevor Steven. After the final whistle there were memorable scenes as some of the away supporters invaded the pitch and lifted several Everton players on their shoulders, with some in fear of their shorts being ripped off in the melee. Twelve months after heartache, there was pure ecstasy[39] and in the dressing room area after the game, Kendall reflected on a job well done:

> *This ends all the ifs and buts and is a greater achievement than our Championship success of two years ago. We have used 23 players this season and every one of them has been a hero and played a full part in our success. They were all down here with us today. I had a feeling it might happen here and wanted them to enjoy it. Losing out to Liverpool in both the FA Cup and the League last season was very hard to take. Today we have produced an emphatic answer.*

For thousands of Evertonians, the long trip to East Anglia was more than worth it.

---

[39]   Everton also became the first club in history to record ten or more away league victories in three successive seasons.

The six-hour journey home for players and staff has gone down in club legend, with the speed of the vehicle rarely getting above forty miles per hour as it was constantly slowed down by supporters' cars and vans. On the coach there was an impromptu disco and song contest hosted by Terry Darracott. One man missed all the fun: the skipper. 'I don't think I realized how much it had taken out of me until we were on the way home,' Kevin Ratcliffe revealed in *The Blues and I*. 'I didn't feel too good. I just flopped out on the back seat of the coach and fell asleep, absolutely exhausted.'

After such high jinks, thankfully there was five days before the home game against Luton Town, when the league winners' trophy – in fact two trophies, the classic original plus sponsor's – was due to be handed over afterwards. As several players have mentioned since, the Hatters were hardly convivial party guests, largely due to a feud between the two squads, which dated back to a brutal affair at Kenilworth Road three years before when Mal Donaghy was sent off for the home team. On that occasion, according to Simon Jones in the *Sunday Telegraph*, there were a 'number of personal vendettas being pursued...Reid, in particular, sometimes allowed his game to become unnecessarily violent.' After the infamous 2-1 loss at Kenilworth Road in March 1986, the usual gentlemanly David Pleat was incensed with the behaviour of the opposition. Three times Gary Lineker had gone to ground and on one occasion, after his theatrical behaviour had got Steve Foster booked, the striker writhed in 'agony' while Luton's David Preece was receiving treatment for an unseen off-the-ball 'challenge' involving Alan Harper. Referee Ray Lewis[40] booked four Luton players in the space of twenty minutes during a contest that threatened to turn into a brawl. No visitors received a yellow card and Pleat was infuriated by their conduct. 'A few Everton players went down as though they were pole-axed,' the Luton boss complained afterwards, 'and then they got up and walked away a few minutes later. I hope we have smashed open the championship race.' 'Managers have been known to be more gracious in defeat,' Nicholas Harling noted in *The Times*.

Luton arrived on the first Saturday in May with the current season's championship race over, but unsurprisingly they proved flinty opponents. In front of a 44,092 crowd – curiously 9,000 below capacity – Mark Stein gave the visitors a shock lead and, although Everton dominated, the champions needed a controversial Trevor Steven penalty to equalise after 52 minutes when Marvin Johnson was ruled to have handled in the Gwladys Street penalty area. Goalkeeper Les Sealey – never the most stable of players and earlier kicked in the face by Graeme Sharp – went into a frenzy and threw the ball at referee

---

40   Lewis delightfully and appropriately being born in Great Bookham.

George Tyson. Luton lost all self-control and by the hour mark they were 3-1 down, thanks to another Steven penalty and Sharp's first league goal on the ground since September. During that time, to make matters worse, feisty midfielder Peter Nicholas was sent off after a second yellow following a fierce challenge on Reid. There were no further goals and, at the end of the game, for the second time in three seasons Kevin Ratcliffe lifted a championship trophy at Goodison. 'After the match, a trophy-laden Ratcliffe led his team on a lap of honour to the euphoric chant of "Champions, Champions." It was an act of mutual respect,' wrote Ken Rogers in the *Liverpool Echo*.

For the second time in three seasons, Kevin Ratcliffe lifts championship silverware at Goodison.

Two days later the league season was complete, Everton triumphing 1-0 over a scratch Tottenham team with an FA Cup final appointment on the following Saturday. A tally of 86 points was four less than in 1984/85, but the gap was nine to Liverpool, which failed to reflect a gripping contest of ebbs and flows. It is worth adding that, although Everton's many injuries are well documented, their deadly rivals also had their own problems in the closing months of the campaign, missing key players like Steve Nicol and Mark Lawrenson. If they had all been fit then the end-of-season battle may have been closer. The counterpoint being, of course, that Kenny Dalglish did not manage the absences with the same efficiency as his opposite number.

Nevertheless, their title duel confirmed the expectation at the start of the campaign that the Merseyside giants were again the teams to beat. The two clubs had now been the dominant forces within English football for four seasons, their hegemony meaning that, for the first time in top-flight history, the same sides filled the top two spots for a third successive campaign.[41] Describing their rivalry at this stage recalls Jerry Izenberg's description of the 'Thrilla in Manila', the brutal third clash between Muhammad Ali and Joe Frazier in 1975. According to Izenberg, the intensity and extent of the rivalry meant the two boxers were no longer fighting for the world heavyweight title but 'were fighting for the championship of each other.' By May 1987 the same applied to Everton and Liverpool. Yet as the season ended there was a feeling that both sides were creaking, like Ali and Frazier a decade before, after engaging in intensive hand-to-hand combat over four seasons.

Consequently, even allowing for diminishing novelty value, there was a clear gap in quality, flavour and personality between the two teams who faced off at Anfield in April compared to those who took part in the titanic League Cup final battles. With Everton undoubtedly in need of some reconstruction, and Liverpool having their weakest squad in the period 1970-1991, there was no way the two clubs could be classed as the best in Europe like twelve months before. Therefore, in playing terms, it was not a vintage duel for the title but that should not diminish Everton's achievement.

Title Management

The background to Kendall's second title was a far more complex affair than 1984/85. Whereas then, after a slow start, the Toffees were always in contention at the top, two years later there was a considerably bigger burden. Injury problems meant they stood eighth in the middle of November and in mid-March Liverpool looked like retaining the title. 'The only time when I felt the pressure to be really on was five or six weeks ago when we were nine points adrift of Liverpool,' Kendall said after the Norwich game, 'I think we all realised that to slip further behind would have proved fatal. Had we lost more ground at that stage I think we would have blown it.' After acknowledging how Kendall and his

---

[41]   Only achieved twice since, by Arsenal and Manchester United (four seasons from 1997/98) and Chelsea and Manchester United (three seasons from 2005/06).

team had overcome adversity to head the field, Donald Saunders summed up the title victory in the *Daily Telegraph* thus:

> *Shrewd buying and selling has enabled Howard Kendall to call on 23 players to counteract injuries and last summer's sale of Gary Lineker to Barcelona. Filtering so many men in and out of the teams – sometimes for only one game – without seriously disrupting the system or rhythm of the side – has called for a high degree of coaching skill. Maintaining a buoyant dressing room spirit among 23 ambitious players – some rewarded with only bit parts – has required expert man-management. Mr Kendall and his chief coach, Colin Harvey, have done the job so well that close observers now remark that the team are playing with the all-round skill, efficiency, confidence and purpose of Liverpool at their best.*

As Saunders remarked, one of the reasons why the gap was closed was the manager's superb marshalling of sparse resources. In his first title-winning season, apart from serious injury to Adrian Heath and Kevin Sheedy's occasional absences, the Everton boss was largely picking from the same group of players, with Kevin Richardson and Alan Harper filling any gaps. Now he was afforded no such luxury until, crucially, the final months of the campaign but even then Paul Bracewell and Graeme Sharp were still injured. Handling the challenge of several absences was a true test of Kendall's management skills but he was lucky that, after the opening weeks, there were always at least eight first-choice players available for selection – the problem was that they were not necessarily the same eight. Kevin Sheedy was virtually ever-present up until February, but the midfielder's absence thereafter was covered by Peter Reid's return. Consequently, nine players appeared in 27 or more league games during the season, just one less than two years before, indicating that, for all the injury problems, there was still a healthy corps available. The injuries in 1985/86 were far more damaging: for most of that campaign Kendall only had one fit centre-half to choose from, twelve months later crucially there were three. Reid started fifteen games in both campaigns but in 1987 was fit and firing from late March. The year before the inspirational midfielder was clearly treading water at the end, as were Kevin Sheedy and Gary Lineker. Most importantly, Southall was out for the final two months of the 1985/86 campaign but a year later he was displaying the best form of his Everton career. One of the reasons, therefore, why the team had a sense of momentum in the spring of 1987 was that the general fitness levels were far greater than among the battle-worn troops of twelve months before.

In addition, it was Kendall's ability to fill the two or three vacancies each week without affecting the balance of the team that marked out the title victory as an exception, not the rule. A glance through the record books shows that teams using 23 players during a campaign tend not to win championships. David Lacey pointed out in the *Guardian* that Kendall's (and Colin Harvey's) ability to mix and match throughout the campaign was the essence of good management. To that end Kendall was lucky to have one of the best utility players in the business: Alan Harper. A notably more confident presence in the team than before, the former Liverpool reserve was outstanding, first as cover for Gary Stevens before Christmas and then partnering Kevin Sheedy in the midfield during the golden period in the middle of the campaign when he showed his true quality as a footballer: a good reader of the game, precise and accurate passing plus a positional sense which acted as a perfect balance for his more esteemed colleague's forward probing. 'Clubs could not survive without men of his calibre,' Ken Rogers wrote in the *Liverpool Echo*, 'talented enough to play in a multitude of positions and big enough to cope with the ups and downs of life in a highly talented squad.' After a transfer-deadline move to Aston Villa collapsed in March 1986 after he was injured in a reserve game, several clubs had made bids – including one of £270,000 from Brian Clough at Nottingham Forest – but Kendall knew Harper's value. 'I would probably have to ask my chairman to spend £500,000 to replace Alan because I would have to buy two quality players to take his place,' he once said.

The low-key signing of Paul Power also proved a masterstroke, the former Manchester City player displaying similar versatility and durability on the left flank. The consummate professional believed he was initially bought as a stop-gap. 'Howard Kendall didn't pull the wool over my eyes; he said he wanted me for cover on the left,' he said at the end of the campaign. But injuries meant Power was an ever-present until the title was clinched. 'Frankly I'm astounded,' he admitted, 'Originally I was lucky to get my feet on the bottom rung of the ladder because of injuries and I've managed to stay there.'

Case for the defence

Contrary to popular belief, the famous statement that 'Attack wins you games, defence wins you titles,' does not originate with Sir Alex Ferguson, the phrase is from the American football coach Paul Bryant several decades before. Going back to his fledgling Blackburn days, Kendall fully understood that maxim. Yet strangely, for a manager committed to the principle of containment, his successful Everton teams initially could be vulnerable. The 1984/85 side conceded four goals in a league game on five occasions and 43 overall during the campaign – a total exceeded only once by the champions –

Derby County in 1974/75 – during the previous eighteen years. There was a suspicion that playing a high line could leave them exposed and during the following campaign a further 41 goals were let in, with injuries adding problems. Those statistics were behind the purchase of Dave Watson.

After some initial teething problems by the mid-point of the campaign the defence was clearly a far tighter unit than previous years. However, that was not solely due to the new arrival. Kevin Ratcliffe and Gary Stevens were more experienced and consistent, being at or near their peak. Behind them, Neville Southall returned from serious injury a more complete goalkeeper, entering the golden period of four or five years when he was the best in the world. Consequently, only 31 goals were conceded during the season – a club record for a 42-game league campaign. There was no way, unlike two years before, that the defence could concede four goals on five occasions. Indeed, they shipped three goals only twice – one game being at Anfield.

Yet that greater defensive stability was not to the detriment of attacking areas. With Trevor Steven and Kevin Sheedy playing in the centre of midfield for long periods, there was greater penetration through the middle than preceding years. One of the reasons why the spread of goals was more impressive following Gary Lineker's departure was the greater threat from all areas of the pitch. While the final tally of 76 goals was twelve less than two years before, the goal difference remained the same at 45. Nevertheless, that was only half the story. The journalist Patrick Barclay used to say that a great indicator of the effectiveness of title-winning seasons is the ratio of goals scored to conceded. For Everton's three previous post-war triumphs that ratio was stubbornly about 2:1, as was 1985/86. However, in 1986/87, thanks to greater defensive stability, the ratio flew up to 2.5:1, right up there with the most dominant Liverpool champions of previous years, as Donald Saunders pointed out. The history of the time shows that, whereas a ratio of 2:1 gave you a chance of the title, one of 2.5:1 from 76 goals scored and 31 conceded almost guaranteed it.

The impressiveness of the numbers highlights the enormous achievement of Kendall, plus Harvey, in carving out a ninth league title largely against the odds. 'Maybe I am not too bad a manager,' the Everton boss said after the Carrow Road victory. The board's problem was that various clubs around the continent thought the same.

12.
TWILIGHT OF A CHAMPION

BY MAY 1987 KENDALL WAS THE MOST SUCCESSFUL EVERTON MANAGER in history, his second league title taking him ahead of Harry Catterick in terms of major trophies. 'I'm a very proud man today,' he said 24 hours after the Carrow Road victory, 'Although I never set out to surpass Harry...My aim was to strive to be the best, not just in one season, but over a long period. It's a building process and we have laid the foundations.'

With rumours of interest from elsewhere, whether Kendall was there to oversee the construction of a Goodison empire was up for debate at the end of the campaign. 'It is our intention to keep hold of him,' Philip Carter said. 'We will fight tooth and nail if anyone does try to lure him away to the continent. If and when an approach is made it would be my intention and that of Everton Football Club to retain Howard's services.'

New camp move falls through

However, such speculation was not exactly new to the Everton chairman. In May 1985 Real Madrid were rumoured to be making a move while eight months later there were stories linking Kendall with the Juventus job, the Italian giants offering £150,000 per year plus bonuses. Although the Everton boss admitted that 'I am flattered to be linked with such a great club,' there was no official contact from Turin, according to Brian Glanville in *The Sunday Times*. In the same period, with Arsenal and Spurs both on the lookout for new blood, according to tabloid speculation Kendall was first among their desired targets. Meanwhile, with Ron Atkinson expected to leave Old Trafford during the summer of 1986, the most coveted manager in British football was also rumoured to be top of the Old Trafford hierarchy's wish-list.

Intriguingly, given these stories, when questioned about his plans in the early spring of 1986, Kendall cryptically responded there was 'every possibility' he would be staying at Goodison, without making any commitment. 'You have to admit that names like Juventus, Real Madrid and Barcelona have a bit of magic about them,' he acknowledged, 'But, then, so has Everton.'

Such reticence was because, infamously, the Catalan club had already made an approach for his services as Terry Venables' replacement. Leading Barcelona officials attended the home match against Chelsea in mid-March and met the Everton boss 24 hours later. Kendall naturally rebutted the story but a Barcelona official let slip to a leading Spanish newspaper that 'We have spoken with Mr Kendall and although he won't confirm that he has spoken with Barcelona he doesn't deny it either. Venables has told us that he feels Kendall would be the next manager of Barcelona.' Pressed for further comment, Kendall responded, 'It's a great compliment that Terry has put me forward for the job,' before adding obliquely, 'There are things happening but I want to do things the right way.'

The Everton boss later revealed that the meeting with Barcelona's president Jose Luis Nunez took place in London's Connaught Hotel – with Philip Carter's blessing – and that following discussions he signed a provisional contract. [42] 'I knew that if the offer was to be confirmed, I would have to think very carefully of the implications, both for myself and my family,' he revealed in *Only the Best is Good Enough*. 'But I also knew that I would accept.' Yet, for all the secrecy, word got out to the *Daily Mirror* and consequently their manager was the target of training-ground humour. 'He's not saying anything,' Peter Reid said in his diary entry for the end of March, 'he just smiles when he's greeted with choruses of "Adios amigo" and that sort of thing.' With Venables expected to return to England or go to Italy during the summer, the assumption was Kendall would fill the gap. Yet by mid-April the trail went cold. Then, in a startling development, Venables and Barcelona performed a *volte face* and announced that the Englishman would remain in Catalonia for another year. [43] 'It was a dream scenario, one lifted from the pages of a fantasy novel,'

---

[42] As ever there are conflicting accounts of events. It is now known that, apart from Kendall, Alex Ferguson and Bobby Robson were interviewed on the same day. 'I was interviewed for the Barcelona job when I was at Aberdeen,' Fergie told the *Sunday Express* in 2008, 'Terry Venables was in charge at the time but he was going to leave. He had recommended me and I met the Barcelona president in the Connaught Hotel, London.' In his 2000 book, *Barça: A People's Passion*, author Jimmy Burns spoke with Jaume Olive, who was one of the Barcelona high command present. 'Both Ferguson and Kendall came across as knowledgeable no-nonsense guys,' Olive told Burns. 'But nothing was offered to them, nor did they advertise their availability.' Of the three, it was Robson – interviewed last – who impressed the most, according to Olive.

[43] Curiously the reports surfacing on the day Kendall informed Gary Lineker's agent of Barcelona's interest at Vicarage Road. Although there has been speculation since that the Everton boss was happy to release his star striker on the basis he would be following him to the Nou Camp, the opposite could also be true: that Barcelona knew they had a better chance of getting Lineker if they provided a further inducement to Kendall. Once the sale has been agreed, they announced Venables was staying after all.

Kendall said of the original approach. Sadly for the Everton boss it remained just that, for the moment. But Barcelona would be back.

Fernando drums up support

That was not the end of the of the Spanish inquisition for Kendall. After turning down overtures from Real Madrid during that summer, in March 1987 there was another approach from the Nou Camp club when, once again, Venables looked like quitting. Yet again the future England boss remained in situ.

However, in April 1987 Kendall took a phone call at home. At the other end of the line was Fernando Ochoa, general manager of Spanish side Athletic Bilbao. As the Everton boss later admitted, the Barcelona approaches had stimulated his desire to work abroad. With UEFA earlier rejecting a return by English clubs to European competition for the 1987/88 season, for a second time Kendall was denied a chance to compete in the European Cup. Following a friendly in Bordeaux two months before, a UEFA official had informed him that there was a strong likelihood the ban would be lifted so the development was a shock. 'This is a serious blow,' the Everton boss admitted, 'Our best players need to be involved in European competition.' Bilbao were certainly not the first side to speak to Kendall at this time. There had been discussions with others: Atletico Madrid was one club he engaged seriously with. 'I have not been hawking myself around Europe,' he told *World Soccer*, 'I have merely been in the receipt of offers and have paid those clubs the courtesy of talking to them. My contract with Everton permitted that.'

When Ochoa started talking, Kendall was in receptive mood and agreed a meeting. When they spoke shortly afterwards 'it quickly became clear that Mr Ochoa was a most persuasive man,' as Kendall said in *Only the Best is Good Enough*. 'If he had been sent over to England to try and "sell" Athletic Bilbao to me, he did a very fine job indeed.' Terry Venables – once more – had recommended him. The reported financial offer was certainly attractive. With an introductory 'golden handshake' of £150,000 followed by a two-year deal worth £130,000 annually, the total package was significantly greater than his existing salary. However, the big attraction was that, under Spanish law, he could only be taxed to a maximum of 22 per cent, a third of the highest rate in England. Effectively he would be doubling his take-home pay. 'The more I thought about the offer, the more it appealed to me,' Kendall said.

Athletic initially demanded that he did not go on the end-of-season trip to Australia and New Zealand – 'I told them they would have to appoint someone else if they were

By the summer of 1987 Howard Kendall was the hottest managerial property in Europe.

not prepared to wait,' Kendall responded – but the Everton boss travelled to Spain to meet club officials on his return. 'They knew what they were doing and they knew what it was they wanted,' Kendall later recalled, 'I was hooked. My mind was made up. I wanted the job.' Although Richard Bott in *World Soccer* claimed that 'Of course, a pot of Spanish gold was the overriding factor,' Kendall later expanded on his reasons for moving in the same publication:

> *It's not just about money. I've always had a bit of an ambition to work abroad and when there was talk of a few clubs being interested in me last year it whetted my appetite…I feel it's right for a change of direction, a different challenge. The pressure is very intense at a big club like Everton. Liverpool have had three managers in the time I have been in charge here. And it has become increasingly difficult for me to devote*

enough time to working with the players. When I first became manager at Everton, Bill Shankly used to pop into our training ground for a cup of tea. He told me: "The first thing you must do every morning is put on your tracksuit and training gear." But I was finding it harder to do that, simply because of the size of the club and the success we were having.

After six years in charge at Goodison, a change of scene was understandable. Aside from coaching in a different environment, the attraction of quitting at the top and preserving his status as, pound for pound, the best manager in English club football would also have been an important consideration. At the end of the season clearly, if not a total rebuilding exercise, there was a certain amount of squad reconstruction required. As Kendall himself admitted, if that failed then all the progress over six seasons could be destroyed in two. Leaving on a high meant that, even if unsuccessful in Spain, opportunities back home would not be in short supply. Contrary to popular belief, the European ban was not the main reason for moving – at the time there were strong hopes sanctions would be removed after the 1988 European Championship. Given Athletic had not qualified in 1987/88, had Kendall stayed at Goodison there was a possibility his side would have been back for the following season, which was also the earliest time he could have featured after moving abroad. Nevertheless, this all seemed like a missed opportunity for both the club and Kendall himself. The manager had spoken just six weeks earlier about laying down the foundations for long-term success at Goodison but now he was departing for a new challenge. Yet supporters could have legitimately argued that the real challenge was creating a dynasty to match that across the park. At the same time those fans had probably contributed to his leaving.

Never forget

There was another, more contentious, reason that made the decision to depart easier. Kendall said in a newspaper article during August 1985 that he had been 'to hell and back' in the dark days before success arrived and considered resigning for the sake of his family. In the week after 'Kendall out' was infamously sprayed on his garage doors, he played in a testimonial match in Flint. Abused by travelling fans on the touchline, the Everton boss stayed in the middle of the pitch to avoid the heckling. 'They were cruel,' he told the *Independent's* Joe Lovejoy in 1993, 'but it made me tougher. If it ever happens again, I'll be prepared.'

Although more than a few supporters subsequently wrote letters of apology, only a saint could have completely blocked out the vitriol handed out during late 1983. As John Roberts noted in the *Daily Mail* on the day after the title was clinched against QPR, 'For those fans shouting "There's only one Howard Kendall" it was one more than they desired eighteen months before.' Such fickleness was never lost on the Everton boss. He was also haunted by the callous way Everton treated Harry Catterick, who had wanted to be paid off after his sacking; instead, the club had him scouting for Billy Bingham. 'They're just waiting for me to die,' Catterick once told Kendall. 'You can't forget something like that,' he later told James Lawton in the *Daily Express* before opening up on the capricious nature of fandom:

> *You remember a lot of things as you go on in the game. When certain people cheer you when you win you remember how it was when you were losing, when they were daubing Kendall Out on my garage back home in Formby and the kids had to go to school and suffer because of what I did. You are made very aware by things like that. You go on your guard. You know you have to be hard to survive.*

The move away from Goodison was an example of that self-preservation. As well as the professional benefits of moving to Bilbao in terms of getting the tracksuit back on, the move ensured enjoyment of the rewards simply not available in England and would thereby help secure his financial future.

Nevertheless, whether Kendall exonerated his detractors from the dark days is a moot point. Although he did not hold grudges, personal slights were not forgotten. Several years later he pointed out that Barcelona still owed him the train fare for his interview in 1986: 'That's a little thing, but it is little things that say a lot to someone like me. It's the way I am and you have to stay with that.' The abuse he (and his family) received before the trophy-laden years remained very much in the foreground. After moving to Spain, Kendall later told Patrick Barclay in the *Independent* that he would never return to Goodison as Everton boss. 'He remembers the preceding tribulations,' Barclay wrote. 'Still waters run deep. And for such a cheerful man Kendall does not forgive easily.'

He would also have been aware of a core who credited the spectacular renaissance to Colin Harvey, given it coincided with the latter's promotion from the reserve team in November 1983. Consequently, Kendall's attitude towards supporters – and theirs to him – was undoubtedly in a different place to later years. Unlike Harvey, his initial ties were professional not emotional. 'The fans who abused him a little over two years ago must take some of the blame for the decision that has rocked the Merseyside club,' claimed Christopher Davies in the *Daily Telegraph*. As Harry Harris said in the *Daily Mirror* when the Barcelona links first emerged: 'It may come as a shock to Everton fans but Kendall has not forgotten the abuse he suffered from them less than two years ago, his family suffered and that might just sway Kendall into leaving.' It obviously did.

Gone

In the third week of June the story broke that the Everton boss was departing. On the evening of Thursday, 18 June, Fernando Ochoa announced Kendall was joining on Spanish radio: 'My president, Pedro Aurteneche has confirmed to me in a phone call from the Canaries [where he met the Everton boss] that Kendall has signed for Bilbao.' On the Friday morning Philip Carter called an emergency board meeting and at a hastily arranged press conference later in the day, the Everton chairman admitted that Kendall had turned down an improved four-year deal, believed to be worth more than £500,000.

With Gary Lineker having gone to the Iberian peninsula, Carter ruefully added 'Spain has had its fair share as far as Everton are concerned.' Kendall's leaving was the latest in a long list of departing playing and managerial talent to the continent: as well as Lineker, Mark Hughes, Glenn Hoddle and Ian Rush would be featuring abroad in the following season, joining more established stars like Ray Wilkins and Trevor Francis. The Spanish top flight now had six British managers. The footballing brain-drain was a concern to everybody, even across the park. 'Howard's move to Spain makes the situation much more serious,' said Liverpool secretary Peter Robinson, 'In fact, the prospect for the future of our game is terrifying. English clubs simply cannot compete with the money the top continental clubs can offer. They seem to have ways of paying certain sums to foreign employees without incurring tax. In England the top money-earners have to pay tax at 60 per cent.' The irony of course, is that it was later revealed that Robinson had recommended Kendall to Athletic after he had rejected Ochoa's attempt to prise Kenny Dalglish away from Anfield.[44]

However, this is where the failure to move to Barcelona twelve months before enters the discussion. Although the Everton boss said this whetted his appetite for a job abroad, seeing the chance of the move of a lifetime going begging meant that the Athletic job was taken on the rebound, as it were. As he reflected to *World Soccer*, if they had not come in

[44] However it would appear Kendall was not the only manager the Liverpool secretary recommended to Bilbao. 'Peter Robinson from Liverpool had recommended me but I didn't know,' Dave Bassett recalled in 2022, 'This chap called and asked to meet at a hotel. I thought it was Vinnie [Jones] messing about…So I went wearing a T-shirt, shorts and flip-flops and hadn't shaved. Then this smart Spanish bloke walks up and introduces himself.'

for him, then Atletico Madrid may have been his eventual destination. There was also a strong possibility that doing a sound job in the Basque region would not harm his chances of Barcelona making a further approach.

Yet, with all due respect to Kendall and the Spanish club, once those factors are removed, the financial aspect was the only facet of the deal that made any sense. Although he later denied moving solely for money – which was undoubtedly true – there can be no doubt that the cash rewards carried enormous influence. It had to. For Kendall, the financial rewards acted as compensation for Bilbao not being Barcelona – a club which he would probably have taken a pay cut to manage. With regards to Bilbao, it was the only way they could have snared Europe's most in-demand manager. Beyond that, to virtually all observers then and more than three decades later the move still baffles. Like Bilbao, Aston Villa were an historically significant club who had enjoyed success in the early 1980s but had struggled in 1986/87. Eyebrows would surely have been raised if, in a parallel universe, the hugely sought-after manager of the Spanish champions had pitched up at Villa Park for the following season.

While the attraction of a new lifestyle with different scenery, away from the pressures of the English top flight, was undoubtedly compelling for the Everton boss – as well the chance of stepping back into his tracksuit – the choice of Bilbao was still strange. The Basque side could only sign players born in their region, something Kendall alluded to in his departing press conference. 'I am aware of the rules of the club,' he said, 'Unless we can persuade Kevin Sheedy and one or two others to turn Basque!' Also, here was a team who needed rebuilding after finishing in the bottom six, one of the lowest points in their 89-year history. Plus, given Kendall had voiced his frustrations over the European ban, joining a club where qualification had been achieved for the following campaign made sense. On the contrary, as he later wrote, 'Bilbao was a club in a very poor state of health when I arrived to take over.' As an elite manager, Kendall could and should have been aiming higher and not acting, as he later admitted, as some sort of footballing trouble-shooter. Again, the financial value of the contract comes into play.

Yet, for all those that doubted the move, Kendall saw things in a different way, both on and off the pitch. 'I wasn't expected to win the league...I was expected to go and prove that Basque football could compete, and also qualify for Europe. I thought it was a great challenge. It excited me,' he wrote in *Love Affairs & Marriage*, 'They were truly lovely people connected with the club and they made me feel very welcome.'

Furthermore, scrutiny of Philip Carter's role is required. Having been informed by Kendall of Bilbao's deal, the chairman waited until the last moment before making a counter-offer to his prized asset. That Carter was hardly proactive whilst Bilbao were wooing Kendall was not lost on his manager, who cryptically remarked on the evening the deal was announced that 'I am seeing the chairman, who I haven't spoken to for a few weeks.' That may seem slightly odd, but Carter's passiveness showed he was not going to break the bank for his manager, given the financial tax advantages of overseas clubs. Kendall was disingenuous when claiming the four-year deal at Goodison offered more security. To match Bilbao and smother the punitive UK tax laws, his chairman would have had to pay close to £250,000 basic a year, not £125,000.

Having said that, Kendall's departure – plus Carter's apparent indifference – also raised the age-old debate over the value placed on managers by their boardrooms. 'Everton lost the big one – badly,' James Lawton suggested in the *Daily Express*. 'The scandal and the sadness is that they didn't lose to Juventus or Barcelona or some Arabian prince dripping with oil money. They lost to Athletic Bilbao, a struggling Spanish club… Everton's board should curl up in shame.' For all their increasing influence and power, most managers were still relatively underpaid and underappreciated – history was littered with clubs treating even the most successful with a certain amount of contempt. In that context, Lawton compared the profit made by Everton on the Lineker deal to what the board were willing (or not willing) to pay their most successful ever manager. While the generous Spanish tax laws and Kendall's genuine footballing reasons for moving may have made any club offer obsolete, there is still a feeling Carter and his fellow directors had fallen into the trap of their peers: a failure to give the most important person at the club the financial security and status they deserved.

However, this was probably a specious argument in any case, as Carter was never going to match Bilbao's terms. So the most successful manager in the club's history was gone – or allowed to go – but not before his departing message. 'Everyone has been absolutely tremendous to me,' he said. 'I'd like to thank the supporters, the staff and the players whom I've handled while I have been manager here. I'd like to think that the fans wish me well.'

At the end of the campaign Kendall had picked up the Manager of the Year award for a second time. 'David Pleat has just said to me to take a year off,' he said in his acceptance speech, before quipping, 'Well David, that was last season!' Now he was making his peers' jobs easier by leaving the country, as a dramatic and hugely successful six-year managerial spell enshrined in the club's history ended.

Legacy

There is a strand of modern psychology called 'flow', defined in *Psychology Today* as a state of absorption arising when as individuals 'we focus our attention on a stimulating and challenging activity, creating a sense of well-being and giving rise to creativity.' When that is applied to a group – say in football – the members of the team 'attune to each other in a subtle unconscious way, and become capable of…athletic (in the case of sports teams) feats. They become much more than the sum of their individual talents.'

As discussed previously, there was nothing complicated or revolutionary about Kendall's Everton. A strong defence, well-balanced midfield and potent strike force are not exactly original constituents of a winning team. Also, in terms of style, compressing the game and the forcing of opposition into errors, as demanded by himself and Colin Harvey, was not an end in itself. As the great Arrigo Sacchi said in *The Immortals*, his brilliant book about his AC Milan team of the late 1980s: 'Tactics are about trying to take an advantage of an opposition weakness and waiting for them to make a mistake. A strategy is a positive plan of action to carry out.' Sacchi subsequently pointed out that tactics 'were for losers' as something more substantial was needed for successful sides. For Kendall that plan encompassed not only pressing tactics but other aspects which Sacchi used so effectively at Milan: work harder than the opposition, support for the man on the ball, maintain a narrow span of grass between defence and attack while deploying a stifling offside trap.

Executing that strategy required discipline and organisation, plus the right personnel. As Alan Ball remarked several years before, Kendall did not have the time or money to build another Liverpool, the Everton boss had to create a 'character' side. However, that just did not entail employing the right people, putting them on the pitch and then telling them to get on with it. Kendall, with Colin Harvey, had to create a togetherness, with everybody treated as equals, as Sacchi himself did later in the decade. As the legendary Italian said, 'The only way you can build a side is by getting players who speak the same language and can play a team game. You can't achieve anything on your own, and if you do, it doesn't last long.'

The key to Kendall's success was down to the fact that, either by accident or design, his management style encompassed several of the key factors needed to generate what is known as 'group flow' and Sacchi's beliefs to deliver his required strategy. Although some requirements of the former are blindingly obvious – setting of goals, and the need for good communication, with Kendall a master of that, both with players and the media – there are less obvious aspects that are the cornerstones of his achievements. First and most important is matching the skills to 'the challenge of the task'. In *Boys from the Blue Stuff* I suggested one of Kendall's strengths in team-building was accentuating a particular characteristic in a single area of the pitch. Wanting to press effectively, he picked two very similar central midfielders – Peter Reid and Paul Bracewell – who could do exactly that. That doubled the intense pressing required in the centre of the park, which initially frustrated and then overwhelmed opponents. Likewise on the right flank. Gary Stevens and Trevor Steven were both tremendously hard workers who could move up and down the wing in unison. At the end of the 1984/85 campaign, Kendall ensured that Andy Gray and Graeme Sharp – essentially aggressive players with similar attributes – were integrated into the line-up, giving extra physicality up top. To balance the hard work and power in the rest of the pitch, Kendall relied on Kevin Sheedy's sublime subtlety and ingenuity on the left flank. In addition, having versatile players like Alan Harper and Kevin Richardson around meant the Everton boss was rarely forced into giving unfamiliar roles to the squad, even during the injury crisis that affected his final two seasons. With a solid defence and one of the best goalkeepers on the planet, the Everton manager was therefore able to optimise the balance of characteristics and skills across the team so they played in the style he – and Colin Harvey – wanted.

Another key aspect of group flow is that the best teams have a blending of egos and 'all participants play an equal role in the collective creation of the final performance'. Kendall's biggest strength – his peerless man-management skills – enabled this. The so-called 'team of no stars' label that in some ways was derogatory pointed towards their key strength: there were stars, but they operated within a collective where everybody's role was given equal billing, and nobody was afforded special treatment. There were people with big personalities in Kendall's dressing room – Andy Gray, Peter Reid and Neville Southall to name three – but to their credit they were all team players and there were no damaging, dominating forces. Credit here too for skipper Kevin Ratcliffe, who helped maintain the equilibrium and ensure there were no hierarchies and cliques. In addition, those who were not necessarily first choice but came in to perform a particular role had their contribution acknowledged. Consequently, Kendall's side were one of the great egalitarian units in English football history.

With group flow, the way teams communicate is also important. As one expert said 'the kind of communication that leads to group flow often doesn't happen in the conference room. Instead, it's more likely to happen in freewheeling, spontaneous conversations in the hallway, or in social settings after work or at lunch.' Kendall's regular Chinese meals for the squad and other events were not there for the sake of it: they were a key part of his team-building strategy for on the pitch, as well as off it. As well as allowing grievances to be aired, they were also part of the familiarisation process, another key aspect of the theory. Teams are more productive and effective if their members know what makes their colleagues tick.

Those structures that the Everton manager put in place off the pitch explain the personality of his teams on it. The 1984/85 side was noted for their resilience and competitiveness, characteristics hewn from the togetherness fostered by the manager away from the game. Two years later, the title won with a squad of 23 players reflected the classless society of the Everton dressing room. Everybody was equal and those who played ten games were regarded with the same importance as those who played four times as many.

For all the words about Everton in the mid-1980s, in simple terms at its heart was the 'human resource' strategy of the Toffees boss which allowed the group to develop. As Philip Carter said at the end of the 1986/87 season, 'Howard has done a remarkable job. One of his main attributes is his ability to weld together a team and produce consistent results. He has a tremendous gift for man-management.' Thankfully that gift brought the most successful team in Everton's history.

13

THE CARAVAN OF LOVE

ON THURSDAY, 18 JUNE 1987, COLIN HARVEY, HIS WIFE MAUREEN AND one of their three daughters, Emma, were enjoying a well-deserved break at the family caravan in Prestatyn, North Wales. Maureen's father was minding their two dogs and when they phoned him to enquire about their well-being, one of Colin's other daughters, Joanna, said that Philip Carter had left a message saying they needed to speak. When they did, he was offered the manager's post. 'I accepted the job with a great deal of pride when the chairman asked me did I want it,' he revealed after taking the role. 'Without a second thought I blurted out "Yes, please."'

Continuity with Colin

Given the suddenness of the departure, to be fair to the Everton chairman he was decisive in selecting a replacement. After all, Carter had reportedly told Harvey that the job was his if Kendall had left twelve months before. Yet the counter-argument was that possibly he was too trigger-happy. Carter should have given himself some breathing space. Perhaps his thinking was that the immediate appointment of Harvey – respected by the players, popular with supporters – would ease any pain following his predecessor's departure.

That thesis hits rocky territory when the other candidates for the role are considered. There was not exactly a wealth of options. Earlier in the year Everton were linked with Watford's Graham Taylor, should Kendall ever leave, but the future England manager still had a reputation as a long-ball practitioner, perhaps unfairly. Ron Atkinson certainly had the personality, but had been sacked at Manchester United and would not have been a viable option, especially considering the Old Trafford club were not exactly flavour of the month on Merseyside. Apart from that duo, other potential contenders were thin on the ground. Brian Clough, a potential option a decade before, was probably past his best.

For all the misgivings, Carter was in no doubt about the decision. 'He has the essential talent for man-management,' he claimed, 'We are fortunate that with his appointment we are able to maintain continuity inside the club.' The magical word: continuity. The elixir of football management for which only Liverpool held the secrets. Carter hoped that Harvey's appointment would stimulate the continuous success which had been the feature of the Anfield dynasty over the previous three decades. But there were flaws in his theory. First, comparing the appointment of Harvey as manager to, say, Bob Paisley in 1974, raised serious questions. Paisley was a decade older and had been first-team coach for fifteen years, whereas Harvey had been in that role for less than four. That wisdom and experience gained from successfully working with many different types of players and characters in a period of great change in football was something that Harvey, for all his natural gifts as a coach, did not possess.

Not only that, continuity is more than just replacing the man at the top. Succession planning worked at Anfield because of the rich depth of coaching ability and experience in the backroom staff, who all played an enormous role in their huge accomplishments: from Joe Fagan to Ronnie Moran, Tom Saunders, Reuben Bennett, Roy Evans and Geoff Twentyman.[45] There was no such depth at Bellefield so Harvey's ascension severely weakened the coaching capacity. Only time would tell whether the new boss could replace his own lost skills at Bellefield. There also was still a feeling that Harvey, for all his protestations to the contrary, was a reluctant replacement. 'To be honest I don't really want it in these circumstances, because I didn't want Howard to go,' he said shortly afterwards, 'He's undoubtedly the best manager in England and I didn't think he would take that [Bilbao] job after what he's built here.'

The coach drivers

It was because of the kingdom built by Kendall that Harvey was inheriting in many ways a chalice that, if not poisoned, had been stained, in the nicest possible way, by the charisma and man-management skills of his predecessor. The new boss, a completely different personality – one which had produced the classic good/bad cop managerial partnership – immediately went to work on shaping the club in his own way. With Mick Heaton[46] - whose role as confidant to the players was vital in maintaining -the squad equilibrium -

---

[45]   The proof in the theory being that Liverpool's success dried up in the early/mid 1990s as that pool of coaching talent started to disappear.

[46]   After departing Heaton gave an exclusive interview to the *News of the World* during which he revealed, contrary to popular belief, that it was the board who forced Kendall to promote Harvey in November 1983. That claim was given credence forty years later when Elton Welsby, who was working for ITV at the time, took to social media to say that 'I have it first hand that Howard was given an ultimatum. Promote Colin and play Reidy...otherwise.' Heaton also claimed that the board were behind the signing of Andy Gray: 'We went to see him at Wolves and it looked as though he had "gone". He was just going through the motions.'

leaving to pursue his own managerial ambitions at Workington Town, Terry Darracott was promoted from the reserves to become Harvey's assistant. Mike Lyons, recently sacked after a sixteen-month spell at Grimsby Town which had resulted in relegation to the Third Division, stepped into Darracott's shoes. But the other appointment raised eyebrows. Twenty-four hours after Peter Reid had celebrated his 31st birthday, he was offered a player-coaching role. 'I was uncomfortable with the idea at first and I said to Colin that I knew certain things went on in dressing rooms and I'm not the type to report back to the manager, but he was great about that,' he wrote in *Cheer Up Peter Reid*, '"If anything's going on out of school, I don't want to hear it from you," he said. "I'll find out about it anyway." That put me at ease and I agreed to step up.'

Although there was no doubting Reid's pedigree, the move was strange. The midfielder held no immediate ambitions to pursue a coaching career, indeed the aim was to regain his place in the England squad with the 1988 European Championship looming. Reid also possessed no coaching badges. 'But then neither did men like Bill Shankly and Bob Paisley,' he quipped. Ideally for the Huyton-born player, promotion to a coaching role should have come under a more experienced manager.

Even without the benefit of hindsight, the new set-up appeared light in terms of coaching ability, at that level, plus experience. None of the appointees – including Harvey – had ever filled their respective roles before and, although they all knew the club and squad, the individual and collective lack of experience had the potential to cause issues. The strength of Liverpool's managerial appointments after Shankly had been that the backroom staff remained largely unchanged whereas, after Kendall, for all the claims of continuity the club was effectively operating with a blank sheet of paper.

To rebuild or not rebuild?

That was the question facing Harvey in the summer of 1987. Although the title had been clinched by nine points, the fact more than twenty players had been used indicated that a certain amount of reshuffling of the pack was needed.

Although the defence was generally in good shape there were still recurring doubts over Derek Mountfield's fitness. Veteran Paul Power – who had missed the end of the previous campaign due to an operation – could not be expected to continue the consistent ever-present form of twelve months before. In the middle of the park there was no immediate return anticipated for Paul Bracewell while Reid – now with added responsibilities – was past his peak years, although still hugely competitive. Ian Snodin was a valuable addition but still in the not-proven category, his main issue being consistency. 'Snodin does everything well,' John Giles said. 'The problem is he doesn't do it often enough.' Kevin Sheedy was another with fitness issues. Up front Graeme Sharp and Adrian Heath were long-time partners, while Wayne Clarke was another, like Snodin, who still had to prove himself. To be fair to the former Wolves player, there was nothing in his track record to suggest he was a consistent top-flight goalscorer.

Although Kendall had enjoyed huge success, Dave Watson was the only proven starter bought in the previous three years: the squad was still built around those who became first-team regulars during 1981-83. Five years later new blood was needed to freshen things up. But the manager thought differently. 'I will not be chasing after players like Peter Beardsley – you can forget that,' he declared, 'We have great players bursting with enthusiasm and ability. Everything has worked well for four or five years so I see no reason to change it now.' That was understandable but the statement pointed to the problem facing Harvey. Stick or twist. Bring in some big-name players but run the risk of it not working? And then stand accused of breaking up a title-winning side? Or leave things relatively unchanged and then charged with letting matters drift whilst rivals progressed? A more confident and experienced manager may have gone with the former option but Harvey, understandably, went with the latter. There were not many dissenting voices. 'Few managers have ever been lucky enough to take over such a well-run organisation,' Ian Hargraves noted in the *Liverpool Echo*. 'Few have been better equipped to adapt and develop that organisation, hopefully making it even stronger.'

Climbing off the floor

At the end of the 1986/87 season, for the first time in several years there was room for optimism in English football. After a decade of declining attendances there was a jump of more than two million spectators coming through the gates across all four divisions. Although the usual suspects were contending the title at the end of the campaign, before Christmas there had been some unfamiliar names near the top. Live coverage of league football had produced some thrilling contests while the introduction of the play-off system had reinvigorated the lower divisions. 'In the years ahead 1987 might come to be regarded as a vintage year for football,' Jimmy Hill claimed in *The Times*. 'Arsenal, Tottenham, West Ham, Nottingham Forest, Luton and Norwich, in different degrees and at different times, gave their supporters a peek at the Holy Grail before the extensive resources of Liverpool and Everton again separated them from the boys.'

The Everton chairman wanted to use some of that resource on redeveloping Goodison. 'Football has spent millions improving spectator facilities, ground security and on other measures to deal with its problems,' said Carter before the start of the season, 'You actually have to be positive about the relationship with people, those living near the ground, hospitals, children, schools, local authorities…make them aware of the club and allow them to relate to it.' At long last football was realising that one way of increasing popularity was improving facilities, increasing choice and building relationships with supporters. Consequently, during the summer the club spent more than £1 million redeveloping Goodison Park: the Gwladys Street End now had a new, extended roof that protected all spectators from the elements, whilst a seated Family Club, situated in the Enclosure section of the Main Stand, was unveiled just before the start of the campaign. Further positive developments off the field included season-tickets sales going beyond £1 million for the first time, on the back of an average league attendance of 32,935 in 1986/87 – the highest for eight years.[47]

Yet although these were encouraging signs, in financial terms the club was still a poor relation among the Big Five. Lacking Manchester United's wider appeal with casual fans, and Liverpool's historical success, the Goodison club's turnover for the campaign of £4.3m was £1m below the Anfield outfit and £2.5m less than entered the coffers at Old Trafford.

That financial disparity – plus Harvey's cautious approach – was in some ways obvious during the summer. With the money received for Ian Rush, Liverpool splashed out a British-record £1.8 million on Peter Beardsley plus £900,000 on John Barnes. With Graeme Souness possessing a bottomless pit of money at Rangers, British clubs appeared to be on the cusp of another transfer arms race previously witnessed a decade before. Asked whether the first £2 million domestic player was on the immediate horizon, secretary Jim Greenwood pointed out that the club had just finished with a surplus of £800,000. 'You are talking in terms of close on three years profits at that level without buying a player to finance one £2m deal,' he admitted, 'I don't believe the Beardsley deal has set new standards. He was available at that figure and is obviously a good player, but I can't see that kind of fee being repeated.'[48] That could have been interpreted as short-hand for the club being circumspect in the transfer market, a policy contrary to a close season which produced a domestic record £22m in transfer fees. Everton's share was zero. Only time would tell whether it was a costly decision.

---

[47]   A slight increase over the previous two seasons, but considerably more than the low point of 19,343 in 1983/84. John Moores used to say that two successful teams in the city was good for stimulating interest – for proof the Littlewoods boss only had to look at Liverpool's attendances in the mid-1980s. In their treble year of 1983/84 just 31,974 spectators on average watched league football at Anfield. Yet during the trophyless following season, with Everton in the ascendancy, that figure rose by 3,000 per game and in another barren 1986/87 campaign there was a further increase to 36,296. Moores, as usual, was correct all along.

48   In Everton's case it was within twelve months.

14
RUNNING TO STAND STILL

SIXTY SECONDS BEFORE HALF-TIME AT GOODISON PARK ON THE LAST Saturday of September 1987, Coventry City's Dave Bennett sped down the right wing and pulled the ball back to David Phillips, who crashed a shot past Neville Southall from twenty yards out. The goal put the visitors 2-0 ahead, as six minutes before Cyrille Regis had taken advantage of indecision in the centre of the home defence to deliver an equally venomous strike. Although there was still time for Wayne Clarke to pull a goal back before the break, the anticipated second-half barrage did not happen and the champions fell to a limp defeat, their first at home for twelve months. Eight weeks before, Everton had convincingly defeated Coventry at Wembley to lift the Charity Shield but for the new boss, less than two months in the job, this was hardly in the script and, while a third loss in five league games was hardly a reason to engage the panic button, events felt different to previous years. Chris James in the *Daily Mirror* certainly thought so:

> *Everton's crown is slipping. The League champions' first home defeat at the hands of Coventry must set alarm bells ringing. New boss Colin Harvey put the blame on three successive home games and skipper Kevin Ratcliffe slammed the Goodison fans for not giving the right sort of backing. What a load of rubbish! This champion-size flop was the fault of Everton's players alone. The flair and fire which brought last May's title triumph has been replaced by a lack of imagination and creativity.*

Worryingly, James' eviscerating analysis had more in common with the newspaper criticism during 1983/84 as the defeat left Harvey's team ninth in the table, with just three victories – and only ten goals – in nine games. To make matters worse Liverpool – 15-8 title favourites with Everton at 9-4 – who initially had been unable to play at Anfield due to repairs needed to the Kop,[49] had started the season in sparkling form, with the irresistible John Barnes adding an extra dimension. Their renewed threat was not lost on the Everton manager. 'I felt sorry for those who turned up to watch us against Coventry especially at the moment when there's a lot going on across the park,' Harvey ruefully admitted.

Not helpful was that Kendall's aura was difficult to replace. There was still a sense that his ghost was stalking the corridors and pitches of Goodison and Bellefield. Harvey admitted to Vince Wilson in the *Sunday Mirror* that he would sometimes ignore shouts of 'boss' and 'gaffer'. 'I've looked around for Howard in that split second, seen that he wasn't there and then realised it was me they were after.'

Charity begins at Wembley

'Harvey is now the captain at command headquarters rather than sergeant in the dugout,' David Lacey wrote in the *Guardian*. 'But all that is likely to change for Everton is their luck with injuries, and that can only be a change for the better.' However, that sadly was not the case as, for the second successive campaign, an early-season glut of enforced absences hampered plans. There were four players missing for an eighth trip to the Twin Towers in four years, when Wayne Clarke's goal against Coventry proved decisive. 'Everton may have lost their manager Howard Kendall to the land of the Basques,' Ronald Atkin wrote in the *Observer*, 'but they have not mislaid the winning habit he instilled in recent years.'

By the time Harvey's team travelled to Plough Lane for their first away league game, no less than six first-team players were absent for the 1-1 draw. However, the new boss was still able to field a team worth several million pounds at Nottingham Forest four days later. Copying the Kendall template on the road of removing any risk, the visitors had one meaningful attack all game against a youthful home team, who in contrast played with real quality. 'Everton, who periodically peek out from behind their medical bulletins,' wrote James Lawton in the *Daily Express*, 'either booted the ball down field or passed back to their goalkeeper.'

Sadly, one name was taken for granted on the Goodison casualty list. Paul Bracewell. After four operations and little sign of progress, the midfielder flew to San Francisco for a procedure carried out by a top American specialist. 'We have come to the end of what

---

[49]   Philip Carter had offered the use of Goodison to help Liverpool avoid a backlog of home fixtures. 'It was very kind of Everton and illustrated the close friendship that exists between the two clubs,' Peter Robinson said. Such an offer is sadly impossible in the modern era, but remarkably not the first of its kind. In 1971 the redevelopment of the Main Stand meant Liverpool were unable to fulfil their home leg of the Fairs (UEFA) Cup final should they beat Leeds in the semi-final. The plan therefore was to play their home game at Goodison. Thankfully, for some, the Yorkshire side went through. Should Liverpool have won, their final opponents at Goodison would have been, ironically, Juventus.

we can do in England,' Colin Harvey sadly confessed, 'This trip is the last throw of the dice for Paul in an injury saga that has drastically hit his career.' The gamble thankfully paid off, the surgeon identifying and removing a piece of bone that had attached itself to the joint, causing massive inflammation. However, the classy midfielder would still be out until the new year. Yet for one piece of good news, there was a setback elsewhere, with Kevin Sheedy out for two months following an Achilles operation. The 27-year-old had played ninety minutes on only two occasions since January and his enforced absence again raised the subject of Harvey's failure to reinvigorate the team during the summer.

Forward failings

The lack of goals was one feature of Harvey's early days in the managerial hot-seat. With Sheedy absent there was a dearth of creativity in the middle of the park. 'Unless Everton's midfield combination is quickly sorted out goals will remain scarce,' one correspondent to the *Football Echo* noted. 'Midfield is where defeat is avoided and success created, but Reid and Power make few attacking runs and are too defensive-minded. Without Sheedy's prompting the balance and shape is lacking. Reid and Snodin played 30 league games last season, but their lack of firepower and midfield impetus is worrying.'

That lack of support and goals from midfield was further complicated by a struggling and injury-hit forward line. Adrian Heath failed to feature in the league until mid-September while Wayne Clarke and Graeme Sharp did not exactly appear to be a natural striking partnership. With three players vying for two places, plus Sharp and Heath now in their seventh season together, unsurprisingly there were stories of restlessness. Sharp had been a rumoured target of both Rangers and Newcastle United while the unsettled Heath was linked with a move to Leeds United. Ironically, when Heath returned, Sharp swapped places in the Bellefield treatment room. Meanwhile Harvey denied speculation he was already trying to offload Clarke. 'They [Heath and Clarke] are not going from Everton…I want to emphasise that they are not playing for a move away,' the manager stated. 'No-one has been in for them and, more importantly, I don't want them to leave.'

But a misfiring and stale forward line also brought Harvey begrudgingly to the negotiating table. For a third time an attempt to buy Manchester United's out-of-favour Peter Davenport failed, with Alex Ferguson curtly replying, 'He's not for sale'. Meanwhile West Ham's Tony Cottee, previously a rumoured target for both Everton and Liverpool, was also attracting attention but his manager John Lyall rejected a £1.5 million bid with Bobby Mimms and Derek Mountfield used as bait. Nevertheless, rumours of a deal would regularly surface over the course of the campaign.

Thus both Harvey and his strike-force were under the microscope when the champions travelled to Southampton on the first Saturday in October, a week after the Coventry defeat. On a beautiful autumnal afternoon, the visitors finally rediscovered the zest and ruthlessness of the title run-in. Star man was a fired-up Graeme Sharp, who enjoyed the most productive ninety minutes of his Goodison career. The start was delayed for five minutes when referee Lester Shapter demanded repairs to the net behind Tim Flowers' goal and within 120 seconds of the start the striker caused further damage, heading home Snodin's flighted free-kick. After sixteen minutes the hard-working Scot intercepted Graham Baker's back-pass and slotted past Flowers again. With less than twenty minutes on the clock, Sharp completed a remarkable hat-trick, firing home on the half-volley from twenty yards after Clarke nodded down Watson's long ball. After Flowers smothered a further one-on-one opportunity, on the hour Sharp made it four, after the Saints offside trap fell apart. Following the game, the man of the match fired a blistering broadside at the doubters. 'They were starting to write us off after losing at home to Coventry last week. That was absolute nonsense,' he said, 'The local papers were calling us chumps last week and that really got up our noses. We stuck those cuttings on the dressing room wall and it's certainly worked for us.'

Not uncoincidental was that the 4-0 victory also featured Gary Stevens' first appearance of the campaign, with Everton benefitting from his muscularity and attacking verve which also, of course, helped make his right-wing partner Trevor Steven more effective. However, for all the positive noises from the south coast, Everton were seven points behind their red rivals, who still had two games in hand. 'A few of the lads went to watch Liverpool play Derby in midweek,' an admiring Sharp admitted after the game. 'They were brilliant. But we're not scared of them.' Which was just as well, as Harvey's side had two journeys to Anfield in the next month.

Gary finds Liverpool's Achilles heel

The new manager could have done without the League Cup draw bringing a trip across the park for the third round at the end of October, with a league game there four days later. However, victory over Southampton was followed by an equally impressive 4-1 home drubbing of Chelsea. Everton 'gave us another reminder yesterday that it would be foolish to dismiss their chances of again pipping Liverpool, the favourites, for the title,' according to Jason Thomas in *The Sunday Times*.

Harvey's side went to Anfield on a run of just one defeat in eight games but they had hardly set the world alight: on the previous Saturday they were booed off at Goodison following a dour 2-0 win over Watford. That sequence paled into insignificance compared to the home team, who had dropped just two points in ten league matches, scoring four goals in half of them. Full houses at Anfield were now the norm and there was another welcoming the champions for their cup tie on a mild, misty Wednesday evening. Beforehand the Everton manager was typically candid: 'The onus is on me and I accept that. The fans will be looking towards me so the buck stops here.' However, the determined Harvey handed out a warning. 'We are running into our best form at the right time,' he said, 'We will show the same attitude that helped us win the championship.' For once, an Everton team did that against their neighbours and, although nobody could realise, produced the last great performance of a golden era.

The supposed underdogs – 'although we don't regard ourselves as such,' Harvey claimed – wound the clock back three years by completely nullifying a team whose attacking extravagance had laid waste to the top flight in the opening months – and had lost just one of their previous 101 cup games on the ground – through intense, but organised, pressing which closed space. After a slow start the visitors grew into the game, with veteran Reid very much leading from the front in one of his finest displays. The midfielder had been intensely irked by the pre-match hype around the opposition, which he referred to in no-nonsense terms after the game. 'Obviously Liverpool have been playing very well,' he said, 'But you would have thought we were facing the Brazilian World Cup side out there.' The only empathy Reid showed all night was to lift a canine pitch invader off the pitch.

With the home team held at arm's length – thanks to Ratcliffe and Watson, who announced himself as a top-class Everton defender – and unable to gain any foothold, the visitors wasted their first golden opportunity just before the break. Mark Lawrenson, in the right-back position, played a suicidal pass across his own box to the prowling Sharp who, caught by surprise, failed to get the ball out of his feet and a weak shot went straight at Bruce Grobbelaar. There was more of the same in the second half until an extraordinary incident with thirteen minutes remaining. Barnes picked up the ball on the left touchline but Sharp anticipated his reckless back-pass and, after the striker and Grobbelaar challenged, the ball ran loose in the Kop penalty area. At a slight angle but with an empty net, Sharp embarrassingly side-footed the ball across the face of goal and out for a goal-kick. In truth, the shot was barely a close shave, not helped by the fact the Everton number nine usually struck the ball with his instep and, as he admitted afterwards, there was time for another touch. 'A miss so blatant that it defied belief' were Stuart Jones' words in *The Times*.

Dave Watson played superbly in the victory at Anfield, confirming his development into a centre-half of genuine stature.

Then just as the Everton fans massed at the Anfield Road end – plus a further 12,000 watching on a big screen at Goodison – were rueing the miss, up stepped a hero for whom recent derby matches had not exactly been happy occasions. With six minutes left, Reid's smart switch of play to the right fell into Stevens' path and, after his right-wing partner had cleverly opened space in front of the middle of the Liverpool defence, the full-back's left-footed swinger struck Gary Gillespie's heel and arced agonisingly out of Grobbelaar's reach for a richly deserved victory. 'Anything less than an Everton win would have been an injustice on the night,' claimed Ken Rogers in the *Liverpool Echo*, 'Because they had total self-belief and a passionate desire to turn the derby tide.' Harvey hailed his team as 'brilliant, the whole lot of them. It was a magnificent performance.'

After the game the players claimed that the recent poor press had acted as motivation

THE END

while for the match-winner there was a sense of redemption. Gary Stevens had been involved in the incident that left Jim Beglin with a broken leg at Goodison in January and taken the rap for Liverpool's first goal in the FA Cup final. Now fortune smiled on him at last. 'This is one of my pleasant memories of derby matches,' he declared. 'I hope it pacifies Everton fans who hold me responsible for one or two things.'

However, that evening's victory indirectly supported the wider viewpoint that Harvey's outfit was underperforming: a team who had lost away games at QPR and Luton could then outplay a side in rampant form. But as the 44,000 supporters left Anfield that night, there was another matter on the agenda, talk of which had largely been *verboten* on Merseyside.

Black and blue

The aftermath of Everton's triumph was sadly noteworthy for criticism of their supporters, specifically concerning the repugnant racist abuse handed out to John Barnes, regarded as being some of the worst of its kind ever seen on an English ground. The Liverpool player was showered with bananas when he took a corner in front of the away 'fans' at the Anfield Road and there was regular racist chanting.

'Their behaviour was absolutely deplorable and I say to them "If you can't conduct yourselves as Evertonians should, then stay away. We don't want you,"' an angry Philip Carter declared, 'How a few hundred senseless people can spoil the enjoyment of thousands is utterly appalling.' The switchboards of local radio stations were bombarded with calls from Everton supporters condemning the actions of their fellow fans while even BBC's *Newsnight* felt compelled to run a feature on the story.

The reasons behind their behaviour were multifaceted but largely rooted in the complexities of the city's ethnicity. In an area characterised by a strong sense of individual and collective identity there was undoubtedly a policy of racial exclusion – even with a six per cent black population there was little evidence at the time of any integration in the main shopping areas or, significantly, football matches. 'I have long got used to the fact that in many grounds, such as Everton, I am often the only non-white in the main stand,' Mihir Bose wrote in the *Daily Telegraph*.

But why was the city, with the oldest black community in the country, way behind most areas in terms of accepting black players? 'Liverpool, as a city, possessed a near unique historic brew of racism, imperialism and conservatism,' according to the authors of *Race, Ethnicity and Football*. Attitudes derived from Bill Shankly's preaching of socialist principles – 'I would be at home with folks of my own kind' he once said – plus the haughty, conservative nature of the Goodison board resulted in the city's clubs and supporters hardly taking an enlightened attitude to race, even by the mid-1980s. By that stage the two sides had employed one black player each, Cliff Marshall and Howard Gayle, who made thirteen appearances between them. In 1981 Bob Paisley was asked why Liverpool had recruited so few black players. 'We don't trust them,' was his response. Four years earlier, Gordon Lee was accused by his former chairman at Newcastle, Lord Westwood, of failing to sign West Brom's Laurie Cunningham on account of his skin colour. Lee naturally denied the claim. 'I have never practised any colour prejudice at any time I have been manager,' he responded. However, in his book about John Barnes, *Out of his Skin*, author Dave Hill claimed that it was well known within the Everton dressing room that Lee would never buy black players – similar to Paisley, for the hackneyed view that they lacked character and buckled under pressure. To be fair, they were not alone in that belief.

Accusations of racism were hardly new. Indeed, alleged abuse of black players by supporters of the local clubs went all the way back to 1956, when a letter from a Doncaster fan to the *Liverpool Echo* criticised Liverpudlians for their racist abuse of Charlie Williams,[50] the home team's winger. Eight years later, the Leeds winger Albert Johanneson was subject to Zulu chants and racist abuse at Goodison. Subsequently, both grounds held the reputation as being among the worst to visit for black players.

Ironically, earlier in the year Liverpool had been dubbed 'the most racist club in the country' by the Merseyside Community Relations Council and had rid Anfield's walls of racist graffiti following the arrival of Barnes. In contrast, one council member caused surprise by asking 'Why is it there is so much racist graffiti at Anfield when you don't see any at all Everton?' But if the inference was the problem existed in one half of the city, that was a mistake. Just a month before the derby game, a letter to the local press complained about the shameful racist abuse of Coventry players during their victory at Goodison.

Curiously, though, as various academics commented afterwards, the chants at Anfield – such as 'Everton are white' – were largely directed towards Liverpool supporters rather than Barnes. Away fans were reaffirming their own white Scouse identity and longstanding pride in their attitudes towards race to the opposition: the chants were aimed to undermine those at the other end of the ground who were likely to hold the same beliefs. To make matters worse, there were only four days to assess whether those Everton supporters,

---

[50] Williams later became a popular stand-up comedian.

whose actions shamed the club, had heeded the criticism. 'Tomorrow's game is going out live on TV,' Carter said on the Saturday, 'so it is even more important that the spectacle is seen to be conducted in the best possible spirit for football in general and Merseyside in particular.'

On the pitch, a loss to Liverpool, even at this ridiculously early stage of the season, would probably leave title aspirations dead in the water. With Wayne Clarke replacing the suspended Heath, who was badly missed, the visitors played with the same verve and determination but a chastened Liverpool showed far more grit and penetration. That said, Everton had the better of the opening half-hour and only Grobbelaar's reflex save at the near post from Steven kept the game goalless. Then on 35 minutes, against the run of play according to Jimmy Hill at half-time, the home team forged ahead. With Rush gone, the Everton defence clearly played a higher line but Barnes' sumptuous through ball fed the onrushing Steve McMahon and the former Goodison ball-boy fired past Southall. The second half brought a similar tale, Steven and Stevens both threatened Grobbelaar before a further goal for the leaders on seventy minutes. John Aldridge's effort was blocked at the Kop end and Peter Beardsley gratefully accepted the loose ball with a sharp left-footed half-volley past Southall.

The damaging 2-0 loss left Everton nine points behind Liverpool having played three games more. 'Everton turned us over on Wednesday... They overpowered us then,' Steve McMahon admitted. 'They showed 110 per cent commitment but we were confident we wouldn't let them do it.' Although Kevin Ratcliffe defiantly insisted the title race was not over, there appeared to be little chance of Liverpool collapsing like Manchester United two years before. 'Yet another televised spectacular left armchair fans and a capacity crowd wondering who will finish second,' Harry Harris declared in the *Daily Mirror*.

However, the football was merely a sideshow for those looking for a repeat of the off-pitch events during the Wednesday evening. The BBC coverage of the game was predictably sanitised, choosing to ignore the racist chants at the start of the game from Everton fans which largely petered out once Liverpool went ahead. After the game Jimmy Hill remarked, 'What we should be grateful for I think is that this was a real local derby with none of the nastiness really of last Wednesday night. It was just what it should be.' But that was not the case and his analysis showed once again that televised football was, and still is, uncomfortable about talking about societal issues.

Centenary circus

The 1987/88 campaign featured several events that marked the Football League's centenary celebrations. Unsurprisingly, the arrangements descended into farce on occasions: a planned pop concert was cancelled whilst the centre-point of the festivities, a sixteen-team tournament at Wembley which took place over a single weekend in April – the so-called Mercantile Credit Football Festival – was poorly attended. Just 41,500 turned up on the Saturday and only 17,000 for the Sunday. Nine of the fifteen games – which varied between forty and sixty minutes in length – went to penalties, with Everton going out to Newcastle via that method. The Football League was therefore determined to eke out as much from the landmark anniversary as possible, with the Mercantile Credit Centenary Trophy being played during the *following* season. That competition is quite rightly consigned to the dustbin of history, with Everton going out to Manchester United in the first round. The eventual winners of the trophy, Arsenal, do not even recognise the triumph on their official honours list. Stuart Jones put it well in *The Times* when he described the tournament as 'the closing debacle of the embarrassing League centenary celebrations'.

The Football League also wished to schedule a 'League Centenary Challenge' match between the reigning English and Scottish champions. With Rangers lifting the Scottish title in 1986/87, Philip Carter understood that Goodison Park would host Graeme Souness' side but the League Centenary Committee, chaired by Chelsea chairman Ken Bates, unwisely selected Maine Road, for reasons of neutrality. However, the thought of policing travelling Scottish and Everton fans, in Manchester of all places, was always going to have a limited shelf life. The possibility of crowd trouble convinced those north of the border that, they too, could follow their English counterparts into European exile and the Scottish League withdrew Rangers' invitation. Left with no opponents for their champions, following discussions with European Cup holders Porto and Napoli, eventually the Football League enticed Bayern Munich to Goodison with a guarantee of £75,000, the same figure paid to the Toffees. Sadly, the only way the game, played on a freezing November evening, rekindled memories of their epic Cup Winners' Cup semi-final was via the scoreline: Everton won 3-1. Elsewhere it was a toss-up who was the more apathetic: the home supporters or Bayern players. Faced with paying £4 for a terrace ticket or £8 for a stand ticket – a third higher than usual prices – a ridiculously small crowd of just 13,083 spectators, against nearly 50,000 two years before, watched little more than a training game. Consequently, the Football League managed to lose £100,000 on one of their glamour events of the celebrations. 'An evening that should have been glorious entertainment became a sad and largely silent commentary on the [centenary] committee's twisted sense of logic,' Stuart Jones remarked about the ticket prices.

Remarkably the laughable sequence of events did not end there. Organised by a Bahrain-based promotions firm, twelve months earlier Liverpool had faced Celtic for an ersatz British Championship match in Dubai. The game was deemed a success and a repeat fixture, officially for the Dubai Super Cup, was scheduled between Everton and Rangers for the December. However, the Football League refused to sanction the meeting, purely as retribution for the Scottish side pulling out of their centenary game. 'I find it unbelievable that the Football League have taken this decision,' secretary Jim Greenwood complained. 'They are in effect telling the Scottish League which team we should play in Dubai.' Embarrassingly Philip Carter was forced to step aside from the League discussion but soon broke his silence as Everton chairman. 'We feel the action is ill-considered and the decision was made without the full facts,' he claimed, 'The organisers are asking what the hell is going on.' Not for the last time, Carter was treading a fine line in his dual roles. However, when Everton appealed, the League was forced to drop its objection.

In the event perhaps Harvey wished they had not changed their mind, following a bitterly disappointing experience in the Middle East. In front of 8,000 enthusiastic British exiles and curious locals at the Al Nasr Stadium, his team dominated for an hour, having gone ahead through sponsors' man of the match Kevin Sheedy after 24 minutes. When Dave Watson uncharacteristically found time and space in the opposition box to fire home with his less-favoured left foot midway through the second half, the Dubai Super Cup appeared to be Everton's. But old nemesis Souness' appearance from the bench changed the whole dynamic of the lucrative fixture. The previously accomplished English champions lost all momentum in the draining heat with Robert Fleck bringing their Scottish counterparts back into the game ten minutes from the end. With three minutes left, Ally McCoist brought parity when he took Fleck's pass and lifted the ball over Southall. With the game ending 2-2 there was no extra time and the destination of the trophy was all down to penalties – sixteen of them, as the contest threatened to take the match beyond midnight. The first fifteen were all converted successfully before the unfortunate Ian Snodin saw his kick saved by Chris Woods. 'We should have won it easily,' Colin Harvey said afterwards. That was an understatement and a possibly unfair indication that some of the ruthlessness of the Kendall years had disappeared.[51]

51   Sadly not the last time Rangers would cause Everton angst. As the month ended, Harvey thought there was a deal with Aston Villa to sign winger Mark Walters – whose middle name was Everton – only for the Scottish club to offer better financial terms. The irony being, given previous criticism, that Walters would have been the club's first high-profile signing of a black player.

Managing the Red Menace

Although the Toffees entered the Christmas period on the back of just one defeat in fifteen games, they had not been convincing. Nevertheless, in normal circumstances a tally of 34 points from twenty matches, leaving them in fifth place, was perfectly acceptable. After all, twelve months before they were only one point and a single place better off with an inferior goal difference. Then, six points behind leaders Arsenal, they had a springboard for a title challenge. The difference now was that Liverpool – who had added Oxford midfielder Ray Houghton to their summer purchases – were producing some of the finest football in Anfield history, reflected in a remarkable tally of 47 points from nineteen games. 'By most normal standards Everton have done quite well this season,' Ian Hargraves wrote in the *Liverpool Echo*. 'Unfortunately, their fans do not tend to judge them in that way, seeing only that their neighbours remain unbeaten in the League and are boosted by what seems an almost bottomless reservoir of talent.'

However, defensively the team was as strong as any Everton side before or since, having conceded just thirteen goals at the halfway mark of the campaign. Watson was unrecognisable from the player who was a victim of terrace abuse in his early days, whilst Ratcliffe was at the peak of his career. 'We've been solid in defence and we've done well in midfield,' Harvey said, 'But outside of Goodison we've not scored enough goals.' Graeme Sharp's form after a bright autumn was patchy while Adrian Heath's lost confidence adversely impacted his finishing, which matched the unreliability of his early years. There was the sad sight of the striker being booed by supporters during the drab goalless draw against Oxford at the end of November, amid a sequence of scoring in only two of seventeen domestic league and cup games. 'Adrian Heath has been unfortunate not to have put as many chances away as he could,' Harvey said. His manager's mood hardly improved when Heath was quoted as saying he would go to Rangers 'like a shot' although the striker said the words to a Scottish journalist were taken out of context.

Not only were the two strikers misfiring – a continuation in truth of the previous campaign, when the duo collectively netted just sixteen goals in 57 league games, half that of 1984/85 when Heath did not play after Christmas – but midfield goals were non-existent. Peter Reid rarely troubled the scorers while, although there was no concern about Ian Snodin's defensive and midfield prowess, goalscoring and creativity had never been the Yorkshireman's forte. Even when Sheedy returned to the first team in November there was no real improvement in output, the Ireland international clearly playing to orders in a more withdrawn role. Trevor Steven had just one league goal from open play.

One of the contributing factors was the manager himself. As a coach Harvey's main strength had been getting the team to press effectively and force the opposition into making mistakes. But as Arrigo Sacchi pointed out, as a tactic that is not enough, further strings to the bow are needed. Harvey was a big admirer of Don Howe, a brilliant coach who possessed a reputation for superbly drilling teams defensively, but at the expense of the creative arts according to his critics. There was something of the former Arsenal and England coach in Harvey and the new manager was finding that one of the hardest tasks to coach in football is co-ordinated attacking play, especially with a squad in real danger of going stale.

That said, home form remained strong, but a lack of goals was hurting on their travels. Damaging defeats at Manchester United and Sheffield Wednesday over the festive period left the reigning champions in sixth place, a frightening nineteen points behind Kenny Dalglish's side. There had only been 21 goals scored in total during the first twelve away league games of the campaign, which was testimony to Harvey's defensive prowess. But Everton's share was a miserly ten – with four in one game. After reaching double figures for away victories in each of the previous three campaigns, the new manager had recorded just two in his first twelve matches. 'Our away form has been diabolical,' Kevin Ratcliffe admitted. 'It does not match up to what has been expected of us.'

Consequently, six months into his tenure there were already some dissenting voices. 'You have, by your statement in the press, said that you will not be buying a striker,' one fan wrote in the *Football Echo*. 'Well, Colin, thanks for condemning us Evertonians to a situation where we have "surrendered" the trophy without a fight. There will be many Evertonians disheartened by your statement.' However, with a League Cup quarter-final berth secured and the FA Cup to come, there was still a chance of major silverware in Harvey's first season.

15

THE LIGHTS GO OUT

EVEN THOUGH, UNDER KENDALL, EVERTON HAD TRADITIONALLY moved up a gear in the new year, Harvey and skipper Kevin Ratcliffe's perfunctory claims that the reigning champions were still in the title race were taken with less than a pinch of salt. Nevertheless, the Toffees had built on their victory at Anfield to progress to the semi-final stage of the League Cup against Arsenal. The Everton boss would also have taken great heart from a 1-0 league win over Nottingham Forest at Goodison on the first Sunday in January, when they 'unleashed some of their best football of the season' according to Chris James in the *Daily Mirror*. Ironically match-winner Wayne Clarke was only in the team because Graeme Sharp was absent with a hand injury after he was bitten by the family dog.

Peter Reid was the star of the show, possibly enjoying the best form of his Everton career, having won four successive *Liverpool Echo* man-of-the-match awards. 'He's brilliant at the moment. His leadership qualities, determination and passing have been magnificent,' his manager said. 'I would say Peter is playing as well as I have seen him perform for Everton.'[52] Against Forest he won a further accolade, after completely dominating England rival Neil Webb. One thing missing from Reid's game had been goals, but that would change in the FA Cup, when Everton replayed a famous fixture.

A Wednesday marathon

The third round produced a tough away tie at Sheffield Wednesday, where the teams were meeting in the competition for the second time since the famous 1966 final. Odds for winning the trophy reflected the difficulty of Everton's task: at 10-1 they were only fourth

---

52   Before Christmas the pair were guests of television presenter Timmy Mallett, who was fronting a televised charity appeal for ITV in Liverpool city centre. The show got off to an embarrassing start. 'Here they are, folks, Colin Harvey and Peter Reeves of Liverpool. Let's hear a big cheer for Liverpool,' Mallett told the disbelieving crowd. Getting Reid's name wrong was bad enough but after Mallett listed a number of Anfield stars, he then asked the Blues boss: 'Well Colin, you've got some tremendous players there. What do you think of them?' Harvey – who was holding an Everton book – responded, 'I don't know, I didn't sign any of them!' A member of the production had to correct Mallett but thankfully for him the show was not broadcast due to an industrial dispute.

in the betting, with Liverpool unsurprisingly 4-1 favourites.

The scrappy game, played in driving rain and wind, was typical early-round FA Cup fare with the most worrying development of the first half an injury to Kevin Ratcliffe, who pulled up with a groin injury and failed to reappear after the break. With a goalless draw on the cards, sixteen minutes from time the home team went ahead through Colin West but, with a rare third-round exit on the cards, the visitors drew level when Reid slid in after Martin Hodge parried Sharp's miscued shot. 'Not what you'd call a classic football match,' was Wednesday manager Howard Wilkinson's observation of a contest broadcast across Europe, 'but it appears to be what the continentals want to see on their screens.'

The replay at Goodison was equally fast and furious, with Lee Chapman putting the visitors ahead on the half-hour mark before a truly memorable goal fifteen minutes from time. Trevor Steven's cross from the right was only partially headed out by Lawrie Madden to a prowling Sharp, fifteen yards out on the left side of the penalty box. The Scot's beautifully struck volley was so ferocious that goalkeeper Hodge stood still before it rattled into the roof of his net. The magnificent effort was Sharp's first goal for eight games. 'That's one of the best strikes I have ever had against me,' an admiring Hodge admitted. 'I couldn't move because it was going that fast. Not many players will better that.' The 32,935 spectators were treated to a fruitless additional thirty minutes before, in the bowels of the Main Stand, Philip Carter called correctly against his Wednesday opposite number, Bert McGee, and the third game was scheduled for Goodison twelve days later. 'It's becoming a marathon and it's still anybody's game,' Ken Rogers wrote in the *Liverpool Echo*.

However, in Goodison's first-ever FA Cup second replay, those home fans in the 37,414 crowd expecting a knockout punch from Harvey's team left disappointed. After going ahead in the tie for the first time, after 58 minutes, when Steven headed home from six yards, Wednesday got a deserved equaliser near the end when Chapman diverted Nigel Worthington's shot past Southall. There were no further goals in regulation time and a further thirty minutes were similarly barren.

The tie was now the most elongated saga in the third round of the competition since Jack Charlton's Wednesday had taken Arsenal to five games nine years before. With yet another replay scheduled for Hillsborough 48 hours later, Harvey was asked for his recollections of that never-ending story. 'I remember those five matches,' he responded, 'It was like Coronation Street and this is getting the same way.'

Incredibly, after five-and-a-half hours of combat in football's War of the Roses, the outcome of the fourth game was swift and brutal. 'We would all like to get it out of the way' Colin Harvey admitted before the game and his marathon men did just that in wonderful style. Thanks to a perfect hat-trick from Graeme Sharp and goals from Heath and Snodin, unbelievably the visitors were 5-0 up at half-time. The second period was understandably anti-climactic, enlivened by the substitute appearance of Paul Bracewell, who received a hero's welcome with seventeen minutes remaining.

Having seen his club earn more than £250,000 from four games watched by 142,000 spectators, Colin Harvey was understandably ecstatic after the final whistle. 'It was quality finishing,' the Everton boss said, 'You expect one goal, two at the most. But all of a sudden it was five at half-time – you'd have got good odds on that.'

Teesside trio

The next round brought a welcome home draw, albeit against a resurgent Middlesbrough outfit who were challenging for promotion to the top flight and a club possessing strong Everton connections via manager Bruce Rioch and coach Colin Todd. In their ranks they had some hugely promising players: Gary Pallister and Tony Mowbray were the best central defensive partnership in the lower leagues while winger Stuart Ripley would later win the Premier League with Blackburn.

Three days after the Wednesday mauling, the attractive but obdurate opponents – Peter Reid needed stitches over a bloodied left eye – made the battle-fatigued home team sweat after Sharp put the home team ahead. Any thoughts of a smooth passage to the next round were scuppered two minutes into the second period when Paul Kerr equalised after the excellent Ripley's shot hit the post.

Harvey's weary foot-soldiers then travelled to the north-east for a sixth FA Cup tie in 25 days with the added complication of a home draw against cup favourites Liverpool for the winners. In front of a 25,235 crowd generating ground-record receipts of £120,000 and a marvellously passionate atmosphere, Harvey's tiring side barely merited their lead acquired after 67 minutes when Dave Watson headed home Alan Harper's cross. A Merseyside cup derby was within touching distance as the game entered the second minute of added time before a towering header from the inspirational Mowbray produced a deserved equaliser.

Yet the first ninety minutes was merely the support act for the main drama in extra time. The rattled visitors had Southall to thank for keeping them in the contest but after 99 minutes the home team finally broke the great Welshman's resistance, substitute Alan Kernaghan hooking the ball home from a prone position after his initial header was cleared off the line by Harper. With the game deep into added time, and with anxious whistles reverberating around Ayresome Park, the Toffees had one last opportunity. Pat Van Den Hauwe launched a long free-kick towards the area, Heath helped the ball on and Steven's header crept agonisingly inside the far post. Ten seconds remained. 'One of the most dramatic, remarkable cup ties we have seen in a long time,' was the considered opinion of ITV's legendary commentator Brian Moore. After a pulsating ten-and-a-half hours and six games of cup action, Harvey's side were still alive – just.

If fatigue was an issue, when the north-east side turned up six days later there was another challenge. There can have been few games at Goodison over the years played in worse conditions – the seventy miles per hour gales circulating around both the ground and surrounding terrace streets, mixed with driving rain and sleet, made a mockery of proceedings. 'A game which had promised so much, coming as it did after two such enthralling encounters, rarely raised itself above the level of farce,' wrote Ian Ross in *The Times*.

The ball could not be confidently kicked into the wind and after one clearance from goalkeeper Stephen Pears' hand initially failed to escape the penalty area, the Boro defence did not clear and Reid played in Sharp before the striker fired home. With the wind easing slightly in the second period, Everton retained control before the Second Division outfit equalised with their only real attack of the evening. Kerr skinned Stevens on the Everton right and his low cross was converted by a sliding Ripley from close range.

Keen to avoid yet another thirty minutes of extra time, the home team turned the screw and got lucky seven minutes from the end when Stevens' hard cross from the right asked searching questions of the Boro defence and the off-balance Mowbray, facing his own goal, could only stick out a boot and watch in agony as the ball sped into the net for the winner. The victors had now played more games than Coventry had in lifting the trophy twelve months before and Rioch paid tribute to their durability: 'If they get to Wembley they'll have trodden the longest road in history – good luck to them.'

Heading out

By mid-February Harvey's prospects of success in his first season as manager were now dependent on the outcome of two tough contests three days apart. His side were due to travel to Highbury aiming to retrieve a one-goal deficit in their League Cup semi-final, following a 1-0 home defeat at Goodison in the first leg, Trevor Steven's missed penalty late on symptomatic of a tired and listless display. 'Everton were always a yard short or a second behind. It was as though they were playing in slow motion,' Stuart Jones commented in *The Times*.

But on the Sunday before the north London trip, there was a small matter of the third Merseyside FA Cup derby in the space of eight seasons. 'We know the next two games could end our season and that's putting the pressure on,' Gary Stevens warned ominously before the clash against Dalglish's side, the full-back still holding the distinction of scoring the winner in Liverpool's only defeat in 32 matches so far. A revered former employee was more positive. 'I believe that Everton can play their part in achieving a treble for the area by going on to win the FA and Littlewoods [League] Cups,' Howard Kendall commented.

After Reid went off after pulling a muscle in his right thigh early on, there was a first half of no corners or chances and even the usual schoolboy enthusiasm of John Motson, broadcasting live on the BBC, was eroded. 'Well, I'm afraid there's not a great deal of style or shape about it at present,' the commentator admitted after an hour. Any viewers who had switched channels then missed the only moment of real quality in the game. Fifteen minutes from time the previously anonymous John Barnes exchanged passes with Peter Beardsley on the Liverpool left and the winger's measured cross was met by derby debutant Ray Houghton, who beat Neil Pointon to the ball and headed past Southall. It was the first headed goal of the midfielder's career. 'A sequence of events totally out of context with the grey spectacle which had gone before,' according to David Lacey in the *Guardian*. Equally noteworthy, the strike was created and executed by three players bought for £3.5 million during a period when Everton had barely spent a penny.

Afterwards a lack of imagination in attack, which had hampered the side all season, ultimately proved costly as Dalglish's side moved into the next round. Meanwhile, Harvey could not hide his disappointment. 'It doesn't help when you lose one of your best players,' he said about Reid's withdrawal, 'but that is no excuse. We created more chances and we defended badly for the goal.' Now, after a series of exhausting cup games during a seven-week period, the whole season depended on dragging a win from Highbury against all odds three days later.

Highbury hangover

'The morale in our camp is still high, the tie is still wide open,' Harvey said after the first leg. However, the interim period of seventeen days had tested that view. Two draining FA Cup games had resulted in one road to Wembley being blocked while Reid's injury kept him out of the return.

With the whole season depending on the ninety minutes, Arsenal took complete control and wasted two golden opportunities before the break, with David Rocastle missing an open goal and Martin Hayes firing wide from the spot. If supporters thought Graham's side had let Everton off the hook, they were proved wrong four minutes after half-time, although there was an element of controversy. Rocastle clattered into Van Den Hauwe, leaving the stricken defender on the ground, but incredibly referee George Courtney did not award a free-kick and Thomas was able to waltz through the area usually patrolled by the Wales international before scoring. More than one observer had said that Howard Kendall was a lucky manager but, after watching a stretcher take the defender off the pitch with damaged ankle and knee ligaments, Harvey may have thought otherwise about his own fortunes.

Early on during his tenure Colin Harvey discovered that the move into the managerial hot-seat brought vastly different pressures from being a coach.

Then, out of nothing, with twenty minutes left substitute Heath equalised on the night with a header at the North Bank after John Lukic had stopped Clarke's effort.[53] To Harvey's frustration, any hopes of a revival were dashed inside three minutes. Groves put Rocastle through a static rearguard and the midfielder fired precisely into the corner. The closing stages were embarrassing and painful for the visiting supporters as the home side ran riot although only Alan Smith added to the scoreline for a 4-1 aggregate victory.

After four years of Merseyside dominance, as many of the huge crowd invaded the pitch it was hard not to feel that the Gunners, and not Everton, were now Liverpool's nearest challengers. 'George Graham's young side indicated during the second leg of the semi-final at Highbury last night that they are a team of genuine stature. Their immediate horizon is bright enough and, considering their average age, so is their distant future,' Stuart Jones commented in *The Times*. 'Everton's lights, on the other hand, have gone out.' It was up to Harvey to switch them back on.

Pushback

Unsurprisingly, supporters used to recent success took to the pages of the *Football Echo* to voice their frustrations. 'We have developed into a team which at best is average, and all too often frequently mediocre. The present team is the worst Everton have fielded for six years,' were the words of one irritated fan.

While there was sympathy for the new boss, in many ways some of the wounds were self-inflicted: the failure to add numbers during the season had proved costly. 'The plight Everton finds itself in is a dire consequence of not strengthening the squad in the close season,' wrote another supporter, '[We] go into important games like Arsenal and Liverpool, battle-weary and running out of ideas and steam in the second half.' Yet Harvey denied that accusation. 'I certainly don't believe that the cup run rebounded on us in the end,' he responded. 'I felt we handled it well. We finished strong in every game, came back with character in a couple and had our moments…The run did take a lot out of us, but it didn't beat us in the end.'

What did beat Everton, therefore, was a failure to make meaningful additions to the squad. 'It's easy to sit down now with the benefit of hindsight and say that we should have possibly bought one or two players,' the manager explained late in the campaign, 'We've had our share of injury problems, but I'm not using that as an excuse.' Harvey had made only one acquisition, that of Leicester City's left-sided midfielder Ian Wilson in the

---

[53] Heath's third goal at that end in three different competitions, after he had netted in the FA Cup semi-final against Southampton in April 1984 and scored the winner in a league game two years later.

previous September for £300,000. The 29-year-old, although neat and tidy, hardly set the pulses of supporters racing and could not be classed as a statement signing by the reigning champions. Unable to replicate Sheedy's flair and potency on the left, the team became increasingly one-dimensional. Most of the attacks originated down the right flank, invariably ending with a cross that was useless for the diminutive Heath. With very little creativity through the middle, unsurprisingly goals dried up. 'The real bone of contention with the majority of fans is the attitude, style and lack of entertainment,' commented one supporter, 'Even the players themselves don't look as though they are enjoying playing.' The lack of firepower was something Harvey was prepared to accept. 'More than anything, you can say that we have not scored enough goals. I am not blaming anyone in particular,' he responded. 'In the past we have shared the load. This season that has not happened.'

Bursting bubbles

There was one final act before the campaign was finished. By late March Liverpool were still unbeaten after 28 league games – indeed their only defeat all season was still to Everton in the League Cup – which was one short of Leeds United's record from the start of a campaign, set in 1973/74. A midweek draw at Derby matched the Yorkshire club's tally and meant the record was Liverpool's should they avoid defeat at Goodison on the following Sunday. Six months before, the Anfield side were 100-1 to go through the league season unbeaten but now they were 6-4 with bookmakers, who were set to lose more than £1 million. Fate not only decreed that their closest rivals provided the final obstacle but also up front for the Toffees was Wayne Clarke, whose brother Allan was such a prolific marksman for Revie's side. The former Leeds striker was at Goodison, commentating for local radio.

In front of a crowd that was 4,000 short of capacity due to the presence of live television, with Sheedy and Reid back Everton looked a better-balanced side than for several months. For neutrals, Liverpool's outstanding season had provided some light in the post-Heysel darkness and consequently, not for the first or last time, Everton were very much the party-poopers in this local skirmish. From the start their plan was to force an early lead and then defend it resourcefully. That tactic worked perfectly as Liverpool unfamiliarly found themselves under significant pressure, with the crucial moment arriving after just fourteen minutes. After Grobbelaar was crowded out at the near post from Steven's corner, a series of ricochets put the ball into Clarke's path and the striker finished from six yards out. As the scorer wheeled away in celebration, the away supporters packed behind Grobbelaar's goal knew that, given the family connection, there was probably going to be a crushing inevitability about proceedings.

The rest of the half was pulsating. Liverpool, having gone behind in the league for only the third time, immediately forced the pace although the outstanding Reid effectively shadowed Barnes. Van Den Hauwe plus the superb Watson[54] – 'a derby player if there ever was one' according to Patrick Barclay in the *Independent* – neutralised their attack. The closest to an equaliser came when Alan Harper kicked a Craig Johnston effort off the line. After the break Everton were continually pegged back but, with no John Aldridge, Dalglish's side visibly tired and Southall had barely a save to make. The nearest to an equaliser came when Beardsley screwed a left-footed strike wide. Unusually, as a fevered game reached ninety minutes, the opposition threat had diminished to such an extent that the home team held on in some comfort. Afterwards it was difficult to decide who was the more disappointed: the Liverpool contingent inside Goodison or ITV, whose cameras were deprived of history. The television company had provided three champagne cases to lubricate celebrations. They remained unopened. 'One goal had made such props pointless,' Michael Calvin commented in the *Daily Telegraph*.

The hard-earned win was a double-edged sword in some respects. Any derby victory is always welcome but it was ironically a painful reminder of a drop in standards. Twelve months before Everton travelled to Anfield knowing a win could effectively clinch the title, now the only significance was depriving their close rivals of a place in the history books. Afterwards Harvey was unconvincing when he said the record had not warranted a discussion in the Everton dressing room. However, in his autobiography Peter Reid succinctly summed up the relative decline: 'It highlighted that we had gone from being better than Liverpool and going toe-to-toe with them to being in a situation in which we were competitive only on a one-off basis.'

Fourth not first

The derby victory failed to act as a springboard for the rest of the campaign and, although Everton were unbeaten in the next eight league games, they produced only three victories and just ten goals. A scrappy and shapeless 2-1 home defeat to Arsenal, for whom Kevin Campbell made his debut as a second-half substitute, on the final day left the Toffees in fourth at season's end, their seventy points twenty less than Liverpool. In usual circumstances a UEFA Cup place acted as compensation but in the post-Heysel world

---

[54]   Watson's brother Alex, also a central defender, was on the Liverpool bench but did not get on the pitch – the closest two siblings have come to facing each other in the fixture. At any level the only brothers to oppose each other in a derby are Paul Lodge (Everton) and Bobby Lodge (Liverpool) in the FA Youth Cup in October 1977.

there was no such reward. Consequently, supporters and those at the club viewed fourth as failure, made worse by the lack of quality elsewhere which forced the former Liverpool manager Bob Paisley to declare 'this is the poorest First Division I have seen in all my years in the game.'

A glance at the table shows where the obvious problems lay: a lack of goals and poor away form. There were just 52 goals scored in forty league games[55] or more than thirty less than each of the three previous campaigns. After a prolific January, Sharp encountered a barren spell of only two goals in the final fifteen games, while strike partner Heath netted only three during the same period. Harvey's inability as a manager to develop a coherent attacking strategy, Sheedy's lengthy absences plus a complete lack of creativity in the centre of midfield all contributed. Those who justify the sale of Gary Lineker on the basis the title was won in the following season forget that the England striker would have made a huge difference to Colin Harvey.

That lack of goals particularly impacted the away record. At Goodison, Everton were imperious, if largely functional, in winning fourteen games and accruing 46 points, only one victory and four points less than Liverpool. On their travels they scored just nineteen goals, down with the worst in the division and one less than bottom-of-the-table Oxford United. That goal tally was half that of Liverpool and the 24 points won were sixteen less than their rivals. Only once in the last 29 league games involving Everton did a team score three times: the Toffees' 3-0 win at Norwich in January. As the season developed games became increasingly monochrome. 'The match between Everton and Charlton [a 1-1 draw at Goodison in April] demonstrated yet again, how negative and short of ideas Everton are these days,' complained one supporter in the *Football Echo*. 'Only two front men throughout the game against a side blatantly happy to settle for a point. This negative approach, especially when playing away, has cost them dearly this season. A draw away is no longer a point gained but rather two points lost.'

There was another aspect of the moderate away record worth considering. Failure to replicate great home form on the road can be down to character and attitude. During the middle of the decade that had not been an issue under Howard Kendall but the mysterious failure in Harvey's first season was perhaps an early indicator of the dressing-room issues which would materialise later in his reign. There was a feeling, rightly or wrongly, within some of the fanbase that several stalwarts of the Kendall era were now picking and choosing their games. Having competed for trophies at the elite end of English football

---

[55]   To help transition the move from a 22-team top flight to one of twenty for 1988/89.

over four or more years, when it was clear Liverpool were uncatchable and with no European reward, understandably motivation for relatively meaningless contests near the end of the season dissipated. Results and performances in the four matches against their biggest rival were very much the exception that proves the rule.

Nevertheless, there were plus-points during the campaign, namely the form of the defence. Just 27 goals were conceded in forty league games, a club-record that stands to this day. Setting aside the peerless Southall, Kevin Ratcliffe (before injury) and the sterling efforts of Pat Van Den Hauwe, player of the season was undoubtedly Dave Watson. Like an ageing test batsman who narrows down his scoring strokes to reduce risk and maximise effectiveness, the former Norwich City skipper had simplified his game to do likewise: sound positioning, strong in the challenge, powerful in the air, keep it simple on the ball. Add in a winner's mentality, apparent even as a youngster, then it was no surprise that Watson was the player of the season and would go on to be the bulwark of the side over the next decade and more. While Watson was progressing, the rest of the squad was doing the opposite and the need for changes was highlighted by Ken Rogers in the *Liverpool Echo* after the final game:

> I believe the Arsenal defeat was the end of an era in many ways. There has been no spark out on the park of late and, as a result, the fans are totally flat. Everton have won two Championships, the FA Cup and the European Cup Winners' Cup – all in the space of four years. It was a glittering spell. But you can't stand still in football, which is what the Blues have done this season. They have failed to strengthen their power base, while a certain team from across the park have captured a string of class individuals to bolster an already formidable squad. There is nothing like a major signing or signings to stimulate interest and get things moving.

16
GET CARTER

GIVEN PREVIOUS DISSATISFACTION OVER THE MONEY OFFERED BY television and with the Big Five keen to have a greater influence on how it was distributed, the new broadcasting deal due to start from the 1988/89 season was always going to cause tremors within the game. The first moves were made eighteen months before when Granada TV approached Philip Carter, in his role as Football League president, on behalf of British Satellite Broadcasting (BSB), a fledgling organisation in which they had shares. 'The machinations that followed were to have cataclysmic consequences,' Joe Lovejoy wrote in *Glory, Goals and Greed: Twenty Years of the Premier League*. Those consequences are still being felt today but resulted in at least one notable casualty during the immediate aftermath.

Dyke floods the market

The starting point for negotiations was broadly the same, the clubs wanting more money for less coverage. Yet television companies could point to the sport being only the fourth most popular in terms of audiences – the 4.2 million who watched the League Cup final live on ITV was fewer than the after-midnight audience that evening who watched golfer Sandy Lyle clinch the Masters. However, there was added intrigue with a third party now interested. Twelve months after their initial expression of interest, in May 1988 British Satellite Broadcasting (BSB) tabled a bid of £200 million over ten years for sixty live midweek matches per season. Ultimately, fears over small audiences and a drop in advertising revenue scuppered the deal, however former *Match of the Day* supremo Mike Murphy presciently warned that in future you would 'see football matches played for television only, or games pulled out of the fixture list and played on Monday night... if (a broadcaster) comes up with enough money for it.'

However, ITV – with head Greg Dyke rejecting the usual duopoly with the BBC – made all the early running but not before history repeated itself. Dyke held secret meetings with representatives of the Big Five with an offer of £600,000 each per season (with an additional £150,000 per featured game) in exchange for exclusive rights to broadcast their home matches. A further five clubs were offered £400,000 each. The £32 million four-year deal – which effectively excluded the other 82 league clubs – threatened a schism in English football and the inevitable creation of a super league. Carter, with an obvious conflict of interest in remaining Everton chairman while having responsibility for the welfare of 92 clubs as Football League president, found himself frozen out as his own Management Committee discussed the deal. They eventually obtained an injunction to stop the clubs signing the agreement while mulling over a joint BSB/BBC offer of £36 million over four years.

Then, in a startling development, Dyke re-emerged with a new proposal of £44 million over four years, the bulk of which would go to top-flight clubs. At the beginning of August, the Football League accepted that deal which took English football into unchartered territory. With eighteen live league games plus three League Cup matches a season, the new arrangement worked out at £500,000 per game. With a £30 million four-year contract for FA Cup games and England internationals later agreed with BSB and BBC, annual domestic television rights previously valued at £3m two years before were now worth six times that amount. 'We think the ITV deal is in the best interests of football collectively and it is the way forward,' Carter said afterwards.

But if the Everton chairman thought the ground-breaking contract would enable him to escape censure over his initial discussions with ITV, he was wrong. There was a storm brewing over the way Carter was secretly negotiating with Dyke for an exclusive deal for top clubs while the Football League thought they were going all in with BSB and BBC. Before an extraordinary meeting of league chairmen, a week after the deal was agreed, sixty of Carter's counterparts handed secretary Graham Kelly a petition calling for his sacking. Unsurprisingly the loudest opposition came from Carter's *bête noire*, Luton chairman, David Evans. Still smarting from his role in the Hatters' exclusion from the League Cup two years before, Evans had a further axe to grind in the way Carter had led the League's eventual outlawing of plastic pitches – Luton being one – during the intervening period. 'Carter has to go – and Arsenal's [vice-chairman] David Dein with him. That's the price they must pay for going behind our backs,' Evans demanded, 'These people were elected to protect the interests of every League club. Instead, they tried to look after the chosen few.' Unsurprisingly, Evans' most vocal cohorts were Oldham's Ian Stott and QPR's David Bulstrode, clubs who had also been told to rip up their plastic pitches by Carter and the Football League. They were not alone though. BSB boss Bob

Hunter accused Carter of behaviour that was 'extremely questionable'. Carter did have the support of one man. 'He's done the best job with football that's ever been done,' Brian Clough claimed, 'And he should be thanked or even knighted.'

Whilst Carter protested his innocence – 'I have behaved honourably, impartially and correctly throughout,' he maintained – there was some sympathy for the aggrieved chairmen who accused him of duplicity. By going alone with ITV, the big clubs had seen a way of forcing through their desired twelve-team top flight, with each side playing each other four times, like had been successfully implemented in Scotland. Ironically therefore, on the basis history repeats itself, there were many similarities – the greed, the secrecy, the complete disregard for the footballing proletariat – between the way the big clubs acted in 1988 and the failed European Super League plans 33 years. As their nominee, Carter still defended his corner. 'I'm the man to lead football into the 1990s,' he claimed, 'At no time did we discuss setting up a Super League we just wanted to get the best deal for televising football.'

However, unlike in 2021 when there were no scapegoats over the European Super League, there was on this occasion. At an extraordinary general meeting in October at Villa Park, the chairmen kicked out Carter and Dein. Humiliatingly, Carter become the first Football League president to be voted off the role in its 100-year history. 'I have done my best to build bridges, and ensure that the interests of all the clubs were considered,' he said afterwards, 'But apparently that was not good enough for some people, so I shall now sit back and concentrate on the much more enjoyable task of supporting Everton.' But that was going to be a more difficult task than anticipated.

TC is boss catch

With increased revenue anticipated from the new television deal, plus the profits from two lengthy cup runs, Harvey had more money available to spend during the summer of 1988 than any Everton manager in history. How it was spent would probably determine his managerial legacy.

With a misfiring forward line, Harvey's main priority was a new striker. During the previous campaign, apart from public links with Tony Cottee, the Everton boss also explored other options. The Sunday tabloid gossip columns were a constant source of speculation, from Gary Lineker being tipped for a return to Harvey keeping tabs on Crystal Palace's Ian Wright. Chelsea's Kerry Dixon and Ally McCoist of Rangers were also in the frame.

However, some reports had more substance. Mark Hughes struggled at Barcelona after moving in 1986 and had been loaned to Bayern Munich and Harvey spoke with the Welsh striker after the German club had played in the FA Centenary game at Goodison. After checking on Hughes with Barcelona in the following spring, the Everton boss fuelled speculation that a bid was in the offing by watching Wales play in Sweden. Eventually any hopes of signing the 24-year-old were extinguished when Alex Ferguson secured his return to Old Trafford for a £1.8 million fee.

The trip to Scandinavia also started rumours about Hughes' international strike partner. Late in the campaign there were reports that the Toffees had set up a £3m deal to bring Ian Rush back to Merseyside. Intriguingly, the Welsh striker, who had endured a nightmare season in Turin, did not exactly pour cold water on the deal, admitting, 'It would be flattering if a big club like Everton were to show an interest in me...I don't know whether Juventus would release me at this point, I don't think they would.' Asked about the rumours, Harvey said they were 'totally wrong'. Yet there was interest from the Everton boss in the previous February[56] when it was an open secret that Juventus would be jettisoning Rush at the end of the campaign. But there were several stumbling blocks, among them that Liverpool had first refusal; Juventus still owed half of the original transfer fee, plus the two clubs had become close post-Heysel so whether the Italian giants would sell to Everton was questionable. Predictably, all the rumours were to put to bed when Rush returned to Anfield in August.

Therefore, early in the summer Harvey's immediate target was Manchester City striker Paul Stewart, subject of a rumoured £850,000 bid earlier in the year. With City placing a prohibitive £2 million fee on his head, there were no takers but when the price lowered to £1.7 million both Spurs and Everton showed interest. Scheduled to meet Harvey at Bellefield, the player infuriated the Everton boss by telling the press 24 hours beforehand that he was signing for Spurs, but then still turned up at the training ground. Harvey called the farcical meeting a 'charade' and that 'basically, he had no intention of signing'.

That took the Everton boss back to his original target, West Ham forward Tony Cottee. When the Hammers agreed to put the England striker on the market at the end of June, the player had a clear choice between the Toffees and Arsenal. Everton's bid of £1.75 million was rejected but when both clubs offered the asking price of £2 million, the choice was down to Cottee. There were several meetings with George Graham and Colin Harvey (plus Philip Carter), but with Arsenal not wishing to break their pay structure to

---

[56]   As reported via a front page exclusive by the *Daily Star* on 12 February, 1988.

accommodate the player's demands, eventually Cottee chose to go north. There was another factor. 'At the end of all the bargaining it was probably the enthusiasm of Everton manager Colin Harvey that won the day,' the player's agent John Smith admitted, 'Colin claimed to be a big fan of Cottee and Tony was very impressed by his attitude.' The one thing that remained confusing was the fee, West Ham quoting £2.5 million on the basis they had asked Everton to pay the VAT element (£300,000) of the deal, meaning the actual fee was £2.2 million, although Philip Carter maintained it was £2 million. But for Harvey, this was not the only big money move of the summer.

Comings and goings

Gary Stevens was one player keen on venturing to pastures new. The England defender had endured a moderate campaign and, in May, Rangers had offered a straight swap deal of midfielder Iain Durrant and Ally McCoist for Stevens[57] and right-sided partner Trevor Steven, which Harvey rejected.

With Rangers' interest still in the background, the matter appeared settled when Stevens told Harvey in early July that he would see out the remaining two years of his contract, but within a fortnight he was up in Glasgow after the two clubs agreed a fee of £1.25 million. Although Stevens admitted after moving that the promise of European football was an attraction, the big increase in salary (plus a signing-on fee) would naturally have been an important factor. Stevens himself later explained: 'I had gone stale. I stayed at Goodison Park too long. The more I thought about the way my form was suffering, the more I realised there was only one solution to move away.' Stories about his private life had been splashed across the tabloids and understandably a move to Scotland would take him out of the spotlight. There was a further reason though: his failing relationship with Harvey. Stevens and his right-wing partner produced a dairy of the 1987/88 campaign, *Even Stevens*, and one of the recurring themes of the book is the number of flashpoints between full-back and manager. 'We had a bit of a fall-out,' he revealed as the reason for moving in James Corbett's *Faith of our Families*. 'It wasn't a massive amount to do with Europe but of course people will look for a reason…it wasn't really because of that.'

To be fair, Harvey realised early on that Stevens would probably be off and had lined up Newcastle's Neil McDonald as a ready-made substitute. The 22-year-old was out of contract and, in pre-Bosman days, could still be sold for a fee. If the clubs disagreed on

---

[57]   Rangers' manager Graeme Souness first expressed an interest in Stevens when they sat together at the same table at the PFA awards dinner earlier in the year. Souness told the full-back to alert him should he ever wish to leave Goodison.

the amount, then an independent tribunal settled the matter. With Everton offering £450,000 and the Geordie club wanting twice that, Harvey was delighted the tribunal valued McDonald at £525,000. The manager would have been less than happy when McDonald's lack of pace made him an unsuitable like-for-like replacement for the England man. That said the Wallsend-born player was more than competent and a beautifully clean striker of a ball.

With Peter Reid reaching the autumn of his career, Harvey was keen to rebuild his midfield and that search had taken him across the Pennines to Bradford City's Stuart McCall. A fee of £850,000 was enough to secure the 24-year-old's services. The strange aspect of the move was McCall's playing style was not dissimilar to Ian Snodin's, which did not go unnoticed by other clubs. Sheffield Wednesday offered £600,000 for Snodin – who was rumoured to be unsettled – but the midfielder told Harvey he was prepared to stay and fight for his place.

The final signing of the summer was more problematical. Like McDonald, Chelsea winger Pat Nevin was also out of contract. The London club ridiculously priced the Scot at £1.7 million but with Everton offering only £400,000 in response there was another visit to the tribunal. The difference in valuations was the largest ever and their final assessment of £925,000 was also a record. Harvey fumed afterwards. 'It is time for a change in the tribunal system,' he complained, 'It is getting to a situation where both clubs are putting unrealistic prices on players' heads.' However, considering Paul Gascoigne (£2 million) and Paul Stewart (£1.7 million) had gone for significantly more money the valuation was not unreasonable. Nevin confidently set out his aspirations afterwards. 'Everton are one of the teams, if not THE team, who will be challenging for honours,' the winger proclaimed, 'You can't let Liverpool run away with everything. Someone has to challenge them.'

Harvey paid out £4.3 million during the summer to meet that challenge but that was partially recouped from other outgoings. Alan Harper went to Sheffield Wednesday for £275,000 while there was sadness when fans' favourite Derek Mountfield left for Aston Villa in a £450,000 move. The centre-half had never really recovered from the cartilage problems which sidelined him for six months at the start of the 1985/86 campaign and Watson's great form meant Mountfield only started four matches in Harvey's first season. The writing was on the wall for the popular defender when the manager preferred Pat Van Den Hauwe after Kevin Ratcliffe's injury.

The final departure was hugely symbolic. Adrian Heath had been subject to much transfer speculation during the previous season, with rumoured interest from Leeds

United, Sunderland and Sheffield Wednesday – £400,000 plus a young David Hirst in exchange – and a reported £500,000 bid from Arsenal in January. Tony Cottee's arrival had put Heath's future under the spotlight and after just six starts in midfield early in 1988/89, the man whose goals revitalised the club in the opening months of 1984 moved to Espanol in Spain for a fee of £550,000. But Inchy would be back.

Potty for Cottee

With Ian Rush added to their ranks, Liverpool went into the new season as the hottest title favourites in history. The bookmakers had installed the champions as odds-on to secure a record eighteenth league title, quoting Kenny Dalglish's team at 8-13, with closest rivals Manchester United at 4-1, Everton 7-1, Nottingham Forest 12-1 and Tottenham with Arsenal at 16-1.

For the Everton manager, having effectively allowed his first season to atrophy, there were raised expectations of delivering a trophy in his second campaign. But previous transfer inertia had left the challenge of assimilating four new and expensive signings on and off the pitch. Thus developing the right blend immediately was essential and time was a commodity Harvey did not have. Consequently, the consensus was that he was a man under pressure.

The Everton boss got a good start and more on a glorious sunlit Saturday afternoon in the opening game against Newcastle United. The two clubs had accounted for more than a third of the transfer fees paid over the summer but after ninety minutes only one looked like obtaining value for money. Within a blink of an eye – thirty seconds to be exact – the vast majority of the 41,560 crowd erupted when £2 million man Cottee opened his account after Sharp's initial shot was saved by Newcastle debutant goalkeeper Dave Beasant. Thirty minutes later Reid put through the new signing, whose cross-shot sped past a beleaguered Beasant and went in off the far post. Just after the hour the striker was in dreamland, reaching Nevin's cross before Beasant and smartly hooking the ball home.[58] With all the new signings making impressive starts – McCall 'played with such assurance in Everton's midfield, you would have thought he had been in the side as long as Peter Reid,' wrote Cynthia Bateman in the *Guardian* – a fourth goal from Sharp near the end acted very much as a postscript. At full time many Evertonians understandably left Goodison believing they had seen the dawn of a new era. 'Colin Harvey, who spent £4¼ million in total had not so much fettled his own model as built a Rolls-Royce,' was

---

[58]   Cottee matching Fred Pickering's feat, achieved against Blackburn in March 1964, of scoring a hat-trick on Everton debut.

Bateman's conclusion.

A week later the new, luxurious Everton spluttered a bit at Highfield Road, returning up the M6 with a further three points, via a first-half Cottee header from a McDonald cross. However, that only tells half the story of an afternoon which witnessed one of the all-time great Everton individual performances. At Upton Park in April, West Ham's Leroy Rosenior had described Neville Southall as the best goalkeeper he had ever seen, after the Welshman produced a display bordering on the supernatural during a goalless draw. What the striker would have made of Southall's exhibition in the West Midlands may have made interesting reading. Now at the apex of his career,[59] he produced a display of such brilliance that calling it world-class would be a disservice. 'Staggering,' was Cyril Chapman's viewpoint in the *Guardian*. The edited highlights include a spectacular stop from Brian Kilcline's fiercely struck penalty after 25 minutes; before half-time he twisted and changed direction in mid-air to miraculously tip Gary Bannister's close-range header over the crossbar (after the game Coventry boss John Sillett compared the save to Gordon Banks' famous stop from Pelé) and on 51 minutes he broke the hearts of the home players and supporters after diving full-length to turn Greg Downes' rising drive over the bar. 'I was walking back to the centre circle to kick off again,' match-winner Cottee admitted. 'Downes had his hands in the air, celebrating.' 'Another extraordinary save,' Chapman commented. Although several in the press box said it would go down as the save of the season, it was arguably not even the best Southall had made in the game.

On the one time he was beaten, the magnificent goalkeeper earned his luck when Cyrille Regis' header struck the bar. Afterwards there was only one talking point. 'One of the best goalkeeping performances I have ever seen in all my life,' Sillett declared. He was not alone.

---

[59] Southall's equally magnificent performance ten days later during a 1-0 defeat by the Netherlands in a World Cup qualifier earned the respect of Ruud Gullit, who subsequently described him as the best goalkeeper in the world.

17
EXPOSURE

TWO VICTORIES, FIVE GOALS, NONE CONCEDED. YET THIS WAS ABOUT as good as it got for Harvey. At the beginning of September there was talk of the championship, four weeks later there was speculation over his future.

Knives out

Alarm bells started to ring when an enterprising Nottingham Forest got the better of a 1-1 draw at Goodison seven days later. Apart from time, the other thing the Everton boss did not have was a fully-fit squad. Kevin Ratcliffe and Pat Van Den Hauwe had not featured at all while Pat Nevin suffered cruciate knee ligament damage against Forest. With Trevor Steven out with an Achilles problem, for the fourth successive campaign there was an injury crisis early on. After a 2-1 away defeat to newly-promoted Millwall, the stark challenges facing Harvey were clearly apparent in the line-up for the home game against Luton Town: Ian Wilson at left-back, Ian Snodin at centre-half with the wantaway Adrian Heath on the right wing. That said, Snodin had impressed with his speed and reading of the game in the middle of the defence. The former Leeds player was powerless as a wholly ineffective team display led to a 2-0 home defeat, one which would have been far worse but for Southall's recurring brilliance. 'Everton were gripped by a fear of getting it wrong, rather than taking a chance on adventure in the hope of getting it right,' commented Phil McNulty in the *Liverpool Daily Post* of a display and result that rarely occurred during the glory years. It was that caution which infuriated the Everton boss in the aftermath. 'We were scared of them every time they got the ball,' an angry Harvey said. 'We were frightened when the opposition had the ball and frightened in front of goal. I don't know why.'

Seven days later a disappointing 2-1 loss at Wimbledon left his expensively assembled side tenth in the table and knives were out, with a familiar name lined up as Harvey's replacement: Brian Clough. There was tabloid conjecture that the Goodison hierarchy were discreetly chasing the Forest boss, who was fancied by an 'influential group' at Everton. Who that 'group' were was not specified, which only added to the speculation. But, at odds of 12-1 Harvey was now among the favourites for the sack. 'Three defeats in a row is a disaster for us,' he admitted, 'Nobody at the club is happy – certainly not me. I'm a winner. I always have been. And I aim to get us doing the business again.' One man who was frankly baffled by all the rumour and innuendo was his predecessor in the Goodison hot-seat. 'It's ludicrous, they have only lost three games,' Howard Kendall claimed, before outlining the main problem, 'There is a big difference between being manager and being No. 2 and that is what Colin is finding out. But he has the ability to be successful.'

Aside from that, why had the early season optimism disappeared? Although there had been injuries, the main problem was the lack of control and mobility in the middle of the park. Peter Reid – never the fastest in the parish – had slowed considerably which also impacted his tackling ability. Also, like Alan Ball before him, a by-product of the dying of the light was a need to follow the play around the pitch, with the midfield losing shape. The extra responsibility following his coaching appointment hardly helped. Meanwhile, with Snodin playing at the back, there was no real ball-winner in midfield, which had featured Pat Nevin, Adrian Heath, Ian Wilson and Kevin Sheedy thus far. Stuart McCall may have been the answer, but the Scot had looked ragged and ill-disciplined.

Also, around this time, stories about dressing-room discontent surfaced. During the previous campaign there were rumours of unrest with some of the squad unhappy with both the style of play and management. However, the summer had brought Harvey an additional but unexpected problem. Due to the riches derived from the massive new television contract, the expensive arrivals had been able to negotiate salaries at least equal to, or more than, most senior pros in the existing squad, which caused understandable turbulence and contributed to the 'them and us' scenario which blighted the dressing room thereafter. However, Peter Reid was keen to dampen down the mounting speculation. 'There's nothing here that warrants the wild accusations which have been in certain newspaper headlines,' he informed the *Liverpool Echo* before admitting, 'Really we have no excuses. We've not been playing well recently – we know that.'

To make matters worse Harvey would be absent for most of October due to a hip replacement operation. As the Everton boss entered hospital, one of the questions was whether Philip Carter would show the same patience and understanding as he did with Howard Kendall. When the Everton chairman delivered the dreaded vote of confidence, the message was murky: was it like that famous 1983 *Daily Express* article in which he offered unconditional support to a beleaguered manager or was it a tightening of the noose on his successor?

Nevertheless, with Ratcliffe and Steven both back, if there was a noose then a much-needed 4-1 home victory of Southampton certainly loosened it. Cottee scored twice after the visitors had taken the lead after 65 seconds, with James Lawton in the *Daily Express* using the striker's goals as a stick to beat Harvey's critics. 'Tony Cottee did rather more than save his manager's neck,' he forcibly claimed, 'He shot great holes in the lunatic proposition that three League defeats are enough to wipe out the career of an honest man, who just a few months ago was entrusted with more than £4 million rebuilding funds…there is no question about their ability to seriously challenge for the title they yielded last year.'

However, even Lawton would have been nonplussed by the 2-0 reverse at Villa Park a fortnight later. Trailing to a first-half Tony Daley strike, the visitors showed that under Harvey they had lost the appetite to fight back after conceding an early goal on their travels. The second goal provided further proof. Southall made two astonishing saves in rapid succession, initially palming away a David Platt effort before racing across the goal-line to stop Daley's point-blank header. That should have been sufficient but within thirty seconds an unmarked Platt was allowed to swivel on the penalty spot and volley past the Welshman. As he kicked the ball away, it was hard not to sympathise with the beaten goalkeeper, who wore the world-weary look of someone puzzled and annoyed at the drop in standards over the previous eighteen months.

And it's live!

After ITV won the exclusive rights to live First Division football, they had a curious attitude to scheduling. Although John Bromley, head of sport, proclaimed coverage 'has leapt into the 1990s. It will be live, pacey and popular', to maximise ratings schedulers waited until the clocks went back before broadcasting their opening game. At the behest of the pools companies, the televised fixtures had to be selected ten weeks in advance and the first game was Everton entertaining Manchester United at Goodison Park. At the start of the campaign, the contest would have naturally been high on the list of priorities for ITV. However, instead of a blockbuster start to the brave new world of glitzy, big screen football, the clash at Goodison was strictly mid-table fare, with Everton in fifteenth and the visitors three places higher at the start of the day.

There was no doubting the broadcaster's commitment. For £11 million a season, ITV promised thirteen cameras instead of the usual seven, with two on the eighteen-yard line at either end, plus better camera angles and action replays. At Goodison they had 55 personnel on site. In addition, at the break there were all the goals from Saturday's matches.[60] With the potential for half-time interviews with managers and dressing-room access, the product was merely replicating coverage on the continent, which for many years had put England in the shade. 'All we can hope to do is to provide as much entertainment as possible and keep our fingers crossed the two teams do the same,' match producer Ted Ayling admitted.

Whether Ayling or the domestic TV audience got that entertainment in the opening period was questionable. With the respective midfields spending most of the half kicking one another – a single camera covering the halfway line was sufficient – the only action of note was a brilliant double-save from Southall, first stopping Brian McClair's shot before blocking Mark Hughes' attempt from the rebound. During an extended half-time break, to accommodate adverts and an interview with Bryan Robson as he stepped off the pitch, Ian St John's observation that the game had been 'tremendous' was more a reflection of the raising of the stakes following the huge deal rather than an objective view of a largely moribund contest. 'Tremendous it was not,' was Davis Lacey's opinion in the *Guardian*, 'It was a fitful struggle between two sides seeking consistency to mount a more serious title challenge.'

The second half was a more positive experience for the 5.8 million viewers at home (as well as a reported seventy million worldwide) and a crowd numbering just 27,005. Midway through the half Clayton Blackmore's in-swinging cross momentarily left Southall out of position and Hughes took advantage of this indecision to instinctively lift a volley over the goalkeeper. Within three minutes Everton were level, Watson headed a free-kick against the crossbar before Cottee fired home from inside the six-yard box. That completed the scoring with a draw seen as a fair result.

But the main talking point of the second half was an infamous challenge by Ian Snodin on wiry Danish winger, Jesper Olsen. As the United player raced clear with only Southall to beat, the Everton player dangerously took away his legs from behind. Not only was the tackle crude but it stopped a clear goalscoring opportunity. Remarkably, Snodin escaped with a booking. United manager Alex Ferguson raged, accusing referee

---

[60]   Very much a revolutionary move and something successfully used in Italian football for many years. Up until the mid-1980s the only First Division goals televised were either on *Match of the Day* or those covered by the various ITV regions, with occasional film broadcast on news bulletins. With contracts also designed to cover lower divisions and midweek highlights prohibited, consequently most games in the top flight were not shown. With the new deal allowing for the screening of all goals from the opening weekend onwards, the home match against Arsenal on the final day of the 1987/88 campaign will go down in Everton history as the last first-team game where no broadcast footage exists.

David Scott of playing to the cameras. 'Because it was live on TV the referee felt he shouldn't send him off,' the United manager fumed. 'He was trying to present the right image. But it didn't do the game any good in front of the watching millions.' Ferguson also claimed there had been an FA directive stating players should be sent off when they stopped an opponent clean though on goal but Scott denied this. 'Why should I have sent him off?' the referee replied. 'There has not been a directive as Alex suggests.' Peter Reid joined Scott in pouring cold water over Ferguson's claims. 'If I had been in the same situation I would have done the same thing, so would all 20 players on the pitch,' the Everton player-coach claimed. 'Ferguson's not saying his players never do that sort of thing, is he?'

Nevertheless, in their first broadcast of the new era of live television, ITV had unwittingly showcased two of the dominant characteristics of television coverage over the next quarter-of-a-century: an exaggeration of quality and, of course, the obligatory Alex Ferguson post-match rant over match officials.

There was another reminder of the dangers of invasive coverage after the game. Neville Southall was ITV's man of the match and when the cameras entered the post-match dressing room, the Welshman was asked for a comment but looked embarrassed. 'I let the gaffer do the talking for me' was all he could mutter. 'It was a much-needed reminder that footballers are instinctive sportsmen rather than instant philosophers,' commented Michael Calvin in the *Daily Telegraph*.

Back in the mix

Snodin may have been the big-screen villain but the bubbly Yorkshireman had been one of the success stories of the season thus far. However, when the campaign commenced, it was fair to say the former Leeds player had still to win over supporters: the talent was clearly there but used sparingly. 'They [the fans] didn't give me much praise last year and I didn't deserve it,' he explained to the *Liverpool Echo*. Now, after an excellent spell as Ratcliffe's replacement, he was moved to right-back, for the first time in his career, before the victory over Southampton. Snodin was a revelation in the 4-1 win, sound defensively while producing an inch-perfect cross for Dave Watson's goal. It was all change on the terraces too. 'The way they have really got behind me this season has really inspired me,' he said.

Nonetheless, for every player on the upgrade there is one whose fortunes dip. Kevin Sheedy had endured difficulties in Harvey's debut managerial season, with the latter's desire to play him wide at odds with the 29-year-old's belief that his future lay in the middle. Before the European Championship in the summer, Sheedy went on record to say he would not kick a ball again for the club. With Pat Nevin's arrival muddying the picture, Sheedy's transfer request was granted in mid-July. 'I pick the team and players play where I tell them,' Harvey said in uncompromising fashion, 'The manager told me again yesterday that he won't play me in the centre of midfield and made up my mind that I want to move away from Everton,' Sheedy responded 24 hours later. Before the season's start there was some sort of reconciliation, albeit temporary. 'He has been outstanding on the left side, but he thinks he's more suited to the centre,' Harvey said, 'At the moment we've agreed to differ on that, but as long as he's with us I'll play the team which I consider is in the best interests of the club.'

Harvey's misguided dogma was hardly satisfactory and after eight goalless and rather unflattering games, Sheedy was dropped for the Southampton fixture. 'At the start of the season I wasn't giving 100 per cent, which was the wrong thing to do,' he later revealed to the *Liverpool Echo's* Ric George. Supporters know when a player is not giving his all and unsurprisingly Sheedy was the target of terrace criticism. To his frustration there appeared to be no end to the dispute, potential suitors put off by a £1 million price tag for a player nearing thirty and possessing a lengthy injury record. Although Benfica, Manchester United and Arsenal were linked, the only club to make an approach were Coventry City, who were eventually deterred by the fee. 'I'm on the transfer list but the manager only tells me what he wants to tell me so I can't say if there have been any offers', Sheedy admitted. To make matters worse, Trevor Steven had filled the left-hand side berth, a decision which Sheedy criticised. Although he had changed home telephone number to put off journalists looking to ignite a war of words with Harvey, his comments on Steven's role – however valid – were hardly going to improve the relationship.

In mid-November there was a further off-the-pitch distraction for the Everton boss. With Athletic Bilbao amid a six-game losing streak there was speculation that Howard Kendall would welcome a move back home, which only heightened when he returned to England on a pre-arranged trip. Cue a national newspaper running a story that Everton wished to reform the successful Kendall-Harvey partnership, should the latter agree to a return to coaching. Philip Carter was enraged. 'You can take it from me that there is absolutely no question of that happening,' the chairman angrily responded. 'There has been no contact with Howard Kendall.'

Problems on the pitch also showed no signs of abating. The Toffees were fortunate to escape with a point in a 1-1 draw at Hillsborough, once again thanks to Southall, who brilliantly saved a Mel Sterland penalty in a game where the visitors had a miserable two shots on target. Writing in the *Independent*, Patrick Barclay – who concluded that the game 'induced despair about standards in the First Division' – was puzzled over the decline of the side:

> They are 15th, their lowest position since the Goodison revival began under Howard Kendall four-and-a half years ago, and it is hard to understand why; always a bad sign. They have spent a lot of money, wisely on the face of it…But the pattern, the instinctive sense of direction that brought two championships, has been disrupted.

Harvey refused to speak to the press after the game but out of nowhere his team produced an unbeaten league run that put them firmly back in the leading pack. A hard-fought 2-1 win over Charlton was followed by a lucky 1-1 draw with leaders Norwich City at Goodison. The Canaries possessed a 100 per cent away record and utterly dominated the contest with Everton offering little and hardly getting a kick. On the hour Malcolm Allen put the visitors ahead and with sixteen minutes left they seemed certain to extend that sequence until referee John Penrose awarded a laughable penalty. Trevor Putney challenged Snodin and got to the ball first. With the linesman flagging for a corner, instead Penrose pointed to the spot. Steven secured a barely deserved point by placing the kick past Bryan Gunn. 'The penalty that John Penrose awarded Everton was like asking Santa for a bike and finding that the stocking contains a Rolls-Royce,' Mihir Bose remarked in *The Sunday Times*.

On the last Saturday in November, Harvey's side returned from Upton Park with another three points, thanks to a Steven shot from outside the box that dribbled under goalkeeper Alan McKnight. After the game – with one eye on Gary Stevens' somewhat acrimonious departure during the summer – Harvey extolled Snodin's virtues. 'Ian is the best No 2 in the country at the moment,' he declared, 'If [Bobby] Robson is looking for a right-back he couldn't go far wrong with Snodin.' On the following Saturday Tony Cottee's 100th league goal was enough to see off Spurs at Goodison and extend the unbeaten run to eight games.[61] But once again Southall protected the three points, thanks to an astonishing save to stop a spectacular own goal equaliser from Dave Watson. Southall's childhood hero Pat Jennings was at the game and appreciated the stop. 'I would have been proud to make a save like that,' he said, 'Neville has shown once again what a brilliant goalkeeper he is.' As a bonus the victory featured a first appearance for Paul

---

[61]   Spurs loomed large in a timeline of Cottee's significant league goals. The striker scored on his debut against Tottenham in January 1983 and sixteen years later netted his 200th career league goal at White Hart Lane for Leicester City.

Bracewell at Goodison since May 1986, the midfielder playing as if he had not been away.

Bracewell retained his place for the visit to Anfield eight days later, for a derby game that once again contained a decision that stuck in the throats of the visiting supporters. Harvey's side performed more than adequately, without really threatening, during the opening period, but found themselves a goal down when Snodin moved up slightly late, allowing Ray Houghton to spring the offside trap and beat Southall. Minutes later the 44,000 crowd thought it was two, but Southall miraculously tipped John Barnes' close-range shot over the bar. Even by the Welshman's stratospheric standards, it was a remarkable save, one that 'left Barnes and the 42,000-plus crowd stunned in disbelief' according to John Keith in the *Daily Express*. Everton toiled without offering much until six minutes after the break, when Steven was upended by young full-back David Burrows in the Anfield Road penalty area. With hernia-victim Graeme Sharp out and Trevor Steven passing over responsibility after missing his previous effort, the transfer-listed Wayne Clark stepped up and buried the spot-kick into the corner. Amazingly, having been on the back foot for most of the game, fifteen minutes later the visiting fans thought they may be celebrating the winner. Some neat interplay around the Liverpool box led to Wilson hanging up a cross to the far post where the predatory Clarke nodded home. But celebrations were short-lived: referee Joe Worrall disallowed the header for the scorer climbing over Burrows. It seemed harsh at the time – the linesman, in a perfect position, seemed content with the goal. Despite some late Liverpool pressure, Southall and the Everton defence held firm for a hard-earned draw.

Afterwards there were talking points aplenty. Although television replays seemed to indicate Worrall had made an error in disallowing Clarke's goal, the Warrington-born official refused to be drawn on the matter and, in a similar scenario to Alex Ferguson's accusation about the failure to send off Ian Snodin, stated the presence of the television cameras did not influence his decision. Goalscorer Clarke meanwhile claimed: 'No way was it a foul. I got up early and just hung there.' Surprisingly Kenny Dalglish agreed the goal should have stood, while also claiming Worrall should not have given the penalty. The other discussion point was the brilliance of Southall. Ray Houghton said he was the pivotal presence in the game, describing him as 'a daunting figure. His save from Barnes was incredible. Had we gone 2-0 up then, we would have won easily.'

A point at QPR and two home victories against Middlesbrough and Coventry City (when the 1985 championship-winning midfield quartet played together for the first time since the 1986 FA Cup final) over the Christmas period left Everton in a surprisingly lofty fourth place at the end of 1988. Thirty points from eighteen games left them seven behind pace-setters Arsenal and two ahead of Liverpool. 'We've put a good run together and it's up to us to keep it going,' Harvey declared. 'The lads are beginning to believe in themselves. However, they've not produced the form they're capable of and I think they can still do better.' Only time would tell.

18

NEW YEAR WOBBLES

DESPITE HARVEY'S ADMISSION THAT THE TEAM HAD LARGELY struggled, the fact Everton stood fourth at the midway point reopened the debate on the quality – or lack of it – in all echelons of English football. Wide-open championship races – like in 1974/75 – usually point to that and Kevin Ratcliffe's belief that ten teams were in contention spoke volumes. Bob Paisley's earlier claims that the quality was the worst in living memory remained unchallenged. Indeed, QPR's assistant boss Peter Shreeves and Leeds manager Howard Wilkinson, two of the most respected and forward-looking coaches in the country, agreed. 'The standard is very average,' Shreeves told Peter Ball of *The Times*. 'Apart from the top few, I don't think any teams have seven or eight quality players these days. Coming back in the coach from away matches, you ask, "Who did you rate from their team?" and you get only four or five names. The rest are hard-working, very fit, athletic footballers, but there aren't too many who can actually change a game.' In the same interview, Wilkinson concurred: 'We are faced with a problem that we are producing fewer and fewer players of exceptional talent.'

There were many reasons for this, such as the lack of European club football preventing English players testing themselves against the elite. Coaching primarily focused on fitness and physical strength, at the expense of flair, caused the most damage. The days of a lower-division player not having enough skill to play in the top flight were long gone. Consequently, Shreeves said it was now the opposite, giving an example of a player who was 'a good passer, but not strong enough for the First Division.' The top flight was increasingly colourless. 'What we are saying,' Shreeves explained, 'is that if you are fit and strong and can get up and down the field you can play in the First Division.'

Bullied at Bradford

One of the by-products of a levelling of standards and playing styles across the 92 clubs was an increased vulnerability for big clubs in cup games, as Everton found to their cost at Bradford City in a League Cup fourth-round tie eleven days before Christmas. The fixture at Valley Parade was notable for Sheedy returning, the midfielder admitting that being out of the first team was damaging his international prospects.

In front of a crowd of 15,055 paying ground record receipts of £55,102, the visitors were outmanoeuvred by a team four places from the bottom of the Second Division and without a victory since October. Harvey had taken the squad to Maine Road on the preceding Saturday, where Terry Dolan's team were soundly beaten 4-0. Following a bright opening Everton went behind after eighteen minutes when Mark Leonard[62] met Peter Jackson's free-kick with a looping header over Southall. Six minutes later it was 2-0. Brian Mitchell swept past Van Den Hauwe and, with Ratcliffe out of position, an unmarked Ian Banks side-footed past Southall. With the centre of defence having its worst game for two years, Bradford constantly broke through the backline and five minutes after the break they were three ahead. A switch of play went to Mick Kennedy unmarked on the left, his cross found Leigh Palin occupying the space between the two Everton centre-halves and the midfielder headed home.

The First Division side struck the woodwork twice but all they had to show for a fightback of sorts was a consolation goal from Watson near the end. Harvey admitted afterwards that the visit to Maine Road had produced a certain amount of complacency on a disastrous evening. 'I think my players were psychologically affected by that,' he said. 'It seemed like a good idea at the time.' The goals conceded also reflected problems in the rearguard. Ratcliffe had struggled since returning to the team, especially in terms of regaining that extra pace which made him such a formidable presence. Pat Van Den Hauwe was also unsettled and his form was suffering – the tough defender reportedly wanting a return to the capital. The Everton boss consequently pointed the finger after the sobering defeat. 'We conceded one good goal and one bad goal in the first half, and their third goal was an absolute disaster,' he declared, 'We let in a couple of goals we would not normally have done.'

Out of the running

The Bradford setback failed to damage the bookmakers' confidence in Everton's title challenge, odds of 6-1 at the turn of the year reflecting their recent championship pedigree. They were third favourites, behind Arsenal at 10-11 and Liverpool at 9-4. However, any

---

[62]   St Helens-born Leonard was an Everton supporter as a child but unfortunately suffered a broken leg after being struck by a hit-and-run driver in November 1981, while on the way to sign for the club from Witton Albion. Everton kept to their commitment and he signed six months later.

aspirations were immediately dented following a 2-0 loss on the banks of the Trent at New Year. Nottingham Forest had won only once at home all season, to Liverpool, and they made it an unlikely Mersey double on an afternoon when Trevor Steven's missed penalty, with the game goalless, proved crucial.

Twelve days later came probably the most important league game of the season, indeed one of the most significant matches of the Harvey era. When they arrived at Goodison in the middle of January, Arsenal had just been knocked out of the FA Cup at Highbury by bottom-club West Ham and although still top, the game was seen as a major test. 'There will never be a better time for Everton to sow a few seeds of self-doubt in Arsenal's mind,' wrote Clive White in *The Times*, 'not to mention reduce the deficit.' Before the showdown there was possibly an unwise attempt at mind games from Tony Cottee. 'I could have joined Arsenal but I didn't,' he declared. 'I made a decision which was the right one, and always will be...I don't feel as if I've got anything to prove to George Graham, Arsenal or their supporters. It doesn't matter to me what Arsenal have done.' He then went on to claim the preference of playing with Graeme Sharp ahead of Alan Smith also influenced his move. However, Kevin Ratcliffe was more circumspect, likening Arsenal to Kendall's championship team. 'We did not have any players who the public, outside Goodison, would have recognised as exceptional. It was a team effort,' he told the *Daily Telegraph's* Colin Gibson. 'Arsenal are very much the same...there's a team spirit when a team grow up like that. Arsenal have been getting stronger and stronger each season.'

Ten points behind, Everton desperately needed a victory but Graham's side confirmed Ratcliffe's assessment, producing a mature display proving that their development arc over the previous two years put them firmly at the same place as Everton in 1984/85. Just as significantly, even without Tony Adams and Steve Bould their performance more than resembled Kendall's team: the Gunners played it tight in the opening period before opening out to devastating effect after the break. Within six minutes of the restart, they were two goals ahead, an unmarked Paul Merson – whose pace and forward threat completely overshadowed Cottee – driving through the centre of defence to open their account before Smith headed home David Rocastle's cross from the right. But there was added poignancy over the identity of their third goalscorer after 72 minutes, which hardly enhanced the mood of the watching home crowd. Although a hugely valuable player, three years before Kevin Richardson could not command a place in the Everton first team but faced with a completely ineffective Toffees midfield – Sheedy showed little interest, Reid and Bracewell (unsurprisingly) were too slow and Nevin lightweight – the

Geordie crowned his man-of-the-match display with a fine goal after exchanging passes with Merson. The manner of the three goals also highlighted the decline of the central defence, which was described as 'astonishingly vulnerable' by Brian Glanville in the *Sunday Times*.

With Cottee running down a series of blind alleys, a Watson goal near the end was scant consolation. The only danger Arsenal goalkeeper John Lukic had faced all afternoon was from an RAF police dog which escaped the attentions of its handler and moved menacingly towards him as he warmed up. When the visitors left the pitch to a standing ovation after the final whistle, the home crowd were indirectly acknowledging the fact Arsenal were everything their team used to be but were no longer: youthful, hungry, ruthlessly efficient, and well organised. Richardson confirmed that impression afterwards: 'It is like history repeating itself for me. The pattern, the team, the balance and the tactics are so similar to the way Everton played when they won the league when I was here.'

'It's a thin dividing line,' Harvey mused afterwards. 'If we had put our first-half chances away...' However, Stephen Brierley of the *Guardian* responded, 'It was not so much that his voice trailed off, rather that most stopped listening. Thin or thick, Everton had been stuffed.' If the League Cup semi-final defeat almost twelve months before signalled that Gunners were now best-placed to challenge Liverpool's hegemony, this comprehensive victory confirmed Everton were now amongst the also-rans.

Understandably, the fanbase was not exactly enamoured following what seemed a defining defeat. 'Colin Harvey has a lot to answer for as Everton fall apart at the back again,' one correspondent to the *Football Echo* groaned. 'He continues to pick Reid and Bracewell who are too slow in midfield, which puts the central defence under pressure. What is Mr Carter doing about this alarming situation. I am afraid Mr Harvey and Co. must go.' That may not have been a viable option but another letter pointed to a wider issue: 'Arsenal were fitter, faster, more skilful and much younger. Increasingly clubs are finding a rich supply of young players. Where are Everton's?' That was a perfectly valid point. Following the ascension of the players in Harvey's reserves to the first team in the early months of Kendall's reign, the supply line from Bellefield had diminished to a trickle. The success of the senior squad obviously was a factor but not the only reason. Kendall, naturally a cautious manager, was never a developer of talent from cradle to first team while there was a feeling that, following Harvey's promotion to senior coach, standards had slipped lower down. The warning signs were there as early as September 1984 when the reserve team lost a two-goal lead on the way to a humiliating 6-2 loss at Bramall Lane. Kendall was furious with the attitude of five players – Darren Hughes, Ian

Bishop, Johnny Morrissey, Rob Wakenshaw and Stuart Rimmer – and put them all on the transfer list. In *An Everton Diary*, Peter Reid wrote that during his comeback from injury in early 1986 he had been disappointed with the attitude of several reserve-team players to the extent of reporting the problem to Kendall. In addition, after reaching two FA Youth Cup finals in 1983 and 1984, the junior team had scarcely made an impression on the competition.[63] With the first team enjoying so much success, the club could be accused of taking their eye off the ball at youth and reserve level. They could escape with that attitude whilst lifting trophies but later in the decade, when rebuilding was required and transfer fees escalated, the lack of homegrown talent made a difficult job even harder.

Seven days later Harvey dropped Reid for the trip to the plastic pitch at Luton which brought familiar headaches and an even more familiar result: a 1-0 loss made it five defeats in five league games on the dreaded surface. 'Everton must have wished they could have been banned from the make-believe world of Kenilworth Road, along with all visiting fans,' quipped Dennis Shaw in the *People*. There was nothing funny about the Toffees' league form, three successive league defeats had left them ninth in the table, fourteen points behind leaders Arsenal. Everton were now 50-1 for the title, not exactly a generous gesture from bookmakers considering the traffic between the two clubs. Just after the halfway point, like twelve months before, the road to glory now rested with the FA Cup.

Baggies, mariners and aircraft carriers
On paper the third-round tie was tricky: a trip to West Brom, leaders of the Second Division. At 16-1 to lift the cup before the game, Everton's odds lengthened a bit in the opening half-hour when the visiting defence – without the injured Watson – was continually breeched by an imaginative Baggies front line led by Don Goodman. After 27 minutes it was the pacy striker's run and cross that led to Colin Anderson heading the home side in front. The lead did not last long, following a controversial incident twelve minutes later. Trevor Steven was clearly tripped a yard inside the area yet referee Alan Gunn bizarrely awarded a free-kick outside the box. After the Everton players implored the match official to speak to his linesman, in chaotic scenes Gunn then pointed to the spot. 'It was the Everton players who got the referee to change his mind,' Goodman claimed. Sheedy then rifled the ball into the roof of the net past the stranded Paul

---

[63]   Of the forty players who appeared in the FA Youth Cup between 1984-88, only John Ebbrell had a lengthy Everton career. Six players appeared in a single first-team game, four at the end of the 1984/85 campaign when Kendall fielded weakened teams after the title had been won.

Bradshaw. 'On the balance of play they do not deserve to be level,' Barry Davies commented on BBC's *Match of the Day*.

The second period was more even and enlightened by two incidents. The first was another incredible double save by Southall, this time diving to parry Goodman's shot before flying across his goal-line to block Robert Hopkins' strike with his legs. Then five minutes from time there was enormous controversy. Tony Cottee broke free and was clearly clattered by Bradshaw inside the area but Gunn, probably to assuage the home fans and players after the Everton penalty, waved away protests. 'That was definitely a penalty,' the Everton striker said, 'I like to think I'm an honest person and I've never dived for a penalty in my life.' Television coverage confirmed Cottee's claims and that the referee had made a calamitous error, leading the *Liverpool Echo's* Ian Hargraves to say it was 'just about the most blatant penalty I have ever seen'. After the game, though, talk was once again about the Everton goalkeeper. Home manager Brian Talbot believed Southall had prevented a West Brom victory. 'Two world-class saves in two seconds,' he claimed. Harvey was not convinced: 'Sure they were great. But Neville usually catches those.'

Despite enjoying all the territorial advantage, the Toffees made heavy weather of the replay at Goodison after dangerman Goodman went off injured in the opening twenty minutes. Following the marathon ties of twelve months before, as the minutes ticked away those home supporters in a 31,697 crowd could have been forgiven for thinking history was in danger of repeating itself but five minutes from the end Wayne Clarke set up Sheedy and the midfielder's explosive left-foot did the rest.

The fourth round brought a tie with a similar feel, taking Harvey's side to the south coast for a tricky encounter with Second Division Plymouth Argyle. The Pilgrims may have been only mid-table but proved just as tricky opponents as West Brom. Out of the title race and with rising criticism, it was a tie Everton, and Harvey, dare not lose.

With Sharp and Steven back from injury, for the first time since December 1984 the Toffees had a fully-fit squad. A hard and heavily-sanded pitch neutralised any advantage in quality and despite being under pressure in the opening half, Southall was rarely troubled. In fact the visitors had the best chance just before the break when Sheedy and Cottee got in each other's way before the former's rarely-used right foot scooped the ball over the bar. Nevertheless, Second Division opponents had caused Harvey no end of problems in his short tenure and the nightmare of Valley Parade was revisited when Sean McCarthy put the home team ahead on 62 minutes.

As the game entered the final quarter-of-an-hour it was looking ominous for the visitors until an unexpected gift. Snodin's cross from the right looked harmless enough but in the flurry of arms, referee Danny Vickers harshly judged that defender Adrian Burrows was guilty of handball – especially as Sharp appeared to manhandle the Plymouth player. It was a case of déjà vu as Sheedy – now off the transfer list – again stepped up to keep Everton in the cup by firing past 18-year-old goalkeeper Alan Miller. 'Everton are having the sort of luck which can win the FA Cup,' Vince Wright claimed in *The Sunday Times*. 'An equaliser was rather more than they deserved.' Although Harvey was a relieved man after the game, he could not hide the displeasure at another passive and lethargic away display. 'We didn't start to play until we scored,' he commented. 'We were too tentative and sat back. In terms of attacking and pressuring them, it was disappointing.'

At Goodison it was a completely different story. Beforehand, Plymouth had trained on the aircraft carrier, HMS Invincible, but four goals from the home side sunk the visitors. Two headers for Sharp, a Nevin tap-in plus the trademark Sheedy strike – a left-foot volley at the far post from the diminutive winger's cross – were enough to see off the south-coast outfit. The reward was another difficult trip to a lower-division side, this time at Barnsley. But by then one of the club's most important and finest players of the post-war era had departed.

PR to QPR

Few players have wielded more influence on and off the pitch at Goodison than Peter Reid. During the mid-1980s if Neville Southall was irreplaceable, then the Huyton-born midfielder was not far behind and to this day he remains one of the most popular players to ever wear the blue jersey. Indeed, there were few more well-liked by fellow professionals and it was not just footballing ability that influenced his peers when they voted him 1985 PFA Player of the Year. However, the injuries and contract disputes that blighted the first half of his playing career meant he was making up for lost time after joining Everton in December 1982. On the pitch Reid's blue-collar approach to the day job chimed perfectly with Kendall's desire for his players to close down the opposition and deny space. With the ball Reid kept it straightforward but, as he showed for the first of Andy Gray's famous diving headers against Sunderland in April 1985, there was no little skill. That said, Reid was far more than a standard footballer, his will-to-win was never far from the surface and the sight of the midfielder coaxing that little bit extra from his team-mates was a regular sight when silverware was on the line. In many ways he was the glue who kept the side together, his presence on the pitch ensuring all the dots in Kendall's team were joined. 'You don't need to get involved in lengthy team talks. You just go out and work to your strengths,' he once revealed. 'That should be good enough to win if you apply yourself in the right way.'

Nevertheless, midway through the 1988/89 campaign it was clear endless months on the treatment table, plus the frenetic years of covering every blade of grass, had caught up with the inspirational midfielder. With younger men – plus a returning Bracewell – now providing options, when QPR offered a way out of Goodison in early February a move was agreed quickly. As a deal it was the opposite of his joining, which had been more than two years in the making, after an earlier move thwarted by a disagreement with Gordon Lee over wages in 1980. As he revealed in *Cheer Up Peter Reid*: 'If arriving at Goodison had been a battle with contract wrangles, career-threatening injuries, aborted moves and failed medicals all intervening in one way or another, arranging my exit was so uncomplicated that it felt totally surreal.'

Appropriately it was Andy Gray, widely credited with helping to turn round the fortunes of Kendall's side with the departing Reid, who paid tribute in the *Liverpool Echo* at the time: 'He tackles like a demon and he hates to be beaten. He's a simple player who never tries to complicate the game. If things were not going well, you knew you can give the ball to Reidy and he would do something with it. He is a player who has that rare quality to turn a match single-handed.' Reid would be missed although, as someone said, his fashion sense less so.

Not so potty over Cottee

The Toffees may have stumbled into the FA Cup fifth round via two penalties and a pair of replay victories but three successive 1-1 draws in the league hardly lifted confidence at Goodison Park either, leaving them trailing in ninth place. During the middle stalemate – at Southampton where Kevin Sheedy scored a wonderful goal from thirty yards[64]– Cottee was substituted after a poor performance. The electric start to the season when Bobby Robson compared him to Jimmy Greaves – 'He could emerge as the nearest England have to the great little man,' the England boss proclaimed – and the bookmakers had installed him as 3-1 favourite to be the top flight's leading scorer, seemed a long way off. The striker had gone eleven games without a goal and by his own admission was not playing well. 'I just hope that I am judged on performances over my five-year contract and not five months,' he admitted. However, his boss saw it differently and came out in

---

[64]   After the game Saints boss Chris Nicholl shook his head and described the goal as 'unbelievable'. The manager had a history of such strikes with Everton, having produced a similar effort for Aston Villa at Old Trafford in the 1977 League Cup final second replay. Coincidentally the Villa goalkeeper that night, John Burridge, was the Southampton custodian beaten by Sheedy at the Dell.

support. 'I would like Tony to be scoring goals and he's obviously out of form, but I'm not putting all the blame on him,' Harvey said. 'We haven't got it right across midfield, and that is as much as a problem as not scoring. We are not getting the supply right.' Cottee himself later recalled those problems in his autobiography *Claret and Blues*:

> *I wasn't getting the service I had been used to at West Ham, which, on the face value of it, may seem surprising when you consider we had two class wingers in Steven and Sheedy supplying crosses. The fact is, Trevor didn't have a particularly good season… and when he or Sheedy did get into promising positions, they invariably looked to pick out Sharpy, who they'd played with for so long. I felt as if I was being by-passed and the team wasn't playing to my strengths. Crosses were generally hit long towards the big man at the far post, few were delivered hard and low for my benefit.*

In many ways that was the flaw in purchasing Cottee. The consensus was Everton were getting the classic big/small striker partnership with Graeme Sharp and the new signing. Ideally for that type of duo the smaller player must be hard-working, mobile and forage around the box. Adrian Heath was a perfect foil for the Scot because he did just that, like Kevin Keegan with John Toshack at Anfield a decade before. That was not Cottee's forte, though. The striker was a finisher pure and simple, who relied on others to do the build-up work: see his statement about crosses 'for my benefit' in his autobiography.

At West Ham he was in the company of Frank McAvennie, a completely different player to Sharp, a natural predator, smaller and more mobile than the Everton player but, in a footballing sense, less rounded and nowhere the same threat in the air. It worked at Upton Park, therefore, because the entire Hammers' output was based on feeding the ball into space or at the feet of the striking duo. When Cottee arrived at Goodison in the preceding summer he optimistically believed his new club would play to his strengths. In many ways he regarded himself rather than Sharp as the target man, which was part of the problem. 'We'll play the game on the ground and that suits the smaller guys like me, Pat Nevin and Stuart McCall,' he said expectantly. Yet, at Goodison, the tradition had usually been to target a big striker with the long ball from deep or crosses from out wide. That approach played to the strengths of Sharp and not Cottee. Even when Sharp was absent, understudy Wayne Clarke was cut from a similar cloth.

One of the reasons why Everton, with Clarke, were so ineffective against Arsenal at Goodison was a constant stream of high balls which were meat and drink for the Gunners' defence. To be fair to Cottee, the service on the ground, from the middle of the park and out wide, was largely negligible as well. As he told author Rob Sawyer for the *Toffeeweb* website in 2015: 'The ball was going out to Sheeds on the left and I was going to show for the ball into feet, or to spin into the channels, but the ball was going straight to Sharpy every single time and I was nowhere near him.' For balance though, Cottee's dislike of defensive duties – 'he was a lazy sod,' McAvennie once claimed – hardly endeared him to the crowd at times, or indeed his team-mates.

Although there were goals, Tony Cottee's first season at Everton was one of ups and downs.

Gary Lineker may have been similarly selfish, but the England international obviously possessed far more sustained pace and offered more outside the box. The former Leicester player was also better in the air and a more clinical finisher, especially when faced with one-on-ones with the goalkeeper. However, one of the strange things about the acquisitions of the two strikers for club-record fees was that Kendall tinkered with the house style to accommodate Lineker, while Harvey failed to do so with Cottee. West Ham had players like the gifted Alan Devonshire and Alan Dickens to feed him through the middle while at Goodison the two creative midfielders were Steven and Sheedy, both of whom could play through the centre but Harvey obstinately chose to retain out wide, only reinforcing the traditional style of play. Perhaps the current boss may have been influenced by the style change to suit Lineker's strengths ultimately proved damaging, but that was three years before and the squad had aged. A reboot was required in terms of personnel and tactics. Cottee's acquisition provided that opportunity but ultimately Harvey was caught between two stools.

Barnsley stormer

In the first game after Harvey's impassioned defence, Cottee promptly netted against Aston Villa in a 1-1 draw and retained his place for the trip to Barnsley. The Second Division side were enjoying excellent form, unbeaten over seven matches, and in the third round hammered eventual divisional champions Chelsea 4-0. Ian Snodin had been injured and Neil McDonald's good form at right-back meant that, for the first time, the former Leeds player and Stuart McCall were central midfield partners.

In front of 32,551 spectators – for the first time ever Barnsley hosted the biggest crowd of the day – the favourites showed more gumption and grit than at Valley Parade before Christmas. Snodin had a superb game and played a key role in the goal which put the visitors ahead after just fifteen minutes. He lost his marker with some smart movement, pulled the ball back for Steven, and Sharp met the cross with a crisp left-footed volley for his eighth goal of a stop-start season. The home team forced nine corners in the opening half but on the only occasion they broke through Southall brilliantly saved Ron Futcher's drive. Harvey, plus his team, had endured six months of pressure and were looking to avoid a defeat which would produce a premature end to the campaign. Consequently, the result was everything. As the wind spoiled any prospects of a footballing contest, the grimly determined visitors held off a limited Barnsley side for a vital win. 'While it was the product of hard work rather than flair, it will have come as sweet relief to a team which at present seems to derive almost masochistic enjoyment from below-par performances,' Ian Ross concluded in *The Times*. The final word goes to the Barnsley boss Allan Clarke, who praised Everton afterwards. 'I hope they go on and win it,' he said, 'They beat us and they always play football.' The fact his younger brother was on the Everton bench was possibly a reason why. Such goodwill was forgotten, however, when the quarter-final brought public enemy number one to Goodison.

Beating up with the Joneses

One person dominated the headlines when the cup draw picked out Everton (11-2 third favourites) to host holders Wimbledon (15-2 fourth) in the middle of March. In fact, the same man had hardly been off the back pages since the first weekend of February when the London club visited Goodison for their league game. With a typically dour struggle locked at 1-1, after 71 minutes self-proclaimed hardman Vinnie Jones produced a shockingly high challenge which caught Graeme Sharp above the knee and, in the melee which followed, the midfielder went head-to-head against Kevin Ratcliffe with the outcome that the Toffees skipper fell, somewhat theatrically, to the floor clutching his face. Referee Mick Peck, standing barely a yard away, immediately showed Jones the red card. Afterwards the Everton skipper was accused of play-acting to get his opponent dismissed. 'Everyone is screaming for Vinny's head,' team-mate Lawrie Sanchez argued, 'but he wasn't guilty this time. Ratcliffe was the villain of the piece for making a meal of it. Kevin wasn't head-butted by Vinny but he went down as if he had been pole-axed. I hate to see a player get another pro sent off.'[65] Yet Sanchez's argument was baseless: the tackle on Sharp had given Peck enough reason to do so in any case. It was the fourth dismissal of Jones' fledgling top-flight career and a second at Goodison in succession: the previous April he was sent off for retaliation against Peter Reid. Coming on the back of team-mate Eric Young's sending-off against Aston Villa, the dismissal again shone a light on Wimbledon's shocking disciplinary record: 32 red cards in eight years.

That attention was only magnified when the cup draw mischievously produced a rematch at Goodison. Although Colin Harvey offered an olive branch – 'Vinny is as welcome here as any other player, and there is no suggestion of a vendetta,' he claimed – PFA chief Gordon Taylor contacted both managers to stress the importance of their players not dragging the game into the gutter. However, the FA top brass had their attention drawn to a provocative article written by Ratcliffe, under the headline 'Come and get me Psycho' that asked of Jones: 'I hope you come to Goodison looking for a vendetta.' There was no further action as the content did not justify the headline. Indeed, the Everton skipper had said the same thing just after the draw, in the context that if Wimbledon came to Goodison to target him, then his team-mates would have more freedom.

Everton were also given a boost when the BBC chose the tie for broadcasting live on the Sunday afternoon in unusual circumstances. Under the terms of their deal, they could show one live match and highlights of three on *Match of the Day* on the Saturday evening. The obvious selection for live coverage was Nottingham Forest's visit to Manchester United but that would have meant one of the two Merseyside giants moving their tie to the Sunday – Liverpool being drawn at home to Brentford – and the BBC losing one of their Saturday night games. As a compromise they selected the tie at Goodison instead, inducing a feeling that the live cameras would curb Wimbledon's aggressive methods.

As it happened the broadcasters probably wished they had travelled to Old Trafford

[65] A quarter of a century later Ratcliffe and Jones were still feuding. In a *Daily Star Sunday* interview the Everton skipper did admit to a degree of play-acting. 'He [Jones] barely touched me. But I went down anyway and he got sent off,' he admitted. Ratcliffe also claimed that after the incident Jones, a fellow Welsh international (although never a team-mate), would not tackle him. Over in California, an angry Jones bit back. 'Come over. Let's sort out our differences,' the so-called hardman replied, 'Let him ring my doorbell next time he's on a Hollywood tour bus and we can put that right.' Ratcliffe responded by accusing Jones of 'not being Welsh...never liked the fella.'

instead. The cameras probably wanted either a decent cup tie or, if not, at least some of the niggling edge which had rarely been far from the surface previously. With Jones (and equally significantly Van Den Hauwe) diplomatically left on the bench, they got neither as the visitors produced their own peculiar crude brand of football whilst reining in some of their excesses. The result was a dreary and tortuous contest in front of a largely quiet half-filled stadium – the 24,562 gate was the lowest of the quarter-final ties – and the watching millions, a contest described by Steve Curry in the *Daily Express* as 'the most tedious game since live television intruded on the Sunday roast'. Yet everything may have been different had Everton not wasted a golden opportunity to forge ahead in the ninth minute. Kevin Sheedy's cross from the right was clearly handled by John Fashanu in the box but Sharp – who grabbed the ball ahead of the Ireland international – saw his penalty easily palmed away to his right by Hans Segers. Before the break there was only one further action of note, a spectacular 35-yard drive from Ratcliffe which the Dutch goalkeeper tipped over the bar.

The second half was an improvement, but only just, with Everton earning reward for forcing six corners in the opening fifteen minutes by deservedly taking the lead. Bracewell – enjoying his best game since returning to the fold – tenaciously drove into the heart of the penalty area, had two shots desperately blocked and when the second rebounded to Sheedy on the left, his hard-driven cross across the six-yard box was turned in by Stuart McCall, for the midfielder's first goal in 28 games. The strike resulted in Jones entering the fray to a mass of jeers but, obviously under orders to behave, the troublemaker did nothing of note. With the subdued visitors going through the motions, the Toffees may have extended their lead but for some acrobatics from Segers. It may not have been pretty but when referee Keith Hackett blew the whistle there was relief all around Goodison, because of the result and the feared bloodbath which did not materialise. Although as Steve Curry noted, 'Just how many armchair watchers had resisted their Sunday slumber long enough to witness the winner might make an interesting survey.'

There was some brutal honesty from the match winner after the game. 'I have still got a lot to prove. My goal record is a disgrace,' McCall said of his decisive strike. 'At one stage this season not only was I not scoring but I was not contributing enough to the team. But recently I've been contributing more.' Meanwhile, nothing summed up Wimbledon's approach to the day more than the attitude of boss Bobby Gould. After the controversial clash in February, Gould spent thirty minutes vehemently defending his side's conduct. This time it was a brusque 'We were not good enough. Full marks to Everton, I wish them well. Good night gentlemen,' as he rushed to the team bus. Twenty-four hours later, for the fourth time during the decade, the FA Cup semi-final draw split the two Merseyside giants, with Everton playing Norwich at Villa Park and Liverpool facing Nottingham Forest at Hillsborough. For many, football would never be the same afterwards.

19
SATURDAY, 15 APRIL 1989

AS MANY HAVE POINTED OUT SINCE, IT SEEMS STRANGE IN THE ERA OF omnipresent mobile phones and instant communication how little was known about the dreadful events of Hillsborough on what was otherwise a glorious spring afternoon in the Midlands. During the first half there was a message posted on the Villa Park scoreboard that the semi-final between Liverpool and Nottingham Forest had been 'suspended'. Inevitably, given the climate of the times, thoughts of those present turned to a problem with hooliganism, with rumours proliferating around the ground. Indeed, Colin Harvey later recalled in *Faith of Our Families* that the first he heard of the incident was when a couple of journalists told him at half-time that 'there's been some crowd trouble'.

After Pat Nevin's first-half goal had won the game and taken Everton to an eleventh FA Cup final, there were the usual mass celebrations by the travelling fans in keeping with the occasion. However, there was an inkling all was not right and that something more serious was happening in south Yorkshire. As he left the pitch in jubilant mood, in *Claret and Blues* Tony Cottee recalled throwing his shinpads into the crowd and then being cryptically told by a visibly aggressive police inspector, who obviously knew more about events: 'People like you should be locked up, you're a disgrace.' In his memoir *The Accidental Footballer* Nevin gave his recollection of the immediate aftermath:

> *As I floated off the park Mike Ingham from BBC Radio Sport was waiting to interview me. The gentleman that he was, before going live he gave me a warning. 'I think you should know, Pat, something awful happened at the other semi-final at Hillsborough between Liverpool and Nottingham Forest, the details are unclear but there are certainly dozens of dead Liverpool fans inside the ground.'*

Nevin wrote that happiness turned to immediate devastation. 'It did take those moments to compute the full horror but it was the highest high of my time in football to lowest low in less than twenty seconds.' After a couple of questions, the winger wisely truncated the interview on the basis there were far more important matters at hand. In the dressing room Harvey told the players about the incident and fatalities but at that stage everything was vague. The scale of the horror only emerged when the players and coaching staff boarded the team bus. 'The full enormity of what happened only struck home when we reached the M62 on the last leg of the journey home and were joined by cars and coachloads of devastated Liverpool supporters,' Neville Southall later said, 'A good day turned into a nightmare.'

More than 150,000 people attended a makeshift shrine at Anfield in the days that followed, where a huge number of blue-and-white scarves reflected a city in mourning. Naturally Harvey offered the hand of friendship. 'It goes without saying that my players will do anything they can to help,' he said, 'Whether it's simply a matter of talking to fans or attending funerals, we will be only too willing to play our part.' The Everton manager and family members attended a service at the Roman Catholic Metropolitan Cathedral while the entire squad went to Anfield where Harvey placed a floral tribute in the centre circle. Within a week the fences surrounding the pitch at Goodison were removed. What had taken eleven weeks to construct took just three days to take away. Meanwhile 4,000 scarves, almost a mile long, formed a link between the two grounds.

While Liverpool and the wider footballing world came to terms with the tragedy, the show had to go on. After Everton cancelled their home game with Derby County, due to be played 72 hours later, they returned to action against Tottenham on the Saturday in a subdued atmosphere at White Hart Lane. Chairmen Irving Scholar and Philip Carter led their respective teams and at 3.06 p.m. there was a minute's silence. Given the circumstances, the subsequent game unsurprisingly resembled a testimonial, with two goals from Paul Walsh giving the home team a 2-1 victory. At that stage whether the FA Cup would go ahead was still in the balance.

Wembley woe

Although the FA gave the green light for the competition to continue, at Anfield there were other priorities. For a while there was a possibility of Liverpool pulling out and Nottingham Forest being given a bye into the final. However, they agreed to continue after a friendly at Celtic two weeks after the tragedy. That said, there was annoyance at Anfield with the FA's diktat that the replayed semi-final would be played on Sunday, 7 May with the final thirteen days later. Chairman John Smith originally wanted the semi-final played on the latter with the final scheduled for the date of the following season's curtain-raiser, the Charity Shield, on 12 August.

Coincidentally, with all the talk of Wembley, Everton found themselves playing under the Twin Towers for the sixth successive season at the end of April. The occasion was the Simod Cup final, ironically against Nottingham Forest. The Toffees had reached that stage by winning only three games, their semi-final victory over QPR at Goodison watched by just 7,072 spectators. The public indifference on Merseyside continued for the climax, Everton selling less than 10,000 tickets compared to 30,000 in Nottingham. Consequently, the crowd for the final was a miserly 46,606 but they got value for money. Frustratingly for Harvey, he was deprived of a first major 'trophy' after his side had twice let the lead slip in normal time. Cottee put Everton ahead after eight minutes and, after Garry Parker equalised, a brilliant Graeme Sharp goal – the striker striding onto a Kevin Sheedy long ball to fire over Steve Sutton from the edge of the box – was answered by a second strike from the Forest player. In the extra thirty minutes Lee Chapman and Cottee traded goals but, with penalties looming, the big Forest striker became the third player to record a brace on the afternoon, with a winner from close range two minutes from time. The Simod Cup may not have been a major competition, but a trophy is a trophy and the failure to capitalise on their superiority when well-placed was in keeping with the first two years of the Harvey reign.

Three days after the Forest defeat, appropriately Liverpool's first official game after a break of two-and-a-half weeks was at an emotionally-charged Goodison for the 140th Merseyside league derby, in front of a live television audience of millions and 46,000 spectators. Beforehand, Harvey pledged it would be business as usual. 'We are playing our closest rivals and it's always a match you want to win,' he said, before dismissing any suggestions of a half-hearted attitude. 'That would be a disgrace and we would be letting everyone down. It would be disrespectful to everyone and everything that has gone on.' On a humid evening Liverpool dominated for an hour before understandably fading. With chances at both ends, an entertaining but ultimately goalless game was the appropriate result in the circumstances. 'The fact that there were no goals provided a reflection of everything the English game ought to be,' David Lacey commented in the *Guardian*. 'The fences were down, Everton and Liverpool fans were fully and happily integrated, the game was fast and positive and played in an atmosphere of mounting excitement.' With Liverpool eventually defeating Nottingham Forest 3-1 at Old Trafford, another all-Merseyside FA Cup final was a reality.

Can't win, won't win

It was described in *The Times* as an FA Cup final 'which has perhaps the most dramatic, certainly the most poignant, background in the whole wide range of the game.' Words not from 1989 but 31 years before when Bolton faced Manchester United three months after the Munich air disaster. 'There is little doubt all the world outside Bolton will lean sympathetically towards the new Manchester United,' the newspaper went on to say. Although that disaster directly impacted their team and not supporters, Everton were in a similar position to Bolton before a final where they ruthlessly cast aside United 2-0.

Their manager, as somebody born in the city, would have felt this more than most. 'Harvey knows that after Hillsborough, he is on a hiding to nothing,' Ian Hargraves pointed out in the *Liverpool Echo*, 'However much both clubs may praise the city's unity, and however frequently they may stress that Evertonians also suffered emotionally from the disaster, they are perfectly well aware than on the big day most of the nation will be looking for a Liverpool victory.' Consequently, it was David Miller in *The Times* who reflected the views of many Evertonians before the game:

> *In all the millions of words that have been written about Liverpool Football Club following the tragedies of Heysel and Hillsborough, the majority in sympathy and some in legitimate anger, there has been little thought for Everton, a club which has innocently suffered in the shadow of its neighbour's tribulations. In all the tears shed on behalf of the city, few hearts have grieved for Everton. There was, indeed, no immediate cause. They were not involved. Yet the tragedies have caused an unfair restriction upon the achievements of the city's 'other' club, have denied the acclaim which its performances over the past four seasons have justified.*

Naturally the Everton boss had the challenge of convincing his team that it was not Liverpool's destiny to lift the trophy. That said, he was in no mood to lie down for the benefit of the widely-desired narrative. 'It would be a disgrace and we would be letting everybody down if we approached this game in the wrong frame of mind – and we won't be doing so,' Harvey said before the final. His side had been victorious in their final three league games, but Liverpool were unbeaten in 22 matches in all competitions, with nineteen victories. 'We've hit some good form recently,' Harvey pointed out, 'But they have been in that form for longer.' The bookmakers' odds before the game of Liverpool 4-7 on and Everton at 11-8 were not unrealistic.

As the teams walked out at a fenceless Wembley the pitch-side thermometer showed temperatures of more than ninety degrees Fahrenheit. There were six Everton players remaining from the final three years before, and only four from the opposition, Harvey preferring Bracewell and Steven in the middle with Nevin playing wide right. Those thinking the game would act as some sort of catharsis for events at Hillsborough were possibly proved correct by the sight of Gerry Marsden pouring out *You'll Never Walk Alone* to the 82,800 crowd before the game. 'In a sense you might see the occasion as some kind of a gigantic memorial celebration for those who died at Sheffield,' Brian Glanville commented in *The Sunday Times.*

Everton made the stronger and more confident start, coming close to going ahead as early as the second minute when Steve McMahon was forced to hook away the ball at the far post from Nevin's corner. But after four minutes they were caught by the classic sucker punch. A poor ball from Sheedy was collected by Steve Nicol in the right-back position, the Scot's long pass picked out McMahon, who had galloped from deep, and John Aldridge took the former Everton player's pass to fire past Southall from just inside the box. Whereas three years before was a classic 50-50 contest, Liverpool were now clearly the better team, having reinforced their ranks with a quality and imagination absent at Goodison. The initial problem was the unbalanced midfield with Bracewell and Steven too slow and lightweight, being out-muscled and out-manoeuvred by the more combative and dynamic McMahon and Ronnie Whelan. Nevin, as was his style, started well but faded and only affected the game fitfully. The winger was not disciplined and physical enough to track John Barnes. Out on the left Sheedy – who had only passed a fitness test in the morning – looked lost and was largely anonymous. With Stuart McCall on the bench, concerns over the Ireland international meant Harvey had to wastefully pick another midfielder, Ian Wilson, as his second substitute, instead of forward Wayne Clarke. With no headway in the middle, service to the forward duo of Cottee and Sharp was negligible and from out wide one-dimensional.

Moreover, the Toffees' defence immediately looked vulnerable, with Ratcliffe's worrying loss of pace, and the associated impact on his overall effectiveness, contributing to an unhappy afternoon for the skipper.[66] With Harvey's outfit slow and predictable, Liverpool were inventive and played with flair in the opening half, constantly finding gaps in the middle of the Toffees' backline and could have added to their tally before, on the hour, McCall came on as substitute for the disappointing Bracewell, who departed stage left in a blue shirt for the final time. That was the cue for the outsiders to make a contest of it as Liverpool uncharacteristically dropped their guard. A barrage of balls into the

---

[66] Ratcliffe became the first player to captain a side in four FA Cup finals at Wembley.

penalty area unsettled their defence but, with the game about to enter injury time, there appeared to be no way back. When the increasingly influential Steven spooned a cross behind the goal, an angry Everton fan ran onto the pitch to confront him, only to be escorted off by that well-known paragon of good behaviour, Pat Van Den Hauwe. Then with the red ribbons being attached the cup, Nevin fed the overlapping Watson, his cross-shot across the six-yard box was pushed out by Grobbelaar to the prowling McCall who slid the ball home. There were just three seconds remaining. McCall's equaliser was the signal for a pitch invasion from jubilant Everton supporters which, although understandable, was one of a number which subsequently reopened the debate about the wisdom of removing fences.

S

tuart McCall equalises for a second time in the FA Cup final, unfortunately celebrations were short-lived.

Parity lasted just four minutes into extra time. After Nicol crossed, substitute Ian Rush sneaked between Ratcliffe and Dave Watson before turning and hooking the ball past Southall. Defensively it was a poor goal to concede. Eight minutes later McCall brought the game even again, this time via a volley from the edge of the box. However, the Scot's achievement of being the only substitute to score twice in an FA Cup final lasted less than 120 seconds as, in an uncanny repeat of the second goal, Rush slipped again into the space between the two Everton central defenders and headed Barnes' cross from the left past Southall. 'From start to finish the Everton defence learned nothing and was surprised by everything,' David Lacey noted in the *Guardian*. From then on it was one-way traffic, with only Southall's heroics stopping a humiliation. At the end of the game there were, thankfully perhaps, no laps of honour because of the pitch invasions, contributing to the feeling that the occasion was all a bit unreal. 'They were all Liverpool songs leading up to the kick-off,' Kevin Ratcliffe said later, 'There's only one team getting all the credit. It was very hard to play in, and take; the build-up about it was just weird.'

In their two previous finals against Liverpool, the Toffees could have felt hard done by but not on this occasion. For all the talk about the game acting as a sort of commemoration, Ratcliffe offered some realism after the final whistle: 'When we equalised twice, we thought we had half a chance, but in the end we knew we were beaten by a better team.'

20
A TALE OF TWO STRIKERS

THE CUP FINAL APPEARANCE EFFECTIVELY PLACED A VEIL OVER A desperately poor league campaign. The distractions of the road to Wembley overshadowed tribulations in the First Division: a 3-2 defeat at Derby County at the end of February made it seven league games without victory, the worst run since a 2-0 home defeat to Norwich City in April 1981 led to Philip Carter announcing a review of Gordon Lee's position before sacking him. Despite some tabloid speculation to the contrary, there was no immediate chance of Harvey suffering the same fate.

Clever Trevor

The three league victories at the end of the campaign took Everton from twelfth in the table to a moderate eighth, hardly a ringing endorsement of the effectiveness of the new signings or form of established players. Trevor Steven was in the latter group and the former Burnley player was another whose performances had been inconsistent. Out of contract in the summer, the club had met his financial demands as early as February but the paperwork remained unsigned. The midfielder was unsurprisingly in demand – Tottenham were lurking in the background and Alex Ferguson had expressed interest twelve months before. Liverpool made an inquiry but Harvey's demand for Steve McMahon in exchange scuppered the deal. A drop in form, like his teammates, during the final three months of the campaign also put off potential suitors. That said, before the cup final it was clear he was in no rush to renew. 'I'm 25 and my next contract will take me to nearly thirty. It's a very important contract,' he admitted.

With Steven clearly keeping his options open, there was no surprise when stories emerged of talks with Rangers boss Graeme Souness – who had been tracking him for three years – before England faced Scotland in Glasgow on the last Saturday in May.[67]

---

[67]   Souness and assistant Walter Smith had attended Everton's last home game of the season and asked to meet afterwards. Rather than speak with the duo at the ground, the midfielder eventually met them in the West Derby suburb of Liverpool – in a back entry, which was probably very brave of him.

Forty-eight hours later the wide man also spoke with Manchester United. The Italian clubs Roma and Sampdoria also retained an interest. Although Everton promised to match the terms of any new offer, by the end of the week Steven had a clear choice between United and Rangers. In the end a lucrative three-year contract at Ibrox and the promise of European Cup football proved the clincher.[68] 'I know people will accuse me of being money-grabbing,' he claimed, 'but I can assure you it isn't the case.' In some respects, Steven's departure was like that of the manager who brought him to Everton – yes, European football was an attraction, but it had to be financially worthwhile too. Four years into the ban, it was not necessarily down to the former. Rangers' offer of a reported annual salary of £200,000 would make him one of the best paid players in Britain. Once again, though, the departure raised questions over the club's immediate prospects. 'Like a lot of Everton fans, he believes the club is in decline and has been since Howard Kendall headed to Spain,' Len Capeling remarked in the *Liverpool Daily Post*. 'Nowadays any player who needs a new challenge turns his face firmly against Goodison.'

From a playing perspective, on paper it was a big loss but, although Steven had been a considerable presence in both title-winning campaigns, there were struggles for consistency under Harvey. Some of the youthful zest that made him such an energetic presence on the right had disappeared – where once he breezed past an opponent the more likely option now was the safe pass inside – while the cup final had showed he did not possess the physique for a berth in the centre. 'There has also been an impression that his play, for all its technical accomplishment, too closely mirrors his understated, almost impassive personality,' Patrick Barclay once wrote in the *Independent*. There was also a feeling that, like some others signed by Kendall, the primary loyalty was with their former manager.

However, the transfer became a saga thanks to a major discrepancy in the respective clubs' valuations. Rangers offered £1 million while Everton priced Steven at £4 million, based on Chris Waddle's £4.2 million transfer from Tottenham to Olympique de Marseille. The case was heard at an inter-league tribunal in August, where Everton lowered their demand to £2.5 million. After a two-hour hearing the fee was set at £1.525 million, a new tribunal record. Harvey was an angry man outside, citing the £2 million fees Manchester United had paid for Gary Pallister and Paul Ince. 'They've got a top-class international at a bargain price if you go by current transfer fees,' he complained, 'Neither of them [Pallister and Ince] has Steven's experience. There is always a winner and a loser

---

[68]   Steven also had a childhood link with Rangers. As a very small boy in January 1967 he watched his hometown club, Berwick Rangers, famously defeat the mighty Ibrox side 1-0 in the Scottish Cup third round.

on these occasions and this time we have lost.'

If Steven enjoyed a fulfilling Everton career, the same could not be said of another departure. Paul Bracewell should have been a fixture in the central midfield for many years but, after returning in mid-season, had looked a shadow of the player who had formed such a formidable partnership with Peter Reid. Bracewell moved to Sunderland, first on loan and then on a permanent deal, and returned to top-flight football twelve months later, before making a major contribution to Newcastle's revival under Kevin Keegan. A further spell at Sunderland – under Reid – followed before wrapping up his career at Fulham. Ironically for a player who had suffered so many setbacks at Goodison, in the ten years following his departure he averaged 33 league games a season. By the end of September 1989 three-quarters of the 1985 championship-winning midfield had left in the space of eight months. More than anything else, those departures effectively signalled that the most successful era in the club's history was now over.

Foreign trade

With the hinges on the exit door at Goodison squeaking continuously, despite his previous signings Harvey still needed to replenish the squad. After a scouting trip to watch Swedish defender Dennis Schiller in action against Brazil, Harvey came away hugely impressed by a different Swede, midfielder Stefan Rehn, and a deal was immediately agreed with Djurgardens for a fee of £400,000. Rehn had to wait until mid-September for his first league start and three further substitute appearances followed. The last of them, at home to Millwall four weeks later, resulted in the ignominy of Rehn being substituted himself.[69] After just three months at Goodison, already the Swedish international's time was up. The main problem was Rehn's slight physique was more in keeping with a winger. Roy Hodgson was managing in Sweden at the time and told the *Liverpool Echo*'s Ric George: 'I'm sure he could succeed in England, but Everton, with their high-pressure and physical style, tend to rely on their two big players up front. Perhaps Stefan wasn't the right man for them.'

The impulsive purchase of a player totally unsuited for the English game was a poor signing and Rehn returned to his homeland in the following January, where he enjoyed a successful career, winning five domestic titles with Gothenburg and securing a berth in Sweden's squads for the 1992 European Championship and World Cup two years later. The theory that Harvey had blown his big chance with the expensive deals in the previous

---

[69] The first Everton player to achieve this unwanted feat in a league game. The first in any match had been debutant winger Neil Adams in the 1986 Charity Shield against Liverpool.

summer was given more substance when he was clearly targeting the cheaper foreign market. Another purchase was utility player Ray Atteveld for £250,000, from Dutch side Haarlem, where he was rated the best prospect from the club since Ruud Gullit.

Whereas Rehn and Atteveld were complete strangers to all Evertonians, a third midfield addition was somebody very well known on Merseyside. Even though Norman Whiteside had been out of the Manchester United side with an ankle injury he had been on Harvey's radar for some time. Ironically interest only heightened when Norwich City midfielder Mike Phelan rejected Harvey's advances and chose Old Trafford instead, leaving Whiteside surplus. Also, before signing Whiteside, Coventry rejected a £750,000 bid for midfielder Steve Sedgeley.

That said, the abrasive Ulsterman came to Merseyside with a certain reputation: the man whose goal wrecked Everton's treble dreams four years was equally unpopular at Anfield.[70] Therefore his arrival for £750,000 in August was not well-received, with callers who flooded a phone-in on BBC Radio Merseyside hardly opening out welcoming arms. 'I propose that Mr Harvey pays a visit one Sunday to my local Sunday League,' said one correspondent to the *Football Echo*, 'where I am quite sure he would be able to obtain another ten Norman Whitesides.' Equally unimpressed was the Everton manager's former sparring partner Alan Ball. 'I scratched my head a bit when I heard the news,' he told the *People*. 'I couldn't believe that Colin Harvey had done it. It was a big surprise, especially after all his injury problems. Whiteside's not the most mobile player.' But that had always been the case. Nevertheless, when fit, the new signing was a hugely gifted powerhouse, possessing a footballing radar and intelligence way beyond his 24 years, one indeed to rank with the very best. 'If it comes off it could well propel him [Harvey] finally out of the shadow of Howard Kendall,' John Giles wrote in the *Daily Express*. The Everton boss also added steel to the defence by spending £750,000 on Aston Villa centre-half Martin Keown, having seen off competition from Manchester United, Derby County and Nottingham Forest.

Tony the lonely

As well as fleshing out the midfield during the summer, Harvey also had an eye on another striker. Having unsuccessfully tried to include Ally McCoist as part of the deal with Rangers for Trevor Steven, the manager had Crystal Palace's Mark Bright top of the

---

[70]   Whiteside had scored the winner there in December 1986 and during the following season produced a still-infamous substitute appearance. In a game where the visitors were trailing 3-1 and down to ten men, Whiteside proceeded to physically lay waste to most of the Liverpool team as United pulled two goals back to draw 3-3. 'His vendetta mentality should have no place in a United side,' David Lacey commented in the *Guardian*.

shopping list but the London club rejected any approach. With Gary Lineker returning home after his three-year spell at Barcelona, Everton understandably were one of several clubs who initially expressed an interest in the England marksman, only to be rebuffed.[71] 'I'd spoken to Jim Greenwood [the Everton secretary] and told him we had taken the decision that Gary didn't want to go back to Goodison Park,' Lineker's agent Jon Holmes told Colin Malam for the latter's book *Strikingly Different*. Surprisingly, the expected interest in this country was non-existent and with few options abroad – the Milan clubs had gone with German and Dutch imports and Juventus' experience with Ian Rush had put them off – Holmes was forced to offer Lineker to Terry Venables at Spurs and eventually the two clubs agreed a fee of £1.1 million. Greenwood then telephoned Holmes. 'We are going to take some stick [from the fans] over this,' he declared about the sale. The agent then reaffirmed to Greenwood that Lineker was not keen on going back. However, later Holmes cryptically told Malam, 'Everton never really came rushing in. They had not made what you'd call a concrete offer largely because I'd led them to believe the transfer wasn't on.' The inference clearly being Holmes' initial claim of not being interested was merely a ruse to test their commitment. If Everton had put in a serious bid then the likelihood is, with no firm offers from elsewhere, Lineker would have been forced to seriously consider a return.

Ironically, Harvey then travelled to Lineker's old stomping ground of Filbert Street to acquire Mike Newell for the same fee paid by Tottenham for the England man, with Wayne Clarke part of the deal. The 24-year-old already had a reputation as a journeyman after being rejected at Anfield six years before. Following a brief spell at Crewe Alexandra there was fruitful time at Wigan Athletic and in the top flight with Luton Town – which included a hat-trick against Liverpool – before he surprisingly dropped down a division with the Foxes. To be fair 21 goals in 81 league games in the Midlands was an unremarkable record for somebody worth a seven-figure fee.[72]

Nevertheless, that moderate tally was forgotten when the new signing made a sparkling start to the campaign, the hugely important third season for Harvey. Beforehand, David Lacey in the *Guardian* was mildly disparaging about the summer's developments.

---

[71] Supporters have since criticised the club for not inserting a 'buy-back' clause in the Lineker deal to Barcelona. But to do this all parties have to agree and, in any case, they are usually used only in the case of young, promising players. As discussed previously, for Everton the clause would have meant a possible reduction in the initial fee received with no guarantee Lineker would have returned in any case.

[72] Prior to Everton's interest Newell had agreed a move to Rangers but the deal fell through in mysterious circumstances, with the striker convinced it was because they discovered he was a Catholic. Then events took a strange turn when the Glasgow club bought their first-ever Catholic player when stealing Maurice Johnston from under the noses of neighbours Celtic.

'Everton, who spent heavily a year ago and not only won nothing but never looked like winning anything…have signed an Englishman, two Irishmen, a Dutchman and a Swede. This is the sort of activity you might find in the Belgian League. At least Pat Van Den Hauwe should feel at home.'[73] In fairness to Harvey, he acknowledged previous failings. 'Our displays in the League have just not been good enough. We have let our fans down,' he said, 'We are making no predictions, but we owe our fans something.'

The main problem for the Everton boss, though, was familiar. 'I now have three quality strikers fighting for just two positions and, as anyone will tell you, three into two does not go,' Harvey said, inferring his record signing's starting place was in jeopardy. And so it proved. With Newell impressing in pre-season, Cottee found himself on the bench for the 2-0 defeat at Coventry on the opening Saturday of the campaign – ironically his favourite opponents, with twelve goals in thirteen games. Seventy-two hours later the former West Ham player was named once again as a substitute for the home game against Tottenham and then selected for the reserves on the following night, coincidentally at Highfield Road. Yet on the night Cottee was a surprising absentee in a team which featured several of the new summer signings. The fallout was immediate and the rumour mill went into overdrive. 'Tony Cottee staged a sensational one-man strike last night, refusing to play in Everton reserves and become the costliest "stiff" in British soccer,' Harry Harris revealed in the *Daily Mirror*, 'The £2 million England forward's point-blank rejection of facing the humiliation of reserve-team football will surely prompt a shock split from Everton.' His manager naturally moved to deny rumours of a damaging division, although an explanation that the club's most expensive signing had been mistakenly named in the squad did not sound convincing, especially when he added that 'if anything has to be said to him, it will be done in the privacy of the dressing room'.

Cottee later elaborated on the events in his autobiography. On the morning after the Tottenham game, he was told he would be playing in the reserves by manager Mike Lyons. Cottee went to see Harvey in his office at Bellefield, angry that his manager had not informed him personally. In his diary the Everton player wrote: 'Within 30 seconds of my meeting Colin, he told me that he didn't want me.' Although the striker later said that was the impression he was given, he added, 'Colin had basically had enough and the conversation ended with me saying I'd put in a transfer request in the morning, as I slammed the door behind me.' Cottee's frustrations reached boiling point when a club letter informing him of a fine of two weeks' wages was lost in the post – the first he knew

---

[73]   Although not for long, the tough defender moving to Tottenham for a £575,000 fee shortly after the season started.

of the sanction was when he checked his pay slip. Still out of the team, inevitably Cottee appealed the fine to the Football League and in early October there was a hearing in Manchester – the forward and his representative on one side, Harvey and Carter on the other – where they upheld Everton's decision. With Cottee still out of the team, such an eventuality was hardly going to end the quarrel between the two parties. Although publicly both denied he was for sale, Cottee had verbally asked for a transfer and, even when the club invited interest, tellingly the only inquiries came from Real Sociedad and Borussia Dortmund.

Newell outshines old boys

Cottee was still in the shadows because of the outstanding form of the man brought in as competition. While the former West Ham player seethed on the bench against Tottenham, Mike Newell took just 97 seconds of his home debut to open his account in an entertaining game won by a typical blistering Sheedy strike. 'It was Newell who emerged as the new Goodison hero, producing an all-action display up front, scoring a goal and proving a constant thorn in the side of the Spurs defence,' wrote Phil McNulty in the *Liverpool Daily Post*. Four days later the expensively reassembled team looked the part in crushing Southampton 3-0 at Goodison, with Whiteside scoring in a game where he added a bit of much-needed steel to the midfield. Newell netted again and there was a first Everton league goal for the reborn Stuart McCall, who looked far more comfortable working with the Ulsterman in the centre of the park. 'Stuart was a great foil for me, a bustling ball of energy,' Whiteside wrote in his book, *Determined*. The main talk after the game though was a brutal tackle by Goodison's favourite pantomime villain, Jimmy Case, which left Sharp with a deep gash in his leg and knee damage, plus an angry Harvey on the pitch. Southampton boss Chris Nicholl showed no compassion for the stricken striker: 'Graeme Sharp lives by the sword. He's kicked plenty of our players, he's kicked me many times in the past.'

Four days later Everton travelled to Hillsborough, the first visit of one of the city's clubs since the horror five months before. Prior to kick-off, Kevin Ratcliffe carefully laid a bouquet of flowers in front of the Leppings Lane End, while the start was delayed fifteen minutes to allow the full complement of Everton fans into the ground. After Sheedy had put the Toffees ahead, Harvey was within 52 seconds of topping the table for the first time as a manager but then new-signing Dalian Atkinson, a one-time target of the Everton boss, crashed the ball home.

Whiteside was excellent again across the Pennines and the midfielder looked forward to the next match, against Manchester United, by declaring that Everton 'were ten times more likely to win the championship' than his former club. Although as one sage pointed out, he was overplaying his own side's chances, as 'ten times nothing is nothing'. The home team certainly proved Whiteside's claim as Alex Ferguson's no-hopers were completely outplayed for the first hour at Goodison, with Harvey's side strolling to a three-goal lead before the Ulsterman's departure with a hamstring injury changed the course of the contest. The visitors pulled two goals back as Everton survived a frantic finish. Before the season started, both Harvey and Ferguson had been quoted at 3-1 to be sacked before the end of the campaign and, as remarkable as it seems now, after five games it was the Everton manager who looked to have the brighter future. 'What no-one who saw this bloodcurdling collision could deny is that it has already come right for Colin Harvey's Everton,' claimed John Bean in the *Daily Express*.

Harvey's men finally took top spot seven days later when a hard-working but unimaginative performance at a lowly and inferior Charlton brought three points thanks to another Newell strike nineteen minutes from time, their only real attempt of the afternoon. Receiving the ball with his back to goal just outside the penalty area, the striker turned his marker and watched his shot clip the post on the way into the net. It was only Everton's second away league win in ten months and they were the fourth different leaders in the space of a month. However, even with something to celebrate, Harvey's press conference lasted less than sixty seconds. 'I thought we did enough to win,' he said, before adding that Newell's form had been 'encouraging'. Asked whether he agreed with the theory that Liverpool being champions was a foregone conclusion, he responded, 'No, not at all,' before saying goodbye. This was typical behaviour of the Everton manager, who should have presented a more positive persona, but that was not in his nature. 'Harvey has found life outside the training ground and the matches altogether more difficult,' Stephen Bierley had previously written in the *Guardian*. 'He often appears tense in public.'

Being a football manager is not character-building but character revealing, with Harvey being an interesting case study. Whereas Kendall would have flourished in that position, his successor was far more reserved and this failure to connect with supporters, many of whom remained to be convinced of his credentials, counted against him. 'Everton will soon take up their rightful position in mid-table,' one wrote in the *Football Echo* on the day of the Charlton game. 'The only way to stop the usual rot developing is to weed out the decayed wood. Colin Harvey should revert to the role of coach and a new manager appointed.'

Although probably a harsh assessment, there was a feeling that Newell's goals – five in seven games – masked deficiencies elsewhere, particularly on the left where Pointon and Sheedy had both been struggling. However, thirteen points from six games was an excellent start before the big test of the season so far: a home Merseyside derby. Understandably, all the talk before the game focused on the Liverpool supporter leading the Toffees attack, especially as Bobby Robson was at Charlton and impressed. 'He looked very useful indeed,' the England boss revealed. 'I shall now be keeping a close eye on him.'

On a sunlit Saturday at Goodison, Newell got off to a fairy-tale start against the club that had rejected him. After the visitors had initially dominated, taking Nevin's chipped pass from just inside his own half, the coltish striker beat both Glenn Hysen and Bruce Grobbelaar to the ball before firing his team ahead. In a thrilling opening thirty minutes both sides also struck the frame of the goal before Liverpool took control of the midfield – 'Rarely can anyone have been visibly less fit than Whiteside,' wrote Stuart Jones in *The Times* – and never let go, with John Barnes heading an equaliser. On the hour Peter Beardsley's pass freed up the England winger – who gave Snodin a torrid time – on the left and his low cross was met by an unchallenged Rush at the near post. Defensively it was a bad goal to concede, showing once again deficiencies in the once impregnable Ratcliffe-Watson axis. Within minutes those were apparent again following a typical Rush derby goal, striding on to another Beardsley through ball to finish past Southall. Thereafter it was typical derby fare, Liverpool retaining possession *ad nauseum* while Everton struggled to lay a glove on the title favourites and, at the end of the 3-1 defeat, the home fans left the ground reassessing their own ambitions.

Out of the shadows

While a first home defeat of the campaign was hardly terminal, a 2-1 loss at Crystal Palace seven days later pointed to wider issues. The timid visitors allowed Palace midfielder Andy Gray to run riot in the opening half and were two goals down at the break. Although Newell pulled a goal back and Everton pummelled Palace in the second half, they failed to obtain the draw their revival merited.

Desperately needing a goal, Harvey did not call Cottee off the bench, much to the striker's frustrations. 'I'll be sorting out a few things when my agent gets back from holiday on Monday,' he warned after the game. 'I'm not happy [with] the way things are.' Curiously, Palace's Gray had his say about the affair. 'Cottee must have been sick when he saw Newell score,' he commented. 'There's no way Cottee can't want the guy to fail.

He's been waiting for him to slip up – after all he's taken his living away from him.' Interesting perception that happened to be true, as Cottee confessed in his autobiography. 'I certainly didn't want to stand by and watch Newelly play a blinder in my place, which would only prolong my absence from the side,' he disclosed. Although a widely-held sentiment by many professionals, Cottee's candid disclosure still provided a fascinating insight into Harvey's dressing room.

However, the former Upton Park favourite was not in the wings for long. Ironically it was not Newell who made way but his more gilded partner Graeme Sharp. Like other strikers at the same age, the Scot was a far better all-round player than in his peak years, yet the trade-off was he was spending too much time with back to goal, outside the box. Like many of his ilk, there was a diminished desire to get in where it hurts in the opposition penalty area. Consequently his threat diminished. 'Perhaps Sharpie has lost a little motivation. After all he's been at Goodison a long time and seen a lot of players come and go,' old sparring partner Andy Gray said in his *Liverpool Echo* column. 'Sharpie must sort himself out and do it quickly before he faces the embarrassment of being dropped.' But only one goal in nine games forced Harvey's hand and Cottee was recalled at the expense of the 28-year-old for a very fortunate 2-1 home victory over Millwall.

Then, out of literally nowhere, came probably the best performance of Harvey's reign, against reigning champions Arsenal at Goodison. It was probably the only game where the much-criticised class of the summer of 1988 collectively justified their fees. Yet the omens were not good beforehand. With Ratcliffe injured, Martin Keown had stepped in for his debut against Millwall and performed well but, against the Gunners, youth product John Ebbrell covered for the injured Ian Snodin while Neil McDonald was at left-back for Neil Pointon. While the somewhat makeshift defence held the visitors at bay, at the other end of the pitch Pat Nevin enjoyed his most enterprising game in a blue shirt, opening the scoring just before the break when Whiteside's clever cross deceived goalkeeper John Lukic and the Scottish winger prodded the ball home. With confidence growing, after the break the home team continually pinned back George Graham's side and got their reward eleven minutes from time. McDonald exchanged passes with the hard-working Cottee and fired past the stranded Lukic. The estranged striker also had a hand in a third goal, feeding Nevin who jinked through the Gunners' defence for his second of the afternoon. Star man, however, was Stuart McCall, whose intelligent and energetic display was a reminder of an Everton legend. 'The fiery redhead is gradually assuming the mantle of another former Everton favourite, Alan Ball,' Ian Hargraves noted in the *Liverpool Echo*.

At full time the cheers of the 32,917 crowd circled around Goodison when news filtered through of Liverpool's 4-1 defeat at Southampton, a result which sent Harvey back to the top. The significance was not lost on the watching James Lawton. 'Colin Harvey deserves some kind of award – maybe a bronze life jacket – for taking Everton to the top,' he declared in the *Daily Express*, 'Less than 12 months ago Harvey looked like one of big-time football's dead men. Seeing his team cut to pieces by champions-elect Arsenal at Goodison, Harvey seemed to be presiding over the last remnants of Howard Kendall's empire. But instead he has boldly reshaped his team and given himself the most vital asset enjoyed by any football manager – the chance to be his own man.'

After more than two years in charge, Harvey finally appeared to have emerged out of Kendall's shadow. The good form of his own acquisitions – not just those of his second summer, but also Newell and Whiteside – lent credence to the belief that, at last, he was stamping his own authority not only within the club but on the First Division. 'I believe that if we do play to our full potential and keep intact our confidence and self-belief, we are capable of going very close to being the best,' the Everton boss confidently predicted. A week later a 1-1 draw at Norwich – when Cottee scored his first of the campaign – kept Everton top. But not for long.

21
WINTER OF DISCONTENT

THE TRIP TO ASTON VILLA ON AFTERNOON OF SUNDAY, 5 NOVEMBER 1989, remains one of the most chilling days in the club's modern history. The result not only made Harvey's earlier prophecy of competing with the best look foolish but has since been widely accepted as the game which signalled the end of the glory days.

Bonfire fall Guys

There were mitigating circumstances which partially explained the extraordinary events played out in front of a watching audience of more than six million viewers.[74] Still shorn of three first-choice defenders, Harvey saw his problems compounded when Watson was unable to train all week because of hamstring problems which left him a doubtful starter. Meanwhile, Keown had a back injury.

Everton's defence had managed to ride their luck in previous games due to a lack of ruthlessness from their opponents but Villa were not so forgiving. The slaughter started as early as the fifth minute when Gordon Cowans put the home side ahead and, fifteen minutes later, Ian Olney scored a second after Southall had parried David Platt's shot. With the visitors losing their shape, spirit, and discipline in equal measure – Whiteside was substituted at half-time to save him from a red card after a sixth booking in thirteen games – Platt made it three with a header over the Welshman before the half-hour mark.

As he strode from the pitch at the break, in front of the intrusive cameras Villa boss Graham Taylor was asked what he wanted. 'Another 45 minutes of the same,' was the response. Taylor got that as, despite Harvey making seven positional changes and substituting the clearly unfit Watson, Villa were 6-0 up before the clock reached seventy minutes. As statisticians sifted through the record books for the Toffees' heaviest-ever defeats, only two underserved late goals from the visitors prevented their possible rewriting.

---

[74] The actual number was 6.4 million, less than the eight million who tuned in for live games on ITV involving Liverpool and Manchester United, indicating that Everton had only limited appeal compared to their rivals.

Although an unfit and untried defence was always going to be a risky proposition, the distinct lack of heart and appetite grated with visiting supporters. 'For manager Colin Harvey it must have been one of the most crushing results of his career,' the always observant John Giles wrote afterwards, 'Victory would have taken him back on to the top of the league and provided some hard evidence that his team is, finally, capable of truly competing with such as Liverpool and Arsenal. Instead he was left with a broken team, one exposed as lacking in competitive heart when the going got tough.' In essence, that was why fortunes were gradually fading under Harvey. Kendall's team possessed no little skill but ultimately internal harmony and character – both individually and collectively – set them apart. When he took over the reins, Harvey had two choices: sign top-quality and proven talent, like Kenny Dalglish, or acquire players who possessed the requisite personality to maintain what Kendall had started. With the Arsenal victory now a flash in the pan, it was increasingly clear the Everton boss had done neither.

Floored by Tyson

Harvey cut a devastated figure after the Midlands mauling. 'This was my worst day as a manager – one of my worst-ever in football,' he understandably declared. 'We'll see a sign of what the players have got under their jerseys when we play Chelsea next Saturday.' The expected positive reaction did not happen as another abject performance resulted in a 1-0 defeat, with a further sign of a looming winter of discontent apparent when Cottee went to the press over being substituted. The angry striker had visibly mouthed to Harvey 'Why have you done that?' after being taken off with 25 minutes remaining, as the crowd booed. Although his boss blamed the mix-up over 'a breakdown in communication', Cottee said, 'When you are losing at home I would have thought the last person you take off is a striker. I am very disappointed. I have not asked for a transfer, but will have to wait and see.' Asked to elaborate, Cottee cryptically responded: 'I have said all that I need to say.'

Neville Southall was usually beyond reproach but even the great Welsh international was falling below his usual high standards and, seven days later, a failure to collect a Carlton Fairweather overhead-kick allowed Wimbledon to scramble a last-minute equaliser at Goodison. Within 24 hours there was a bombshell for the club and supporters when news leaked that the goalkeeper wanted to leave. 'I just don't feel right any more,' he confessed at an impromptu press conference after the game, 'Maybe I've been here too long. I've been giving the situation a lot of thought for some time and now I believe it might be right for both me and the club if I left.' Even considering Southall was still shellshocked after the Villa drubbing, they were surprising words considering he had signed a lucrative seven-and-a-half-year contract less then twelve months before. To make matters worse, the first Harvey knew about his discontent was in the newspapers.

Subsequently the two reportedly smoothed things over after 'heart-to-heart' talks at Bellefield but it was hardly convincing stuff. 'I was out of order in saying what I did without telling the manager,' Southall admitted, although he justified his expressed desire to leave as 'fair comment in the mood I was in'. Meanwhile, Harvey said that Southall 'is frustrated at the way we've been playing – as we all are. We all feel down. We all feel frustrated.' Although the goalkeeper had not asked for a transfer, they were hardly encouraging words intended to lift morale. Indeed, as the legendary Len Capeling wrote in the *Liverpool Daily Post*, Southall was merely reflecting the current mood. 'He was only echoing the sentiments of most of the fans who've seen the Kendall era drift away on a tidal wave of bad signings and bad man-management. Colin Harvey has bravely accepted that the buck stops with him, but despite numerous appeals for more fire and fury, too many Everton players appear to have lost their appetite for battle.'

Capeling's point about man-management was well-made. Just two-and-a-half years into his reign, there were few players in the squad who had not had some sort of public quarrel with the Everton boss and/or requested a transfer. Even Peter Reid had been rumoured to have fallen out with Harvey before leaving the club. Yet it is easy to have some sympathy with the struggling boss. Southall was a senior member of the squad and well-rewarded as reportedly one of the three highest-paid players in the country. Rather than be supportive of Harvey, with his ill-timed outburst he had only undermined the Everton manager further. To make matters worse, the out-of-favour Graeme Sharp told the Sunday newspapers that he would give things another month before reviewing his position, with Leeds having a bid refused and Tottenham also circling. Such disunity off the pitch was always going to impact performances.

Nevertheless, on the Wednesday after the Chelsea loss, Southall's difficult month only got worse eight minutes from the end of a closely-fought League Cup tie against Nottingham Forest at the City Ground. With all the attention on the goalkeeper after his weekend outburst, in the first half the Welsh international made brilliant saves from Steve Hodge and Stuart Pearce and those heroics looked to have earned the visitors a replay at Goodison Park, until the bizarre intervention of fifty-year-old referee George Tyson. The Football League's oldest match official had become increasingly frustrated with Southall's perceived time-wasting so, when the goalkeeper kept hold of the ball for thirteen seconds with the final whistle in sight, his patience snapped. In a highly unusual move, Tyson penalised him for retaining the ball for too long and awarded an indirect free-kick at the edge of the six-yard box, to the right of goal. From the set piece, Nigel Clough fed Lee Chapman who turned the ball in at the near post. That was enough to clinch victory and, at the end, furious Everton players and their manager had to be shepherded away from Tyson, who was given a police escort from the pitch. In his book *Everton Secrets*, the Everton manager admitted that he had uncharacteristically told Tyson: 'They're calling you a cheat – and, by the way, you are.' Harvey was subsequently fined £1,500 for bringing the game into disrepute.

In the aftermath, Tyson had some explaining to do. 'By the letter – if not the spirit – of the law, the referee was correct,' the *Daily Telegraph* pointed out. However, referees rarely chose to apply sanctions on goalkeepers keeping hold of the ball, a policy that continues to this day.[75] That said, the man in black showed no remorse. 'I'm not worried, I've done nothing wrong. I did my job well,' he said afterwards, 'He [Southall] was whistled at, and he was spoken to and waved at by me…all to no avail. I had warned him about time-wasting.' Yet as Harvey claimed afterwards, what he meant by 'warned' was a moot point: 'He may have shouted something to him from the halfway line, but I certainly didn't see him go up to Neville and issue any kind of a formal warning.' With a quarter-final appearance at stake and a run to the final worth anything up to £1 million, Tyson's expensive foible had repercussions. 'That free-kick decision was a sickener for us and what it has potentially cost us is incalculable,' chief executive Jim Greenwood said. The final word on the whole sorry and unusual saga goes to David Lacey in the *Guardian*. 'Goalkeepers will dally and dawdle to a greater degree and get away with it,' he wrote, 'To be effective this kind of refereeing has to be consistent. Otherwise the letter of the law is an ass.'

Kendall makes his point

After traumatic times against Aston Villa and Wimbledon, Tyson's headline-hogging decision made for another difficult outing for Southall in the Midlands. 'It has been an eventful few days for Neville but they say things go in threes, so hopefully all his troubles are behind him,' Harvey said. Conscious of his previous emotional outburst, Southall made a point of saying 'I'm not fed up.' To compound matters there was a return to the City Ground three days later, resulting in another 1-0 defeat via a Nigel Clough penalty.

Harvey's side continued to be inconsistent, the next six league games bringing three victories and two defeats. The drawn game brought a returning hero to Goodison.

---

[75] In 2000 the law was amended allowing goalkeepers up to six seconds to release the ball. Typically the first to be penalised was Everton's Thomas Myhre, playing for Norway in that year's European Championship.

Howard Kendall had been sacked – or left by mutual consent, according to the former Everton manager – by Athletic Bilbao in November after three successive defeats, the last ironically a 4-0 loss to John Toshack's Real Madrid. He had been linked with a move to Manchester United, among others, and inevitably a return to his former home was also mooted. 'That frankly, sickened me. And goodness knows how Colin felt,' he later said. Kendall then surprisingly accepted a three-year deal at Maine Road and poignantly the first full game in charge of City was at the scene of his greatest glories. Before the game Kendall noted that Harvey's managerial career was at the same stage as his own difficult period exactly six years before, when Philip Carter came out with his famous message of support. 'I think he needs that from the club. Something to reassure him that all the dreadful speculation is just a load of nonsense,' he told the *Daily Express*, 'When you know someone so well, you just hope they ignore some of the more hurtful comments that build into an intense and unfair pressure.'

Nevertheless, in the wake of the goalless draw at Goodison, the only comments Harvey needed to avoid were those scathing match reports containing almost unanimous criticism. In front of a live TV audience and a frozen but barely conscious 21,737 spectators, the two teams produced a classic of its kind – if your kind of contest balances pure ineptitude with negative, soulless tactics. 'Newly-promoted City were bottom of the table, without a win on the road all season so their new boss used some familiar names to form an effective blockade of Harvey's team,' wrote Phil McNulty in the *Liverpool Daily Post*. 'Whilst Peter Reid marshalled their midfield resources, Kendall deployed Alan Harper as a sweeper and the latter had a magnificent game, shutting out the Everton attack before deservedly winning the man-of-the-match award. This was one of the worst football matches ever screened. To describe it as sheer unadulterated rubbish would be to err on the side of generosity.'

'Too many of us let ourselves down last season, including myself. And Everton will not tolerate a mid-table outfit,' Kevin Ratcliffe claimed before the start of the season. But now Harvey's team were exactly that. League leaders in mid-October, the draw against City left the Toffees in a moderate eleventh place. Graeme Sharp came out in support of his manager after the bore-draw. 'There is no crisis at Everton,' he declared. 'It is the not the manager, it is the players involved on the day who get results.' However, the Scot could have been referring to himself. Sharp was one of ten players dropped thus far during the campaign – for six matches in October when he publicly expressed dissatisfaction – and his manager must have been hoping that a spell on the sidelines would rekindle the hunger of the glory years. Disappointingly that did not happen and a goal against Luton on New Year's Day took his tally to just two in 22 games. For Mike Newell it was a similar story. Dropped for five games in December, the local-born player had not scored a league goal since September. Moreover, the forwards were not necessarily all to blame. The midfield was still lightweight and spending £750,000 on Stoke winger Peter Beagrie in November was strange when strength, not guile, was required. Although he was talented, spectators quickly established that his main flaw was to delay crosses because of an almost pathological desire to beat the opposition full-back two or three times. The winger was quickly down the pecking order and unsettled, especially after the coaching staff took him to one side to criticise his style.

After the 2-1 victory over Luton, one supporter represented the views of many over the lack of creativity: 'The problem is that they get so few chances they've forgotten how to take them when one comes along.' Unsurprisingly, the other member of the forward triumvirate was also struggling. Tony Cottee asked for a transfer after being dropped for the fourth time against the Hatters, one which the club granted. After beginning his Goodison career in a blaze of glory, only three goals in seventeen games pointed towards the end of the forward's time, just eighteen months into a five-year contract. Harvey said, 'I have no regrets about signing Cottee because I still regard him as a top-quality player. But unfortunately it has not worked out for him.' After thanking supporters, Cottee's words also sounded like a valedictory message. 'It became obvious some time ago that the team were not playing to my strengths,' he claimed. 'It is in everyone's best interests that I now look to continue my playing career elsewhere.'

Nevertheless, with Harvey wanting a reported £1.5 million fee and Cottee's wages of £3,000 per week outside the reach of all but the biggest clubs, the number of suitors was small, especially as he wanted to move back to the capital. But Arsenal were never going to be interested – 'Too much, too late,' snapped George Graham – while Terry Venables thought that a partnership with Gary Lineker was not ideal. Crystal Palace did show interest and, intriguingly, the original plan was a straight swap with Ian Wright but that fell by the wayside when the Palace striker broke a leg. Even then a Palace loan bid for Cottee to cover his absence was turned down by Everton. Despite rumoured interest from Bayern Munich and Hamburg, there was no obvious outlet abroad either and, in the end, any quick exit was scuppered when Harvey put the blocks on a straight swap with Tottenham's Paul Stewart due to the latter's failing form. With all routes out of the club blocked off, the wantaway striker unexpectedly found himself back in a blue shirt as Harvey tried to rescue another disappointing campaign.

22
BEYOND A BOUNDARY

THERE WAS A SENSE OF DREAD AROUND GOODISON PARK WHEN THE third round of the FA Cup produced a difficult away tie at Second Division Middlesbrough, with memories of the three games at the fourth-round stage two seasons before still fresh. The Toffees were 12-1 third favourites for the cup, more a reflection of their pedigree over the previous decade than a current status as a team who could not win on their travels.

A freezing cold north-east Saturday in early January is not the most attractive proposition and, to be fair, so was the match – a dour goalless draw where neither goalkeeper was seriously threatened. At Goodison four days later an apathetic 24,352 crowd were equally unlikely to be endangered by quality entertainment, a drab 1-1 draw where Sheedy's first-half goal was equalised by former Everton trainee Gary Parkinson. Philip Carter won the toss for the second replay and that was an altogether more attractive affair with the visitors creating a host of chances: Southall made three great saves, a Keown header came back off his own upright while Snodin kicked a Mark Brennan effort off the line. Everton were not without their own opportunities before, just 73 seconds from another period of extra time, Norman Whiteside crashed the ball home after Nevin's shot struck the bar. 'I was the right man in the right place at the right time,' said the Northern Ireland international. Coincidentally, the draw for the next round also revisited the other 1988 FA Cup marathon.

Sheffield Wednesday (a), FA Cup fourth round

On their previous cup outing the sides had taken four games, and seven hours, to settle their differences so both managers were hoping to avoid a replay. Like January 1988 there was a league meeting preceding the cup tie, with Everton winning 2-0 at Goodison. At Hillsborough – where the Leppings Lane terraces remained off limits and police delayed the start by thirty minutes due to the delayed arrival of some of the 3,800 visiting supporters – it was a more uncomfortable afternoon for Harvey's team.

The visitors were on an unbeaten sequence of seven FA Cup matches against the Owls, dating back to 1954, and made it eight in ninety minutes of fast and furious football. Wednesday were managed by Ron Atkinson and fates decreed it was Norman Whiteside, having helped the colourful boss lift the FA Cup twice, who applied the rapier thrust. The midfielder, who had scored four times in five games since returning from an Achilles operation, opened his account on ten minutes after Sharp's header crashed against the underside of the bar and he was on hand to smash home the rebound. The lead lasted only two minutes. Dalian Atkinson tussled with Southall at the edge of the box and the ball ran loose for David Hirst to fire home. But Everton were back in front before the half-hour mark. Neil McDonald's corner – Everton's only one of the game – spooned into the air via Peter Shirtliff and when Sharp's shot was cleared off the line by Nigel Worthington, Whiteside, showing his old forward instincts, was again inside the six-yard box to double his tally. 'That twerp has only gone and scored twice on about the only two occasions he's been across the halfway line,' an unhappy Atkinson said afterwards.

Thereafter Harvey was protected by his defensive shield. He had strung five men across the back and, in a display of anti-football, rarely strayed into opposition territory. At the core was Neville Southall, the Welshman producing another scintillating display of the goalkeeper's arts. Included in his tally of saves was a stunning effort from David Hirst on 53 minutes, when he clawed a goal-bound header over the bar, a stop that brought even the Wednesday fans to their feet. After his side's 2-1 defeat, Atkinson paid tribute to the great Welshman: 'I couldn't fault our team for effort – but unfortunately we came up against one of the world's best goalkeepers on song.' The next round brought a tie against another familiar face.

Oldham Athletic (a), FA Cup fifth round

The Second Division Lancashire side were, pound-for-pound, one of the form teams in the country. Although critics claimed their plastic pitch at Boundary Park gave an unfair advantage – they were 32 games unbeaten at home – the Latics were significantly better than the average outfit at their level. They were an excellent footballing side featuring fine players like striker Andy Ritchie, winger Rick Holden and outstanding full-back Denis Irwin, destined for greater achievements elsewhere. Also in the ranks were former Everton players Neil Adams and Ian Marshall, who was fated to play a pivotal role in the tie.

The biggest connection was of course Oldham manager Joe Royle. Everton's then post-war leading scorer had crafted a side enjoying a season bordering on the epic. Fourth in the Second Division, they were forging a two-pronged attack on Wembley, not only in the FA Cup but also in the League Cup, having reached the semi-final stage where they had just destroyed West Ham United 6-0 in the first leg at home. Whether it was the plastic pitch, Oldham's excellent cup pedigree or Everton's poor away record – perhaps a combination of all three – but the bookmakers had the home team at 11-8 favourites to progress, against 7-4 for Harvey's side. 'Forget about Oldham's plastic pitch and get your own attitude right,' Harvey told his players on the eve of the game.

In the opening half-hour, his squad undoubtedly heeded that call. Having ditched the unpopular five at the back, Harvey's underdogs made a mockery of the bookmakers' odds in icy, Lancastrian drizzle. The much-criticised forward duo for once showed a real purpose together, with Cottee singlehandedly intent on exacting revenge for West Ham's humiliation three days before. 'Not the least awe-inspiring thing about Everton was the understanding of Sharp and Cottee,' wrote Clive White in *The Times*, 'The Oldham supporters will be relieved to hear that that is not always the case.' The visitors opened the scoring after 22 minutes when a cross from the right was miskicked by Earl Barrett and Sharp's beautifully struck right-footed shot went under Jon Hallworth in the Oldham goal. Four minutes later it was 2-0. Cottee's clever header put his forward partner clear and, after being illegally scythed down by Marshall, Sharp and Hallworth collided and the ball ran clear for the club-record signing to knock it in. Everton had succeeded in making Oldham look both second-rate and Second Division and could have sealed the tie minutes later when Hallworth pulled off the save of the match to stop Cottee.

Totally in command at the break, Everton reverted to their Hillsborough tactic of containment afterwards, one that failed miserably. 'At three goals up, the tie might have been over,' Clive White wrote. 'The trouble was that Everton thought that it was at two goals up.' Not for the first time, Royle pushed Marshall up as an auxiliary attacker and the former Everton player caused enormous discomfort to the hitherto untroubled backline. For all that, it took a soft penalty on the hour mark to start the Oldham fightback. Veteran striker Roger Palmer appeared to fall over Neville Southall but it was enough to convince referee Tony Ward to point to the spot. Ritchie converted for his 25th goal of the season. *Match of the Day* proved conclusively it was an error but Everton lost both their shape and heads in the fall-out as, in a portent of things to come, three visiting players were booked for dissent and several other protests, as frustrations built with referee Ward. With gaps growing at the back, Palmer ghosted in to head home Holden's precise cross seven minutes later and earn a replay at Goodison. At the end of the game Snodin, Sharp and McCall could be seen haranguing the referee in a particularly unpleasant manner.

Setting aside the loss of discipline, Harvey could be satisfied with the quality of the first-half display and achieving the objective of at least forcing a replay on Goodison's organic grass. Royle, however, could not resist a dig at the critics. 'It should be a good tie on Wednesday. I believe the pitch is quite flat there, isn't it?' he asked rhetorically.

Oldham Athletic (h), FA Cup fifth round replay

Royle also quipped that his players may need gumshields for the replay after the visitors lost their discipline at Boundary Park. His hunch proved correct as referee Ward once again took centre stage in another pulsating and feisty cup tie. In contrast to the disciplined visitors, Harvey's side produced another volatile display which forced Ward into booking five of their players, the tetchiness a by-product of rising pressure after another poor season. Following a goalless opening 45 minutes, the major flashpoint came when Whiteside, already on a yellow card and burning the shortest of fuses, swung a leg dangerously at midfielder Mick Milligan and was sent off.

Although a man down and losing the corner count 12-3, the home team created the two best chances of a goalless ninety minutes, Sheedy's free-kick striking the foot of the post before, moments later, the midfielder shot straight at Hallworth from close range. Then, ten minutes into the extra period, the Second Division cup specialists went ahead when Holden found space on the left touchline and Marshall met his delicate chip with a header past Southall. But with Everton's entire season resting on the result, they got a lifeline three minutes from the end. After Ratcliffe's clever chip caused hesitation in the Oldham defence, Sharp beat Hallworth to the ball but was then hauled down by the goalkeeper and, as the Evertonians in the 36,663 crowd held their breath, Ward pointed straight to the spot. Sheedy sealed a replay with a fierce drive into the roof of the net.

Afterwards, Royle refused to be drawn on the home team's hot-blooded approach, one that left Ian Marshall with a broken nose and three players nursing leg injuries. He did admit, though, that 'I'm just grateful that we came out of Goodison Park without a serious injury.' However, Graeme Sharp showed somewhat less diplomacy in launching an attack on referee Ward's handling of the game. 'Thirty-six thousand people can't be wrong,' he claimed. 'They saw his performance and it was poor, very poor for a match of this stature. He has to get control of it, and if he lets it slip it is his fault.'

Oldham Athletic (a), FA Cup fifth round, second replay

Before the third game between the teams, delayed for seventeen days until the first Saturday in March, the wider focus was on the ill-discipline displayed by Harvey's team thus far. Stephen Bierley in the *Guardian* focused on Sharp's outburst, particularly as he had been booked twice for dissent in the tie, labelling it 'blatantly absurd, given Sharp's dreadful behaviour in both matches'. He then added, 'What shocked Everton watchers… was the team's lack of discipline and their reliance on the physical. There were puzzled, worried and sad faces in the carpeted main stand after the replay. In no way had Oldham attempted to rough Everton up; quite the reverse, in fact.' There were stories in the aftermath that the directors were dismayed with their hostile approach. Although unseemly, that merely was the consequence of the desperation to win a trophy in Harvey's third season, something the Everton boss reflected on before a second trip to Boundary Park. 'We realise the importance of the game to our fans,' Harvey said, 'There is a big prize at the end of it so we must get something from the tie.'

With the quarter-final promising a home draw against Aston Villa, the visitors went ahead on 13 minutes when Cottee latched onto McDonald's perfectly-weighted pass and slipped the ball over Hallworth. However, the Everton full-back would journey from hero to villain over the course of the game. Royle's side had laid siege to the Everton goal and on the half-hour McDonald's suicidal back pass was left short and, as Roger Palmer and Southall both challenged, the ball rebounded in off the Oldham striker. Although the Everton defender was to blame it was uncharacteristically weak goalkeeping by Southall, who was clearly uncomfortable diving at Palmer's feet on the plastic surface.

With Royle deploying only a single centre-half in a high-risk attacking 3-4-3 formation, Oldham overwhelmed the First Division aristocrats and should have had the game won in normal time. However, they got their reward three minutes into the extra period, with Everton punished for the folly of playing a right-back on the opposite flank. Ian Marshall moved outside McDonald and, whereas a left-footed full-back would usually scoop the ball out for a throw-in, the Everton player lunged dangerously with his right leg and only succeeded in unlawfully bringing down the Oldham player inside the box. Marshall, released by Harvey two years before, exacted some sort of retribution by scoring from the spot.

Southall more than atoned for his mistake by making three world-class saves as the crowd witnessed more one-way traffic towards the Everton goal. Apart from a John Ebbrell shot that went wide, there was little to threaten the home side, who deservedly cruised into the quarter-finals. 'This match was decided purely on footballing merit, and the First Division team were outclassed to an almost embarrassing extent,' wrote Peter Ball in *The Times*. One of the reasons was the clear lack of character and passion in the team, when compared to the mid-1980s. The watching Tommy Docherty was both an interested observer and scathing towards Everton. 'I feel sorry for Colin Harvey because the level of commitment shown out there was pathetic,' 'The Doc' said. 'With one or two exceptions I don't know how those players can look at themselves in the mirror tonight. To call them appalling is to flatter them.'

Missing the boat

The defeat in Lancashire raised further questions about Harvey's managerial tenure and style of play. 'This team is an absolute disgrace, playing high ball, hit and hope, clueless football,' complained one angry supporter in the pages of the *Football Echo*, 'There is no skill, no movement off the ball, no heart, no passing ability – nothing.' That may have seemed harsh but was certainly not an isolated view. Having blamed the defence for the defeat at Oldham, Harvey issued a rallying call 48 hours later: 'I was deeply upset for the supporters on Saturday, not least those who have watched us in all of the cup ties. We must get something out of the remainder of the season... for them.'

However, unlike the four previous campaigns there was possibly something more tangible to play for than just the title – which was heading to Anfield for the eighteenth time. Lennart Johansson, the new UEFA president, had recently announced that he would welcome back English clubs into Europe. Although contingent on the good behaviour of supporters at that summer's World Cup, the glimmer of hope at least offered an incentive for managers and players during the final two months of the campaign. The expectation being that, with Liverpool serving an extended ban, a place would be made available in the UEFA Cup for the runners-up. That seemed a distant dream for Harvey, especially when a goalless draw at Old Trafford, four days after the Oldham loss, left his side tenth in the table albeit with games in hand on those above.

However, a run of five wins in six games lifted Everton to the lofty heights of third in the table with five games left – five points behind second-placed Aston Villa. Although there was still a possibility of snatching second, the elevated placing acted very much as a mirage. The single defeat in that run, 1-0 at Arsenal, was a fairer reflection of the team's standing, a dreadful performance featuring not a single shot on target. Only one victory in the last five games left the Toffees finishing the season in a moderate sixth place.

Results-wise, like the previous campaigns the main issue was away form. No team in the top flight accrued more home points (45) and home goals (40) than Harvey's outfit. On their travels the same disparity existed: just three victories and seventeen goals. In Harvey's three seasons there had been just twelve away league victories, the same as in the 1984/85 campaign alone – and all against moderate opposition, with five against teams who were ultimately relegated. 'Quite simply, away tactics in recent seasons have been inept and unadventurous – and most perplexingly unchanged,' said one correspondent to the *Football Echo*. This continual inequality between home and away results and performances was a reminder of the perceived lack of character and spirit among the squad. In front of a home crowd, under favourable conditions, they possessed sufficient quality to overcome most teams. On the road, when required to dig in and show more resilience, they were found lacking. It was no coincidence that some of the poorest displays came at places like Wimbledon, Millwall and Crystal Palace, teams who would reduce games to a purely physical battle. Consequently, at the end of a third below-average campaign, the Everton manager was under pressure. 'If I left Goodison without winning anything, it would be the cause of great personal regret,' Harvey admitted during the Oldham cup saga. 'This is a tough job but I feel I am the right man for it.' If the statement was intended to bring support from his chairman, it did not as Philip Carter pulled no punches in the club's annual report, published during the summer:

> The 1989/90 season was extremely disappointing, both from the point of view of League position and Cup performance. The final League position of sixth once again reflected an appalling away performance. With the exception of Luton Town and Millwall, we had one of the worst away records in the League, winning only three games, following an equally poor performance the previous season, when we won only four games. The Manager and Board acknowledge that the situation away from home is quite unacceptable.

The Everton board was not the only interested party unhappy with developments. Shortly afterwards Shareholders' Association chairman Peter Parry delivered a letter to Carter expressing their 'Apprehension at the present situation at Goodison,' and a 'Lack of confidence in the present set-up.' The message followed a motion, passed at their annual meeting, of no confidence in the club's management. Parry outlined 'a general feeling of frustration because we seemed to be back in much the same situation that we were in 12 months ago.' One of two main concerns was the set-up below first-team level, with the ridiculous situation in some games of the coaching staff making up the numbers. The other was the constant stories appearing in the press of players being unsettled.

The association was probably thinking of one in particular.

23
UP AGAINST THE POST

IF SUPPORTERS THOUGHT THE KISS AND MAKE-UP BETWEEN HARVEY and Southall after the Wimbledon game in November 1989 was the end of the goalkeeper's travails, they were sadly mistaken. In the following months Southall's future was never far from the back pages.

Neville ending story

On the final weekend of 1989 there were further reports that he was unsettled, with growing differences between goalkeeper and manager. Not only that but John Toshack at Real Madrid was preparing a £3 million bid for the Llandudno-born number one, with rumours Harvey would use the money to fund purchases of QPR's David Seaman and Celtic midfield maestro Paul McStay. Published on the morning of an away fixture at QPR, Harvey was not happy with the timing: 'It was done for maximum effect on the day of a game. First of all, there is absolutely nothing in it. Secondly, talk of a rift is ridiculous.' Southall set aside the off-pitch speculation to produce another man-of-the-match performance in a 1-0 defeat at Loftus Road, although an untypical rush out of the area led to a booking for bringing down Roy Wegerle, when a red card could have been tendered.

If those stories were merely conjecture, a month later a report by Bob Russell in the *Daily Mirror* appeared to have more legs. Russell claimed that, on the final Friday in January, Southall met a representative from Barcelona at a Manchester restaurant. The deal on the table was a reported £700,000 over three years, with a signing-on fee added on. '£2m Adios for Southall' and 'Supersaver on the gold trail' screamed the back pages. The offer from Barcelona was £2.2 million, or more than twice the world record for a goalkeeper. This time it was Jim Greenwood's turn to issue a denial: 'The lad has signed a seven-year contract giving him everything he ever wanted. He has made it quite clear that he has no intention of leaving so why do they persist with the speculation?' Southall had claimed that he would never move to Spain because of his hatred of the sunshine in southern Europe. 'Neville has not spoken to Barcelona, Real Madrid, Frickley Athletic or anybody and nor have I,' said his agent, Neil Ramsey.

The Everton goalkeeper was so incensed by the story that he sought libel damages from the newspaper in the High Court. His solicitor said the words 'meant that he was disloyal and in breach of contract in that he was not prepared to honour his contract with Everton and had attended a meeting outside Liverpool with a representative of Barcelona FC at which he agreed to play for them.' Interestingly, the meeting with Barcelona was not disputed. But Mr Justice Michael Davies ruled against the Everton goalkeeper in July 1990, on the basis the article was not 'capable of being defamatory' and he should pay costs. However, Davies also said that there was no suggestion the Everton player had agreed to play for Barcelona in contravention of his contract, affirming he 'has done nothing discreditable'. Southall felt the judge's latter comments left him vindicated.

By that stage the unhappy Welsh international had already expressed a desire to leave via more traditional means. In early May, the club revealed Southall had asked for a transfer two weeks before, citing 'personal reasons'. With Real Madrid and Manchester United circling, Harvey turned down his demand. 'Southall has been told that his request is totally unacceptable to the club,' the Everton boss responded. 'Only a few weeks previously the player issued a statement through his Leeds-based agent Neil Ramsey saying that he was perfectly happy at Goodison.' Southall still had six years left on his agreement. 'All parties are required to honour that contract,' Harvey asserted. 'No further discussions are necessary.' Four weeks later Southall was refusing to comment on the matter but, when asked if he still wanted to leave, his agent responded: 'Neville's views are the same now as they were when he made the transfer request.' A meeting between Harvey and Carter at the end of May resulted in them slapping a £3 million fee on their errant goalkeeper.

Manchester United were in pole position to take Southall but they found demands from both club and player prohibitive: not only Everton's valuation but Southall wanted a four-year deal that topped his £190,000 basic salary and included bonuses. For a club £5 million in debt, the £4 million package proved an expensive step too far. Having said that, with the real possibility of Southall leaving, the Everton manager unsurprisingly wanted options and during the summer gave a two-week trial to Egypt's international stopper, Ahmed Shobeir, who had just excelled at the World Cup. The 28-year-old made a positive impression at Bellefield and Harvey was keen to push through a £275,000 deal, one that needed a work permit, which in turn depended on Shobeir being first choice. On that basis Harvey was happy to let his wantaway star go, but only at the set price. However, with Alex Ferguson failing to sell Mark Hughes to fund the deal, Southall remained at Everton. Consequently, the goalkeeper's frustrations resurfaced in early August, with a second transfer request, which was once again turned down – effectively meaning the Shobeir deal was off. A third made just before a trip to Turkey a fortnight later suffered the same fate. Although how long the two parties could continue this public game of cat and mouse was debatable, as the odds of Southall leaving appeared to be slim. After the opening game, they had shortened dramatically.

The incredible sulk

A gloriously sunny Saturday on August Bank Holiday weekend was the setting for a famous, or possibly infamous, Goodison moment, one that still resonates. The visitors were Second Division champions Leeds United and typically, like any newly-promoted side on the opening day, they asked searching questions of Harvey's team, who soon fell into disarray. The scene for a disastrous ninety minutes was set early on when a long throw from Gary McAllister caused chaos in Everton's central defence and Chris Fairclough stepped in to head past Southall. After Neil McDonald had fired wide from the penalty spot, Southall looked nothing like the world's best goalkeeper when colliding with Martin Keown to gift Gary Speed a second. After the break a ghost of Goodison afternoons past returned to haunt the home team, when Imre Varadi[76] made it three. Despite a brave fightback with goals from Pat Nevin and John Ebbrell, an undeserved equaliser proved elusive and Everton's crucial season was off to a damaging start on a day when there were three separate pitch invasions from home supporters.

Nevertheless, there was only one story in town over the next 48 hours. With the bulk of the 34,412 crowd making the most of the sunshine during the half-time break, five minutes before the teams were due to return puzzled looks filled the stadium. Southall had surprisingly emerged from the players' tunnel and headed towards his goal, in front of the Leeds fans at the Park End. The goalkeeper, looking thoroughly dejected, then plonked himself down and sat with his back against the post. The Everton manager said before the game he hoped to give fans something to shout about but the jeering of one of his own players was not what he had in mind.

Incredibly Harvey also claimed to have no knowledge of the surreal development. In *Everton Secrets* he said, 'When we got back in I had a few words with the players – not shouting but trying to sort things out – and then told them to get ready to go out for the

---

[76] Varadi's erratic finishing in a blue shirt did not go unnoticed in the Goodison press box, which used to hold a sweepstake for which pitch-side advertisement would be the first on the receiving end of his shots.

second half. I had no idea that Neville had left the dressing room early.' Harvey was only made aware of the incident by ITV's Clive Tyldesley after the game. Southall kept his own counsel, only opening up to the *Liverpool Echo's* Ken Rogers a week later. 'People thought that I had come out to make a point about my transfer request and that I'd sat down to make my feelings clear,' he admitted, 'That had nothing to do with it whatsoever…I didn't realise the implications of the half-time incident. I put the boss in an awkward situation.'

Southall described the dressing room during the break. 'I didn't want to sit down to listen to anything. I was wound up,' he revealed, 'I just wanted to get back onto the pitch and get going again. It had nothing to do with the other lads.' However, an unnamed teammate leaked some candid details to the *People* on the following weekend. 'As soon as the team walked in the manager made it clear he was angry,' the source revealed, 'He made straight for Neville and pointed the finger at him for losing the goals. He told Neville he should have come to collect the long throw-in that led to the opener. Then he put the second one on Nev's toes too. Neville was boiling but he kept his cool and bit his lip. He just turned round and walked back out.' The players and staff initially thought Southall had gone to wait in the tunnel outside. In the context of shareholders' previous concerns over player unrest, the public sit-in combined with tabloid leaks indicated those problems were spilling over into the new campaign. Unsurprisingly the reaction to his perceived protest was damning. James Lawton in the *Daily Express* wrote:

> The behaviour of Everton goalkeeper Neville Southall shames every pro-footballer in the land. His loutish breach of discipline and public contempt for those people who pay his generous wages makes a travesty of values like loyalty and team spirit…It is a grab-all mentality perfectly expressed by Southall. Less than two years ago he signed a seven-year contract. No-one held a gun to his head. He signed it with the usual platitudes of Everton being his club, etc, etc. Now he severely embarrasses his manager, who has given a lifetime of service to his beloved Everton.

Lawton, as ever, was correct and it is easy to feel sympathy for Harvey. A struggling, inexperienced manager publicly undermined by his senior – and best – player. The incident would never have happened under his predecessor. Gordon Taylor, the chief executive of the PFA, was at Goodison and claimed Southall's conduct was 'unprofessional and not fair on his team-mates, the manager and those who pay his wages.'

Southall's summer of discontent led to one of Goodison's most memorable images.

For all his protestations to the contrary, over the previous eighteen months Southall appeared to relish occupying the space at the eye of the storm, possessing a growing sense of self-entitlement which needed to be contained. Rather than take his grievances outside to the watching public, the Welsh goalkeeper should have aired them in the privacy of the dressing room. To be fair, Southall had always spoke glowingly of his respect for Harvey but then clearly undermined his manager with a truculent 'protest' on the opening day. Consequently, he was guilty of behaviour best described as contradictory. That contrary behaviour extended elsewhere. 'I'm happy to be playing for Everton and I could be here for the next ten years for all I know,' he told Brian Reade in the *Liverpool Daily Post*. Yet in the next breath he reaffirmed his desire to leave: 'My transfer request is a personal matter between myself and Colin Harvey, and I've made a decision for the future of myself and my family.' The Everton boss fined the player a week's wages – £4,000 – for the display of indiscipline although he denied the protest was due to a bust-up at the break. Inevitably the contretemps only accelerated the chances of Southall leaving Goodison, with Manchester United still believed to be in the box seat. That said, Serie A side Torino spoke with Southall's agent and were believed to have bid £2.7 million for his services.

For all the relationship difficulties, Southall was irreplaceable and retained his place for the midweek away game at Coventry. Beforehand, Jim King, secretary of the Everton Supporters' Club, also laid into the goalkeeper. 'The fans are disgusted in these so-called superstars,' he said, 'They think the world of Neville but are upset by that disgraceful incident.' Those strong feelings manifested itself in hate mail to the goalkeeper and a banner in the Highfield Road away end of 'JUDAS SOUTHALL ONCE A BINMAN ALWAYS A BINMAN'. Although Southall played reasonably well, the lack of pace in the new central defensive partnership of Watson and Keown left them vulnerable against the home team's speedy attackers during a dispiriting 3-1 defeat which left Harvey's team bottom.

The opening two league games had been lost in 1984/85 and, poignantly, for their third match the Toffees travelled to Maine Road where their former manager lay waiting. Even more poignantly, like six seasons before, Kendall's team won 1-0 but this time the boot was on the other foot. The circular narrative was completed by a winner from Adrian Heath, one of a colony of former Everton players in Moss Side. To end a miserable week for Southall, and perhaps an indication of his state of mind, after being warned for using bad language by the police at Highfield Road he was booked for dissent in Manchester. After the game Kendall came out in support of his former coach: 'When you win something, the fans expect you to win more and that put Colin in a difficult position. It doesn't work that way, but you try telling that to supporters…but I'll know he'll get it right.'

Nevertheless, the defeat left Harvey's team rooted to the bottom, three defeats confirming the worst start to a campaign for 33 years. If things could get worse, they sadly did, when there was much to take away from a visit to a Chinese restaurant in Southport.

Chinese whispers

Togetherness was seemingly one of the great strengths of Kendall's team but that appeared to quickly dilute under his successor. The perception of a split dressing room has since been put down to new arrivals during Harvey's second summer. However, within Kendall's side there had been two groups with more intangible differences, which only became apparent after he left. The first were those whose loyalty was primarily towards Harvey because of his role in their development: Kevin Ratcliffe, Graeme Sharp and, to a lesser extent, Neville Southall. Allegiance to Kendall came from those he had signed – players like Trevor Steven, Peter Reid, Pat Van Den Hauwe and Kevin Sheedy. Within two years of Harvey taking the managerial seat most of the latter group had departed while, notwithstanding the occasional outburst from Southall, the former remained and were the most vocal in their public support.

Harvey's relationship with Sheedy was a recurring problem during his managerial tenure. Aside from the differences over his best position, there were other issues. 'I had difficulty communicating on a personal basis,' Harvey admitted in *Everton Secrets*. 'I wouldn't say we had a clash of personalities but there was something not right between us. We'd never quite hit it off and I'm sure Kevin would say the same.' Sheedy talking openly about his issues in the Irish press hardly helped. In that context, unsurprisingly, Harvey had accepted another transfer request during the summer but an asking price of £650,000 scared off potential suitors.

The Ireland international was also a key player in the incident used as exemplifying the dysfunction in the Everton squad. In a tradition first started by Kendall, the squad would sometimes go out socially in midweek – the so-called 'Chinese Tuesdays' – with the bill paid via the various fines incurred during the season thus far. Previously the events had been seen as a valuable way of allowing players to air grievances and get things off their chests.

Needing a morale-lift after three straight defeats, in keeping with the custom Harvey took the players to a Chinese restaurant in Southport[77] and afterwards several went for a drink in the Red Rum Bar at the Carlton Hotel. Sheedy – who claimed his drinks had been spiked – took up the story in his book *So Good I did it Twice*:

> *I ended up in the company of Martin Keown…I was speaking double Dutch. Martin and I had a row over football issues. I must have said something he took offence at and he pushed me over, kicked me in the face and split my eye. A fall out is one thing, but you don't expect a team-mate to kick you in the face.*

The incident – over in a matter of a seconds before the two were separated by teammates – was across the back pages within 48 hours. The eyewitness accounts of a group of drunken Everton players arguing in public scarcely countered the theory that here was a disunited and mismatched squad. Stuart McCall hardly helped by telling the press that 'it was just playful' before admitting that he was not present.

Creditably, Sheedy took full responsibility when the two miscreants were summoned to Harvey's office and the manager fined both. Yet that was not the end of Harvey's problems for, when still in the office, according to Sheedy his assailant launched into a full broadside. 'I was shocked and embarrassed as Martin laid into Colin, saying that the players didn't rate him and that he wasn't a good manager,' Sheedy revealed in his book,

---

[77] Ironically the day out was paid for by Neville Southall's fine following his opening game sit-in.

'It was just unbelievable for a player to be talking to a manager like that.' With the press circling outside Bellefield, Sheedy – wearing dark glasses to hide his black eye – was driven out of the training ground in the boot of his own car by Terry Darracott. Although Harvey made the usual noises about morale being high and the players working hard, with Neil McDonald now wanting a move after being dropped for the Manchester City defeat, the walls were closing in on the Everton boss.

24
HURT

THERE WAS AN OLD (AND PROBABLY APOCRYPHAL) STORY WITHIN American politics concerning President Gerald Ford. On leaving office in 1977 he left successor Jimmy Carter three envelopes. The first, he said, should only be opened when there was an emergency, the second only in event of a disaster and the third when there was a catastrophe. When Carter had reason to open the first envelope it said 'blame me'. Later in his presidency when there was a crisis, the second was opened and read 'blame the other party'. In 1980, after the attempt to rescue the hostages in the American embassy in Tehran ended in disaster, Carter opened the third. It said 'Prepare three envelopes'. Had Howard Kendall handed Harvey three envelopes in June 1987, the first two would probably have read 'blame the press' and 'blame the players'. However, even though the team was struggling in the early part of the 1990/91 season, there was still no reason for Harvey to open the mythical third envelope.

Sheffield shocker

The first point of the campaign duly arrived four days after the tear-up in Southport, Mike Newell's equaliser earning a deserved outcome against Arsenal at Goodison. A further draw at Sunderland was followed by a 3-2 home defeat to Liverpool, when even a stirring second-half fightback could not disguise the fact that their previous close rivalry had now all but disappeared. 'The gulf between Everton and Liverpool is now so great that no freak of the form book could rescue Colin Harvey's strugglers from their inevitable fate,' opined Phil McNulty in the *Liverpool Daily Post*. Even the first league victory of the season, at the seventh attempt, 3-0 against a desperately poor Southampton at Goodison, could not disguise the decline. The apathy amid the largely silent 23,000 crowd told its own tale. 'Something is wrong and on Saturday's evidence may not be right again until a new manager arrives,' muttered Martin Thorpe in the *Guardian*.

Three further winless games left Harvey's team in eighteenth place, with just one victory in ten league games. Unsurprisingly there was already speculation about his position. Crystal Palace's Steve Coppell was considered favourite, with Sheffield Wednesday's Ron Atkinson and Joe Royle – who had reportedly turned down the Manchester City role – also highly fancied. Not helping Harvey's position was that his contract was up in the summer.

Nevertheless, there had been some relief in the League Cup, the second round producing an 11-0 aggregate victory over Wrexham. The draw gave, on paper, a reasonably kind tie at newly-promoted Sheffield United – the only top-flight team without a victory thus far. With both seeking solace in the cup to compensate for a combined record of one victory in twenty league games, Harvey issued a warning beforehand. 'They have not been doing really well and neither have we. It's up to us to be ready for them. It sounds simple but we know this is going to be a hard 90 minutes.' As it happened the aftermath proved even harder.

There was no sense the match would prove so significant in the opening hour, with the visitors the better of two poor teams. Ironically the best chance had fallen to Martin Keown, who shot wide from six yards with only the goalkeeper to beat. Then came the pivotal moment, when it all went wrong for Harvey and his side. Brian Deane was put through on goal but was knocked to the ground by Dave Watson. Although the challenge was awkward rather than malevolent, referee Alf Buksh deemed it a professional foul and sent off the unlucky Everton defender. Perhaps sensing that events were conspiring against them yet again, the visiting side fell apart. Five minutes later a suspiciously-offside Carl Bradshaw put the home side ahead and ten minutes from time an unmarked Deane added a second. A consolation strike from Pat Nevin was not enough to rescue a lost cause. Like any other manager on borrowed time Harvey blamed the footballing fates: 'I thought the sending-off was a bit harsh…We have said both goals were offside, but the linesman hasn't given it.'

Realising perhaps that the game was up Harvey was in defiant mood 24 hours later. 'Why should I walk away from it?' he told the *Liverpool Echo's* Ken Rogers at Bellefield, 'I'm not the type of person to give in. I'm still very determined.' But a later comment about the defeat in many ways summed up Harvey's tenure and how his desire for success was not necessarily shared within the dressing room. 'Because of circumstances, last night's match was very important to everyone at the club,' he said. 'But I didn't feel it hurt certain people enough when we lost. No football manager can tolerate that, certainly not me.'

As it happened, unsurprisingly, neither could the board. Like Jimmy Carter, Harvey would now have had reason to open that fabled third envelope. Thirty minutes after speaking to Rogers, Harvey was summoned to a meeting with Philip Carter and came out a short time later as the former manager of Everton. The rather curt club statement said: 'Chairman Philip Carter thanks him for his contribution over 14 years, but stated that the team's recent performances were quite unacceptable.' Harvey admitted, 'It wasn't to be. The opportunity was there to be successful. There was always money available so I never had any problems in that respect. I just didn't knit it all together.'

Hiding to nothing

Like most things in life, timing is everything. And it was for Colin Harvey. 'Nobody needed to tell me the name of the game in Merseyside football,' he said after taking over. 'You start the season on the basis you have to win something big. My problem is following Howard Kendall. I can only go down because I am expected to win the championship again.' However, the new incumbent's job was even more challenging: the only scenario worse than taking over the recently crowned champions is doing so when they have just been crowned champions *and* require something of an overhaul.

All teams, however successful or unsuccessful they are, have a lifespan of three or four years, at most. A glance at the Liverpool sides of the 1970s and 1980s and Manchester United under Alex Ferguson shows that. Harry Catterick had previously gone one better, claiming that the cycle was five years based on the view schoolboys joining at the age of fifteen were ready for first-team action at twenty. However, increased mobility of players two decades later brought that timespan down. By the time Harvey took over the reins the cycle had already reached a natural end – Kendall had started to build his great side five years before. The club's most successful manager probably realised this in 1987. 'Howard Kendall saw the writing on the wall three years ago and got out,' Brian Reade wrote in the *Liverpool Daily Post* after the Oldham FA Cup defeat. 'He knew the side had passed its peak and rather than start the painful rebuilding process he moved on.'

In many respects history was repeating itself. The supposed opportunities for Harvey were like Harry Catterick's in 1970, when the expectation was this 'is a young side that will dominate for the next five years'. But that was not the case, their best years were behind them. Players such as Brian Labone and Johnny Morrissey were in the autumn of their careers. Injuries to key players proliferated whilst previous stalwarts went stale and lost form. Catterick had previously failed to add quality from a position of strength to reinvigorate the squad.

For Harvey it was a similar scenario. Of the inherited squad the only established player brought to the club in the previous three years was Dave Watson, whose transfer was paid for by the Gary Lineker sale. 'A manager should always be looking for signs of disintegration in a winning side and then sell the players responsible before their deterioration is noticed by possible buyers,' the great Peter Taylor wrote in *With Clough by Taylor*. Kendall failed to do this and instead of, say, two other top-class additions – including a striker to replace Lineker – there was a make-do-and-mend approach. In his final three seasons as a manager, from a position of real strength, Kendall's net spend was remarkably just £400,000, against more than £1 million in his first three years, when money was significantly tighter. Players such as Paul Power, Paul Wilkinson, Neil Adams, Wayne Clarke, Neil Pointon and Kevin Langley were good professionals but not individuals to build a title-winning side around.

Consequently, Harvey inherited an unbalanced squad with a surplus of journeymen. 'I wasn't interested in chasing Peter Beardsley,' he said shortly after becoming manager, 'Why because our squad is as good as any in the country.' That belief was his first – and probably biggest – mistake. He failed to acknowledge there was a rebuilding challenge like the ones faced by Graeme Souness at Anfield in 1991 and David Moyes at Old Trafford two decades later. With the lifespan of teams being four years at most, his statement after taking over that 'Everything has worked well for four or five years so I see no reason to change it now' was a costly misjudgement. To keep things working well, changes are regularly needed. By the time he made them the rot had well and truly set in.

The myth of Heysel

Subsequent claims that the break-up of Kendall's team was due to the Heysel ban do not stand up to scrutiny. Blaming the close neighbours – or more specifically their supporters – for the decline during the second half of the decade has always seemed far too convenient. Every player who started the 5-0 victory over Manchester United in October 1984 was still at the club *three years* after the ban was announced. Even without Heysel, the team would have needed restructuring in any case. Momentum does not sustain itself indefinitely, it always requires replenishment.

Peter Reid and Andy Gray were ageing and always had a limited shelf life. Gary Stevens eventually left to take himself out of the tabloid firing line and a failing relationship with Harvey. Trevor Steven, an intelligent, well-advised individual, always maximised his earning potential. Still at Goodison four years after the ban, he found the lure of the Scottish pound irresistible. Elsewhere there was a natural turnover of players: Bracewell's injury problems proved insurmountable, the injury-plagued Mountfield left to improve his chances of first-team football while Van Den Hauwe wanted a return to his capital roots. 'Priorities change,' John Giles once wrote in the *Daily Express*. 'Players who once were willing to run through brick walls of the club who gave them their first chance look to the financially rewarding moves.' Gary Lineker may have been the exception that proves the rule, although the magnetism of Barcelona would probably have been too much whether there was a ban or not. Therefore, contrary to popular belief the European exile did not lead to an immediate mass exodus from Goodison.

Such an argument would have been unnecessary had Harvey's recruitment worked. That initial failure to rebuild was exacerbated by three further years of transfer activity best described as moderate. One of the danger signs was the complete lack of interest from other big clubs – always a red flag – for virtually all his purchases. Of the fifteen players Harvey bought, only Martin Keown was subsequently sold at a significant profit before enjoying a top-class career in England. Too many were also-rans and not good enough. Even the two additions during the summer of 1990 hardly helped. Midfielder Mike Milligan had starred for Oldham but was palpably out of his depth while attacking full-back Andy Hinchcliffe, bought from Manchester City, was weak defensively, which only added to the long-standing issues on the left flank.

Apart from the distinct lack of quality there was the question of personality. Kendall had built a team full of talent but their success was also due to deep reserves of character and resilience. One of Harvey's tasks, therefore, was to ensure continuity in that aspect of recruitment. However, apart from Keown and, possibly, Stuart McCall there were obvious shortcomings in that department, which contributed to a lack of fight when under pressure and manifested itself in dreadful away form. Erratic and inconsistent players such as Pat Nevin and Peter Beagrie were strange signings for a man who was a hard taskmaster as a coach.

'The directors have backed me to the hilt. And it can't be their fault or the fault of the players I've bought here, if it doesn't work out,' he said after the £4.5m transfer splurge in the summer of 1988, 'It will be an error of judgement on my part. The buck stops at the manager's door.' It certainly did.

The old, new and blue

Harvey's time as Everton boss was set against a backdrop of changes in the game that ultimately led to the multi-billion-pound industry of today. Central to that growth was the new £11 million-a-year TV contract signed during the summer of 1988. That huge amount of money – heavily weighted towards the Big Five clubs – naturally ended up in the wallets of the players. The financial implications were immediately apparent. In

Harvey's first season the club's pay bill was £2.2 million with nobody earning more than £100,000. In his final season, after three years of the TV deal, this had almost doubled to £3.9 million with no less than nine employees earning six-figure-plus salaries.

Like his appointment, for Harvey this timing was awkward. Step-changes in salaries had historically proved problematical – *Money Can't Buy Us Love* documented the unrest following the lifting of the maximum wage in 1961 as players, with a greater awareness of their own worth, wanted that value reflected in their pay packet. In 1988 the huge TV deal was announced at a time when Harvey was making his first serious foray into the transfer market. Players (and their representatives), knowing clubs were newly cash-rich, negotiated substantially larger contracts than available twelve months before. Tony Cottee, for example, was earning a higher salary than senior colleagues who had brought unprecedented success earlier in the decade. 'The size of my pay packet was proving a constant source of speculation to the media and, no doubt, my team-mates too,' the former West Ham striker wrote in his autobiography.

As a tough, man-marking central defender, Marton Keown was one of Colin Harvey's rare successful forays into the transfer market.

229

If the new signings had proved top-class – like John Barnes and Peter Beardsley – then the dressing-room equilibrium could have been maintained. Sadly, for Harvey that proved not to be the case. It was no coincidence that, with recent acquisitions struggling, the first rumours of unrest appeared during the autumn of 1988. If older players understandably took umbrage with the pay situation then that was human nature. As indeed was the fear that their first-team places were under threat.[78] However, a strong and experienced manager would have just toughed it out. Harvey was unfortunately neither and the turbulence remained. 'It became obvious that some of the more senior players, who had been at the club a long time, were keen to get a slice of the action themselves,' Cottee wrote. And that eventually happened midway through the 1988/89 campaign as Kevin Ratcliffe, Graeme Sharp, Kevin Sheedy and Neville Southall were given new contracts. As a means of maintaining a fragile dressing-room equilibrium that may have worked but awarding improved and lucrative long-term deals to a corps of ageing players, eager to cash in on their previous glory but collectively past their best, made no sense at all from a footballing and financial perspective. However, Harvey had little choice if any sort of harmony was to be maintained.

The unrest over personal rewards may have been quelled but disunity within the squad remained. Dressing rooms are sensitive pieces of machinery and, as many have commented, there was very much a 'them and us' situation between the old, successful guard and the younger, expensive recruits. There were many factors at play here. First, it is certainly not a given that everyone in the workplace should get on – that is not an issue if performance is unaffected. In addition, immediately before the class of the summer of 1988 arrived there had been tales of discontent, with Harvey's style of management differing from his predecessor and a split between those players he developed and those purchased by Kendall. 'There were clearly some players who didn't get on with each other at all,' Pat Nevin reflected in *The Accidental Footballer* on his initial impressions. 'When I first arrived, there was obviously tension in the dressing room... That tension at the start of the [1988/89] season that I put down to healthy competitiveness was clearly more than that.' Add another group of younger and better-paid players into that environment and there was no surprise deep divisions appeared.

---

[78]   As an example, Cottee felt Wayne Clarke was under pressure after his arrival. Clarke's esteemed older brother, Allan, subsequently wrote two articles in the *Daily Mirror* criticising the club-record signing. Then in a *Match* magazine article published after he left the club in July 1989, Clarke junior let rip about Cottee: 'In my view he's been a complete waste of money...Few people will be surprised if the club off-load him this summer, although they might struggle to recoup the £2 million they paid for him.' Furthermore, Clarke claimed club directors had forced Harvey to field the former West Ham player in the FA Cup semi-final against Norwich. Harvey denied the claim but the story reflects the perceived dysfunction in the dressing room.

In addition, that collective unity required by Kendall naturally made an entrenched group suspicious of outsiders. Newcomers can feel intimidated in that environment. The different age groups ensured varying lifestyles: the older guard, 'encouraged' by Kendall to use alcohol as part of the team-bonding process, were social animals while the younger brigade, perhaps newly-married or with young children, wanted a quieter time. 'We tried to include all new players in everything we did but this particular group didn't want to know,' Graeme Sharp said in his autobiography.

The manager and coaching staff could have sorted out those differences but the harder they tried, the worse they became. Apart from the infamous Sheedy-Keown rumble in Southport, there are several accounts of team-bonding sessions ending disastrously. A four-day golfing holiday in Marbella before Christmas 1989 descended into near anarchy. With continuous rain putting pay to time on the course, players retired to the bar and proved the theory that footballers and alcohol are a combustible combination. 'That led to more sniping and the unbelievable situation, at one stage, where a fight between an older and younger player seemed inevitable,' Cottee recalled, 'Strong words were exchanged, with one set of players blaming the other for the team's poor form, and the mood of unrest continued throughout our stay.' The ill-feeling continued at that year's Christmas party, with the ridiculous sight of the younger players booing the drinking-party songs of the old guard. 'The atmosphere went from frosty to icy between the groups,' Nevin revealed.

Consequently, when things began to go wrong on the pitch, the two factions blamed each other. 'Team spirit had been the foundation of our success. Because we got on so well we felt so comfortable in each other's company that we could criticise one another too,' Neville Southall wrote in *The Binman Chronicles*, 'Now there was tension and infighting.' The older players felt the younger generation were not good enough while the latter felt their senior counterparts were not as competitive as during the glory years. Incongruously, both parties were correct. Equally true is that collectively they should have made the situation work but did not and, as Kevin Ratcliffe admitted, the players never stood up to be counted. 'Many are happy to take the credit when things are going well,' he claimed, 'but they are just as happy to let the manager take the flak when things are going wrong.' Ratcliffe's injury problems did not help. A strong captain at his peak could have helped pull the dressing room together but the Welshman had enough concerns over his own form and fitness and this probably undermined his authority. As he told the *When Shorts were Short* podcast: 'You weren't getting anywhere as a captain, it's as if I wasn't being listened to.' With no appetite to build bridges, by the final year of

Harvey's reign, Nevin claimed the differences were clearly affecting on-field performances. 'Simple things like certain players celebrating more, or indeed only, if one of their mates scored a goal,' he wrote, 'There were times when I felt that I could wait forever to get a pass from certain players because they would always look for their mates first. This is the sort of thing that shouldn't happen beyond the age of eleven.'

Harvey may not have been totally to blame for that incompatibility but it is fair to say his man-management skills did not help. The intensity and demanding nature that were huge attributes as a coach were only half the story for a manager, when the requirement is for both light and shade. His problem was following Kendall, an absolute master in the field. Consequently, from early on, with an inexperienced manager who lacked the softer skills required for the role, there was little surprise when there appeared to be a constant stream of unsettled players or those wanting to leave. Paradoxically, for a hard taskmaster Harvey also lacked ruthlessness and found it awkward making difficult decisions – several players have since claimed he was visibly nervous when delivering bad news. 'He had to leave me out the side once and I could tell he didn't enjoy doing it,' Peter Reid wrote in *Cheer Up Peter Reid*, 'That approach transmitted itself to the players.'

Moreover, a more experienced and confident manager may have offloaded those senior players who were past their best at the end of the decade, rather than offer new deals. Others probably would have implemented stronger sanctions on Southall after his misguided sit-in against Leeds. There is also the feeling that, as a fan since childhood, Harvey craved success *too* much and failure affected him more than others who were more emotionally removed. 'We all desperately wanted him to succeed,' Len Capeling wrote in the *Liverpool Daily Post*, 'but in the end the job almost brought him to his knees. A happy-go-lucky guy became introverted, miserable and, at times, downright abusive.' Harvey later opened up to Rob Sawyer in 2023 for an article on the *Toffeeweb* website about those pressures. 'I didn't manage it particularly well in terms of myself,' he disclosed. 'It was a burden and it got to me. Maybe for other people it would have been a breeze, but it wasn't for me. I was in charge of my own club, and everything got too much for me, I do admit. I would bring it home to Maureen, so it wasn't a good time.'

As Reid said, that burden must have transmitted itself in the dressing room and at Bellefield. Pep Guardiola talks about the loneliness of leadership – the feeling that in hard times it is down to you and you alone – and this was apparent in Harvey's final eighteen months. Following a 1-0 defeat to Chelsea in November 1989 he said afterwards, 'If we didn't do it, it was my fault. I'll accept the responsibility. We let ourselves down in certain positions, but if that is a problem it is mine because I picked them to play there.' Harvey later reflected on the pressures to James Lawton in the *Daily Express*. 'What did I learn?' he said. 'Well, only that managing a football club is an extremely tough job. It could destroy you if you let it.'

That said, a strong coaching team could have provided a buffer but his original selections were unimaginative and lacked gravitas. Harvey should have picked a respected coach from outside as his replacement, somebody who could act as an experienced sounding board for a rookie manager. Don Howe was available in the summer of 1987 and would have been an ideal appointment – Harvey was a huge admirer of his methods and as such he would have provided continuity on the coaching side after working previously with those England internationals in the squad during his time with the national team. Sadly, the hugely knowledgeable and respected coach went to Wimbledon where he was the architect of their FA Cup final victory over Liverpool. By the time Harvey decided to address the issue, by appointing 1960s favourite Jimmy Gabriel as first-team coach in the summer of 1990, it was too little, too late. Also, how much support Philip Carter offered is open to debate. Whereas with Kendall there appeared to be a shoulder to lean on, that never appeared to be the case with Carter and Harvey. Indeed, Carter's 1990 public criticism of performances and cold words after Harvey's sacking indicate that the opposite was true.

All those issues ultimately impacted performances. Kendall's successor never really got to grips with maintaining and developing the style of play he had helped create earlier in the decade. As personnel aged and changed, the torque of the pressing game, so central to the team's strategy, diminished. With Sheedy in constant dispute and Steven failing to restore the inventiveness and quality that had illuminated two title-winning campaigns, their influence lessened. With Gary Stevens' departure also hampering the attacking potential of the side, they effectively became flat-earthers, revisiting the age-old strategy of knocking it long to Graeme Sharp and taking it from there. Although Nevin offered the occasional piece of inventiveness, the outcome was all a bit one-dimensional with the goals output between 25-30 per season less than in the glory years.

Everton remained competitive because defensively they were, for the first two seasons at least, better than during the middle of the decade. Not only was Southall at the apex of his career but Ratcliffe and Watson are still probably the club's finest central defensive duo. 'Dave Watson became my favourite defensive partner,' the club skipper later admitted. 'He had a little bit more technically than Mark Higgins and Derek Mountfield and I could rely on Dave more if I made a mistake.' However, their influence waned following the long-term effects of Ratcliffe's hernia problem, due to his injury at

Sheffield Wednesday in January 1988. 'I remember going through my rehabilitation with the physio and he was outsprinting me,' Ratcliffe said, 'I just didn't have that gear. All of a sudden what was natural wasn't there anymore.' Martin Keown was a valuable addition but his main attribute as a hugely-effective man-marker disturbed the defensive equilibrium. That said, the overarching on-the-pitch problem was that the new recruits were inferior to those they were intended to replace.

Harvey failed for all those reasons, from the detrimental timing of the appointment to his own poor decisions. He was also let down by his squad, of that there is no doubt. 'Harvey's managerial dream was put to a long, lingering death by the inertia of players who feuded and fiddled while the legacy of Kendall simply haemorrhaged,' James Lawton later wrote in the *Daily Express*.

Ultimately he was joining a long list of top-class coaches who found the challenge of moving into the responsibility seat too much. As a coach you are both confidant and critical friend, capable of issuing a rollicking one minute while putting an arm round players' shoulders the next, of massaging bruised egos and then emphasising how good they are. At that time, a coach skirted round the two biggest headaches of the manager's role: what to pay players and who to select. Consequently, your sphere of power is limited. Managers take the big decisions and must put a distance between themselves and those who once trusted them. Like Harvey, the former Chelsea, QPR and Manchester United manager Dave Sexton was a gifted coach who never really felt comfortable when promoted. His former striker Don Givens once reflected on Sexton:

> He always gave me the impression that he would rather do without certain aspects of a manager's job. He loved to work with the players and put all his ability into practice and I don't think he wanted the aggravation caused by having to leave players out of the team, which is an essential part of the job. The only criticism we could have of him was that he wasn't strict enough with certain players.

All those statements apply to Harvey during his time as manager. He was not the first to learn that whereas coaches make players better, managers need to make teams better. There were few more accomplished at the former but the latter required a different mind- and skill-set entirely, for which his predecessor, in his peak years, possessed all the right cards. Consequently, Harvey was always fated to operate in the half-light of Kendall's shadow. Having said that he was admirably candid about the experience. 'Not having won anything was the biggest disappointment of the lot,' he told Simon Hart for *Here We Go*,

'The whole tenure was not good enough.'

That was sad. One of the greatest Evertonians of all deserved far more.

25.
DER KAISER TO
'ER INDOORS

THOSE DISAPPOINTED EVERTON SUPPORTERS SCROLLING THROUGH the BBC's Ceefax service on the afternoon of Tuesday, 6 November 1990 were greeted by the headline news that manager Graham Taylor had recalled the 32-year-old Aston Villa midfielder Gordon Cowans to the England squad for the forthcoming game against the Republic of Ireland. Elsewhere, in the small print there were early previews of Villa's and Manchester United's European games – a cruel reminder of how events elsewhere had conspired against them five years before. Although cynics could have reasonably argued sustained progress should have ensured an Everton return when the ban was lifted in the summer of 1990. Sadly, there was no update on Harvey's replacement.

The latest news on the managerial position had been delivered by Jim Greenwood on the day before: they expected to fill the vacancy in the next 48 hours. Among the early front-runners, Steve Coppell and Ron Atkinson had been ruled out, so there was only one logical candidate remaining. 'Royle ascent expected at Goodison' proclaimed the *Guardian* on the Tuesday morning. It had always been an awkward position for the club's former striker – his close friendship with Harvey precluded him from making any comments on the role. Indeed, that respect meant Royle did not speak to the press after Oldham had removed Everton from the FA Cup, fearing he would be asked about Harvey's future and his chances of getting the job.

Yet, according to the *People*, the post could already have been filled by one of the biggest names in the game. The Sunday tabloid claimed that in April there had been a startling, largely unknown, development, with club officials meeting with Franz Beckenbauer[79] in Stockholm with an agreement for the legendary German to take over

---

[79]   The German was not the only international skipper linked with the role. Bryan Robson was in the final year of his contract at Old Trafford and an approach was made on his behalf. However, the England great was only interested in taking up the job at the end of the campaign and the Goodison hierarchy were not prepared to wait.

after the World Cup. 'I understand one of England's leading clubs has already set up a summer deal for the fabulous Kaiser of West German football,' reported Bill Bradshaw. 'My information is that Everton want Beckenbauer to mastermind a renewed assault on the game's top prizes.' Then the trail sadly went cold before Beckenbauer eventually took over at Marseille. Naturally, later in the year the now World Cup-winning manager denied the story. 'It was just a rumour,' he assured Ric George of the *Liverpool Echo*. 'No-one asked me to come. It was mentioned in some of the newspapers but I said: "No, sorry." Nobody has asked me about it. It was just speculation.'

But when the Ceefax service eventually delivered the name of Harvey's successor at about 4.30 p.m. that evening it was a move even more eye-opening than Der Kaiser wandering into Goodison Park.

Returning to the marital home

'You'll always be welcome back here,' said one Everton supporter when Howard Kendall left for Bilbao in June 1987. And that was the case when the club's most successful manager was unveiled as Harvey's successor in one of Goodison's lounges to a shocked media at just before 7 p.m. on that night. To say the Everton board had pulled off a sensational coup was a complete understatement. 'It's the world's best-kept secret,' Jim Greenwood told the packed room. The assumption within the media that Joe Royle was the near-certainty worked in Everton's favour. By not denying the story they could use it as a smokescreen, enabling them to work on bringing Kendall back out of the spotlight. Royle's link was 'just media speculation,' Philip Carter revealed. 'Howard Kendall was always our first choice.'

Although Royle had been the expected appointment, when Greenwood asked each of the directors who they wanted as the manager, they all responded in turn: Kendall. However, at the welcoming press conference there were some discrepancies around how the return came about. Carter said the first contact with anybody had been with Peter Swales on the Monday and the City chairman rejected the approach. With Kendall having a release clause in his contract, Swales allowed Carter access to his manager after a second phone call, before informing Kendall of Everton's interest. Nevertheless, the new Everton manager contradicted Carter's statement, claiming the initial approach had been in the previous week, something Swales was obviously unaware of.

Kendall later revealed in *Love Affairs & Marriage* that Everton's interest had been made known to him by an unnamed journalist friend, who had originally told him about Harvey's sacking. Although denying there was anything untoward in that conversation, he claimed the journalist then took it upon himself to inform the club that Kendall was keen on returning.[80] Within 48 hours he was approached by a go-between who asked whether the vacancy would be of interest. That timescale fits in with the claim in his first book, *Only the Best is Good Enough*, which stated that he telephoned Everton on Saturday, 3 November – three days after Harvey was sacked – to inform them he wanted the job. Carter claimed at the press conference that Everton had 'to observe all the proprieties which we were scrupulous to do so.' That was obviously not the case.

The remainder of the press conference was notable for two reasons. The first was the presence of a familiar face at Kendall's side. Like the new manager, a beaming Colin Harvey also contradicted the chairman, saying that 'he had heard a bit of something' in the previous week. 'I just hoped it would come to fruition,' the recalled first-team coach revealed, 'Obviously it has and I am delighted about it. It took me two and a half seconds to decide.' Everybody found it hard to decide which was the bigger shock: Kendall's return or Harvey's re-instatement to a post he had filled with distinction, a week after being sacked as a manager. Asked for his reasons for leaving, Kendall responded: 'After fourteen years at this club I could not refuse to return.' Then there was one of the most famous quotes in the club's history: 'If it was a love affair with Manchester City, it was a marriage to Everton.' As David Lacey delightfully put it in the *Guardian*: 'Or put it another way, Manchester City had been Howard's bit on the side but it was time to go back to 'er indoors.'

Coming full circle

One of the surprises of the move was Kendall left a Manchester City outfit very much on the rise. Lying fifth in the table and unbeaten in ten league matches, the side possessed quality young talent like Paul Lake and David White – unlike the team he was renewing acquittances with. That said, Kendall had recruited some familiar faces in Peter Reid, Adrian Heath, Alan Harper, Neil Pointon and Wayne Clarke. Ten days before, on the eve

---

[80] The journalist in question being the late Bob Cass of the *Mail on Sunday*. In his 2017 autobiography Cass revealed his version of events which begin in the Copthorne Hotel in Salford on the evening of the Sheffield United game, City having lost at home to Arsenal on the same night. With the belief that Harvey would be sacked, Kendall told Cass that 'I wouldn't mind going back there if I got the chance.' Indeed Kendall spoke to Harvey on the phone. Cass claimed he was asked to act as go-between and on the following lunchtime, after Harvey's sacking, he telephoned Jim Greenwood – in Kendall's presence – from his hotel room. After putting forward Kendall's case, the Everton chief executive responded, 'I might have a word, do you know where he is?' Cass gave him the Copthorne's number. 'True to his word he [Kendall] telephoned me around nine o'clock that evening,' Cass wrote, '"I've spoken to the Everton people and I think I've got a good chance of the job," he announced. "There's one or two things which need tidying up."' In 1993 Jim Greenwood confirmed the call in the *Liverpool Echo*: 'Within ten minutes of Colin's departure being announced, I had received a call advising us that Howard was ready, willing and available to come back to Goodison Park. From this it was a one-horse race.'

of the Manchester derby, he had proclaimed that 'I would not want to manage any other club.' But now he was back. Kendall returning to Goodison three-and-a-half years after leaving was perhaps an indicator of a career path that had not developed as expected. Indeed, departing after just eleven months in the City job left a bad taste in the mouth for many. 'There is a cynical taste about the whole 11-month episode. A lot of careers, both on and off the field, have been disrupted,' David Lacey commented.

Nevertheless, the unexpected development proved that Kendall was still a manager very much in demand. At Bilbao there had been two attempts from Newcastle in the autumn of 1988 to capture his services and chairman Gordon McKeag even flew over to Spain with an offer of £1 million over five years. Kendall rejected their overtures and a job offer from Leeds United suffered the same fate. Kendall also turned down the Juventus job during this period, according to Brian Glanville – who had long-standing connections with Italian football – in a June 1990 syndicated newspaper column.

Additionally, Barcelona were always in the background, even when he was established in northern Spain. Terry Venables had been sacked in September 1987 and, with successor Luis Aragonés viewed very much as a stop-gap, four months later the Nou Camp giants made a third effort to snare their prey. Kendall rejected their offer but a fourth – £1 million over three years – was more appealing. Following four rounds of talks the likelihood was the former Everton boss would finally journey to Catalonia but ultimately his loyalty to the Basque club, and their people, won the day. 'They did make it very hard for me to say no but in the end I asked myself what was most important,' he told James Lawton, 'I decided it was to do a job for the people here – the people who did everything right by me.'

There were other potential job opportunities for Kendall. He was perennially linked with Manchester United when Alex Ferguson was struggling and Arsenal were rumoured to be lining him up at Highbury should George Graham jump ship. However, the manager of the national team prompted most discussion. With Bobby Robson under fire after a disastrous European Championship in 1988, the former Everton manager was naturally associated with the job. To be fair Kendall always played a straight bat. 'While Robson is still in charge I refuse to comment on whether I would like to be the next England manager,' he said in October of that year, before pointedly adding, 'If the situation changed then so would my attitude towards discussing the England job.'

At that stage Graham Taylor was odds-on betting favourite with Terry Venables at 4-1 and Kendall third at 5-1. Twelve months later the momentum had shifted. With Taylor and Venables struggling at Aston Villa and Tottenham Hotspur respectively, the exiled

Bilbao boss held the upper hand. 'If Kendall really wants the job – and by a process of elimination he is now an overwhelming favourite – he should stay in virtual hiding,' John Giles wrote in his *Daily Express* column, 'And if things do go wrong between now and the end of his contract – and next summer's World Cup – he should stay in the shadows.'

But choosing the England manager has long been a case of musical chairs – select the flavour of the month rather than somebody possessing years of experience and wisdom – and to an extent that subsequently happened. Firstly, the manner of Kendall's departure from Bilbao counted against him. Then, rather than wisely following Giles' advice and becoming a better manager *in absentia*, he pitched up at Manchester City, coincidentally run by Peter Swales, also vice-chairman of the FA's International Selection Committee. With Taylor and Venables now having rejuvenated their clubs – Aston Villa were challenging for the title – Kendall was now fighting relegation with City. In terms of managing England, it was not the smartest career move as by the end of the season Taylor had been reinstated as the front-runner and was 2/7 on favourite for the job, with Venables 4/1 and Kendall 7/1. On the last Friday of May 1990, 24 hours after Bobby Robson's departure was announced, Kendall revealed he had turned down the FA's opportunity for an interview. 'It is no secret that at one stage I was very interested in becoming the manager of England,' he admitted to the *Manchester Evening News*. 'That is why when I took over at Maine Road I insisted on a release clause in my contract…There would seem little point in going along to the FA to be interviewed if in my heart I knew that didn't want to leave Maine Road.'

Yet in *Love Affairs & Marriage* Kendall suspected interference from Swales: 'Peter was one of the key people in the selection process for the job, and although I was on the shortlist…I was never under serious consideration by the FA.' Kendall then recalled a conversation with Swales: '"You didn't want the job, did you, Howard?" he [Swales] said to me slyly, thus dismissing in a sentence all those hard-fought negotiations.' Like several matters with Kendall after 1987, this strange sequence of events leaves many unanswered questions, such as why did Kendall believe Swales could block him having agreed a release clause in his contract? Also why did he feel the FA would not treat his application seriously when he clearly had the best CV of any candidate and they had already put feelers out for him at Bilbao before offering him an interview?

Perhaps he thought, with Taylor being the strong favourite, that the whole process was a *fait accompli* and rejection after an interview would damage his reputation and relationship with the players. As he said at the time: 'I cannot preach loyalty to them with one breath and then with the next walk out to take up a job elsewhere.' Ultimately, there was a sense that, like on other occasions, the wrong man got the job when Taylor was appointed. 'This was a blow to those who believed, like myself, that England badly needed someone with continental experience,' Brian Glanville concluded in *The Sunday Times*, 'Kendall seemed an excellent choice in many ways.'

In retrospect there was one twist of fate in the selection process, which occurred in the unlikely surroundings of the Polish mining town of Katowice in October 1989. With England needing a draw to guarantee participation in the following summer's World Cup finals, the game was still goalless when in the final seconds the home side struck the underside of Peter Shilton's bar. Had that gone in, there would have been no memorable Italia '90 and Bobby Robson was out of a job. At that moment in time Kendall was the favourite and the likelihood is within days the FA would have been putting in a telephone call to northern Spain. But England survived in Katowice and Kendall's big chance had gone.

The challenge

'The re-appointment of Howard Kendall at the Goodison helm is nothing sort of a master stroke,' proclaimed a *Liverpool Echo* editorial on the day after his appointment. 'It is excellent news that the Kendall-Harvey partnership is back in harness at Goodison. They have brought glory days to Goodison once before. They can do it again.' Yet, once the romance and novelty aspect had been forgotten, there were many questions marks over this multi-dimensional reconciliation.

There were no prizes for guessing what was Kendall's first test: healing a fractured squad. 'I arrived back in November 1990 to an unhappy dressing room,' he later wrote in *Love Affairs & Marriage*, 'It was cliquish, and I just felt there were two different groups going out to play together, going out to train together, but changing in the same dressing room.' However, appointing somebody whose first job was to heal a dressing-room schism, while being closely associated with one of the groups, did not seem a wise choice. Rather than wounds healing, there was always the risk of them widening. That was one of the reasons why confidants had told Kendall not to take the job, while several within the Goodison hierarchy were reportedly not exactly enamoured by Harvey's return. Consequently, a neutral choice may have been more astute, but the Everton board were hoping the old magic would return.

Kendall may have said that 'I'll be ruthless to put it right' but the club he was joining – and the footballing environment in which they were all operating – was a different beast to the one he had left just three-and-a-half years before.

26

MERSEYSIDE'S MONUMENT TO FOOTBALL

'BEFORE HOWARD KENDALL'S TRIUMPHANT HOMECOMING, EVERTON looked demoralised and disorientated,' David Hopps wrote in the *Guardian* following a disheartening 2-0 defeat at Leeds United in mid-December, 'Now, more than two months later, they look, well, largely the same.'

The defeat left Kendall with just one victory in his opening six games while there was still a debate whether the new manager was the right choice to heal a wounded dressing room. That said, the consensus was the appointment was welcomed by senior professionals. 'It is great news that Howard and Colin are back together again,' Neville Southall declared. Others were more sceptical. Some of the younger players felt threatened because, at Manchester City, Kendall had gone back to the tried and trusted he had worked with before. The 'them and us' scenario that had infected the Harvey years also showed no signs of abating, according to Tony Cottee. 'My fears soon proved well founded,' he wrote in *Claret and Blues*. 'When Howard arrived for training the next morning [after his appointment], he went round shaking hands with all the players who had played under him in his previous spell in charge, virtually ignoring the rest of us.'

In some ways that behaviour, initially at least, was understandable. However, if Kendall ultimately proved there were no favourites then there was also a possibility of changing fortunes. That eventually happened, thanks to an unlikely intervention from one of the heroes of Italia '90.

Take Platt

Ironically Kendall's first game in charge of his second coming came at Bramall Lane, where his predecessor had crashed and burned. Strangely, a tepid goalless draw started a war of words between Kendall and the Blades boss, Dave Bassett. In the programme notes for his first home match, a televised 1-1 draw against Spurs, Kendall remarked that 'games with Sheffield United are never the most entertaining.' The comments provoked a sharp response from Bassett. 'If the match was disappointing, then it takes two to tango,' he wrote in United's next programme, 'It has always been known that Howard's teams have never been the most attack-minded in the country…And I am disappointed that he should have a go at us.'

The spat was merely a sideshow to what had been a poor start. After a 2-1 defeat at Wimbledon at the end of November saw them back in the drop zone, Kendall warned: 'There have been a number of clubs in the past who have said, "We are too good to go down" …I don't want to create panic or anything like that, but you look at the league table and realise you are in a serious position.'

The problems were familiar. There was a lack of pace at both back and front. The midfield failings were still there – a painful absence of quality and creativity in the first instance. However, the misfiring, unbalanced forward line was still the biggest issue. Like Harvey, the new boss was struggling to get the best out of the Sharp-Cottee-Newell axis, so much so that for his fourth game – a 1-0 home defeat to a rising Manchester United – Kendall was already testing his fourth different striking combination. At least by jettisoning Sharp against Alex Ferguson's side, Kendall was showing past reputations counted for nothing. Although recent signings may have been assured that there were no sacred cows, issues were still there. Having been sold by Kendall at Manchester City because of concerns over his defensive capability, Andy Hinchcliffe was more vulnerable than most. 'Howard was an incredible guy, and what he did for Everton was fantastic, but he just didn't rate me,' the full-back later said. For the 1-0 defeat at Norwich three days before Christmas, presciently Kendall played the Mancunian on the left-hand side of midfield. Above all, though, even at this early stage the manager must have realised the extent of the decline. 'The players were doing my job for me when they saw things happen on the field they didn't agree with,' he had said about the glory years after re-joining, yet there was no sign of that in his opening six weeks in charge. The mix of personalities was now completely different. 'Kendall has tried almost every combination of available players with very little improvement,' Cynthia Bateman concluded in the *Guardian*.

Howard Kendall greets the fans in the first game after his shock return, but the decision to re-appoint his predecessor as coach was not necessarily well-received by the Everton board.

By the time Everton faced Aston Villa at Goodison on Boxing Day they were sixteenth in the table, a point off the relegation places with just three league victories all season. Unusually for a home game, Kendall played Sharp as a lone striker and packed the midfield with five players. 'You don't expect too much from the Blues these days which, in itself is an indictment of their current form and standing,' Ken Rogers commented in the *Liverpool Echo*.

Making a debut at right-back was a local-born twenty-year-old, Eddie Youds, who eventually provided the crucial intervention during a mind-numbing contest in a howling gale before 27,804 frozen spectators. While Southall was at his outstanding best, twice thwarting pacy winger Tony Daley, the home team produced few moments of inspiration. Summarising on local radio, Brian Labone feared Everton were serious relegation candidates. Then with twelve minutes remaining came a goal as welcome as it was unexpected. The novice Youds galloped down the right, kept cool and looked up. His accurate cross picked out Sharp who had the easy task of heading home. But with the game deep into injury time, there was one of the most extraordinary incidents in Goodison's long history. Gordon Cowan's corner was flicked on by Kent Nielsen and sailed towards the goal-line at the far post. As the away fans were about to celebrate the late equaliser, England international David Platt, in wishing to make sure, only succeeded in hooking the ball back into play as it was about to cross the line. 'It was a great clearance,' a relieved Kendall quipped after a second win in nine games, 'Perhaps he wants to play for us; perhaps he doesn't want us to go down.'

The vital win acted as the long-awaited catalyst for an upturn in fortunes. Three successive victories followed before Manchester City – now managed by Peter Reid – arrived in mid-January for a game televised live on ITV in frozen conditions. The visiting supporters hardly welcomed the brief encounter. Several offensive banners were removed by the police although one – 'Even our cat hates Howard Kendall' – remained on the terraces at the Park End, as did another simply saying 'Judas'. However, it was the home side who ran off with the silver following a dominant 2-0 victory. The highlight was the final great strike of Sheedy's distinguished Everton career. After Peter Beagrie's headed pass bounced up awkwardly at the edge of the box, the midfielder simply altered his body shape, twisted in mid-air and hooked the ball over his right shoulder past Tony Coton. It was another worthy entry into his canon of sublime goals. Beagrie had earlier opened the scoring and celebrated with his customary double-somersault. 'He must have been practising it at home, we've never seen it before,' Kendall pointedly remarked afterwards. Everton's recovery was confirmed by five successive victories which had last happened in the title run-in four years before. 'For the first time in many weeks, players whose skill has never been in question but whose application has been dubious, combined as a unit,' Ian Ross declared in *The Times*.

Man of the match, though, was John Ebbrell, the graduate of the FA's School of Excellence completely overshadowing the City player-manager in midfield. Ebbrell was becoming an increasingly influential figure, his rich vein of form featuring goals which started a cup run ultimately signalling the end of a glorious era.

Collision course

The FA Cup third round had produced a tricky away tie at Lennie Lawrence's Charlton Athletic and Ebbrell's brace secured a deserved 2-1 win. 'It is difficult to imagine the Everton of a few months ago coming from a goal down on a squally day against such lively Second Division opponents,' said Paul Wilson in the *Guardian*.

With cup-specialist Kendall at the helm, Everton were attractively priced at 16-1 before the visit to London and those odds reduced when the draw produced an away tie at non-league Woking, who had just shocked West Brom 4-1 at the Hawthorns. The Vauxhall Conference side – six leagues below their opponents – set aside cup romance by moving the tie to Goodison where they benefited financially to the tune of £90,000 – ten times more money than they would have received if they had used their home ground – from a 34,724 gate paying £220,000.

They certainly acquitted themselves well with a mature, intelligent display which embarrassed a nervous Everton – incongruously clad in their all-blue away kit. With Woking creating several half-chances, the big favourites produced only one moment of quality befitting their status: just before the hour mark Neil McDonald's cross reached Sharp and the Scot set up Sheedy to fire home. Six years before non-league Telford had left the pitch to a torrent of abuse after a brutal display had left several Everton players booking time on the treatment table. In contrast Kendall's side remained on the pitch for three minutes at the end of the game so they could congratulate their opponents at the players' tunnel, after the vanquished heroes had first taken the plaudits of supporters. 'We said Woking would make it difficult and they did,' admitted an unhappy Kendall after the game. 'We didn't have that many chances and we didn't have many stars on Sunday.'

But twenty-four hours later in the fifth-round draw came an unwanted tie – a visit to Anfield should Liverpool beat Brighton & Hove Albion in their replay.

The Nevin upending story

Three days later Dalglish's side duly won on the south coast to book a first FA Cup tie on the ground between the two rivals since 1905.[81] On the first Saturday of February they staged a dress rehearsal at the same venue. Although Liverpool had started with twelve victories in thirteen matches, their form faltered following a notoriously defensive team selection which contributed to a 3-0 loss at nearest challengers Arsenal before Christmas.

Indeed, like their rivals across the park, the bumper 1988 television deal had a similarly destabilising effect, forcing the Anfield hierarchy to offer inflated contracts to several players past their best. With the ageing team creaking, there had been just one win in six league games while Dalglish had just signed Millwall winger Jimmy Carter and a 31-year-old David Speedie – strange acquisitions which raised eyebrows but carried more significance in the light of later events.

On another freezing cold day, the home team went ahead with a fortuitous goal. Poor defensive headers by Ratcliffe and Watson led to Jan Molby receiving the ball at the edge of the box and the big Dane's left-footed strike struck Watson with the deflection wrong-footing the unlucky Southall. Rather than shrivel, the visitors went on the offensive. 'To their great credit, Everton were not a bit demoralised by what might have been a

---

[81]   The fourteen previous FA Cup encounters between the clubs having been split equally between Goodison and neutral venues.

demoralising goal,' Brian Glanville wrote in *The Sunday Times*, 'There is plenty of talent, abundant skill, in their team.' That ability resulted in Sharp's header being brilliantly stopped by Grobbelaar before one of the Everton goalkeeper's greatest moments, at the Kop end. 'The save with which Southall answered was simply astonishing,' Patrick Barclay wrote in the *Observer*. Steve Staunton's cross was met by a beautifully-struck John Barnes volley which the Welshman somehow pushed over. 'No wonder Barnes and Speedie instinctively patted the keeper's head,' Barclay remarked.

Although Nevin equalised on the stroke of half-time, two Speedie goals in the second half clinched a fifth successive derby victory for the red half of the city. That said, the defeat was harsh on the visitors, who had the better of play for long periods. 'We know where we went wrong and, hopefully, it won't happen again, for a couple of weeks, at least,' Kendall quipped, referencing the return visit eight days later. Consequently, before the fifth-round tie, the Everton boss was optimistic. 'There has been a bubble about the place,' he said, 'If we had lost 3-1 and been over-run for 90 minutes we would have been going back with some apprehension, but that wasn't the case.' The bookmakers, as expected, thought differently: Everton were 7-2 outsiders against Liverpool's 6-5 on.

On a beautifully sunlit Sunday afternoon, for a match broadcast live on the BBC,[82] Kendall's optimism proved well-founded in a brilliantly entertaining game. With Nevin enjoying a free role behind Sharp, the winger had one of his best outings for the club as well as being involved in an infamous incident that still resonates. Surprisingly, the visitors had Liverpool on the ropes for long periods after Steve McMahon had left the fray in the opening fifteen minutes. The former Everton player's lunge from distance at John Ebbrell was both dangerous and reckless but, with the Toffees midfielder not backing off either, McMahon only succeeded in damaging his own knee ligaments. Jimmy Hill, presenting the BBC coverage, told a nationwide audience it was McMahon's fault: 'There's a line over which professional players should not transgress, even in a local derby.' In a clear case of the biter bit, Ebbrell miraculously escaped serious injury. 'His shinpad,' joked Kendall, 'is going into hospital for treatment.' With the three-man central defence nullifying the Liverpool attack thereafter, if not exactly one-way traffic, a determined and enterprising Everton enjoyed as positive a half at Anfield as any in recent memory. 'The Liverpool defenders frequently shielded their eyes against the western sun,' Stephen Bierley wrote in the *Guardian*, 'That sun must have looked blue.'

---

[82]   Much to the chagrin of Alex Ferguson. The man from Govan was not impressed: 'The decision shows a lack of imagination from the TV people. There were plenty of interesting ties, such as Portsmouth against Tottenham and Notts County against Manchester City.'

Neil McDonald twice forced Grobbelaar into good saves from distance whilst Glenn Hysen's blind back-pass went straight to Sharp but the striker – not for the first time on the ground – failed to take advantage of an opponent's error and the Liverpool goalkeeper smothered his weak shot. Just before the break Grobbelaar had to be equally on his toes when steering a close-range Martin Keown header over the crossbar.

However, Everton's attempts to pull off an audacious coup were undermined by a quite unbelievable incident five minutes before the break. The hugely experienced and capable referee, Neil Midgley, was taking charge of a sixth derby game but usually sound judgement deserted him and baffled millions watching at home. The dangerous Nevin skipped past Gary Ablett inside the penalty area but the Liverpool defender slid in and sent the winger flying and tumbling to the turf in front of the visiting fans who packed the Anfield Road end. 'The referee has pointed to the spot,' commentator Barry Davies exclaimed with no surprise, 'No, he's pointed for a goal kick!' he then added incredulously. Meanwhile co-commentator Trevor Brooking was equally nonplussed. 'You'll never see a more clear-cut penalty,' the former West Ham midfielder admitted.

Why one of the best referees – if not the best – of the era failed to award a spot-kick still perplexes to this day. Perhaps because of a similar incident involving both players in the preceding league derby when referee Lester Shapter did not award a spot-kick when Ablett clearly clipped Nevin's leg in virtually the same spot. Shapter could only have thought Nevin made the most of it and Midgley obviously felt the same. The referee admonishing Nevin for diving only rubbed salt into the wounds. 'If you wanted to look up the rules of what is and what isn't a penalty,' the winger wrote in his autobiography, 'then a video of that incident would be a perfect example of a "stonewaller."' Interviewed by the BBC after the game, Dalglish declared: 'I don't care what the TV evidence suggests. I certainly think it wasn't a penalty.'[83]

Even so, within seconds of the restart the maverick winger had a great chance to put Everton ahead. The Liverpool central defence failed to clear a Southall goal-kick and the ball bounced invitingly for Nevin just inside the penalty area; however, the winger watched in anguish as a lob over Grobbelaar fell inches wide of the post at the Kop end. But then Kevin Sheedy's departure through a hamstring injury led to a midfield reshuffle. 'When Pat Nevin dropped back we also lost our effectiveness up front because he had

---

[83] Nevin went on to describe a humorous epilogue. Sitting in a restaurant that summer, he recalled the comment to his wife, who said she thought Dalglish was talking nonsense. Nevin asked whether she would tell him directly that was the case. 'Absolutely!' came the reply. She, however, was unaware that Dalglish and his wife were sitting behind her. When he came over, Mrs Nevin politely voiced her opinion. Dalglish laughed and said, 'Obviously it was a penalty, but I had to back my player.'

been causing them problems,' Kendall said afterwards. 'Our system worked well until Sheedy went off.' Meanwhile, Liverpool only threatened after Peter Beardsley entered the fray with twenty minutes remaining. Ratcliffe had to kick off the line with Rush prowling and the substitute struck the outside of the post with a fierce drive near the end. 'The Kop were finally on song,' Ken Rogers wrote in the *Liverpool Echo*. 'But the noise at the other end on the final whistle suggested the visitors had got their tactics and their attitude exactly right on the day.'

A delighted Kendall refused to dwell on the penalty that never was 24 hours later. 'What happened yesterday has gone,' he said. 'We can't keep going on about it…By bringing them back to our place, we have gained a little psychological advantage.' Although nobody could realise at the time, the butterfly effect of Midgley's decision caused ripples that are still felt today.

Game of a lifetime

If there had not been an equaliser forty seconds from the end of normal time, then the FA Cup fifth-round replay would have been largely remembered as a wonderfully entertaining and dramatic contest where the extra quality possessed by the Anfield outfit counted at the end. But the sixth goal of the evening changed that narrative completely and ultimately helped elevate a magnificent replay into the pantheon of truly great domestic skirmishes.

However, all that was merely a pipedream in the days beforehand. For Kendall there was a question of changing tactics and forcing the issue with home advantage or retaining the three-man central defence which had operated so effectively at Anfield. Typically, caution reigned and the Everton boss went with Keown as sweeper behind Watson and Ratcliffe. With Beardsley recalled, the decision did not sit well with his skipper. 'I wasn't too happy with Howard,' Ratcliffe said. 'He was asking me to mark Peter Beardsley who would drop deep and end up on the right wing. I wasn't happy going out there when I knew the danger was behind me.'

Ratcliffe had previously been playing that role and felt that he should swap with Keown, even then renowned as a very good man-marker, but Kendall refused. 'Howard wanted to give us some balance and he gave Martin Keown a free role,' Ratcliffe told the *Guardian* in 2018. 'The worst thing you could do was give Martin Keown a free role. He was probably one of the best markers in the game, think of all the man-marking jobs he did brilliantly for Arsenal, but you didn't want to give him too much to think about.'

With Sheedy and McMahon out injured, there were several changes for the replay.

Neil McDonald moved into midfield to replace the Ireland international and, with Andy Hinchcliffe back from injury, John Ebbrell – who played left-back at Anfield – switched with the dropped McCall. Kendall also recalled Mike Newell so was effectively playing a 3-4-3 formation. Unsurprisingly, referee Midgley entered the arena to large-scale boos and one Everton fan jokingly put a Liverpool scarf round his neck as the referee posed for pictures with mascots before the game. It is largely forgotten now, but with no Ronnie Whelan or McMahon the centre of the Liverpool midfield featured the unlikely partnership of Jan Molby and David Burrows. Nevertheless, the odd pairing gave Liverpool extra bite and fluency missing at Anfield and, whereas in the first game Everton gained the upper hand, they were quickly on the back foot on home turf. The visitors' chances materialised immediately. Southall surprisingly failed to gather Beardsley's shot but made up for the error by blocking Rush's attempt on the rebound. John Barnes then fired into the side-netting when well-placed at the edge of the six-yard box. In between Ebbrell shot wide from Sharp's knockdown.

Then on 32 minutes came the first goal after two hours of compelling combat. And ironically the source was a mistake by Everton's disgruntled central defender. Ratcliffe went out to the right-back position to pick up a long pass but, instead of putting the ball into touch, he tried to push it past Rush, who nicked the ball off his international team-mate. The Liverpool striker homed in on Southall but was denied by a miraculous goal-line clearance by Hinchcliffe. Unfortunately for the defender, this found its way towards Beardsley who scored with a half-volley. For the remainder of the half the home team struggled to get a kick as their rivals settled into their familiar passing rhythm.

However, it was a different story after the break. Kendall attempted to disrupt Molby's midfield dominance by bringing on McCall for the struggling Ray Atteveld and was rewarded within two minutes. Hinchcliffe's cross from the left picked out Sharp and Grobbelaar – whose starting position was too deep – only succeeded in parrying the ball into his net. With McCall cancelling out Molby, for the first time in the game Everton gained a beachhead and Nevin wasted a glorious opportunity to put them ahead. After a mix-up between Hysen and Gary Ablett at the edge of the area, the ball fell perfectly for the winger but his trademark shovelled chip went over Grobbelaar and, sadly for the home fans, over the bar too. At the other end, Beardsley was playing like a man on a personal crusade to show that his manager was wrong to jettison him at Anfield and on 71 minutes put Liverpool ahead with a superb second goal. The England international brushed aside Nevin with ease, moved across vacant space at the edge of the penalty area and his vintage left-footed strike arrowed past Southall. Everton suffered for not taking advantage of their second-half ascendancy for precisely two minutes. Grobbelaar should have allowed Steve Nicol to clear Newell's flick but only succeeded in making a harmless situation catastrophic by obstructing the defender and allowing a sliding Sharp to knock the loose ball home before it ran over the line.

'I'm sure we haven't seen the end of the goals,' said an admiring Andy Gray in his fledgling BSkyB co-commentary role and the former Everton hero was proved correct within minutes. The home defence failed to close Molby down from a corner and the Dane's cross was met by the familiar head of a poorly-marked Rush, who rekindled the Wembley nightmare of two years before by glancing the ball past Southall. With their arch-tormenter looking to have scored the winner yet again, as the game drifted into the final minute those agonised Everton fans in the 37,766 crowd – 3,000 tickets ironically remaining unsold for the match of a lifetime – could have been forgiven for thinking the screenplay was following an all-too-familiar script. Tony Cottee had come on for Nevin with five minutes left, with the former West Ham man on a mission. 'Howard wanted me to play like Ian Rush – chasing everything down,' he told *the Athletic*, 'but in reality, I was more of a poacher. Given that we were up against Rushy in the cup match, I felt as though I had a point to prove.' But, as so often happened in derbies, he had barely a kick.

That was about to change with dramatic effect. Liverpool remained in the competition because of a last-minute equaliser at Blackburn in the third round and after an extra-time comeback at Brighton. Now their fortunes would balance out. Everton were awarded a free-kick following a soft-looking foul in the left-back position, Ratcliffe passed back to Southall – illegally as it happens, as the ball was bouncing – and his long clearance was headed back to Neil McDonald on the halfway line. The forward pass was helped on by McCall into the space behind the stranded Ablett where a lurking Cottee pounced to side-foot past Grobbelaar. Three times Liverpool had taken the lead and three times Everton had annexed it. After ninety breathless minutes, where incredulity had been stretched to breaking point, the teams were effectively back to where they had started three days before.

Ironically, John Barnes was the one player on the pitch who had remained largely anonymous but the winger came to life during the first period of extra time. After Southall had made two stupendous saves from headers by Rush and Barry Venison, three minutes before the break Barnes fashioned a quite brilliant fourth goal for his team. Taking the ball to the left of the penalty area, he produced a beautifully curling right-footed shot that looped over the imperious Southall into the far corner. That should have been it but the Liverpool defence had left one final act of *hari-kari* six minutes from the end of extra time. Hysen inexplicably believed Molby's pass back would reach Grobbelaar and allowed the ball to pass through his legs – but straight to the prowling Cottee. 'On my left foot again, I took a swing at it, connected very well and the ball went through Bruce's legs before nestling in the corner,' the striker wrote in his autobiography. Unbelievably Everton had come back from the dead one final time. They did not need to do so again. When Midgley blew for full time the crowd's four-minute standing ovation reflected that they had just witnessed a match for the ages. 'A monument to the modern game was built at Goodison Park on Wednesday night,' Stuart Jones wrote in *The Times* two days later, 'Wednesday night's all-encompassing drama, nevertheless, has sunk into the memory of domestic fixtures and promises to remain forever.'

Understandably both managers looked for superlatives after an emotionally draining game that was physically demanding but ultimately unforgettable. 'It must go down as one of the greatest ever cup ties,' Kendall said, 'I cannot speak too highly of my team for coming back four times. They showed tremendous character.' Kenny Dalglish admitted he had never seen a game like it, acknowledging, 'If there has ever been a better one I wish someone would send me a video of it.' Setting aside their resilience, in the cold light of day Everton could count themselves lucky to have survived the replay. Liverpool were largely the more coherent side and, apart from a brief period at the start of the second half, had been in the ascendancy. Nevertheless, their central-defensive frailties, first apparent in the semi-final defeat to Crystal Palace twelve months before, had repeatedly let the home team off the hook. 'We gave three great examples of how to score goals and we gave three bad examples of how to defend,' Dalglish said afterwards. But within 48 hours the Scot was creating headlines which dwarfed those associated with a game remaining in the collective memory of those lucky enough to be present.

Resigned to defeat

The resignation of Kenny Dalglish on the Friday morning following the replay remains a JFK moment. At a time when football had not crossed over into wider culture the shock news dominated both front and back pages.[84] The Liverpool manager had looked pale and drawn at Goodison and, remarkably, the images of one of the strongest personalities in the game, arm rested on the dugout as another defensive calamity unfolded, have a certain 'rabbit in the headlights' quality.

Significantly, there were untypical arguments and shouting in the Liverpool dressing

---

[84]   The PA system at Euston station even interrupted their messages to passengers to announce Dalglish's departure. 'Kenny Dalglish has resigned as Liverpool manager; just thought you'd like to know,' was the mumbled statement over the tannoy according to the *Sunday Times*.

room after the game. 'After we took the lead for the final time I knew I had to make a change to shore things up at the back,' Dalglish later revealed. 'I could see what needed to be done and what would happen if I didn't. I didn't act on it. That was the moment I knew I was shattered. I needed to get away from the pressure.' That managerial burden, plus the pressures arising from the Hillsborough disaster, eventually overwhelmed the Scot. 'I can understand the reasons he has given,' Kendall commented. 'I felt the pressure of the job a few years ago. I needed a break. I took my break by going to Spain, a working break.'

First-team coach Ronnie Moran took temporary charge and, unsurprisingly, the exhausted teams lost their league game on the following Saturday, Everton at home to Sheffield United and Liverpool at Luton, before part three of their cup saga at Goodison four days later. Kendall left an unhappy Cottee on the bench for the second replay, with McCall replacing Nevin. The Everton boss went back to Ratcliffe about changing his role but got a frosty reception, as his skipper later recalled to the *Guardian*: 'For the second replay he asked me to be sweeper but I'd seen my arse by then and played where I did in the 4-4. I told Howard I'd stay where I was.' Yet the events of five days before cast a long shadow. 'It was a poignant night for this fortress of football strength,' Steve Curry wrote in the *Daily Express*. 'For if the personnel were much the same on the Goodison Park pitch, there was a significant absentee from the dugout.'

On a freezing cold and rainy evening in late February, with both teams tighter defensively, the game was the most typical derby of the four played during the month. The crucial moment occurred just twelve minutes in when the home team went ahead for the first time after almost four hours. Atteveld's free-kick was flicked on by Sharp before Keown's drive was brilliantly saved by Grobbelaar's legs. Molby failed to clear and the inspirational Watson slammed the ball home from by the penalty spot. Thereafter it became a case of how long Southall could keep Liverpool out. In the opening period he had produced a smart save from Rush but in the second half there were further brilliant stops from the Welsh striker and two from Steve Nicol. 'The prodigious hands of Neville Southall throttled a little more of the life out of the faltering legend of Liverpool last night,' Colin Wood wrote in the *Daily Mail*.

However, a moment after 66 minutes signalled it was Everton's night. Nicol produced a great cross from the right which an unmarked Rush met with a header. The 40,201 spectators held their breath but the striker surprisingly glanced the ball wide of the far post. Under constant pressure, the three-man central defensive wall and the brilliant goalkeeper kept their rivals out and secured a quarter-final tie at West Ham United.

Nothing symbolised the erratic nature of Pat Nevin's Everton career than the trilogy of FA Cup games against Liverpool. Man-of-the-match in the first game at Anfield, by the second replay he had been demoted to the substitutes' bench.

Afterwards both sets of players were united in tribute to one man. Ian Rush had been the one forward who had made Southall look mortal but even the great striker had to admit defeat. 'I have always thought Neville was the best in the business. Number one in the world,' he said. 'We played ever so well, but Neville was called on and was just outstanding.' Opposite number Bruce Grobbelaar echoed his team-mate: 'What can you say when a goalkeeper plays like that…he is an inspiration.' The final word on five hours of epic combat goes to the victorious manager. 'People say we lost on the night in terms of general play,' Kendall said, 'but I thought that over 300 minutes of Cup football against Liverpool we just shaded it.'

Ending the seven-year itch

Liverpool and Everton's fight for the league title in 1987 may have recalled the epic

'Thrilla in Manila' between Muhammad Ali and bitter rival Joe Frazier but the same goes for the trilogy of FA Cup games four years on. It was said later that by 1975 neither of the boxers was the best heavyweight in the world, but what made the bout unforgettable was the two curves which mapped out their respective declines intersected at exactly the right time and place. The same could be said about the Merseyside rivals in February 1991. Everton's fall from grace following the glories of the mid-1980s may have been more visible but Liverpool's decline over the same period – notwithstanding the 1987/88 campaign – was not as evident. By the end of the season, Arsenal were crowned champions and within six months Manchester United and Leeds United had also overtaken the Anfield side.

Poignantly the trilogy ended almost seven years to the day since a 1-1 league draw on the same ground signalled Kendall was building an outfit to challenge the Anfield side, something confirmed at Wembley three weeks later. The previous quality may have been missing, but those seven years of deadly competition came to a natural conclusion when, like Ali and Frazier in Manila, the two clubs drew on all that intensity, understanding of mutual strengths and weaknesses, plus shared experience, to produce something extraordinary.

In many other ways the tie also marked the passing of an era. Graeme Sharp's goals in the first replay were his last for club, cementing the Scot's place as Everton's leading post-war goalscorer. On the other side of the coin, Peter Beardsley's brace in the same game were also his final goals for Liverpool, although the forward's career would then take an interesting twist. Kevin Ratcliffe and Kevin Sheedy appeared in one more derby apiece. With ground improvements scheduled for the summer, it was the last derby played in front of a standing Gwladys Street terrace.

Away from the pitch there were signs of change. The tie had more in common with the future than the past. Shifting priorities and a move back to a 22-club top flight meant it was the last FA Cup contest in history to go to three games, with ties requiring penalties after the first replay from the following season. Instead of being broadcast to millions live on terrestrial television, both replays were transmitted to a miniscule audience on the fledgling BSkyB satellite channel, as they flexed their muscles in the domestic football market, with the drama on show hinting at the untapped potential they would use as a negotiating tool twelve months later. 'It was the game that changed football as we once knew it,' match commentator Martin Tyler told Simon Hughes of the *Athletic* on the thirtieth anniversary. Tyler also believed that the footage, because of the association with Dalglish's resignation, extended its shelf-life – an aspect not lost on his employers. 'It was pivotal,' he told Hughes. Consequently the production values and the familiar commentary duo of Tyler and Andy Gray gave the broadcast a feel of the Premier League years that followed.

Additionally, under the terms of the new deal the broadcaster had live rights for one cup game on a Monday evening – commonplace now, but ground-breaking then. When the draw sent Everton to West Ham on the second Monday in March there was a deluge of complaints from supporters about the disruption to travel arrangements. With big changes going on behind the scenes of English football, that was something they would soon have to get used to.

27

THE NEW DEAL

HAVING EVENTUALLY OUTFOUGHT THEIR RIVALS OVER THREE compelling matches, Everton travelled to Second Division West Ham as 9-2 third favourites for the FA Cup. However, Kendall made the mistake of paying the Hammers too much respect and got his tactics wrong by again picking a defensive line-up with three centre-backs, a packed midfield plus Sharp as a lone striker. But West Ham were not Liverpool and the watchful approach gave the initiative to home team, who quickly got a grip on the game. Centre-half Colin Foster opened the scoring with a rare volley after 33 minutes before man of the match Stuart Slater, who had run the visitors ragged all night, made it 2-0 on the hour. With Cottee and Newell on from the bench, Everton showed the folly of previous cautious tactics by penning the Hammers back before Watson scored four minutes from time. But there was a painful lack of ingenuity and creativity and the home team held on for a semi-final tie against Nottingham Forest. 'It was galling to watch such a stunningly ordinary performance after those epic battles which saw off Liverpool,' Phil McNulty said in the *Liverpool Daily Post*.

'It's a bit disappointing after coming through all those games with Liverpool,' Kendall said, 'but that's football.' Yet other remarks pointed at some early problems. Tony Cottee was clearly unhappy at not being picked on his return to Upton Park and provided some adverse comments afterwards. 'It's not for me to criticise selection,' he said, 'because the boss picks the teams, but after I came on we were just belting the ball forward and you can't play football in that situation.' While Cottee was not exactly towing the party line, around the same time neither were the most important figures in English football.

Premier prophecy

In its role as one of the most historic venues in English football, Goodison has been home to many influential meetings over the years. None were more significant than one staged around the time of the West Ham game. 'Those present in the boardroom at

Goodison Park, Liverpool, in March 1991, could have been mistaken by some for a rogues' gallery of football's hierarchy,' proclaimed Alex Fynn and Lynton Guest in *Out of Time: Why football isn't working!*

They were describing a mixed cast, including Philip Carter and David Dein, both removed in shame from the Football League Management Committee two-and-a-half years earlier. Manchester United chairman Martin Edwards was there, as was his Liverpool counterpart, Noel White, plus Anfield chief executive Peter Robinson. The newly appointed FA chief executive Graham Kelly was also present. 'This diverse though undoubtedly influential crew, was on the verge of taking a decision which would bring about the biggest changes in English football since the formation of the Football League in 1888,' Fynn and Guest wrote.

The background to the meeting went back three years to the signing of the exclusive broadcast deal with ITV and at its heart were power-grabs by both the Football League and the FA. The £44m contract in 1988 had heavily favoured the top-flight clubs but they still had to give 25 per cent to the lower divisions even though ITV's John Bromley later admitted, 'There are only about eight teams in the First Division which are attractive to the nation.' With the TV contract up for renewal in 1992, the big clubs were keen on further changes in their favour – as were the powerbrokers. In October 1990 the Football League had produced their own policy document, *One Game, One Team, One Voice*, which proposed an elite division under the unified stewardship of the League and FA, but with the former being the senior partner. The big clubs were hardly enamoured by remaining under the League's arcane structure while Liverpool chairman White, himself an FA councillor, knew his organisation was equally unhappy. Sensing a possible, mutually beneficial partnership, in December White and Dein visited the FA at Lancaster Gate to seek collaboration on the formation of a new league. Surprisingly the governing body was receptive and Dein then set out convincing colleagues in the Big Five of the way forward. Hence the meeting at Goodison where the unanimous and historic decision was taken to form a breakaway Premier League. 'Well gentlemen, that seems to be satisfactory,' Philip Carter concluded at the end.

Still a Big Five club?

That breakaway was only possible because, off the pitch, the game was heading in a different direction. However, the narrative that Italia '90 saved English football from itself is not strictly true. Although the Hillsborough tragedy had showed up the inadequacy of stadia and policing, fans had slowly returned after the nadir of the mid-1980s and, with television now recognising live games as a valuable product, by 1990 the sport was on a more positive track. That progress was propelled further with the enhanced interest due to the sporting and cultural impact of the World Cup. By the end of the 1990/91 campaign, an average of 23,000 spectators were watching a top-flight football game, three thousand more than five years before. In addition, the tournament stimulated awareness in the game from new groups of people with more affluence and diversity, who had previously shown little interest. Then there was the Taylor Report, the official inquiry into the Hillsborough tragedy published in January 1990 which included 76 recommendations, the most significant being the introduction of all-seater stadia.[85] All these spectator-friendly developments pointed to a brighter future.

Yet those positive changes would not have been possible but for the changing nature of fandom. By the end of the 1980s football hooligans now immersed themselves in the growing rave culture rather than cause mayhem on matchday. If it was not for Hillsborough the biggest talking point of the 1988/89 campaign would have been the widespread phenomenon of supporters turning up at grounds carrying various inflatable objects – injecting some much-needed humour into the matchday experience after a decade of disaster and misery. Those developments went hand-in-hand with fanzine culture, a by-product of the Heysel disaster, which gave supporters an independent platform for their voice to be heard. At Goodison titles such as *Speke from the Harbour* and *When Skies are Grey* became essential reading.

On the pitch, by 1991 the Big Five's dominance over English football was well established. During the previous decade only Liverpool (six times), Everton (twice) and Arsenal (twice) had lifted the title. Although the two domestic cup competitions did offer a ray of hope for those outside the elite, only two from that group – Coventry and Wimbledon – had won the FA Cup in that time. Such was their supremacy that by the late 1980s more than twenty per cent of all gate receipts for league games were banked by five clubs.

However, the Big Five was a relatively recent construct, dating back to the mid-1980s when Everton's run of success was beginning. During Everton's title-winning season of 1986/87 the two Merseyside clubs and the north London duo all enjoyed turnover in the £4-5 million range with Liverpool the highest with £5.1m. However, they were all outdone by the £6.7 million earned by Manchester United.

But where Everton sat within the hierarchy of English football in 1991 was now open

---

[85]   It was later mandated that all top-flight clubs should have all-seater stadia by the start of the 1994/95 campaign.

to question. They lacked the countrywide and international support of Manchester United and Liverpool plus, as the sport began the move away from its working-class roots, their largely localised support from some of the most deprived areas of country had to be weighed against Arsenal and Tottenham, who could access the wealth of gentrified fans in the more prosperous south-east. Consequently, rather than being able to move forward from the post-1990 boom, compared to their rivals they were vulnerable in a more monetised sport. Whereas four years before Everton were financially competing with their so-called Big Five peers that was no longer the case – a position laid bare in the financial results for the 1990/91 campaign. Manchester United earned £17 million, Arsenal and Spurs £11 million each[86] while Liverpool's income was £10 million. In comparison, Everton's was £7 million, more in line with the numbers of Leeds United, Aston Villa and Manchester City, who all enjoyed bigger home attendances during the campaign. The only way Everton were going to ensure the Big Five did not become the Big Four was by lifting trophies again.

Clearing out the deadwood

Everton finished ninth at the end of the 1990/91 season, an acceptable end to a difficult campaign. In his first period in charge, Kendall had got it right after three years but Kevin Ratcliffe later recalled a conversation on the team coach just after he returned. 'We'll get this back,' Kendall said. Ratcliffe turned to him and said 'maybe in two years.' But his manager disagreed, saying twelve months. Ratcliffe, cognisant of the dressing-room issues, responded: 'It'll take more than two years to get this back to where it was.' But apart from healing a wounded squad and plugging the growing financial gap with their so-called peers, on the pitch Kendall was facing a far bigger challenge than ten years before. Then there was effectively only Liverpool to overtake at the summit but this time, apart from the Anfield side now managed by Graeme Souness, reigning champions Arsenal were formidable and down the M62 a resurgent Manchester United had just lifted the European Cup Winners' Cup and were expected to mount a championship challenge. Leeds United had finished a menacing fifth in their first season back. Within two months of the start of Kendall's first full season, Kenny Dalglish was appointed Blackburn Rovers manager with the task of spending owner Jack Walker's millions. In early 1992, under the visionary direction of John Hall, Kevin Keegan took the reins at Newcastle United. While

---

[86]   Because the north London duo could charge increased prices, by 1991 Everton earned the same money from five home games as Arsenal and Spurs did from three. That factor, plus that Arsenal's average home gate was 10,000 more than Everton, and Spurs' 5,000 higher, largely explains the income gap.

Kendall was busy trying to re-establish the club near the top of the table as they were dropping out of the financial elite, there were several unexpected and richer contenders waiting to take Everton's place should they fail.

The Everton manager's task was also made harder by the unbalanced and poorly recruited squad. 'There's so much deadwood at this place it's a fire risk,' muttered a Goodison insider to the *Liverpool Daily Post's* Phil McNulty at the end of the 1990/91 season. Consequently, it was easier to list who were the fireproof players in the bloated squad. Dave Watson certainly fitted into that category, as did John Ebbrell, who enjoyed an excellent campaign. The other was Polish winger Robert Warzycha, a successful trialist from Gornik Zabrze who signed for £500,000 in March.

Kendall offloaded the hapless Mike Milligan back to Oldham while Graeme Sharp ended a gilded Goodison career featuring a post-war record of 159 goals in 446 games by following the same path. One of the club's great survivors, the Scot had had a total number of forward partners well into double figures, commencing with one British-record signing in Bob Latchford and ending with another in Tony Cottee. Yet his departure was an example of Kendall's occasional callous streak, first apparent in treatment of players like Alan Biley and Billy Wright a decade before. Informed on holiday of potential interest from Oldham, on his return Sharp was accused by Kendall of discussing a move with Joe Royle behind his back, which the Scot naturally denied. When Royle, having got Sharp's phone number from Kendall, did make an approach, he rejected a move to Boundary Park. With Kendall eyeing other forward options, Sharp then told his manager he would fight for a place only to be told that Everton would not match Oldham's wages. 'That was the last straw. It was just pathetic,' the striker said in his autobiography. 'It really did confirm that I had no future at Goodison Park.'

But that was not the end of the whole sorry farrago. After telling Royle of his intention to move, Sharp was then informed by Kendall that, having just sold Mike Newell, he could not be released. But Sharp was off, for a fee of £500,000. 'I was hurt and disappointed at the way Howard had handled my departure,' he said. 'I felt it was a scandalous way for my Everton career to end…We'd shared some wonderful times over the years, but – and I don't say this lightly – I lost a lot of respect for him during the summer of 1991.' That did not stop his manager paying tribute afterwards. 'His contribution here has been tremendous over ten years,' Kendall eulogised. 'People will look back and say he was one of the most popular and successful strikers we've had.'

Graeme Sharp scores against Chelsea in January 1991. His departure from Goodison
was an example of the occasional unpleasant side of Kendall's man-management.

Over the next eight months Stuart McCall and Neil McDonald departed while Peter Beagrie and Pat Nevin were both sent out on loan. Sadly, Norman Whiteside's injury-plagued career ended with premature retirement at the age of just 26. Kendall also failed to offload Tony Cottee to Blackburn Rovers. Meanwhile, rumours continued to circulate that Neville Southall would be departing, with Manchester United the likely destination. In his place Kendall was considering the purchase of the young Watford goalkeeper, David James, for a seven-figure sum. Although the Welshman had been at his brilliant best since Kendall returned there had been some typical peculiarities. Everton had battled their way to Wembley for the final of the Zenith Data Systems Cup against Crystal Palace in April and, after the game went into extra time with the teams locked at a goal apiece, he was beaten by two brilliant Ian Wright finishes and a John Salako header as the London club strolled to a 4-1 victory. Southall's refusal to collect his loser's medal was indicative of both his single-mindedness and the lowly status of the competition. As for Kendall, with Everton's midfield overrun and their defence torn apart by Wright, the game was a salutary lesson about the restorative work needed. 'Everton are a team going nowhere unless gallons of new blood are pumped in,' Len Capeling wrote in the *Liverpool Daily Post*.

As part of the rebuilding process, in May the Everton boss travelled to Madrid to negotiate a loan or permanent deal for the 26-year-old Gheorghe Hagi, who was out of favour at the Bernabéu. But the Romanian superstar was not keen on a transfer. 'A move to England does not appeal to me,' he admitted. 'The game there is of a very high standard, but I don't think it would suit my style.' Six months later Real Madrid contacted Everton again with a view to Hagi moving to Goodison for the remainder of the campaign. Sadly the mouth-watering prospect remained just that, with Madrid rejecting Kendall's offer. 'Unfortunately, the package deal I put together with my board's permission does not seem to be acceptable,' a frustrated Everton boss said as Hagi ultimately moved to Turkey.

However, Kendall had identified his number one target: Derby County striker Dean Saunders. The pacy forward, valued at anything up to £3 million, was the hottest property in English football and initially Everton's rivals for his signature were believed to be Leeds United, Arsenal, Barcelona, Real Madrid – plus Liverpool. However, in June, with Leeds and Arsenal not wanting an auction and reportedly withdrawing from the race, the road appeared clear for Kendall, who showed his commitment by delivering Everton's offer to the Baseball Ground personally in early June. Four weeks later, knowing other clubs were circling, Kendall increased the bid to a reported British record fee of £2.8 million, which Derby accepted. 'I am delighted that the first hurdle has been cleared,' Kendall said, 'If everything runs smoothly this will prove a signing that will excite our supporters, who have been waiting patiently for something to happen on the transfer route.'

With Nottingham Forest having matched Everton's offer and Liverpool back in the picture, Kendall spoke with Saunders for four hours a day later. The offer on the table to him was £250,000 per year, making him comfortably the highest earner. 'I have tried to convince him that he is going to be part of a successful Everton team in the future,' Kendall said. 'While nothing is guaranteed, the fact that I was sitting down with him yesterday, ready to pay a British-record fee, proves just how ambitious we are.' While Kendall's words were encouraging, in many ways they reflected the decline over the previous four years. It was a conversation that, say, would not have been needed with Gary Lineker.

Yet, within 24 hours of their conversation, Graeme Souness swooped and signed the Welsh international for Liverpool. 'If Dean Saunders doesn't end up at Everton, no one can point the finger at this club and say we didn't do our level best to try and sign him,' Kendall had said during negotiations. Saunders choosing Liverpool was another reminder that Everton, unless they were enjoying a successful spell, could not attract elite players at their peak. The club's name was not a drawing card for the best and, barring a period during the mid-1980s, had not been for nearly twenty years.

Blue Peter

However, there was an upside to the rejection. Across Stanley Park, Peter Beardsley was at the crossroads of his career. Like several Liverpool players, nearing thirty and with one last big contract left, Beardsley told new manager Souness that unless first-team football was guaranteed, with improved terms, he would be looking for a move. That said, in his autobiography, Beardsley claimed Souness obviously did not rate him as a player. According to tabloid speculation, the England international's difficult relationship with Kenny Dalglish in his final months – or allegedly their wives' as the couples were neighbours – had been a factor in the latter's surprise departure. Beardsley even went on to speculate whether Dalglish had marked his card to close friend Souness.

Kendall had already registered an interest before Souness spoke with the forward but, understandably perhaps, the Liverpool manager alerted Leeds and Newcastle about his availability. Surprisingly, neither took up the offer. Consequently, on a pre-season tour of Sweden at the end of July, Souness pulled Beardsley aside and told him of Everton's interest and that Kendall had requested the player should fly to London immediately. Surplus to requirements and feeling ostracised, Beardsley's interest was piqued and he did just that. Curiously, when they did get together, the Everton boss told him that he would have rather met in Manchester 24 hours later, but Souness wanted Beardsley out straightaway. After the two parties agreed a fee of £1 million – the biggest between the two clubs – Kendall revealed optimistically: 'We are not messing about at Everton. We want to win the championship. I want Everton Football Club back on top again.'

For his part, Beardsley proved equally as popular at Goodison as across the park. 'To be fair, the people of Merseyside were very receptive and respectful,' he later said. 'I must have received about a thousand letters from both Reds and Blues when I moved and only one was bad. Howard revealed that even in his wildest dreams he didn't think that Liverpool would make me available to Everton but he tried his luck and the gamble paid off.' It certainly did. The Geordie wizard's individual brand of trickery and professionalism proved an instant hit with supporters and teammates alike. 'He would do things in training and I'm thinking, "I've not had this quality before,"' Pat Nevin revealed, 'For me I thought he was world-class.'

However, with Souness needing to recover the £5 million outlay on Mark Wright and Saunders, Kendall was on the lookout for other pickings at Anfield. Also in the manager's sights was Jan Molby, who was out of favour. Kendall was prepared to pay £1.5 million for the burly Dane and, with the midfielder more than willing to cross the great divide, a second transaction within a month between the clubs was on the cards. With Souness reported to have agreed the deal, Molby unfortunately picked up a knee injury in a reserve game, one which ultimately needed an operation and, by the time he returned, there was an injury crisis and any chance of reviving the move had gone.

Kendall was also a long-term admirer of their utility man Barry Venison, having made inquiries when he was at Sunderland five years before. With Kendall lining up Venison for a midfield role, following discussions with Liverpool in December the two clubs agreed a fee of £425,000. 'I liked him from the early days when he was with Sunderland. I have always admired his attitude and commitment,' Kendall said. 'After talking to him, it's clear that he is relishing the chance to play for us.' However, despite the manager's optimism, the two parties could not agree terms and the move floundered. However, Kendall would return to Anfield again with more success a fortnight later.

28
GOING NOWHERE FAST

THE PRE-SEASON TITLE ODDS SHOWED HOW THE BOOKMAKERS believed Howard Kendall's return would reinvigorate the club. Liverpool and Arsenal were joint-favourites at 7-4 with Manchester United at 8-1 and Leeds United 12-1. But Everton were fifth in the betting at 16-1. A difficult start to the campaign showed these odds to be a tad optimistic. Unsurprisingly, aside from interest in the Anfield dressing room, Kendall had also returned to Maine Road for perennial favourite Alan Harper, signing the utility man for the third time, and for a Huyton-born player shown the door at Goodison a decade before.

Back to the Mark

Mark Ward joined the Everton youth ranks in 1978 but in Gordon Lee's final days three years later departed with damning words from the soon-to-be-sacked Everton boss: 'Mark, we believe you're never going to be big enough, strong enough or quick enough to establish yourself at the highest level.' However, replacement Kendall was more sympathetic and, after taking over, played Ward with the senior squad in an end-of-season testimonial at Halifax to provide a platform for his talents. After thriving under Tranmere Rovers legend John King at non-league Northwich Victoria, Joe Royle took the diminutive winger to Oldham Athletic for £9,500 and such was his progress over two years that in August 1985 he was on the way to West Ham for £250,000. After the Upton Park outfit were relegated four years later Ward was in demand. Kenny Dalglish offered £1m to take him to Anfield – according to Ward in his autobiography *Hammered* the move failed because his manager Lou Macari wanted players, not cash. Then Manchester City boss Kendall had more luck and Ward was back in the north-west in December 1989. Such was the close relationship between the two that when Kendall's replacement, Peter Reid, told Ward that his former boss wanted him at Goodison, he told the player: 'Your dad wants to sign you again.' Ward duly moved for £1.1 million in August.

Ward made his debut at the City Ground on the opening day when a late Nigel Jemson goal gave the hosts a fortunate 2-1 victory. But three days later the returning homeboy got his dream date at Goodison, which was thirteen years in the making, against reigning champions Arsenal. During first-half stoppage time, the former Goodison ball-boy moved in from the left flank to fire home from almost thirty yards out past David Seaman. After Tony Cottee added a second with a tap-in during the second half, Ward struck again, albeit from a free-kick which took a wicked deflection. The eventual 3-1 defeat was Arsenal's heaviest since the 3-0 loss at Goodison two years before. Kendall took Ward off early to ensure he received a standing ovation from the 31,200 crowd, before saying, 'It was a fantastic night for the lad. Hopefully you get what you deserve in this game and Mark Ward deserves what he enjoyed here.' For Ward, in *Hammered* he wrote of the night: 'This is, without doubt, my biggest and happiest memory in football.'

Morecambe not wise

Yet that victory over the champions was the only highlight of the first six weeks of the season. Just three points were garnered from the next five league games – one a 3-1 defeat at Anfield. But the most damning headlines followed a reserve-team game at Manchester City in early September. After a second string featuring more than £4 million of talent in Tony Cottee, Neil McDonald, Peter Beagrie, Ray Atteveld and Eddie Youds was on the wrong end of a dreadful 4-1 loss, Kendall was seething. 'I've told the players that it is just not good enough,' he said afterwards. 'I was desperately disappointed with what I saw from senior Everton players. We need to get it right at all levels, not just the first team.' Their reward was a Friday evening visit to the footballing outpost of Morecambe for the A team in the Lancashire League, not before a memorable anecdote recalled by Tony Cottee in *Claret and Blues*:

> It was degrading for me, the club's record transfer, being forced to play for the third team, while Neil [McDonald] showed his feelings by throwing his team sheet in the bin! My anger turned to laughter, though, when I saw 'Scan' – an ex-Everton apprentice, run out to play for the other side. A couple of weeks earlier, 'Scan' had been cleaning the windows at our house in Birkdale with Roly Howard, the manager of non-league Marine, who was our regular window cleaner!

If Kendall thought the rest of the squad would note the wake-up call he was wrong. Less than 24 hours after the punishment trip to the seaside, the first team produced a similarly feeble display at Sheffield United against a side without a victory all season and with five successive defeats. A goal up through Beardsley, the visitors capitulated in the second half and, after the 2-1 defeat left his team just one place above the relegation places, the Everton manager was irate. 'We are not good enough and something will have to be done about it,' he declared. 'It was like watching a practice match.' Everton had now lost all four away games and Kendall's comments perhaps reflected that the questionable attitude of the squad under Harvey had not yet been eradicated. 'I've seen Kendall keep his cool in a thousand and one post-match situations, even in the dark days going back to 1983,' Ken Rogers wrote in the *Liverpool Echo*. 'When he lets fly with such a powerful attack on his own men, it means the afternoon has been the proverbial can of worms.'

The main problem was the team was too small and lightweight. At Bramall Lane the midfield featured two wide men in Robert Warzycha and Ward plus John Ebbrell and Kevin Sheedy in the centre. Both Harvey and Kendall failed in attempts to get Andy Townsend and the Ireland international's dominating presence would have been a benefit in the middle, as would have Kevin Richardson – Everton expressing an interest in re-signing the midfielder on his return from Real Sociedad before Aston Villa stepped in. In addition, with Mike Newell shortly to depart for Blackburn Rovers, the forward options were Beardsley and Tony Cottee, players who liked the ball played into feet and not in the air. One of many attributes of Kendall's best team was their physical prowess but strangely in his second spell he was taking an alternative route. Consequently, following a difficult start, supporters were realising that success, anticipated as a given following Kendall's return, would not be easy to come by. 'Once again an Everton defeat is greeted by the manager talking of unacceptable performances,' one fan wrote in the *Football Echo* after the loss at Sheffield United. 'Well, he can go on describing things as unacceptable until he's blue in the face, but it won't change a thing. It is also pointless to talk of threatening changes for the next match when all that means is swapping one of Kendall's has-beens for one of Harvey's never will-bes.'

Peter the Great

A player beyond criticism was the one who swapped the red of Liverpool for the blue of Everton during the summer. Peter Beardsley had enjoyed a brilliant start to the campaign, his repertoire of silky skills standing out in a series of poor performances. Yet the Geordie's speed of thought and vision could sometimes be wasted. 'Peter was a truly great player, probably too brilliant for us at the time and too advanced for the players we had,' Neville Southall later wrote in the *Binman Chronicles*, 'He often ended up giving the ball away because the others couldn't see what he could see.'

And the former Liverpool player came to the rescue when Kendall returned to Maine Road for the first time since controversially jumping ship ten months before. Prior to the game Kendall attempted to diffuse the situation by quipping, 'I think I should get a tremendous reception. They should be saying "Welcome to Everton Football Club. You know what they're like away from home!"' The humour was well-timed, as the game itself was a comedy of errors. After a mundane opening period, the contest came to life on 67 minutes when City centre-back Keith Curle misread Atteveld's speculative pass and Beardsley nipped in to score. Both City substitutes struck the crossbar in the last minute of normal time but then, with the final whistle looming, Ward fouled Colin Hendry and referee Mike Reed awarded a penalty. Michael Hughes, a twenty-year-old midfielder playing in his first full game, was amazingly entrusted with the kick but blasted the ball over the bar.

With Beardsley in the international wilderness, England manager Graham Taylor was an interested spectator in Manchester but unfortunately not present at Goodison three days later when the former Newcastle player produced a masterclass against Coventry City. After a lucky opener when a clearance struck him and bobbled past Steve Ogrizovic into the corner, on the hour the thirty-year-old produced a venomous left-footed shot that left the goalkeeper motionless. 'It was the type of goal he used to score against us,' Kendall joked afterwards. The striker subsequently completed a hat-trick from the spot with fifteen minutes remaining.[87] All the subsequent talk was about Beardsley with Ogrizovic joined the growing chorus who felt he should be back in the international reckoning. 'He was brilliant,' the big goalkeeper declared. 'He would be in any England team I picked.' Goals in the League Cup at Watford and in a 2-2 draw at Chelsea took his tally to eight in six matches, before a sparkling, creative performance during a 3-1 home win over Spurs left those on the pitch salivating. Tony Cottee netted a hat-trick but was in no doubt who should take credit. 'Peter was fantastic,' he drooled. 'He is so unselfish. He set up my first goal when he could have shot himself and he's a joy to play with.' Former international partner Gary Lineker, a scorer at Goodison, was equally effusive. 'Peter's a class player and always has been,' he said. 'I see no reason why he shouldn't be in the England squad.' Thankfully, Taylor too was convinced and included Beardsley for the international against Turkey, but unfortunately left the returnee on the bench.[88]

---

[87] Beardsley becoming only the second player to score hat-tricks for both clubs, after David Johnson.

[88] The striker thus missing his only opportunity to become the first player capped by England with Everton and Liverpool.

Going for Mo

After selling Mike Newell for £1.3 million to Blackburn Rovers, there was no shortage of potential striking options for the Everton boss. Southampton had previously rejected a British-record £3m bid – with Newell as a makeweight – for Alan Shearer. Similarly, there were links to Crystal Palace striking duo Ian Wright and Mark Bright, with the former's £2m plus price tag viewed as prohibitive. A £900,000 offer for Chelsea's Kerry Dixon was also turned down with the sellers wanting £1 million. (Seems strange why Kendall would not have then paid the extra £100,000.) Cambridge United also rejected an approach for Dion Dublin.

By November, the need for a new striker was paramount, with Everton's season littered with games full of territorial domination but little return in front of goal. The search took the Everton boss north of the border to Rangers where Maurice Johnston was unsettled, having been sidelined for the favoured duo of Ally McCoist and Mark Hateley. Kendall had first shown an interest in the player when he was at Partick Thistle in 1983 and since then Johnston had been well-travelled: a move to Watford was followed by transfers to Celtic, Nantes and in 1989, infamously, to Rangers when he became the club's first major Catholic signing just weeks after agreeing a return to Parkhead. Kendall's first offer to Rangers was turned down but the Glasgow club accepted an increased bid of £1.5 million for a 28-year-old who had scored 46 goals in 100 appearances there. Chelsea were also interested and Johnston's preference was to go to London, but they were unwilling to meet the increased asking price.

The Scottish international signed a three-and-a-half year deal after agreeing personal terms. Yet there were issues. For all Johnston's claims that he would be seeing out his career at Everton, the move was a fifth in eight roller-coaster years. On the pitch, for a team needing a target man the new signing stood 5ft 9in tall. 'Mo is quite capable in the air,' Kendall insisted. 'You don't have to be six feet two to cause problems upstairs.' As a bubbly character who had earned a reputation for some off-the-pitch excesses – 'And for all that's been written about me, I've never let a manager down on the pitch,' he said defiantly on arrival – Kendall was clearly aiming for Johnston to rekindle the dressing room in the same way Andy Gray had eight years before. But Gray was of a different temperament and joining a squad populated with talented young players who just needed direction and the guiding hand of experience. The squad eight years later was older and had substantially less potential. Kendall also had Peter Reid in 1983. For a player of Johnston's repute, attempting to imitate Gray's influence was always going to be a gamble.[89]

Mid-table mediocrity

The remainder of the campaign was frustrating and, to say the least, tedious. Johnston's introduction – which forced Beardsley into a deeper role – added very little to the firepower of the team. The visit to top-of-the-table Leeds United at the end of November typified their profligacy. Everton largely dominated the game and seemed certain winners when home centre-half Chris Fairclough was red-carded on the hour with the game goalless. But several chances were squandered and three minutes from time Rod Wallace netted an undeserved winner for the hosts. 'It was the traditional Everton hard-luck story with the usual ending,' Phil McNulty pointed out in the *Liverpool Daily Post*. 'Everton, quite simply, played the leaders off the park…[they] have cast aside points like confetti this season, and this was the most criminal waste so far.'

However, any goodwill generated in West Yorkshire on the Saturday was eradicated four days later, on a disastrous evening against the same opponents in a League Cup tie at Goodison. For reasons best known to himself, the manager played three at the back with the full-backs pushing on. Unfamiliarity led to no shape and playing pattern and Leeds ultimately ran out easy 4-1 victors before the home crowd angrily jeered Kendall's side off the pitch. The ragged nature of the evening was exemplified at half-time. When Kendall asked the players for their views, Tony Cottee pointed out the left side was unbalanced. Kendall seemed to agree and then told his striker to take off his kit as he was substituted. The other change at the break was hugely symbolic. Cottee was correct, Rod Wallace had run riot against an exposed Kevin Ratcliffe and the skipper too was replaced and never played for the club again.

Although the manager issued a *mea culpa* afterwards – 'If anyone's going to be criticised about the way we played or team selection, it is going to be me,' he declared – the shattering defeat once again highlighted the gap between Everton and the new elite of English football.

That chasm was reinforced in the next month. Even though they were seventh, Kendall, ever the optimist, was still harbouring title aspirations prior to a trip to Arsenal and a Boxing Day visit of Sheffield Wednesday, before a Merseyside derby two days later. 'It is entirely in our hands. If we have a successful Christmas period people will start to

---

[89]   One group who agreed with the signing was academics at the Liverpool Polytechnic (now John Moores University) Centre for Sport and Exercise Sciences. Using one of the first computer analysis systems for football, they claimed that the data from the 1990 World Cup showed Johnston had been one of the best players and likened his contribution to 'Diego Maradona's for Argentina in the 1986 World Cup'.

talk about us,' he promised. 'It would be nice to think we could be nearer to giving our fans something to look forward to in the New Year.' Those aspirations looked foolish as recent signing Ian Wright struck four times at Highbury in a 4-2 win for the Gunners and a David Hirst goal clinched Wednesday's first victory at Goodison for thirty years. The latter defeat was built on the usual foundations. 'By half-time Everton had had 99 per cent of the chances, nearly all the possession but none of the luck,' Cynthia Bateman wrote in the *Guardian*. 'Indeed, the message from Goodison is that Everton still need a striker to stick the ball in the back of the net.'

Dropped Kevin Sheedy was another from the Class of 1985 who ended his association with the club and Kendall on sour terms. One legacy of the unhappy Harvey years was that the midfielder was still on the transfer list six months after Kendall returned and, although Sheedy took himself off, he fell out with the manager after being dropped for the Wednesday defeat. To be fair, Sheedy's one goal in sixteen league starts as part of a series of lacklustre performances was probably reason enough. In truth he had endured a largely difficult time, both on and off the pitch, since his halcyon days of 1986/87. Harvey failed to identify that the centre of midfield was now his best position and the bad feeling that engendered carried forward to his successor's tenure. Put back on the transfer list, he joined Kevin Keegan's Geordie revolution two months later. 'I really could have done with going three years ago. I was in and out of the side all that time and things did not go well for me,' Sheedy admitted after leaving, 'Since the World Cup [in 1990] it has been very bad and playing in the reserves hastened my departure. I was not very happy.'

After three decades where the derby meant something nationally, now, with Liverpool and Everton thirteen and fifteen points respectively behind leaders Manchester United, the game was very much a sideshow. With the departure of many of the big names that made it the biggest fixture in domestic football during the previous decade, the two line-ups had the feel of reserve teams in comparison. 'Today, for the first time in years, the outcome of a Merseyside derby will be of parochial interest only,' Ian Ross pointed out in *The Times*. Ironically, with the pressure off, the two sides produced a hugely entertaining contest at Goodison. 'Altogether, a derby of distinction,' Brian Glanville wrote in *The Sunday Times*. Liverpool went ahead in the first half via Nick Tanner's scrambled shot at the Gwladys Street End, although Mark Ward vociferously claimed he had cleared the ball before it had fully crossed the line. Ward, in central midfield, became the game's outstanding player and started the move that led to Everton's equaliser. His crisp pass fed Peter Beagrie on the right and the winger's cross was nodded down by Beardsley into the path of new signing Matt Jackson, whose miscued shot went across the six-yard box with

Johnston poking the ball home. The striker had been booked for over-celebrating after scoring his first goal for both Celtic and Rangers in Old Firm derbies and as he started a tour of Goodison after netting the equaliser, referee Vic Callow was probably tempted to make it a treble.

Thereafter it was all Everton. Within minutes the new striker had struck the outside of the post before Ray Houghton's acrobatic goal-line headed clearance stopped Marin Keown from putting the home team ahead. There were no further goals and although a draw was widely accepted as being a fair result, Kendall saw much to admire, such as the burgeoning understanding between Beardsley and Johnston. 'This match was the perfect advert for football,' he said afterwards. But with Everton still in mid-table, whether 1992 could bring an improvement was up in the air.

Paying the penalty
When Neville Southall proclaimed in early January that 'I do not see any reason why we cannot win the League...we have the players who can win the League and the support who can help us win the League,' there were more than a few casual observers who thought the teetotal goalkeeper had lapsed over the New Year. However, Southall's over-optimism could not hide the fact that a decent run could still produce a UEFA Cup spot and an FA Cup third-round victory over Southend United provided a possible gateway to Wembley.

Nevertheless, with the season at a crossroads Kendall's side revisited a familiar script in the visit to championship-chasing Manchester United. 'Last time I saw Everton, in the Merseyside derby, I said that all they needed was a little luck,' Brian Glanville wrote in *The Sunday Times*. 'They have two little men up front, both of them very quick and clever, a midfield which has been given greater guile with the moving of Ward to a central position and a defence which does well when Keown is present.' At Old Trafford the visitors did everything to prove Glanville's point. Several chances were wasted but the difference was in the two wide men. After a glorious start to his Everton career twelve months before, Robert Warzycha had been hugely disappointing. At Old Trafford he rarely took the full-back on and constantly shifted the ball to a colleague at the earliest opportunity. But Andrei Kanchelskis was the opposite, the Ukrainian remaining a constant danger, attacking with pace and that direct approach paid dividends when, after 56 minutes, he latched onto Steve Bruce's pass, galloped from the inside-left position and poked the ball past Southall. Everton had no immediate answer but in the final minute looked to have grabbed a potential lifeline when Bruce brought Johnston down on the edge of the area.

'No penalty, no free kick. Again, you can see what I mean about Everton's luck,' Glanville reflected.

With the team now in tenth, the rest of the campaign depended upon an FA Cup trip to Chelsea on the last Sunday in January, televised live on the BBC. The game, a finely-balanced affair always going to be settled by a single goal, summed up the entire campaign. After Cottee – standing in for the injured Johnston – missed an early opportunity, on the hour the record signing was equally careless. After Chelsea's Gareth Hall slipped thirty yards from goal, he was left with only Kevin Hitchcock to beat but his right-footed shot went straight into the goalkeeper's chest. Twelve minutes later the visitors paid for such generosity. Kendall had managed Chelsea's Clive Allen at Manchester City and afterwards the striker revealed, 'I saw Howard before the game and he said: "I see things are going well for you, but don't get one against us."' But when Dennis Wise's free-kick was headed out, the striker, standing at the edge of the box, met the clearance with a perfectly struck volley that arrowed past Southall.

The visitors pressed the panic button but, as the tie entered the final ten minutes, grabbed a lifeline when Hitchcock pulled down Beagrie in the area. Cottee's penalty summed up the entire campaign: struck too straight, it was easily stopped by the goalkeeper[90] and Everton had nothing to play for by the end of January. Kendall rued his luck afterwards. 'It has been the story of our season,' he said regretfully. 'My players have given everything. They have done their utmost to get a result.'

Drifting off

For the first time in sixteen years, Everton went into the final months of the campaign with little to play for. Paradoxically, ITV, who had been accused of favouring the Big Five in return for their support in the past and possibly the future, immediately thought it apt to showcase Kendall's team on three occasions in the space of a month, each resulting in a spectacularly drab bore-draw. After a goalless stalemate at Villa Park ensured the nation could enjoy a decent snooze, Neil Robinson in the *Guardian* was forced to admit: 'Much more of this and Sunday afternoon television will again be the province of black-and-white films.' While the exposure guaranteed an unexpected windfall of £400,000 for the club, the downside was that the lack of quality displayed to an audience of seven million viewers caused a certain amount of reputational damage. As

---

[90]   As he was walking up to take the kick, Dennis Wise bet the Everton player £5 that he would miss. 'Cottee told me to f--- off,' he revealed after the game. The Everton striker accepted the bet but, by his own later admission, never paid up.

one TV critic quipped: 'Yet another appearance by Everton in the line-up shows that whatever criteria are used by ITV in picking its games, football ability is not included.' Although European ambitions were now thwarted, in his programme notes against QPR in February, Kendall wrote 'there's plenty to play for yet'. However, a dreadful display in the goalless draw exposed wider issues within the club, according to Phil McNulty in the *Liverpool Daily Post*:

> *This wretched excuse for a football match only confirmed the fear that has grown inside experienced Goodison observers in recent weeks. That is the Howard Kendall rebuilding programme still has a long way to go. Everton must now finally come to terms with the fact that harsh reality and the truth both hurt. The blizzard of optimistic messages coming out of Goodison Park cannot disguise a stark and simple fact: Everton are not good enough. Not good enough to be considered among the so-called Big Five of English football.*

Although Beardsley had undoubtedly been a very good signing, the sound piece of business had disguised failings elsewhere. Mark Ward had tailed off after an encouraging start while, by the middle of March, Johnston had scored just four goals in his first seventeen games. In January, Kendall had gone across to Stanley Park to sign Liverpool defender Gary Ablett for £750,000, a purchase which hardly set the fans' pulses racing. Kendall was repeating the errors made when first appointed a decade before, that of signing players who were not going to collectively improve and no better than those sold. 'Everton were an embarrassment during those years,' one correspondent to the *Football Echo* said, before claiming, 'and I feel with the signing of the likes of Ablett, Ward and especially Alan Harper, those nightmare days are upon us again. What we need is a manager with vision and new ideas, not one who looks to the past and buys players who are, frankly, yesterday's men.'

That was a fair point, especially as Kendall had failed to address the two most pressing concerns: a domineering presence in the middle of the park and a tall striker to act as a focal point. The Everton boss had tried to rectify the latter by making two offers for Arsenal's Alan Smith, but was rebuffed as the Gunners were holding out for £2 million and, with money tight, that was beyond the Goodison coffers. There was also talk of arranging a short-term deal for John Aldridge, who had made a prolific return to English football with Tranmere Rovers after a spell in Spain. In the *Liverpool Daily Post*, Len Capeling memorably described the attack as possessing 'the cutting edge of marzipan scissors, the firepower of a one-legged midget.'

The worsening position was complicated by the fact that there was continuing talk in Spanish newspapers of a return to the Iberian peninsula, which increased when Kendall journeyed to northern Spain to visit, in his words, 'old friends' in late January. Jim Greenwood naturally denied the rumours, claiming the trip was to tie up some loose ends from a pre-season friendly with Real Sociedad. That may have been true but Kendall met with Athletic Bilbao club president José Larrauri – whose club were struggling in sixth from bottom – and was seated in the directors' box when Barcelona visited. The timing of the trip was both odd and intriguing: the Saturday evening prior to the FA Cup tie at Chelsea less than 24 hours later. Everton officials knew about the visit and it seemed strange to sanction one when the squad should have been preparing for a season-defining game.

Naturally the tabloid rumour mill also went into overdrive, especially when representatives from Benfica also sounded him out. Kendall responded by denying the gossip: 'Stories about my imminent departure have been flying around for weeks now – but I have a job to do here and I aim to finish it.' Interestingly, there were claims the club would not stand in Kendall's way with Andy Gray, Joe Royle, and Peter Reid – on the brink of a second top-five finish at Maine Road – on the shortlist.

Kendall and Harvey leave the pitch after the drab goalless draw at Notts County in March 1992 – their demeanour perhaps reflecting the fact that rekindling the old magic was proving difficult.

After the Chelsea defeat the season nosedived. Against a severely weakened Southampton side at the start of April, a 1-0 home defeat brought unhappy memories. 'The lowest league crowd of the season - a paltry 15,201 - delivered what is becoming a now customary chorus of jeering at the final whistle to let Kendall and his players know exactly what they feel about the present slump,' Phil McNulty wrote. A fourth successive loss ten days later, 2-0 at home to Sheffield United, was the worst sequence of results since the final days of Gordon Lee. Having fallen to a lowly sixteenth and with home gates dropping to the level of the dark days of 1983, the anticipated renaissance was not transpiring. 'I honestly think that Kendall has to go. If he was a man he would resign,' one fan wrote in the *Football Echo*. 'I honestly think he wants the sack so he can go to Spain. Everton are devoid of anything on the pitch and off the pitch, there is no leadership. Nothing in the club.' Harsh words perhaps but reflecting the concerns of the fanbase. Although seven points from the final four games took Everton twelfth, it was their lowest league placing for more than a decade. 'Howard Kendall's first full season back in charge has gone badly,' Christopher Davies concluded in the *Daily Telegraph*.

End of an era

After the woeful showing against Sheffield United, the Everton boss warned ominously, 'Certain players are not playing to their strengths. After a few years in management, you know who they are, and it will be put right.' One player never in that category was Kevin Ratcliffe. With Martin Keown's excellent form ensuring any first-team options were limited, the club's most successful captain largely ended his Goodison career where it had started – at left-back. However the fall-out from the disastrous Leeds home defeat in the League Cup meant his departure was inevitable, especially with Gary Ablett's arrival in January further limiting opportunities. Ratcliffe was dissatisfied with his manager, though. Told by Kendall that he could leave only for a fee before Ablett came, afterwards the former skipper – the captain's armband had been passed to Dave Watson – was informed that he could leave on a free transfer. 'I'd been injured and [I thought] "what are people going to think now?",' Ratcliffe later said, 'I was disappointed with Howard and the way he dealt with it.'

That was not the end of the matter, though. Knowing it was his last season after fifteen years at the club, Ratcliffe asked to be selected for the final game, a meaningless encounter at Goodison against Chelsea. Kendall refused and played an eighteen-year-old David Unsworth instead. 'I was fit for the last game of the season but he wouldn't play me. I was disappointed,' Ratcliffe told the *Across the Park* podcast. Like Graeme Sharp, and to a lesser extent Kevin Sheedy, the way Kendall handled the departure of his dressing-room leaders showed the darker side of his personality. There is a time for being ruthless but this was not the case and, as with his team-mates, Ratcliffe deserved far better treatment from his manager.

For all that, Ratcliffe had never recovered from the problems arising from the after-effects of the injury suffered at Sheffield Wednesday in January 1988. 'There were games when I wasn't even fifty per cent fit but I went out there,' he told the *People* after leaving. Sadly, for somebody rated among the best defenders in Europe just three years before, the Everton captain's decline mirrored that of the club itself.

29

A WHOLE NEW BALL GAME

ALMOST A YEAR AFTER THE FOUNDING MEETING AT GOODISON PARK, and following months of negotiations and fraught discussions between football's governing bodies, the green light was given for the formation of the new Premier League in February 1992. On Merseyside the move was welcomed, with chairman David Marsh echoing John Moores' previous complaints about the ambitions of the big clubs being thwarted by the perceived short-sightedness of those further down. 'The essential advantage is that our members will, at long last, be responsible for their own destiny,' he explained. 'That has to be an improvement, because in the past every time a change has been proposed, it has almost invariably been thrown out by the representatives of the lower divisions.'

For supporters a 22-team division operated by the Football League replaced by another under the auspices of the FA appeared seamless. However, the signs of the winds of change within English football became apparent when the contract for television coverage was awarded three months later.

Sky's the limit

Planning for the renewal of the contract, in November 1990 ITV's Greg Dyke invited Philip Carter and other representatives from the Big Five for dinner at London Weekend Television. During the meeting Dyke reaffirmed ITV's belief that in future they would only be interested in showing the big clubs, while warning that terms would not be as good as last time should they remain with the Football League. Dyke's view was the Big Five would be better served financially by breaking away. Also helping ITV's cause was that the big clubs resented the way David Dein and Carter had been treated by the League.

What is not open to debate is the award of the television contract for the new Premier League in May 1992 is the stuff of legend. With Sky also in contention, ITV knew the fledgling rival would likely go bust if they lost the auction, so their bid was raised to an unbelievable £262 million for thirty live games a season over five years. However, Spurs chairman, Alan Sugar, who stood to personally gain from an alliance with Sky on account of his Amstrad satellite equipment manufacturing business, emerged as the key player. With ITV in pole position, his intervention on the morning of the award has gone down in folklore. 'I went to the public phone cubicles opposite the meeting room and called their [Sky] chief executive Sam Chisholm,' he recalled in *What You See is What You Get.* 'There's only one way to clinch the deal – you'll have to blow them out of the water! Make your final bid £60m per season and blow them out of the water.' Within minutes a fax was received from Sky offering a mouth-watering £304 million over five years for sixty games a season (which included a £44 million contribution from the BBC for highlights). When the 22 clubs eventually voted for the deal a two-thirds majority was required and, with two abstentions, a 14-6 result in favour of Sky changed the landscape of English football forever.

Nevertheless, there are several myths about the deal. First is that the clubs received the full amount over the term of the contract – the final figure, thanks to issues with overseas rights and sponsorship, was a significantly less £191 million. A second is that the move to Sky for an unprecedented sum was the Big Five being greedy. However, four of them voted *against* Sky and for ITV.[91] Unsurprisingly, Tottenham were the exception. The clubs who did vote for Sky were the so-called 'Bates/Noades' axis[92] who had blocked the recommendations of the Chester Report a decade before. Collectively they supported the Sky bid as it allowed a more equitable share of the spoils than ITV – 'As soon as the small clubs knew that fifty per cent of Sky receipts were to be shared equally between all the Premier League clubs, the deal was irresistible,' the *Guardian* said at the time – and twice as many live games per campaign gave them a chance for more exposure. Most significantly they had not forgotten how ITV and Dyke attempted to freeze them out entirely four years before. For the big clubs, the irony of opposing a deal only made possible because of their desire to breakaway was not lost. The reality was that the original split, with the support of ITV, was intended – rightly or wrongly – to put clear financial distance between the Big Five and their rivals. Although the Sky contract gave Everton more money, they and the rest of the Big Five would have received a much higher figure with ITV, as well as greater exposure. Sponsorship deals were worth more if games were broadcast on terrestrial television to audiences of seven million rather than 500,000 on a

---

91 For the record the other two were Aston Villa and Leeds, significantly clubs included in the ill-fated deal Philip Carter and David Dein tried to put together with ITV in 1988 which ultimately led to their sacking by the Football League.

92 Yet the two clubs who abstained from the vote were Chelsea and Crystal Palace.

subscription-based satellite channel.[93]

That was a very much unspoken truth when chief executive Jim Greenwood put on a brave face 24 hours later. 'We are concerned over what we fear will prove to be over-exposure, and we don't like the number of Monday games, which are likely to cause problems,' he pointed out. 'However, we were outvoted so we have to get on with it.' As it happened, they needed all the money available.

Tightening the purse strings

New chairman David Marsh took over from Philip Carter in August 1991, having been on the board for three years. An outstanding golfer – twice English amateur champion, twice Walker Cup skipper as well as captain of Cambridge and England – the 57-year-old had also qualified as a doctor thirty years before. At the time he was also captain of the Royal and Ancient, the most prestigious role in world golf. Therefore, in many ways, it was a strange and uninspiring selection. Marsh had no corporate business or football administration background, although he was an Everton supporter. Marsh's statement on becoming chairman – 'I saw nearly all the home matches last season because the surgery is only five minutes from the club and I'd luckily combined some dinners with away fixtures' – were hardly the words of somebody appearing totally committed to the cause.

As well as steering the club through the transition out of the Football League, Marsh also had the challenge of rebuilding while competing against others with more financial clout. 'I have been most impressed with the signings he [Kendall] has made, particularly at the price,' he admitted before the start of the 1991/92 campaign, the emphasis on the latter indicating that the club were not exactly cash-rich. The other priority was ensuring they met all the stadium changes mandated by the Taylor Report, primarily the provision of all-seated grounds. Having made several changes in that direction over the previous decade – such as making the Enclosure and Paddock all-seated – Everton were better placed than most in meeting the construction and financial challenges. The first change had taken place during the summer of 1991 when seats were installed on the Gwladys Street terraces, with the other project being the planned replacement of the Park End stand by 1994. Although there was a £2 million grant available from the Football Trust, the club still had to contribute £3 million from its own coffers to meet the bill.[94] Everton

---

[93]   As an example, pitch-side advertising was usually worth £50,000 per televised game but this fell to £5,000 for matches on BSkyB.

[94]   In comparison Liverpool needed £10 million to redevelop Anfield whilst Arsenal required £20 million for Highbury, funded by a debenture scheme.

were obliged to pass on some of those costs and a season ticket for the lower Gwladys Street terrace that set fans back £68 for standing was now £105 for a seat in 1991/92, much to the chagrin of some, who found their season ticket did not even guarantee them the same seat each game. Supporters also lost the 'spec' that many had stood in for many years.

Elsewhere, although the most expensive season ticket of £155 was comparable with Liverpool (£165) and Manchester United (£172), those two clubs took far more at the gate due to their traditionally larger crowds. And, whereas Everton's attendances had usually matched the north London clubs, now both Arsenal and Spurs were enjoying significantly higher crowds. With their most expensive season tickets in the £300-400 range, the two clubs were also forging ahead when comparing matchday revenue.

Consequently, with some dissatisfaction over prices when measured against the available fare on the pitch, Everton's home league attendances dropped to 23,141 in 1991/92, the tenth highest in the division – behind Nottingham Forest and just ahead of Sheffield United – as the Toffees bucked the general upward trend, with league attendances exceeding twenty million for the first time in more than a decade. The accounts for the season did not make good reading and a lack of success pushed them further behind their rivals. Income was £7 million, with matchday receipts being £5 million, half that of their near neighbours who, in a season where they won the FA Cup and enjoyed a lengthy European run, had revenue of £15 million.

Equally significantly, with a high wage bill, Everton lost £2 million for the year, with the debt to the bank now standing at £3.6 million. The pressure was therefore on Marsh to deliver but at the end of the campaign the new chairman was hardly convincing during an interview with Phil McNulty in the *Liverpool Daily Post*. Marsh stonewalled questions around finance and was vague around the club's aspirations. 'If a player becomes available and the board and the manager think he represents good value, we will do our best to make that money available,' he said, which hardly inspired confidence. Asked whether Everton would be attractive to players elsewhere, he was candid. 'If you look at the league position of twelfth you might have difficulty convincing them you are going to win something,' was the response. However, when asked if the club was falling behind their rivals his reply was more worrying. 'We've had to rebuild haven't we?' he responded, 'The team that played in FA Cup finals and League Cup finals have nearly all gone. Only Neville is left. Rebuilding takes time.' Yet it had been five years since the Goodison trophy room had been furnished with new silverware and Harvey had been sacked after failing to expensively reconstruct the championship-winning side. Kendall had spent a considerable amount of time and effort attempting to offload those expensive mistakes and consequently the team was nowhere near the finished article. Marsh's response was a reminder of Harry Catterick's words when he was struggling in the middle of the 1960s. 'The manager has been quoted as saying it is a transitional period and Everton will be good in two or three years' time,' one supporter responded. 'What good is that to an Evertonian? Is "transitional" a new word invented for mediocre?'

Len Capeling, in his column in the same newspaper, remarked, 'I'm sorry to say this but chairman Dr David Marsh did not persuade me that Everton have either the funds or the appetite of a genuine top-class club.' That lack of ambition was exemplified in Marsh's comment that he was only 'marginally disappointed' in the twelfth-place finish. Consequently, without a rich benefactor, the huge national and international support of Liverpool and Manchester United or the north London clubs' access to the *nouveaux riches*, Everton were doomed to exist in the shadows when the Premier League started.

Sir John Moores was still around but in too poor health to contribute. 'I never ever asked him for a penny of his money and nor would he have given it to me,' Marsh later admitted in *Faith of Our Families*, 'It was just an unwritten rule: you didn't ask. So from that point of view we knew we had to survive and we had to generate the money without him actually going into his pocket and giving it.' But with clubs still largely reliant on home gates for revenue and Goodison attendances having dropped by a third during the previous five years, they needed investment as a priority, and this was proving difficult. 'Jim [Greenwood] and I went on various trips to try and arrange finance,' Marsh later revealed. 'You could get the finance, but the people who were prepared to give it would not have been approved by the rest of the board or probably by the FA. You needed millions not just the odd few hundred thousand, and that wasn't enough.' The increased focus on the cash side of football was not lost on Howard Kendall. 'They were talking about finances, which never came up in the past,' he later wrote in *Love Affairs & Marriage* about the first board meeting of his second spell. 'The club's debt was brought up. Philip Carter joked, "Nothing changes, Howard, does it?" I always remember that statement: "Nothing changes, does it?" But it had changed.'

In the bargain basement

The club's spending during the summer of 1992 reflected that lack of drive and hard cash. Although the hierarchy were insisting money was flowing in, season-ticket sales down by twenty per cent were a product of a disillusioned and increasingly disenfranchised fanbase. Although the returning Everton boss had made mistakes, the board had failed to provide sufficient financial support and, after two moderate seasons, David Marsh had been proved correct in one way. With little chance of immediate success then the most highly sought-after players were giving Goodison a wide berth. There was no chance of Everton being part of the battle for the summer's prize-asset, Alan Shearer, who went to Blackburn Rovers for £3.6 million and an annual salary of £450,000 which was twice that of Goodison's highest earner. However, Jim Greenwood claimed that the club was not alone. 'Our situation is no different to the rest of the Premier League with the exception of Blackburn, who have got a rich backer pumping money in,' he explained. 'The situation in football remains tight. To spend £1.5 million on an individual wipes out our season ticket money for an entire season. To pay £3 million ties up that income for two years.' Not only that but the rise in salaries over the previous four years meant they, rather than transfer fees, were becoming the primary source of expenditure.

Even if Everton had money, the lack of quality in the squad would hardly have whetted the appetite of the best players. With Manchester United and Chelsea, the Toffees were one of three clubs who met Cambridge United's £1 million price tag for striker Dion Dublin but the 23-year-old understandably felt Old Trafford was the best option. Having offered better personal terms than Chelsea for Luton Town's Mick Harford, Kendall was left frustrated when the hardman striker still chose Stamford Bridge. The Everton boss was also interested in re-signing Trevor Steven after the midfielder's twelve months at Marseille ended during the summer. '[He] is one of the most outstanding footballers I have ever managed. He is the sort of top-quality player I am looking for,' the admiring Kendall said. Yet the £2.5 million transfer fee and Steven's huge salary proved prohibitive and another dead end was reached. Long-term target Paul McStay of Celtic also rejected a move to Goodison. 'Could it be that the Blues are no longer the prestige club they would like us to believe they are,' said one correspondent to the *Football Echo*. 'Everton have dropped down the ladder and I don't know what it will take to get them back up there.'

Kendall's signings in the summer reflected the financial *realpolitik*. After an inquiry for Dundee United's Duncan Ferguson, the search for a target man finally ended in Scotland when £500,000 clinched the signature of Rangers' Paul Rideout. A schoolboy prodigy at Swindon Town, the forward turned down a move to Liverpool in the summer of 1983 before two years at Villa Park. Thereafter he became something of a wanderer. Everton were his sixth club in nine years and, remarkably, the move to Merseyside was a third transfer in the space of eleven months. The other major signing was Wales skipper Barry Horne, bought for £500,000 from Southampton. Although the midfielder would bring much-needed leadership and grit, more was needed if Kendall's claim that 'For the first time in his career really Barry is going to be expected to win something' was realistic. The signing of a 28-year-old journeyman striker and a thirty-year-old midfielder did not really justify the Everton manager's optimism in truth. As did the initial loan signing of Predrag Radosavljević who, thankfully for copywriters everywhere, was known by his nickname, Preki. The skilful left-footed midfielder had enjoyed an unusual career. After a brief period with Red Star Belgrade he became a big star in the US indoor soccer league either side of a year in Sweden. A free agent as his side, St Louis Storm, had just gone out of business, eventually the Yugoslav was granted a work permit after impressing in pre-season and signed for a reported £300,000. Just four summers after Everton had broken the domestic transfer record for Tony Cottee, they were now trawling the footballing wasteland of North America for bargains.

Welcome to the Big League

More than thirty years later the opening day of the Premier League is seen as a giant leap forward for English football but at the time it was very much a step into the great unknown. Indeed, just four days before a ball was kicked in earnest, the new body was in disarray over a familiar subject – money – between familiar adversaries – the big clubs and their smaller counterparts. The original plan was for brewery giants Bass to sponsor the league in a £9.5 million deal but this was blocked by Liverpool, Arsenal and Nottingham Forest on a technicality. In a counter-offensive, those three clubs, with Everton, Manchester United, Leeds, Aston Villa and QPR, formed their own exclusive group, the Platinum Club, and negotiated perimeter advertising and sponsorship packages for themselves. Collectively their eight votes also blocked the Bass deal but six months later one club broke rank, which was sufficient for the Premier League to agree a £12 million deal with the brewer over four years. In doing so, the power of the traditional big clubs was diluted. 'Football's new Premier League kicks off next weekend with many of its 22 clubs still trying to fathom whether it will be a financial bonanza or a banana,' *The Sunday Times* claimed before the season started.

One reason why the clubs were desperate to maximise commercial deals was because talk of a financial jackpot was premature. The guaranteed income from domestic TV rights was £35 million a year – a steep increase from the previous £11 million paid by ITV, but for Everton – like the rest of the Big Five – the deal offered very little in comparison, with the club receiving just £1.4m.[95] The figure did not exactly fire the

---

[95]   Champions Manchester United getting £2.4m, while generating £10m in gate revenue for the season, showed that for all the rewritten history, the early years of the Premier League were not exactly a cash cow.

imagination. 'We lost two million pounds last year, so it's not that much,' Jim Greenwood pointed out ruefully.

With clubs still facing the pressures of meeting the costs of the Taylor Report, plus rising wages and transfer fees, for all the new riches flowing into the game there was still a familiar source of income to be tapped even further: the spectators. Fans of the new league were faced with an increase of up to twenty per cent for both terrace and stand tickets, as all but three clubs put their prices up. At Goodison the more expensive tickets went up by fifteen per cent. With Sky expected to introduce a monthly subscription for Premier League games, access to live top-flight games was no longer a free service. The gentrification of football had commenced. 'Now traditional fans fear they will be left on the sidelines when a new breed of middle-class football followers become the only people who can afford to watch soccer,' the *Daily Mirror* warned.

The other issue was the plans for games on a Monday evening, with both Merseyside clubs continuing to express their dismay over the provision. 'I think the whole principle of Monday night football disrupts the social life of British society,' David Marsh said. 'We have people coming from far and wide. They won't be able to leave work early on Monday to travel to the game.' The two clubs subsequently agreed that season-ticket holders unable to attend games played on that day would receive refunds – how times change.

30

NEW DAWN FADES

'WE HAVE THE ABILITY TO WIN ANYTHING WE ENTER AND AFTER A few seasons in the shadows we might well surprise a few people.' Howard Kendall greeting the new season with a call to arms. Yet there was nothing off the pitch to support such optimism, given the financial position. 'It's the story of a club that has lost its way, of a club that lost its appetite for the big time,' Len Capeling commented in the *Liverpool Daily Post*. 'Of a club that recruited a former messiah in Howard Kendall – and then promptly clapped him in handcuffs.' The bookmakers also had different ideas, odds of 33-1 to lift the title putting them on a par with Premier League new-boys Blackburn Rovers and Nottingham Forest.

Meanwhile, the Sky promotional film may have attempted to promote the Premier League as a new product but many saw through the razzamatazz. 'The new "Premier" status is just a sham,' said one supporter in the *Football Echo*, 'but the fans are no fools and they recognise that.'

Meet the new league, same as the old one

The opening day of the new Premier League on 15 August, 1992 had more in common with the previous history of English football than the future. There were just eight overseas players within the 22 teams. At Goodison it was very much business as usual when Sheffield Wednesday provided the opposition in front of 27,687 spectators – the second-highest attendance of the day – with the visitors' Nigel Pearson becoming the first to score on the ground in the new league, before debutant Barry Horne equalised before the break.

'We're already a point ahead of the Premier League favourites,' Kendall joked after the game, referring to Manchester United's defeat at Sheffield United. And it was to Old Trafford that his side travelled for their first away game, against an outfit who had blown the chance of a first title in 25 years during the previous spring. In the surreal setting of a stadium holding only 32,000 spectators due to reconstruction of a deserted Stretford End, the rampant visitors put United to the sword with a series of sucker punches. In the opening half Ablett's headed clearance went to Warzycha on the right, the Polish winger's cross-field pass picked out Beardsley, who had sneaked through a gap in the middle, and the England international scored past Peter Schmeichel. Despite enjoying huge territorial advantage, United failed to breach the sturdy Everton rearguard and when Beardsley released Warzycha ten minutes from the end, the Pole turned Gary Pallister inside out before finishing past Schmeichel from twelve yards.[96] At the end the Danish goalkeeper blundered when his fluffed clearance went straight to Maurice Johnston, who curled home a third. 'We must keep killing teams off,' the delighted Kendall said afterwards. 'When we had chances last night, we tucked them away, whereas last season we were dominating games and letting teams off the hook.'

A week later when a late Johnston goal secured a 1-0 victory over Aston Villa after a dominant display, the Toffees stood second in the table, with the promise of renaissance after several years' disappointments. 'Four games and 11 days is too early in the season to assess whether Howard Kendall has fashioned his second Goodison Park championship team,' Dennis Shaw surmised in *The Times*, 'but there can be little doubt that he has Everton on the move again.' New signing Horne had proved an astute signing, his ball-winning capacity adding some much-needed vigour to the midfield.

Eleven minutes from the end of the visit to Spurs on the first Saturday of September there was further tangible evidence of progress. Leading through another Beardsley goal, who galloped clear to put Everton ahead three minutes before the break, the visitors dominated the hapless home team but retreated further and further back as the game progressed, depriving the scorer of meaningful service. Under increasing pressure, the defence eventually crumbled when, on 79 minutes, Paul Allen equalised after two shots had been blocked. With the home team appearing to have settled for a draw, they garnered an undeserved victory when the seventeen-year-old Andy Turner volleyed home via a deflection off Horne. 'White Hart Lane's jubilation carried more than a tinge of incredulity,' Patrick Barclay wrote in the *Observer*. 'Everton could blame only themselves.' Having seen defeat snatched from the jaws of victory, the visiting boss cut a frustrated figure. 'It's easy to say it was a hard-luck story,' he said, 'but we've said that before. We are dominating games without killing the opposition off.'

The unfortunate defeat was a signal that the early-season promise was merely an

---

[96]   Thus becoming the first foreign player to score in the Premier League. It was more than twenty years before the next Polish goal in the top-flight – Marcin Wasilewski for Leicester City in January 2015, curiously also as Old Trafford.

illusion. When Manchester United easily gained revenge at Goodison in mid-September by cantering to a 2-0 victory, Kendall let slip afterwards that several players had fallen below the 'required standards'. This was shorthand for saying the team was largely incapable of meeting his desired level of performance. 'This is a squad riddled with misfits, cast-offs and cut-price overseas gambles, many forced on the club out of financial necessity,' Stephen Bierley pointed out in the *Guardian*. The situation was because the largesse of the Harvey years – expensive fees and high wages making it difficult to move players on – was still being felt. There were very few saleable assets and even scarcer takers. Andy Hinchcliffe had been on the market with no interest and for another player it was a familiar tale of exclusion.

Tony's trouble

'I've still got a year left on my contract but Kendall has told me if he gets an offer he's happy with, he'll accept it,' Tony Cottee said during the summer. 'That tells me I'm not wanted in the long term.' Injured at the start of the season, he had been on the transfer list for twelve months with no interest and his immediate prospects looked bleak especially as there were four forwards chasing two positions.

But Kendall's gamble of dropping Maurice Johnston and recalling the striker for the trip to Blackburn Rovers, three days after the United defeat, paid off. With Kenny Dalglish now managing the Lancashire club, Cottee returned to haunt the Scot after his injury-time intervention at Goodison eighteen months earlier had started a chain of events that led to his Anfield resignation. The visitors endured a dreadful start when Mark Ward was carried off with a broken leg after eight minutes and Alan Shearer put the home side ahead shortly after. But after substitute Warzycha struck the bar with a header, Cottee followed up to score. Then five minutes later the Polish international's cross went beyond the lurking striker and was met perfectly by John Ebbrell to put the visitors ahead. After Shearer stabbed home a second-half equaliser, nine minutes from time Cottee was left with a simple tap-in at the far post after more good work from Warzycha.[97]

The former West Ham striker was understandably jubilant after his brace had secured a 3-2 win. 'I feel I am the person to score the goals for Everton,' he proclaimed 24 hours

---

[97] In a season celebrating their Goodison Park centenary, Everton were keen to acknowledge the landmark. Between 1881 and 1902, Everton had worn pink shirts before changing to blue so when their marketing manager, Derek Johnston, met representatives of their kit manufacturer, Umbro, to discuss the new away kit, there was a natural choice. 'We wanted a kit as close as we could to our original one, so pink got the vote,' Johnston said. Surprisingly the move was well received. 'The lads like it,' said Dave Watson at the start of the season. They liked it even more after winning at Ewood Park on its first outing.

later. 'If anyone doubted my ability, I proved a point last night.' But after being given a hero's reception at Goodison on the following Saturday, Cottee and his team-mates were outplayed by a Crystal Palace side without a win all season. The visitors netted two identical goals in the opening half, both initiated by the menacing John Salako on the left. He fed the excellent Chris Armstrong – a player Kendall had tried to get on loan from previous club Millwall – to first score via a header and then with a dribble past Southall. The home team's display was strangely characterised by little passion or commitment. 'Everton's passive attitude was hard to fathom. Merseysiders usually know better than most that a football match is civil war conducted by other means,' Sue Mott pointed out in *The Sunday Times*.

After a 2-0 defeat at Leeds seven days later left Everton in distinctly mid-table territory there was a growing feeling of unease amongst supporters. The defence was leaking goals and increasingly dependent on Southall for protection. At right-back Alan Harper was now past his best and struggling. The attack was lightweight. Cottee looked lost whilst Paul Rideout had failed to open his account. 'I honestly think that Everton's manager has taken leave of his football senses,' wrote one correspondent in the *Football Echo*. 'As a consequence he is fast losing any remaining credibility.' When Everton travelled to Boundary Park to reacquaint themselves with the plastic pitch and Joe Royle, it was a piece of history as the first Everton game shown live on Sky television under the new contract. Graeme Sharp enjoyed an excellent game and set up the only goal for Richard Jobson after eight minutes. Thereafter only the home team's generosity prevented a landslide, with another former Everton player, Ian Marshall, particularly profligate. 'To say it was a poor performance is an understatement,' Kendall said afterwards. 'What was disappointing yesterday was the way we defended.'[98]

Dropped for the trip to Oldham, by the end of October Cottee had failed to score a league goal since Blackburn and was brooding on the sidelines. Recalled to the team, he was poor in a 2-0 defeat at Arsenal and afterwards Kendall attacked some players – although not singling out Cottee – for producing performances that had fallen to 'unacceptable levels'.[99] But when the striker was then dropped for a League Cup game against Wimbledon four days later, it was clear who was the scapegoat. 'I don't think he's done enough,' Kendall said about the axing. 'Some players, not just Tony Cottee, have

---

[98]   The audience for the match on Sky was just under 500,000, compared to more than two million who watched live coverage of Serie A on Channel 4 on the same afternoon. When top-flight football was on ITV the viewing figures for a game averaged seven million.

[99]   At least the Everton boss had not lost his sense of humour. When a reporter mentioned after the game he had not seen Everton play before this season, Kendall responded, 'I haven't seen them play very often either.'

been giving performances that have dropped to unacceptable levels.' The manager's rather personal comments provoked an understandably angry response from his striker. After replying with a hat-trick for the reserves, Cottee struck out. 'I'm always the scapegoat. It's always me and it always has been. I was certainly very disappointed by the manager's comments before the Wimbledon game,' he angrily claimed. 'I think I'm mistreated. Not at times but most of the time.' But when Cottee stated that 'Until we get a Gary McAllister or someone who can pass a ball and create chances, we are not going to create that many openings,' Kendall was always going to take umbrage. 'He can have a go at me whenever he pleases,' the furious manager remarked, 'but he committed the cardinal sin of criticising his team-mates and fellow professionals.' Ironically, the striker had been part of Kendall's plans for the following home game against Manchester City but the outburst meant he spent the game kicking his heels in the stands. 'Four years ago, Cottee believed that Everton, under Colin Harvey, were more likely to be more successful than Arsenal under George Graham,' Ian Ross wrote in *The Times*. 'His judgment was faulty then and, according to Howard Kendall, the present Everton manager, it is not too good today.'

Cottee may have spoken his mind in criticising the team but he was probably correct. The usual central midfield of Barry Horne and John Ebbrell were defensively-minded while creative players like Warzycha and Preki were woefully inconsistent. 'He [Cottee] wasn't telling the fans something they don't know already,' Len Capeling pointed out in the *Liverpool Daily Post*. 'This Everton side has been allowed to slide into mediocrity and that the values of the old "school of science" have been allowed to melt away like snow in the Sahara.' Tellingly, the striker largely had the support of fans too.

Nevertheless, Kendall's assessment of Cottee contained an element of truth. Although a tally of seventy goals from 171 appearances was perfectly reasonable and the striker could argue that service had been moderate at best, the record signing had failed to influence big games and worryingly his weaknesses – poor positioning and first touch, tame heading, and inability to beat his marker – had largely remained unaddressed in four years at Goodison. Furthermore, his continued failure to engender any sort of empathy with a steady flow of striking partners counted against him. 'We were in and out of love together,' Cottee told the *Athletic* in 2021. 'There was a conversation where Howard told me he knew that I scored goals, but he wanted more than that. I wondered why he wanted me to try and do something that might detract from what I'm good at.'

However, by dropping his striker, Kendall's sensitivity to criticism was a major error. With the team averaging less than a goal a game, he should have left Cottee to do his talking on the pitch and then deal with the matter afterwards. Ironically, against Peter Reid's excellent side, Everton created a surfeit of chances but were let down by poor finishing from replacement Stuart Barlow as the visitors strolled to a 3-1 victory, which planted the Toffees firmly in the relegation zone.[100] 'The dwindling support are wondering if Howard Kendall can repeat his rescue act of nine years ago,' John Keith admitted in the *Daily Express*.

Troubled times

Pressed on the worrying position, chairman David Marsh was phlegmatic. 'We are less than a third of the way through the season,' he pointed out. 'We are not about to panic. Every team goes through a bad patch.' With fans imploring the board to enter the transfer market, Marsh cautioned that club finances were still perilous while Kendall bemoaned the absence of quality. 'If you do find it, it is difficult to prise people away. When clubs have got good players, they are very reluctant to lose them,' he revealed. 'Today there is a shortage of the type of player I brought in during my first period as manager. Everybody would like a young Peter Reid and a young Andy Gray...or an old Andy Gray for that matter.' In the dark days of almost a decade earlier, Kendall would continuously talk about the real quality on the training pitch and how it was a matter of time before that was transferred to matchdays. Now the manager was making no such claims. Indeed, some of the off-the-pitch discourse indicated that the camp was not exactly brimming with happiness. 'The indications are that Everton's class of '92...are by no means as united behind their manager as were the class of '83,' William Johnson pointedly reasoned in the *Daily Telegraph*.

But those mitigating circumstances could not hide the fact that, for a club £4 million in the red, a further £1.7 million had been spent by Kendall during the summer for very little reward. 'The marriage he talks of may not yet be on the rocks,' Johnson added, 'but it will need all the counselling skills of the manager, a sympathetic approach from the boardroom and a positive response from the dressing room if another separation is to be averted.' Kendall certainly drew support from his chairman, though. 'There is no question of resignations,' Marsh claimed. 'We have every confidence in Howard, who is a good manager and proven one.'

---

[100] There was a humorous but temporary truce to the hostilities between the two parties. Unusually Cottee visited his local pub on the Sunday after the City game and the first face he saw was his manager, who met him with a smile and a big handshake. The Sunday newspapers were full of stories that Cottee would be fined £6,000 – two weeks' wages – and when the striker offered to buy Kendall a drink, quick as a flash he responded: 'No, save your money, you're going to need it.' In the end Cottee had to pay for a team meal in Southport – and that came to £1,000, with the champagne paid for by Mark Ward, who was also being punished.

The first tentative steps towards a full reconciliation took place a week later at the City Ground, where Everton had not won for more than a decade. Given the respective managers' trophy-winning history, there was some poignancy in the fixture: if Kendall was having a hard time, then Nottingham Forest were in an even worse situation – Brian Clough's side were bottom. 'It was billed as the crisis showdown,' Jim Holden wrote in the *Daily Express* after the game. On an afternoon when Cottee, Johnston, Hinchcliffe, Preki and Beagrie were in the A team at Oldham, the visitors withstood a frantic first-half barrage and won the game on 52 minutes with a sharp counter-attack which ended with Rideout heading his first league goal for the club. 'A very, very important game for us,' Kendall admitted afterwards, 'especially after the way it had been built up in terms of managers' positions. After this, I assure you neither of us is going to be resigning.' But in the following game there was another home setback with a 1-0 defeat to Chelsea. Kendall eschewed offensive players like Peter Beagrie and Robert Warzycha and selected a midfield featuring Barry Horne with two converted full-backs in Alan Harper and Andy Hinchcliffe. The latter pair had dreadful games as the visitors dominated for long periods of the game. 'Only the amazing Southall, at 34 still Britain's premier goalkeeper, kept the score from resembling a rugby result,' Malcolm Winton said in *The Sunday Times*. The Toffees had not won a home league game since August and had scored just four goals there all season. 'There is a lack of confidence, especially at Goodison,' Kendall said afterwards. 'It's incredible. I've never experienced home form as bad as this either as a player or manager here.'

Seven days later it was the same story, a 1-0 loss at Ipswich leaving Everton in nineteenth place. But the Toffees boss made the back pages for a bizarre quote after the game. 'We have shown people here we are in a false position and not far off a championship side, never mind a relegation side,' he claimed. 'It's not right yet and I'm not trying to kid people it is. But we are not far off.' Although he said 48 hours later that the press had misquoted him, for a side with one league victory in eleven games the manager became any easy target. 'Mr Kendall did not say which championship,' the esteemed Bryon Butler wrote in the *Daily Telegraph* of a manager fighting a relegation battle. 'It must be assumed he has a crack at next season's First Division in mind.'[101]

The defeat raised the question of why there had been no progress in Kendall's two years back in the dugout. In many ways the problems started there. The manager was not alone in believing Harvey's recruitment was flawed. He had jettisoned Neil McDonald,

---

[101] With the formation of the Premier League, the new name of the second tier.

Mike Newell, Mike Milligan and Stuart McCall. Andy Hinchcliffe and Tony Cottee were also up for sale. The inference being, of course, that Kendall obviously did not rate Harvey's judgement. That was no issue if Kendall had selected a new coaching team but, with the previously successful partnership back together, their professional relationship may have been compromised and Harvey could have felt undermined.

That may have been a justifiable strategy if results had improved but, if anything, they were getting worse. The turnover in players had not strengthened the squad: was Paul Rideout – who was playing centre-half at his previous club – really an improvement on Newell? The ageing Alan Harper did not provide an upgrade on McDonald in terms of youth, ability and versatility. Likewise, Mark Ward with Stuart McCall. Maurice Johnston had not played for the best part of two months. Yes, there were financial issues but unimaginative recruitment was like Gordon Lee's at the end of the 1970s where, for example, a player like an ageing Martin Dobson made way for Asa Hartford, who was nearing thirty. Kendall's recent selection of a midfield with no natural width was reminiscent of Lee's strategy in the 1979/80 campaign which brought widespread criticism.

However, in a familiar tale, supporters – while acknowledging the below-par performance of the manager – also targeted the board. The continuing fall in attendances hardly helped finances and expected riches derived from the Premier League barely compensated. 'They [the board] have presided over mediocrity for far too long,' said one frustrated correspondent to the *Football Echo*. 'If Dr Marsh's repeated statements that no money is available for new players is true, Everton must cease to claim to be a big club, and we must all resign ourselves to forever being also-rans…Unfortunately Dr Marsh looks destined to be the chairman that presided over relegation.'

31
NOTHING IN THE POT

NOT MANY PEOPLE HAVE A STAGE SHOW ABOUT THEIR LIFE STORY BUT *Whatever Happened to Billy Kenny* played at Liverpool's Royal Court to critical acclaim in April 2023. The subject – an Everton player whose namesake father had made thirteen appearances a half-century before – once appeared to have the world at his feet before a harrowing descent into addiction. Kenny was a hugely talented midfielder who had attracted the attention of both Kenny Dalglish and Alex Ferguson. When on trials for the England Under-16 team at Lilleshall he had roomed with Ryan Wilson, who later changed his name to Ryan Giggs.

Billy do be a hero

Kenny eventually signed for Everton and made his debut against Coventry in October 1992. There were 23 appearances before the end of the campaign. But then problems started. Kenny had shin splints and needed a hernia operation. 'Compartment Syndrome' followed – his muscles were growing but the surrounding skin was not and another operation was needed. With no football, boredom followed and for Kenny, who had previously been virtually teetotal, that eventually led to a chaotic lifestyle built around an addiction to cocaine and extensive alcohol abuse. Out injured, Kenny did not have to perform so the secret remained just that. 'That's my biggest regret – not telling Colin or Howard Kendall earlier because they would have sorted me out or tried to stop me,' he told the *Liverpool Echo* in 1998. By the time he was back at Bellefield the game was up. 'I couldn't run. I was taking it [cocaine] when I was coming home,' he revealed. 'I had blood and urine samples taken and the club realised I was on coke.' After a spell in rehab and a move to Oldham that ended in another premature exit, there was a further 25 years of drug and alcohol addiction which ended after the death of his mother. 'I've had a second crack at life,' he told the same newspaper in 2023. 'I played for Everton and no-one can take that away from me. I enjoyed it.' But Kenny would have just been another of the game's lost peripheral talents but for one performance at Goodison Park on the first Monday in December 1992.[102]

Like their neighbours, Liverpool had endured a moderate 1991/92 campaign and in early September the feeling was that Graeme Souness was in danger of the sack.[103] Going into the game the home team languished in nineteenth place with their rivals standing ninth, an indication of the rebuilding job required at Anfield. Kenny was one of seven players making their derby debuts while Johnston returned to the fold. If the home team required motivation, then they needed only to turn the pages of the *Liverpool Echo* on the evening before the game: Liverpool's sponsors, Carlsberg, took out an advert featuring a spoof betting slip for the first goal-scorer – the Anfield side had five lines available, Everton had one.

In front of 35,826 spectators – 3,000 empty seats demonstrating that fears over the negative impact of Monday night football were not unfounded – Kendall deployed Ian Snodin as a sweeper to counter the wasteful Ronny Rosenthal. But this left the midfield short and the dominant visitors had enough opportunities to fill several of those betting lines in the opening hour. 'They played us off the pitch in the first half,' Peter Beardsley admitted afterwards. Although substitute Peter Beagrie and a move to a four-man backline produced a more attacking threat after a dreadfully negative opening period for the home team, there was no surprise when Mark Wright's powerful header from Mike Marsh's corner put Liverpool ahead after 62 minutes. The deserved lead lasted all of ninety seconds. With the visiting fans encamped at the Park End chanting 'going down' at their rivals, Snodin fed the returning Johnston at the edge of the box and the Scot turned and his left-footed shot curled past the scampering Mike Hooper, who really should have done more. It was only Everton's fifth goal in nine home league games.

The equaliser opened out the contest and John Barnes struck a post before forcing a brilliant save from Southall. Then eight minutes from the end came the winner – but not at the end supporters were expecting. Beardsley's perceptive pass fed Ablett on the left flank and his former Liverpool team-mate returned the ball to the Everton striker, whose right-footed drive skidded across the turf and past the dive of a despairing Hooper. Amazingly, the home team would have been lucky even to share the spoils but Beardsley's first Goodison goal for seven months secured a derby victory after a four-year gap and the first after trailing since 1932. The fireworks in the vicinity of Goodison Park and the

---

[102] The first Premier League game broadcast live at Goodison Park.

[103] Joe Royle was fifth in the betting to replace Souness at 12-1 with Kendall at 14-1.

sound of *Land of Hope and Glory* on the tannoy at the final whistle only added to the feeling of unreality, for both Kendall and disbelieving home supporters. Meanwhile the match-winner summed up the prevailing mood. 'I'm very pleased although overall I don't think we deserved to win,' Beardsley admitted. 'But in derby games it's not always the best team that does win.'

Peter Beardsley's winner made him only the second player, after David Johnson, to score for both sides in a Merseyside derby.

For Kenny the fortunate derby victory was the highlight of an Everton career strangled at birth. However, like the angler's tale of the one that got away, the impact of the midfielder's performance has grown over the years. Snodin was the *Liverpool Echo's* man of the match while Kenny's performance failed to trouble the scorers in any national newspaper reports. But the matchday sponsors were impressed enough to award the nineteen-year-old a bottle of champagne as their star man. In fact it was a double celebration for the precocious talent: earlier in the day he had signed a new two-and-a-half-year deal. 'He had earned it and he fully justified it on the night, passing the ball superbly and looking a top-class prospect,' Kendall declared 24 hours later. But Kenny would sadly remain just that: a top-class prospect.

Johnston jaw dropper

The derby win offered only temporary salvation, as five days later a dreadful performance in a 1-0 loss at Sheffield United meant any confidence derived from the victory disappeared. Maurice Johnston symbolised the fall from grace after the derby win better than anyone. 'He was the epitome of Goodison joy and relief that night,' Oliver Holt wrote in the *Liverpool Daily Post*. 'Against Sheffield United he was an anonymous figure again. In fact he was worse than anonymous.' Substituted just before the hour mark, Johnston slid out of sight at the back of the dug-out by the end of the game. 'It was just a nightmare,' he just about mumbled after the match. But the striker was not the only player below par at Bramall Lane. 'Judging on this game, their motivation is a frankly terrifying question,' James Lawton asked in the *Daily Express*. Afterwards Kendall angrily laid into his squad:

> *The players are letting themselves down and everyone connected with the club. Our fans are normally very noisy away from home. That was the quietest they have been all season and rightly so...That was the biggest hammering they [the players] have had off me for a long time. The way we played, particularly in the first half, was totally unacceptable.*

The Scot was dropped for the League Cup defeat at Chelsea in midweek, with the added humiliation of turning out for the reserves at Mansfield on the same evening. He was joined by Preki, equally anonymous at Sheffield and somebody whose Everton career, when starting, read: played four, lost four. Johnston remained on the sidelines for the festive period before a bizarre sequence of events which summed up his turbulent time at Goodison. Over Christmas the striker reportedly sustained a broken jaw, following a domestic incident, which only came to light on the first weekend in January. 'I understand the explanation he has given to me and what happened to him,' Kendall remarked. 'I know what people are going to think. It was over the Christmas period. You are talking about someone with a facial injury and people are going to jump to conclusions. I don't want that to happen.' Speculation unsurprisingly followed, especially when tabloid stories emerged of Mark Ward being involved in a brawl outside the Fisherman's Rest, a pub close to Johnston's home, on the same weekend. Although further inquiries established the Scot was not present, he literally remained tight-lipped. Meanwhile his manager's silence only added to the air of mystery, which was not helped when Johnston's wife cryptically told the press: 'He is a footballer and he has a football injury.'

Events then took a slightly farcical turn when chairman David Marsh – a doctor, of course – was quoted on local radio as explaining Johnston's injury had come via a collision with his daughter's rocking horse. Much mirth naturally ensued. However, the real story was never going to linger in the shadows for long. 'Maurice had a few drinks and had to be carried home,' a club source told the press. 'He got up in the middle of the night and fell, smashing his face at the bottom of the stairs.' The actual damage was a depressed fracture of a cheekbone, which required an operation keeping the striker out for a month. Having misled and ultimately undermined his manager, Johnston did not exactly have Kendall's sympathy. 'I've accepted it but I'm not happy,' a furious Kendall blustered. 'We get enough injuries and suspensions on the football field without this.'[104] With Paul Rideout suspended, Kendall had pencilled in Johnston for a return to the side for an FA Cup third-round replay against Wimbledon but that was no longer an option.

The Everton boss was never the forgiving sort over such matters and Johnston only played two more games. Yet there was still more controversy. In early May Kendall allowed him to finish the season early and go to Florida with his family for a month, after newspaper reports of an armed robbery at his home. However, subsequent stories indicated the intrusion had been exaggerated and there had 'only' been an unsuccessful burglary attempt with no weapons. The ruse, if there was one, seemed to work. Subsequently, the misfit remained at Goodison for a further four months before returning to Scotland.

The feeling is that Johnston was bought too late in his career, the sharpness and hunger of his peak years missing, although he could also point to a midfield that failed to play to his strengths. For a club with financial difficulties a £1.5m loss – as well as two years as the best-paid player – was a calculated gamble which failed. There was a lack of good judgement on Kendall's behalf: at a time when English football was becoming more athletic and muscular, he sold two strikers – Graeme Sharp and Mike Newell – suited to that environment while acquiring one with more technical gifts.

'I have to hold my hands up and admit Mo has been the biggest disappointment of my management career,' Kendall later admitted. 'Mo was my most expensive signing – it's big loss and it does hurt.'

[104] In his memoir *Hammered*, Johnston's partner-in-crime Mark Ward lifted the lid on the whole shoddy affair. Johnston HAD been present on the night of the brawl in the Fisherman's Rest but Ward revealed he had been sent home beforehand for being too drunk. Ward claimed that, after returning home, Johnston fell over a shoe on the landing and ended up tumbling down the spiral staircase and hitting his face on the wall. On the next day at training, Johnston turned up looking like 'the Elephant Man' according to the former West Ham player. Both miscreants were carpeted by Kendall who fined them two weeks' wages. After Ward tried to convince Kendall that Johnston was not involved in the brawl, the manager responded, 'Well, how the f--- has he got a face like that.'

Vote of confidence

Nothing smacks more of passive-aggressive behaviour than a chairman's vote of confidence. So when Goodison chief David Marsh announced that 'We're not panicking and we believe Howard is still the right man for the job,' there were the usual nods from sages within the game. The words followed a 1-0 League Cup defeat at Chelsea just before Christmas with Everton eighteenth in the Premier League – one point off the relegation zone – and with a paltry fifteen goals, the lowest in the top flight. With one trophy-winning route removed, only the FA Cup remained to salvage a dispiriting campaign.

However, Marsh's next statement was more worrying: 'Howard brought this club a lot of success in the 1980s and we hope he will do it again. But just as important is the fact that he has won the League and Cups and that he has also experienced the bad times before. And he has come through them.' But that was a decade before. The club and playing staff – plus, ominously, Kendall and Harvey – had significantly changed in the interim. The game was different, moving on even since the last title victory six years before. Taking the lead from the long-ball disciples who had come to prominence during the middle of the decade, the top flight had become less about individual technique and more about speed and power.

This change accelerated with the outlawing of the back-pass to goalkeepers from the start of the 1992/93 season – they could receive the ball to feet but could no longer pick it up. Kendall had traditionally copied Liverpool's template of liberally using the tactic away from home, especially early on to take the sting out of games, and he was forced to change time-honoured methods. Also, the tempo of the game increased and much of the skill squeezed out. Sides attempted to exploit the law change by playing the ball over the top even quicker and more frequently than before. 'A lot of clubs have gone for a certain type of player who is effective under the new rule,' Kendall explained to Joe Lovejoy in the *Independent*. 'He may not be able to control the ball, his first touch may be useless, but he's quick and strong, and he can turn defences and leave them facing their own goal.' Kendall always liked his players to pass, rather than kick, the ball so such tactics were anathema to him and he was struggling to adapt. 'Nowadays you've got to look for effective players rather than just technically good players. We've got to try to marry the two styles,' he admitted.

The impact of the law change was one of the reasons why Kendall was struggling: identifying and then incorporating those strong-arm players into the squad was not his speciality. If anything, the bias had been towards smaller players with technical skills during his first two seasons back, with the team receiving plaudits more for attractive performances than results – ironically during the glory years the opposite was largely true. That said, there was justifiable criticism that the search for the right blend was hampered by constant tinkering.

Elsewhere, when strong, direct leadership was required all Marsh could offer was the word 'hope' to supporters. That vain expectation effectively extended to waiting for a turnaround in fortunes, as had happened in the winter of 1983, but unfortunately for Marsh there was no League Cup quarter-final tie at Oxford on the horizon. Furthermore, the squad was nowhere near capable enough to take advantage of any good luck which fell into their laps. Then there was a solid backbone to build from but now a mishmash of players with long and extravagant contracts made them difficult to move on. 'Can Mr Kendall turn another unpalatable mixture of playing ingredients into another irresistible formation of all-conquering heroes?' asked William Johnson in the *Daily Telegraph*, 'The answer appears to be No.' With the club in the red and losing money every week, Marsh also confirmed there was nothing in the pot. 'There's no chance of us bringing anybody in,' a wistful Kendall responded. 'There's no money available. We've got to get out of this with the players we've got.'

After four points had been taken from two home games, the players would have argued they gave their all at Loftus Road in the final game of 1992, especially following Neville Southall's bizarre early dismissal. After nineteen minutes, the Welshman rushed out to collect a headed back-pass from Dave Watson but a look of horror filled his face after realising he had caught the ball outside the area. Referee Gerald Ashby could have kept the goalkeeper on the pitch as it did not look a premeditated act to stop a goalscoring opportunity, but he thought otherwise and showed the red card. Southall left to a standing ovation from the home support – reflecting both sympathy and the esteem in which he was held – while hand-shakes with several opponents spoke volumes. There was no such compassion for Paul Rideout just before the break, his uncharacteristically reckless challenge on Darren Peacock left the visitors both two goals and two players down. Substitute goalkeeper Jason Kearton was powerless to stop a third after the break but then inexplicably Rangers stopped playing. Stuart Barlow scored twice for the nine-man visitors and a remarkable comeback was only thwarted when Andy Sinton completed a hat-trick at the death. Kendall wisely refused to speak to reporters about the game, but referring to a tough FA Cup assignment at Wimbledon, quipped: 'I will be delighted if Paul Rideout is suspended for the FA Cup fourth round.'

Wombling out

The two clubs had already met three times during the campaign, goalless draws at Goodison in both the Premier League and League Cup followed by a 1-0 win for Everton at Selhurst Park in the replay. With just one goal in three games, those expecting a classic in south London numbered significantly less than the 7,818 hardy souls who braved the impenetrable, freezing mist which eventually enveloped the pitch in the opening half. 'Hopes were high of this wretched game being put out of its misery,' Clive White scathingly noted in the *Observer*. 'Unfortunately, the fog wisely decided not to hang around and the agony went its full distance.' Nothing summed up the dire fare than Vinnie Jones being the most accomplished player on the pitch, while White's comments on Everton were a sad reflection on the current state of play at Goodison: 'Who would have thought that dourness would be the prevailing quality of a side managed by Howard Kendall?' Following Southall's brilliance in the opening half and a Beardsley shot that smacked the top of the crossbar near the end, the third goalless draw in four games between the clubs produced a largely unwanted further meeting at Goodison ten days later.

With Southall incurring a one-match suspension, for the first time in 216 games and four years there was another goalkeeper starting a game, with Kearton donning the gloves. The replay followed the pattern of previous encounters, full of niggles and physical confrontations. With the watching Southall powerless, the deputy stopper failed his first big test when not blocking John Fashanu's poorly-struck shot after 35 minutes. But the crucial passage of play occurred five minutes into the second half. Preki's wonderful free-kick struck the angle of crossbar and post and, after bouncing back, Wimbledon took the ball up field and Robbie Earle slalomed through the home defence to score a second. 'Everton's season fell apart in the twinkling of an eye,' Ken Rogers summarised in the *Liverpool Echo*. A late flurry saw auxiliary striker Dave Watson pull a goal back but it was not enough and the Toffees went out at the third-round stage for a second successive season. Just as worrying, the crowd of 15,293 frozen spectators was the lowest in the FA Cup at Goodison since before the First World War. With the season falling apart, twenty-four hours later the *Liverpool Echo* published an open letter:

> *Everton's season hit rock bottom last night. Defeat in any game is bad enough but defeat in the third round of the FA Cup against Wimbledon was disastrous. It signalled the end of trophy hunting this season. It signalled the demise of the Blues to the position of also-rans. Everton fans were looking forward to the first Premier League season with hope, anticipation and the prospect of success. What they have had*

to endure throughout a totally disappointing campaign is frustration and failure. All that Everton are left with is a dog-fight for survival in the Premier League basement. The club is in crisis – the fans (those who turn up, anyway) are in utter despair. The big question is: WHAT IS THE BOARD GOING TO DO ABOUT IT?

Marsh responded to the questions by trotting out the usual excuses: the problems would not be solved by waving the cheque-book and game-changing players were not readily available. 'We will do everything in our power to bring about a revival,' he concluded, 'but I must warn again there are no magical solutions.' One immediate answer to rapidly rising debts was to sell Martin Keown to Arsenal, his first club, for a fee of £2 million. With Kendall planning to move Gary Ablett into the centre to replace the England international, and Andy Hinchcliffe injured, there was a vacancy at left-back filled by 34-year-old Kenny Sansom on a free transfer. Keown would go on to enjoy a decade of huge success at Highbury, including three Premier League titles. Meanwhile the signing of Sansom seemed horribly in tune with the financially straightened times and the perceived lack of ambition within the Goodison hierarchy. Kendall's argument that Sansom's arrival was like Paul Power's hardly sounded convincing and so it proved, the left-back making just seven appearances before departing.

Despite Marsh's words of support rumours of a change in the dug-out gathered pace. 'Under-fire Howard Kendall has three weeks and three games to avoid reaching what he admits would be crisis point in Everton's season,' Richard Tanner wrote in the *Daily Mirror*. With more stories that the Goodison chief was thinking of returning to Bilbao, the usual suspects such as Peter Reid and Joe Royle were trotted out as replacements, but there was surprising interest in Hearts' manager, Joe Jordan. Kendall came out fighting for his part, being forced into a statement that very much sounded like a defence against the sack. 'I accept that the present situation is not good enough,' he admitted, 'but surely it is better to have someone in the job who understands how they [the fans] feel and knows exactly what is needed to put things right.' His best protection was, naturally, the goodwill engendered in the boardroom and terraces because of his past success, but that stretched only so far.

Such unease off the pitch was temporarily forgotten when, in the final week of January, a 3-1 victory at Wimbledon brought a third successive league victory and the haven of twelfth place. Nevertheless, the game was noteworthy for the then lowest top-flight attendance in history, with only 3,039 hardy souls bothering to attend at Selhurst Park – after five turgid encounters between the teams already, one cynic observed it was a miracle that that many turned up. But four days later a fluent and confident Norwich City left Goodison with a fully-deserved 1-0 victory. 'Everton fans could not hide their disgust,' said one correspondent to the *Football Echo*, 'They felt openly snubbed and let down by the administrators of their club.' Yet that did not exclude the manager, whose decisions continued to baffle. For the vital FA Cup replay against Wimbledon neither Beagrie or Cottee made the substitutes' bench and there was a woefully unbalanced selection against Norwich, with Alan Harper and Billy Kenny occupying the left flank and Ian Snodin overrun as a sole central midfielder. After that game one supporter presciently asked: 'If a team reflects its expression of its manager then the needs of Everton FC are more for a Mike Walker than any new players.'

Crisis mismanagement

'It's a crisis when you are out of both cups and still in the bottom six of the League in February,' was a stock phrase of the Everton boss. He used it in the dark days of his first tenure and repeated it again a decade later. So when Spurs inflicted a 2-1 defeat at Goodison in the second week of that month, Kendall was under no illusions about the seriousness of the position. A third successive loss, plus shock victories for three other teams below the Toffees on the same evening, left the club fifth from bottom. More worryingly the attendance was a paltry 16,164 – 25,000 less than Liverpool had attracted for their most recent home game against bottom-of-the-table Nottingham Forest. 'Six years without a trophy has clearly taken its toll on Everton's pulling power,' Ken Rogers suggested about the gate in the *Liverpool Echo*. 'This performance will have done nothing to encourage people to return.'

Ten days later the away game at Villa Park produced the same result but an even worse performance. The Everton boss had learned nothing from the Norwich defeat by playing Barry Horne in front of Sansom on this occasion, with Snodin remaining in the middle. With Warzycha nominally playing right midfield but effectively acting as a de facto winger, Horne constantly got pulled into the middle to support Snodin leaving enormous spaces on the left to tempt the home team. 'Howard Kendall, the manager, must take full blame for sending out his side with the most inviting imbalance I can recall ever seeing at this level,' Rob Hughes declared in *The Sunday Times*. Sunk by two goals in the first seventeen minutes, the eventual 2-1 defeat could have been much worse but for Villa's deterioration in the second period, when they were, according to Hughes 'dragged down to the level of Everton, whose decline in economic terms, in playing strength, in belief and leadership is horribly apparent.' Forty-eight hours later Kendall admitted:

'We've got to scrap for results now. What I'm looking for at the moment is to have as many players with battling qualities out there as I can.' Those qualities were certainly absent when a reserve team featuring several from the first-team squad conceded ten goals in a Central League game at Derby County two days later. The only consolation for the Everton boss and supporters was that, with Liverpool having their worst campaign for more than a generation, the newspaper column inches dedicated to their own perilous decline were not as great as expected.

Safe

On the first day of March only goal difference kept Everton out of the relegation zone at the expense of Middlesbrough – the Toffees' lowest placing after Christmas since 1984. Two days later at Goodison, when Blackburn Rovers right-back David May casually strolled through the home defence to volley the visitors ahead just before the break, the relegation trapdoor opened that little bit wider. But the recall of long-term injury victims John Ebbrell and Mark Ward had restored some much-needed balance to the midfield and the home team got the luck their endeavour deserved after half-time. Colin Hendry had cleared one Stuart Barlow effort off the line before the Rovers centre-half then unluckily turned Matt Jackson's cross into the net. After Tim Sherwood aided the home cause by stupidly getting sent off for swearing at a linesman, Everton smelt blood and Tony Cottee ensured that Kenny Dalglish's return to Goodison was a miserable one. The diminutive striker nipped between two defenders to reach Barlow's headed flick and finished perfectly past former Goodison custodian Bobby Mimms.

Three points from a determined second-half fightback proved a turning point in the campaign. Four days later a superb Ward volley after just eight minutes secured another vital victory at Highfield Road, in a game broadcast live on Sky. Four further wins in the final eleven games meant Kendall's team scaled the unlikely heights of thirteenth in the first Premier League table.[105] There were two notable games during the final months. At Anfield near the end of March, Everton went down 1-0 in a game where substitute Stuart Barlow missed three straightforward chances before Ronny Rosenthal struck a painful injury-time winner from what looked like an offside position. In the difficult press conference that followed the Everton boss was informed Andy Hinchcliffe was playing the match-winner onside and, as the inquisition was nearing the end, a Hungarian

---

[105] Strangely, given the Premier League was brought into existence to help create an elite in English football, the first season was anything but – just ten points separated those teams who were relegated and sixth place. Everton in thirteenth finished only four points ahead of the drop zone.

television journalist thrust a microphone under an exasperated Kendall's nose and asked: 'Which of the teams do you think is going to win the championship?' The Everton manager's reply was deadpan: 'You certainly didn't see them here today lad.'

Contrary to popular belief, the start of the Premier League did not immediately herald a new, glamorous era for English football. Just 3,039 spectators watched Everton's visit to Plough Lane to play Wimbledon in January 1993, the then lowest recorded gate in top-flight history.

A bizarre game at Maine Road on the final day was, unexpectedly, a happier experience. Rookie home goalkeeper Martyn Margetson had a nightmare opening half. Unnerved by a series of demanding Andy Hinchliffe corners, the Wales Under-21 international was beaten for the first time when Matt Jackson's left-foot volley put the away team ahead on just six minutes. Twelve minutes later Margetson could only partially clear another Hinchcliffe corner to Peter Beagrie who crashed the ball straight back past him. On the half-hour the hapless stopper fumbled at the near post but was lucky when Cottee was flagged offside after hammering the ball into the roof of the net. Three minutes later Margetson's nightmare continued when his botched clearance went straight to Preki and though the Serb's shot struck the woodwork, Beardsley joyfully put away the rebound.

David White pulled a goal back yet, with the youngster being cruelly barracked by his own supporters, Peter Reid had no choice but to bring on substitute goalkeeper Andy

Dibble at the break. But his fortunes were no better and on 51 minutes a twenty-yard screamer from Preki flashed past him. Twelve minutes later history was made. Neville Southall left the pitch with a back injury and when Jason Kearton took the gloves, for the first time ever a competitive game featured substitute goalkeepers for both sides. The scoring continued – Keith Curle pulled a goal back from the spot before Beagrie wrapped up the game, and Everton's season, with another crushing strike from twenty yards. Strangely Kendall was not the only target for abuse on the day. City chairman Peter Swales was also in the firing line as both men ran the gauntlet of egg-throwing home supporters.

Aftermath

In the tropical climes of Mauritius on Everton's post-season tour Kendall gave a wide-ranging interview to Steve Bates of the *People*. The Everton manager sounded like somebody who knew the odds were stacked against him, after two relegation skirmishes, falling gates and with a shortage of money hampering any squad reconstruction. 'Time is running out on me at Goodison,' he admitted, 'Yes, things look difficult but we have to get on and make the best of it. People expected me to wave a magic wand when I returned but that was never possible.' This, of course, begged the question of why he came back in the first place.

Kendall then gave an honest appraisal of a disappointing campaign. 'I wanted to field a settled side but I never could,' he explained. 'Players lacked consistency and when that happens so does the manager.' Kendall's honesty reflected his own inability to extract the best out of available funds and, by extension, the squad. Although adequate at the back, the midfield had no balance whatsoever. Barry Horne, John Ebbrell, Ian Snodin and Billy Kenny were of similar physical stature and playing style. Like their defensive counterparts, collectively they offered no goal threat – mustering just four from 95 league appearances – and only limited creativity. That would have been just about acceptable if there had been Trevor Steven and Kevin Sheedy out wide but Peter Beagrie and Robert Warzycha were not direct enough and unreliable. Both appeared incapable of getting in behind the opposition defence. Up front Johnston and Rideout had disappointed while Beardsley drifted too much into the middle of the pitch and a tally of ten goals was five down on the previous campaign. Even in his peak years at Newcastle and Liverpool, the gifted attacker rarely enjoyed a consistent run over a season – his goal on the final day was the first since January – and it was the same at Goodison where he increasingly struggled to fit into the preferred 4-4-2 system. Kendall never really decided whether he was a midfield schemer or a forward. 'I was encouraging him to go in the penalty area, but often he wasn't there,' he later said.

That the manager had underperformed was undeniable but, in his defence, English football now stood in the era of the increasingly symbiotic relationship between owner wealth and trophy-winning potential. Although the Premier League has subsequently been credited with the new-found domestic riches of the early-1990s, its initial financial impact was marginal. The tectonic shift in the transfer market had been caused by the arrival of David Murray at Rangers and then Jack Walker at Blackburn Rovers. That a relatively small Lancashire club was able to compete – finishing sixth – in the opening season was testimony to the fact cash-rich owners still trumped inflated television contracts. Either way, Everton were now being left behind. 'Everything has been done financially to help me in terms of doing the job but if money's not there, it's not there,' Kendall told Bates. 'Our current situation means there's no way I can compete for big-name players like Roy Keane,' he added wistfully, 'and that's not just down to cash. We have to convince the quality players we are going places but first we have to make an impact. Then we can challenge for the big names.'

32
THE KISS OF LIFE

ALTHOUGH KENDALL DESIRED A BIG NAME, THE SEARCH FOR A BIG
striker was the priority over the summer. Despite interest in Mark Bright, Chris Armstrong,
Brian Deane, Stan Collymore, Niall Quinn, David Hirst, and an offer for Paul Wilkinson
to return, there was no luck for the Everton boss. To increase spending power Beardsley
was controversially sold to Newcastle United for £1.5 million but that made little
difference. Kendall was a long-term admirer of Dundee United's Duncan Ferguson and
bid £3.25 million for the striker only for Rangers to clinch the deal with one of £4
million. 'There are no instant cures in football,' Kendall admitted, 'unless, like Blackburn,
you have a Jack Walker and that's what Everton and me need right now.' The Everton
hierarchy obviously thought the same.

For sale

'Everton is up for sale,' the *Liverpool Echo* exclusively revealed in a front-page headline
during the middle of May 1993. John Moores had purchased forty per cent of the club's
shares for £100,000 more than thirty years before, but the former chairman was now 97
years of age and in poor health. Consequently, his family was reported to have instructed
merchant banker Hill Samuel to seek ways of refinancing the club by selling their holding
for £2.5 million, effectively valuing the shares around the £2,500 mark, or to draw up
plans for a share issue. Although the club naturally denied the story, there was belated
recognition in the Goodison boardroom that, even to stand a chance of competing,
further capital investment was imperative. 'I can assure you something has to be done
before the annual shareholders' meeting in mid-August,' David Marsh said. 'If I can't go
to them and say this is being done to arrest the problem, then I'm failing in my job.'

'It promises to be lively,' Kendall said in advance of that meeting – and he was correct.
One shareholder announced to the board that 'We are a laughing stock in this city. What
are you going to do to put things right?' Kendall was then asked searching questions

about the lowest league position for twelve years. 'I don't blame you for not being happy with my management for the last eighteen months,' he responded. 'Because I'm not proud to report on last season's efforts.'

Meanwhile, the shock refusal of John Moores' nominees to take part in the re-election of Desmond Pitcher and Alan Waterworth as directors indicated a developing split between the major shareholders and some board members. That the Moores family was the real problem within the club was increasingly apparent. Their shareholding had once been a positive but now deterred outsiders from making a significant investment, as they could not hold the controlling interest. Any further share issue would dilute the strength of the family holding – unless they were prepared to take up most of it themselves, which was not going to happen. Then there were two further issues. Why would anybody want to invest in Everton in any case? The club were saddled with debts of £4 million and possessed few saleable assets. Shareholders were rarely paid a dividend. The worrying financial position was put into context by Kendall to David Prentice at the season's end. Asked whether the £2 million received for Martin Keown had been made available for squad strengthening, he responded, 'I will be as honest as I can, but that's an internal thing which I don't feel I should answer.'

The other problem was a local one: the absence of wealth on Merseyside was not conducive to external investment. When Liverpool made a share issue to finance the building of their Centenary Stand two years before there was little interest and Sir John's nephew, David, ended up buying the bulk of them for £2 million.

Come August, the chairman's failure to deliver a financial package, as he had promised, plus the strange move by the Moores family to opt out of voting for the re-election of two directors, pointed to a growing feeling of inertia and lack of accountability. Regarding Moores' nominees, they either supported the directors or did not and, as the major shareholders, should have been displaying leadership and direction. 'I think they should be told to either put up more money or sell out to someone who will,' Ian Hargraves demanded in the *Liverpool Echo*. The latter scenario was ultimately a drama that would run and run.

'We'll surprise a few people'
Away from the boardroom, the bookmakers made Everton a rather ambitious 50-1 to win the Premier League title. However, of more relevance for supporters they were also an alarmingly slim 13-2 to go down. Kendall, with typical optimism, was more interested in the former scenario. 'I am quite optimistic we'll surprise a few people,' he promised in

the opening home programme of the season, against Manchester City.

Such positivity was well-founded. At Southampton on the opening day the visitors produced a vibrant display against a backdrop of the off-the-pitch turmoil. Peter Beagrie opened the scoring after just ten minutes[106] and their dominance was rubber-stamped when John Ebbrell added a second just before the break. With their team producing neat patterns of possession and enough goal attempts to win by a landslide, the travelling fans ironically chanted 'We're going to win the league.' Afterwards the Everton boss was delighted: 'It was particularly pleasing because before today there has been talk of new faces and how disillusioned the fans are.'

A dominant display against Manchester City at Goodison brought a richly-deserved 1-0 victory four days later and on the following Saturday evening Everton supporters stared incredulously at the embryonic table, with their team sitting astonishingly at the summit. Despite conceding a goal at Goodison to Sheffield United's Dane Whitehouse after just 53 seconds, Dave Bassett's side found the home team's slick passing style uncomfortable and when Tony Cottee completed his hat-trick in the final minute, the 4-2 victory was enough to send the Toffees top following their best start in fifteen years. 'If this carries on Howard Kendall's team might be dark horses worth backing,' Louise Taylor proclaimed in *The Sunday Times*. Asked why fortunes had changed so dramatically, Kendall cryptically responded: 'They're all having a go now.' Indirectly he was citing those previously criticised for lacking application like Peter Beagrie and Paul Rideout, plus the hat-trick hero, who were all now prepared to do the dirty work.

For the former West Ham striker it was another peak in five years of ups and downs. Only the lack of buyers had kept Cottee at Goodison and signing a three-year contract during the summer seemed very much like an extension of this marriage of convenience. After renewing, Cottee revealed that, although accepting some of Kendall's criticisms in the past, he felt some of the adverse comments were uncalled for. 'The boss is right in that I must do the work,' he explained, 'but there's no point in me chasing back to the left-back position to win a tackle if I'm not back in the right position to score a goal at the end of that move.' However, the two parties had reached a compromise. Cottee agreed, in his words, to 'help the other lads more'. In return, the manager would cut out the public criticism. Kendall, however, was always prepared to have the final word on such matters. After awarding the striker full marks for his performance at the Dell, he pithily remarked: 'He's now showing what he can do, which he didn't always do last season.'

---

[106] The only time in the first thirty years of the Premier League that an Everton player scored the first goal of the season.

But the good start could not last. Three successive defeats left the side in mid-table. And David Lacey in the *Guardian* handed out an ominous warning after a 2-0 loss to Arsenal at the end of August. 'Everton did not do much from start to finish,' he wrote, 'and ended up reminding everyone that last season they lay fourth in the league at the end of August but 20th by late October.'

Grievous Angell

The dip in form also highlighted the continuing need for a big striker, with Kendall's transfer torment continuing. Middlesbrough rejected another £1.1 million bid for Paul Wilkinson and a £1 million offer for Mark Bright was similarly turned down by Sheffield Wednesday. However the main target was Manchester City's beanpole frontman Niall Quinn, whom Kendall had brought to Maine Road from Highbury more than three years before. In early August there had been a £2 million bid which City had waved away but there was an opening when the Ireland international publicly displayed his anger over the surprise sacking of Peter Reid early in the campaign. However, replacement boss Brian Horton was unmoved and even an improved offer of £2.3 million failed to prise the big striker away from Maine Road.

The rejection led to one of the more infamous playing spells in recent Goodison history. Southend's burly striker Brett Angell had been a man in demand after a goal every two games at Roots Hall. Indeed, two years before the 25-year-old had rejected a deal to join Kenny Dalglish at Blackburn Rovers. At 6ft 4in he was the perfect fit for the totemic striker Kendall craved but the warning signs were there when the Everton boss only agreed an initial month-long loan before committing to a £1.5 million deal. As it was, Angell made just one substitute appearance and returned to Southend. But that was not the last Goodison would see of the big striker.

The new arrival was on the bench for the first derby match of the season, at Goodison in mid-September when, in the early-autumn sunshine, Kendall's side overran their rivals, with the opening period as one-sided in Everton's favour as any derby in living memory. 'In more than thirty years watching Merseyside football I have never seen a derby challenge as feeble as Liverpool's in this 149th league meeting,' the hugely experienced John Keith asserted in the *Daily Express*. With the visitors offering only token resistance, Barry Horne and John Ebbrell dominated the middle of the park, completely overshadowing Jamie Redknapp and Ronnie Whelan. The non-stop Horne was superb. 'That's the best game he has had so far and will hopefully help him,' Kendall said afterwards. 'We won everything in central midfield.'

The home team opened the scoring just before the half-hour mark. Hinchcliffe's poor delivery from a corner was met with an equally bad clearance from Steve McManaman at the near post, the ball reached Mark Ward at the edge of the box and the former West Ham player blasted his shot past Bruce Grobbelaar. The Liverpool goalkeeper then played a starring role in an extraordinary incident during the aftermath. Annoyed by his team-mate's shabby clearance, Grobbelaar slapped McManaman in the face and was then on the receiving end of a retaliatory strike. Fighting a former soldier[107] was not necessarily the best course of action for the local-born player and the unseemly argument continued until the restart. Seven years earlier a similar dispute between Grobbelaar and Jim Beglin in the FA Cup final was seen as the catalyst for a Liverpool revival, however such was Everton's complete dominance there was no chance of a repeat. The Zimbabwean's heroics kept the score down until four minutes from time when Cottee took advantage of sloppy defensive work to score his first league goal against Liverpool in a blue shirt. 'That's our most dominating display against Liverpool in my five years at Everton,' he said afterwards.

The deserved victory was Everton's fifth out of eight league games, leaving them fourth in the table. 'An acceptable return,' said Peter Jardine in the *Liverpool Daily Post*. 'Although Everton have specialised in false dawns since the sun set on their last championship-winning side.' It took exactly seven days to establish the victory was yet another one.

Efan unbelievable

Born in Manchester in 1967, Efan Ekoku lived in Toxteth – growing up as a Liverpool fan worshipping Ian Rush – until he was sixteen before joining Norwich City in the summer of 1993 from Bournemouth. Without a goal yet for his new club, the striker found himself leading the line for the Canaries at Goodison on the final Saturday in September. Supporters would barely have noticed that the matchday programme reported that his eight goals in a friendly game against a Swedish Fifth Division club were 'thought to have created a record for English clubs in Scandinavia.' By the end of the afternoon the Everton defence looked like they had not taken note either.

That was for later as before the game Kendall wanted to build on the feel-good factor following the derby victory. 'Let's have thirty thousand today against Norwich,' he said. 'We've had good backing this season and we'd like the few thousand extra who saw the

---

[107] After being conscripted into national service during 1978, Grobbelaar spent eleven months in the Rhodesia Regiment during the Rhodesia Bush War.

derby to come along.' Disappointingly that plea fell on deaf ears, the paltry gate of just 20,531 spectators on a sunny afternoon a sign supporters remained cynical over talk of renaissance. Nevertheless, they watched the home team control events for nearly an hour with the same bite and determination that characterised the derby victory. But warning signs were there when, after Paul Rideout had put Everton ahead, Ekoku took advantage of slack work at the back and levelled just before the break. 'Norwich were run ragged in the first half, outplayed to the point of embarrassment by Everton's nippy forwards and ludicrously fortunate to reach half-time level,' John Farrell wrote in the *Observer*.

Then after the hosts had struck the woodwork for a second time, the makeshift central defensive pairing of Gary Ablett and Matt Jackson – so solid against Liverpool – fell apart. On 57 minutes an unmarked Ekoku netted a second with a header. Thereafter the more Everton pressed, the more dangerous the visitors looked when they broke out of defence. Ekoku and Ruel Fox evaded the offside trap on 63 minutes with the striker completing a hat-trick. Six minutes later Ekoku became the first player in the fledgling Premier League to score four goals in a game, after skilfully lifting the ball over Jackson's head and rounding Southall, who promptly threw his cap into the net in disgust. Chris Sutton made it five as the roof fell in on the centre of the home defence.

The humiliating result and the manner of the collapse was barely believable. 'If you defend badly you expect to be punished,' Kendall said. 'We defended badly today.' However, the unbalanced display was typical of a side struggling for consistency over several years. Good performances were usually followed by below-average displays. The response to the previous derby victory nine months before had been the dreadful performance in a 1-0 loss at Sheffield United. The defeat of Liverpool in the FA Cup in February 1991 was ultimately wasted thanks to the lacklustre showing at West Ham in the next round. Only once in two years had there been three consecutive league wins.

On the following weekend there was yet more disappointment at Tottenham. Twelve months before, the visitors wastefully threw away three valuable points when leading late on and never recovered the early-season momentum. Everton somehow managed to produce a repeat performance. Ahead 2-1 with 75 seconds remaining, poor defending allowed the home team to equalise via Darren Anderton and then force a winner from Darren Caskey ninety seconds into injury time. 'Two seasons running they have blown winning positions at White Hart Lane,' David Prentice pointed out in the *Liverpool Echo*. 'Like last season, Howard Kendall must pray that this doesn't turn out to be a watershed defeat.'

Whether it was or not certainly depended on better defending. Dave Watson had crucially been absent since mid-August and the side was missing his leadership and organisational skills, as well as that will-to-win. Kendall was counting the cost of not adequately replacing Martin Keown, being forced to deploy a central defensive partnership of Ablett and the inexperienced Matt Jackson, who were effectively full-backs operating in the middle. At right-back Paul Holmes, signed from Birmingham City for £200,000 six months before, was steady but hardly inspiring while on the left Hinchcliffe, as ever, offered an attacking threat but was vulnerable when pressed. The defending in north London during the final five minutes was chaotic and disorganised while Everton even managed to surrender five goals across the ultimately successful two-legged League Cup tie against fourth-tier Lincoln City. 'We are conceding too many goals,' Kendall said after the Spurs game. 'There has never been a side in football that has won anything letting in goals like we did today.' At promoted Swindon two weeks later, Jackson was at fault when they conceded a last-minute equaliser after dominating a team without a league victory all season.

Although Kendall was correct to point out defensive lapses, one of the contributory factors to two poor results was strange substitutions by the manager: at Spurs the dangerous Beagrie had just struck the crossbar with twenty minutes remaining but was immediately replaced by the ineffectual Preki, while Cottee went off for Stuart Barlow. That handed the initiative to the home team. In Wiltshire he took the unusual step of substituting a substitute, removing Barlow after the striker had been on the pitch for 52 minutes. Barlow had an unusual ascension to the first-team ranks. Plucked from non-league obscurity at the age of 22 the forward had developed a reputation as a pacy player but one whose finishing could best be described as unreliable. At the County Ground he spurned two golden opportunities, one literally underneath the opposition crossbar. 'Stuart Barlow was not brought off because of the missed chances,' Kendall said. 'He gets into a fair share of goalscoring opportunities but it was not his day.'

However, there were positives. Paul Rideout, possibly piqued by the potential acquisition of Angell, was a rejuvenated figure, scoring six times in four games. The striker was leading the line impressively, finally forming a productive partnership with Tony Cottee – as a pairing their twelve games together had generated fourteen goals – and Kendall at last appeared content with his options up front. 'The way our lads are doing at the moment,' he explained, 'means I am not looking to spend any money. I am looking for my players here to do what they are capable of doing more consistently.' Consistency, the word defining Kendall's second spell, was proving increasingly elusive.

33

HOWARD TAKES THE WRONG TURN

THOSE SUPPORTERS VAINLY WISHING FOR AN 'OXFORD UNITED' moment, to offer at least some comfort during an increasingly dispiriting campaign, may have thought their prayers were answered when the Toffees faced second-tier Crystal Palace in the League Cup. 'Our biggest match of the season,' Kendall admitted beforehand. Two goals down to the superior underdogs in the second half, they earned a reprieve via a Dave Watson equaliser two minutes into added time. 'Everton were fortunate,' wrote Stephen Brierley in the *Guardian*. 'Mortified Palace had deserved more than a replay.' At Selhurst Park it was a different tale. Watson added two more goals to his collection as the visitors strolled to a 4-1 victory – the same result as the replay win over Oxford a decade before.

Stomach for a fight?

The similarities ended there. On the Saturday before the replay win Everton had lost 2-1 at Coventry City – a team without a win in seven games – following a dispiriting display. 'They were hopeless,' said Andy Gray, now filling the pundit's chair at Sky Sports. Shortly after, David Prentice interviewed Kendall on the third anniversary of his return. Prentice handed out a warning: 'The honeymoon period is long over. Kendall has a grim job on his hands as he strives to keep the club's head above water.' To his credit the Everton boss pulled no punches in response. 'If you look at records in the past, people would be looking on this as a very important season in terms of how we have progressed,' he admitted. 'At the moment you could look at it and say there has not been great, if any, improvement.'

The following game, at home to QPR, sadly provided no counterpoint to Kendall's opinion. The lowest league gate of the season, of just 17,089, witnessed rookie visiting striker Bradley Allen rip through the home defence on the way to a hat-trick, as the London club eased to a 3-0 win, their utter dominance an embarrassment to the home team. 'Rangers were given time, and very often the ball, by Everton, whose passing would have embarrassed the average Sunday side,' wrote Alex Spillius in *The Sunday Times*. After the crowd booed his players off at both the break and full time, a shell-shocked Kendall was close to tears after the game. 'That's my lowest moment since I came back here. I saw people walking away after their third goal and that hurts,' he said, before adding defiantly, 'If anything, this makes me determined to get it right.' Kendall may have put on a brave face but five defeats in seven games left his side tumbling to thirteenth place and he now accepted his job was on the line before the visit of Leeds three days later. 'If there are many more [games] like Saturday there is only thing that will happen – and I'm well aware of that,' he admitted. One supporter's letter to the *Football Echo* about the reaction to the QPR defeat summed up the prevailing mood:

> *The management and the board of directors must take full responsibility, for that is where the boos and jeers were directed…for all the mediocrity and incompetence that has been Everton for the last six years. It is an indictment of the management that good players look bad and not so good look awful…Right now at Goodison Park, Liverpool 4, football is in need of the Kiss of Life.*

With Kendall's head close to the chopping block, the next two league games brought draws but a more pressing concern was, with Paul Rideout needing a stomach operation, the Everton boss was down to just two fit strikers. An initial request to Manchester United for Dion Dublin was rejected by Alex Ferguson. 'We've told everyone Dion isn't available at the moment,' he responded. 'We're not interested at present.' Although Kendall had previously admitted that the issue with searching for players was not money but the absence of quality, the ball was in the directors' court if Dublin became available. As David Prentice wrote, 'If the board has belief in Kendall – and his quality as a manager is proven – they must back him up with more money.'

Black and not blue

The fact that Everton were now the only one out of the 92 league clubs without a black player had not gone unnoticed, yet the bid to land Dublin was conveniently forgotten in the ongoing debate about racism in football. Rightly or wrongly, the club had not shaken off the accusations of possessing a racist element since the abuse of John Barnes several years before. While they were certainly not alone, home fans ensured that Goodison still had a reputation for being one of the worst grounds to visit for black players. After the Arsenal trio David Rocastle, Michael Thomas and Paul Davis were victims of shocking terrace abuse during their visit in September 1990, Philip Carter stated that the perpetrators 'bring shame to everyone connected with the club'. However, with Barnes, again, and Southampton's Rod Wallace the target of terrace abuse in the following two home games, the club was forced to threaten offenders with prosecution.

Although Paul Davis welcomed the move as progress, a Channel Four documentary on racism in football twelve months later again pointed accusing fingers at the club. With virtually all top-flight sides having several black players – Liverpool now had four – Everton were edging towards pariah status on the issue and unsurprisingly conspiracy theories started. 'There are whispers in the game that Everton operate a colour bar,' the *People* claimed. Understandably the club rebuffed those claims, with Kendall referencing the attempts to sign QPR's Paul Parker in 1991 before the defender went to Manchester United. 'I was upset by the accusations,' Kendall later said.

Yet, perhaps unfairly, while there were no black players at Goodison murmurs around the game continued, especially as a section of support off the pitch continued to bring shame on the club, even in the Premier League era. The *Guardian* reported on the abuse handed out to Southampton's Ken Monkou in August 1993. 'The accusation of racism isn't levelled at all Everton supporters, just a violent minority,' was their viewpoint. John Fashanu was never one to remain silent on such issues and he told the Commission for Racial Equality nine months later that 'Something is happening there that isn't right.' Newcastle United had been a club with a similar reputation but the signing of Andy Cole was seen as helping to remove barriers. Thankfully for Everton, a similar move in the summer of 1994 had the same impact, as we will return to later.

Dublin costs a packet

Paul Parker was in the Manchester United side who visited Goodison for their League Cup fourth-round tie on the final day of November 1993. Kendall could take solace from the previous league meeting on the ground five weeks before, when his side proved more than a match for the champions, deserving at least a draw following a competitive encounter settled by the visitors' only shot on target – albeit a stunning volley from Lee Sharpe. For the cup game, Kendall chose his default tactical option on significant occasions: play it tight, stifle the opposition and take it from there. But with a five-man midfield and Cottee playing a lone striker role, he paid the price for such a negative game-plan against top-class opponents. 'Even with a full house, there was little feeling of a cup tie or a local derby atmosphere, Everton looking as if they knew their cause was hopeless almost from the start,' Peter Ball noted in *The Times*.

United immediately settled into a smooth groove, going ahead on thirteen minutes when Watson uncharacteristically misjudged Paul Ince's through ball and Mark Hughes chested it down before a ferocious volley left Southall with no chance. The home team's response was more spirited than effective and, a minute after the break, they were caught cold when Southall could only parry Andrei Kanchelskis' angled shot into the path of Ryan Giggs, who fired home. The goal appeared to have eased United into the next round but substitute Stuart Barlow's pace rattled their defence and when Gary Pallister dragged the striker down the referee awarded a spot-kick. Typical of Everton's luck at this time, Cottee had given up penalty duties after several high-profile misses but the new inductee was Ward, who was now off the pitch. To his credit Cottee stepped up – 'I didn't see many rushing to take it off him,' Kendall commented – but his kick was easily saved by Schmeichel.

That ended Everton's resistance for the evening and only the bizarre sight of three United goals being disallowed in the final ten minutes prevented a scoreline in keeping with their domination. 'United are an excellent side,' the Everton manager said ruefully after the game of a team fourteen points clear at the top. 'I fancy them for the championship, actually,' he quipped. After repeated bids for Dion Dublin, in the bowels of the Main Stand he also spoke to Alex Ferguson about the striker. 'Look, it needs to be an exceptional offer to even consider parting with the player,' the United boss told him. The Everton manager asked Ferguson what he thought would be 'exceptional' before adding, 'Would £1.5 million do the trick?' Fergie responded: 'That is not exceptional enough, £1.8 million is the price.' It was one of the more significant conversations in Everton history.

Over and out

Everton were now thirteenth in the table, with just three wins since the flurry of victories in the opening week. Southampton were the visitors on the following Saturday and before the game Kendall gave an update on the frustrating search for a target man. 'Believe me, I'm doing my upmost,' he explained. 'The financial situation isn't great, but I must stress that it's up to me to find a player who is available and who will move first.' A changed team gave a spirited performance against the Saints with three points sealed via a Tony Cottee winner. The most notable aspect of a grey day was the crowd: a paltry gate of just

13,667 spectators was the fourth-lowest of the post-war era in the top flight on the ground. After the game Kendall climbed the stairs to the old pressroom in the Main Stand and, after saying his team should have scored more and praising several players, commented: 'I take it you have not been too excited today gentlemen but I'm all right tonight.' Nick Hilton in the *Liverpool Daily Post* wrote 48 hours later, 'No-one thought anything of it at the time. They sounded like the words of a manager relieved to have won for the first time in five games.'

But those words took on a different meaning when, at precisely 5.34 p.m., Kendall climbed the stairs for a second time in less than half an hour, this time accompanied by chairman David Marsh, plus deputy chairman Desmond Pitcher. Marsh pulled out a used white envelope and read a simple thirty-word statement on the back: 'Everton Football Club jointly announce that Mr Kendall's position at the club has been terminated by him in accordance with the terms of his contract.' With the attendant press hastily rewriting their copy, Marsh added, 'We had an inkling of something towards the end of the match and Howard told us of his decision shortly afterwards.' A muted Kendall simply added: 'We will talk another time and I would rather talk tomorrow.' And that was that. 'A messy, untidy ending that left so many questions to be answered on another day,' Nick Hilton wrote.

That was on Sunday when Kendall returned to Bellefield to collect his belongings. He refused to be drawn on reasons for leaving other than to say, 'I didn't say anything to the players after the game because I would have broken up in front of them. I desperately wanted to do well here for the supporters, but I haven't been able to do what the fans wanted, and that hurts.' However, stories simultaneously emerged that his resignation was due to the failure to land Dion Dublin. 'Howard Kendall walked out on Everton because the board blocked the purchase of striker Dion Dublin,' the well-connected John Keith reported in the *Daily Express*, 'Kendall…believed he could do a deal at £1.5 million. But when the board said he could have only £500,000 Kendall decided it was time to quit.'

Naturally Marsh denied that theory, saying it was just speculation. After pointing out the board had underwritten a bid of up to £4 million for Duncan Ferguson during the summer, he denied there was no money. 'If people want to know why Howard resigned they should ask him,' he told the press. 'I don't think it's right for me to speculate on why Howard resigned. I don't know.' After trying to talk Kendall out of quitting, Marsh intriguingly said there was another conversation with his manager 'that was a personal and private thing…I would rather not say any more about that.' The contents of the conversation were never revealed. Kendall subsequently gave his version of events, commencing with the aftermath of the League Cup defeat, in *Love Affairs & Marriage*:

> *I resurrected the idea of a deal for Dion Dublin with Alex Ferguson. To my delight he was quite receptive and we sat down and agreed a transfer…I called David Marsh the next day, the Thursday, to tell him about the transfer. He neither said yes or no and that was that until the next morning when I received a call at Bellefield…It was Marsh. "We don't like the deal," he said. "The deal's off." "I've agreed everything with Alex," I protested. "We don't like the deal," he repeated. "The deal is off." "As far as I'm concerned then I'm no longer the manager of Everton Football Club," I answered. "See you."*

In some respects, Kendall's recollections provided more questions than answers. Firstly, there was no transfer deal agreed with Manchester United, Ferguson admitted as much in the aftermath of the sacking. Fergie was willing to sell, but only if Everton raised their bid to £1.8 million. That said, that was irrelevant in the context of the resignation. Whatever the 'deal' was, the Goodison board vetoed it according to Kendall. But why? Kendall proffered the theory that they rejected the transfer because he once expressed the opinion that Dublin appeared to be a bad buy, after seeing him with a slight limp during a recent game against Everton, when still recovering from injury.[108] A much likelier scenario was boardroom misgivings over the fee involved for a player still in the unproven category. Memories were still fresh of the £2 million spent on the more experienced Maurice Johnston for his transfer and wages, which produced 39 largely below-par performances and a free transfer. Some went further than that. Aside from Johnston, Kendall's recent dealings had been moderate: the big fee of the summer, £850,000 paid for Chelsea striker Graham Stuart, also appeared to be money wasted. 'With the kind of signings he has made over the last eighteen months, the board was probably justified,' said Peter Parry, chairman of the Everton Shareholders' Association. Peter Beardsley's brilliant contribution to Newcastle's blistering return to the top flight under Kevin Keegan also cast further doubts on his judgement.

In addition, although Kendall felt undermined, the board could have felt equally put out because he was agreeing deals with other clubs assuming funds were available. Perhaps they were just reiterating who was in charge. Kendall lamented the days when

---

[108] However, Dublin never featured against Everton during his time at United. Kendall may have been talking about a reserve game against the Toffees at Old Trafford in early October when the rangy striker did play, but he was not recovering from injury and had recently been included in several first-team squads. It would seem highly unlikely for the board to reject the deal on the basis he was injured.

Philip Carter and Jim Greenwood would 'wave things through' in his words but football had changed – as more money entered the game, clubs naturally became more corporate in approach. The irony being, of course, that in this new environment the club was now being run by a GP, not a Littlewoods executive.

The other issue was why the Everton chairman appeared to be genuinely surprised by the shock development, even though his manager had reaffirmed the intention to quit on the morning of the game. Possibly he believed Kendall was not serious and after giving himself some breathing space would return to the fold. 'Kendall needed a stronger and wiser counsel on Saturday,' a *Liverpool Echo* editorial suggested and that was correct. However, in *Only the Best is Good Enough*, Kendall provided some clues about his mindset:

> *If the money I feel I need is made available to me and I am able to bring to the club the players I think we need, then I feel we will have a fairly good chance of achieving success. However, if my judgement proves to be faulty and things do not go well, no-one will need to tell me when it is time to go, because I will know.*

Kendall possibly just felt his time was up and the Dublin tale was a smokescreen. He fully understood Everton managers were usually on borrowed time if there were no signs of progress after three years in the dug-out. That happened to Billy Bingham, Gordon Lee and Colin Harvey. The revival in the early months of 1984 kept the managerial guillotine at bay but now that landmark had just passed. 'People will naturally be looking at next year as The Big One,' he had said in the preceding summer. 'It's time to do something again.' But as the year ended there was nothing happening at all and the immediate future was relatively bleak. However, having been ruthlessly discarded as a player by Billy Bingham in 1974 and suffered at the hands of supporters a decade later, Kendall was only too aware that, to survive the fickle and callous nature of football, you had to look after your own interests first and foremost.

Looking after those interests in turn led to a series of somewhat baffling decisions from the summer of 1987 onwards. 'Nothing in football surprises me, but I must confess Kendall's decision hit me for six,' Brian Clough said about the return to Goodison. 'I should have known better because Kendall has always been something of a surprise package. After all, he upped and left Everton after winning a second Championship medal – not to go to Real Madrid or Barcelona but to Atletico [sic] Bilbao.'

Yet perhaps the move was no surprise as there had been stories during the summer of plans to move Kendall upstairs into an advisory role. Speaking on the *Across the Park* podcast in 2019, Colin Harvey claimed the board were ready to sack Kendall before he resigned. Also, with the possibility of a new owner keen on making an immediate impact, the club's most successful manager may have been jumping to avoid being pushed – the departure was by 'mutual agreement' – to ensure his reputation remained intact.

If Kendall had any doubts, perhaps developments elsewhere helped make up his mind. England manager Graham Taylor had been sacked and there was no obvious replacement, with the FA having little desire to poach from a domestic club during the season. Kendall, with first-hand experience of clubs locking down their manager when the national team job was available, was fully aware that being a free agent was a huge advantage.

The FA were employing Jimmy Armfield as their kingmaker and as he travelled the country canvassing opinion from those within the game, Terry Venables emerged as the favoured choice. But the former Spurs boss had several off-the-pitch legal issues to contend with, including accusations of making illegal payments at White Hart Lane, so the consensus was the FA would bide their time until the end of the campaign and appoint an interim boss. 'We need someone who is available – someone like Howard Kendall,' Armfield encouragingly admitted. The two had spoken but Kendall would only say, 'Any contact I've had I consider to be confidential. I am not touting myself for any job.' After being an also-ran in the summer and 50-1 in November, he was now 8-1 to get the post full time but favourite for the interim role. 'Venables and Kendall vie for England job,' ran the *Daily Telegraph* headline on Christmas Eve. But when the FA charges were dropped and some of the smoke around Venables' business dealings began to clear they, somewhat reluctantly it must be said, offered the 51-year-old the role. Not for the first time the man from Dagenham had blocked Kendall's path to one of the big jobs.

Running out of road

In assessing Kendall's second reign it is essential to distinguish between wider changes that affected the club's standing and those over which he exercised some management control. For the former, the dramatically increased revenues that arrived via the ITV deal in 1988 and then the start of the Premier League four years later – although this took time to drip through – changed the financial environment. Also, the arrival of ambitious Blackburn Rovers and Newcastle United in the first two years of the Premier League added both enormous wealth – particularly from the Lancashire side – and competition which was simply not there in Kendall's first tenure, when Liverpool's domination neutered the opposition and football's economic decline provided a more level financial playing field.

Consequently, the more his second spell progressed the more Kendall referred to the club falling behind. 'Blackburn are a one-off,' he told David Prentice, 'But Manchester United and Arsenal have been able to compete for those [expensive] players, simply because of their involvement in Europe.' Yet, with the principal source of income still from the turnstiles, there was a feeling that the successful years of the mid-1980s had acted effectively as a mirage, the average gates then of around 33,000 were reflective of a fanbase drawn to winning football – by 1993 they had returned the norm of Kendall's early years. Liverpool had enjoyed similar attendances during the mid-1980s but their bigger and wider support offered protection in leaner times: during a poor season in 1993/94 they averaged just under 40,000. The Everton manager was particularly hurt by the gate of just 20,000 to watch the Norwich City game at Goodison, a week after the derby victory. 'Liverpool have not been involved in Europe this season, but their attendances are double what we are attracting,' Kendall lamented. The impact was felt at the bank: Liverpool pocketed £9m from Anfield in 1993/94, against only £5 million for Everton at Goodison.

With commercial and sponsorship revenue intrinsically linked to matchday gates and wider appeal, Everton were now falling way behind: their overall income in 1993/94 of £9 million was, at most, half that of their supposed Big Five rivals. Although Kendall would, not unreasonably, refer to the gap as limiting their trophy-winning potential that did not explain his team's lack of competitiveness. Over five seasons from 1989/90 onwards Aston Villa, historically and demographically in a similar space to the Toffees, earned only £6 million more in income yet twice finished runners-up in the top flight and won the League Cup. Unfashionable clubs like QPR, Crystal Palace and Norwich City had been outperforming Kendall's outfit. In that context, the Everton boss – one of the highest-paid in the country – should have been offering considerably more than two full seasons where relegation had been a possibility and a third where they were mired in mid-table mediocrity. Also, apart from the memorable FA Cup win over Liverpool, there had been nothing of note in cup competitions.

Furthermore, managers set the agenda for their tenure in the opening twelve month in charge. In the opening season of his first spell – more by accident than design – the core of his mid-1980s side emerged from the reserve team as youngsters and became first-team regulars, supported by the acquisition of Adrian Heath. At no point in his second incarnation did Kendall appear to make a similar breakthrough – he may have argued the board should have supported him more financially but money spent failed to light the blue touch paper. The acquisition of Maurice Johnston proved disastrous and defined his second spell in the way Andy Gray did his first. Unlike first time around, there were no talented youngsters to fall back on, with the alarming lack of a meaningful youth development policy. On the pitch, if Kendall's great team featured a superbly balanced midfield then his early-1990s vintage was anything but. Workhorses like Barry Horne and John Ebbrell were complemented by inconsistent wide men like Peter Beagrie and Robert Warzycha. Consequently, the team not only lacked shape but had a shortage of creativity through the middle. Up front the failure to land an effective big striker eventually proved fatal.

However, the overarching issue was Kendall himself. The history of football in the second half of the twentieth century shows that successful managers had, if they were lucky, a decade at the top before their star went into decline or they were wise enough to get out. That applied to Sir Alf Ramsey, Don Revie, Bill Nicholson, Bill Shankly, Harry Catterick, Ron Saunders, Bob Paisley and even Brian Clough. There are many reasons for this. Extensive pressure has a debilitating effect. The tactics and style that originally brought success can become outmoded in a changing game. Teams need rebuilding. On a personal level the age gap between manager and players becomes greater which affects relationships. New and younger management rivals (and other competitors) emerge. The clubs they manage change culturally. Now a decade after his extraordinary revival of Everton's fortunes, for Kendall all these factors applied to a degree. Consequently, the inner confidence and self-belief that had sustained the Everton manager over the previous ten years was deserting him.

The finesse of his man-management had also disappeared and probably the biggest mistake was expecting the team-building methods, used to such great effect during the mid-1980s, would produce the same results. The group in Kendall's second spell were completely different as individuals, and a more professional approach to diet and lifestyle meant such methods were now unfashionable. Kendall could have legitimately argued that the huge uplift in money also diminished their motivation and ambition, compared to those who had brought success in the previous decade.[109] As Tony Cottee also pointed out, greater rewards brought cynicism and mistrust in the dressing room. 'There seemed to be some sort of friction among the squad which had to be sorted out as quickly as possible,' Kendall noted late in his second spell. By the latter days of his second tenure,

---

[109]   Graeme Souness took over at Liverpool five months after Kendall's return. Speaking on the *Off the Ball* sports show in Ireland in 2018, he noted a difference in players' attitudes to when he had left Anfield seven years before. 'They don't listen anymore,' former team-mate Ronnie Whelan told him, 'It's all changed, everything's a joke today.' Souness blamed money for shifting attitudes. Kendall probably had the same experience.

that mistrust extended to the relationship between players and manager. During an interview with Len Capeling in 1997, Kendall admitted realising he was running out of road following the disastrous 3-2 loss at Spurs in October 1993:

> *I remember a game at Tottenham and we were winning 2-0 I think and I took off Beagrie or something like that. Then it was 2-1 and they were bombing us down that side so I went a little bit negative and Tottenham equalised. The players came in and it was one of the first times they had questioned something I'd done tactically or whatever. You've always got a reason for doing things but I just felt then that they weren't believing in what I was doing or my reasons for doing it. Maybe I lost them a little bit. I think all managers go through that stage but that hurt. I think we eventually lost the game 3-2 and of course I'm the one to blame because I made the substitution.*

David Lacey in the *Guardian* claimed Kendall 'had gone to seed' and although that may have been harsh, he increasingly looked like a manager whose time had gone. As an example, the Everton boss had reintroduced bottles of wine on the night before the game but, in *The Real McCall*, Stuart McCall alleged that, although many were happy with an odd glass, on occasions drinking got out of hand. He recalled that several members of the team who played in the ZDS Cup final against Crystal Palace had over-indulged the night before while two players who appeared in the televised 2-0 loss at Leeds in December 1990 took to the pitch with serious hangovers. 'There was often a drink about when you least expected it,' McCall revealed. 'I picked up a cup in the dressing-room before a game and thought it was half full of Lucozade. I took a swig and had to spit it out. It was whisky.'

Pat Nevin was more explicit in his criticism of the atmosphere around team management. 'The drinking culture was being, to put it kindly, tolerated more again,' he wrote in *The Accidental Footballer*. 'The manager seemed perfectly happy with that…but a bottle of wine the night before a match isn't a great idea for most players. I was uncomfortable with the way certain standards were slipping.' The elephant in the room here is the manager's own drinking. However, Nevin's recollections of the 2-1 FA Cup defeat at West Ham in March 1991 provide an insight into how this was possibly becoming problematical. 'Howard was not absolutely on the ball for this vital game,' he wrote. 'There had been a few drinks taken beforehand and when he read out the team, he actually named the same player, Stuart McCall, at least twice in two different positions.' During the first half it was clear that West Ham winger Stuart Slater was running riot after being allowed too much space and, with Kendall passive, Nevin took it upon himself to provide cover. At half-time, with Everton 1-0 down, Kendall asked who had changed the system and Nevin admitted it was him. In his book he recalled what he said next to the manager: 'I didn't think you were capable of doing it, because your judgement is impaired.' Nevin then wrote: 'The insinuation was clear, even if it was unspoken by me and the others: he had had a few too many.' The question here is how aware the board were of the issue and whether it played a role in Kendall's departure. One reader's letter to the *Football Echo* summed up the trajectory of Kendall's post-1987 career perfectly:

> *His record as a manager since 1987 clearly indicates his best years are behind him. He was sacked from Athletic Bilbao, walked out on Manchester City after a year and his last three years at Goodison were a major disappointment with no challenges for honours. This dismal picture extends to the club's other teams. The Youth team have not had a run in the Youth Cup since 1984. No wonder we are incapable of bringing youngsters through into the first team…Mr Kendall's record in the transfer market in his second spell was disastrous. None of his signings has [sic] been an outstanding success.*

All this begged the question why Kendall had returned. There are similarities here with Malcolm Allison. Like Kendall 'Big Mal' was a charismatic and extrovert figurehead with a liking for the social side of the game. With Joe Mercer, the pair had taken Manchester City out of the shadows of their more successful and glamorous local rival by winning four trophies in three seasons before departing in 1973. When the club was struggling six years later, the allure of a return was too much to resist. However, during his time away, Peter Swales had become chairman and the boardroom landscape had altered completely. Likewise, the squad was nowhere as potent as first time around. Supporters expected Allison to rekindle the excitement of a decade before but the magic had gone and within two years the love affair was over, his fraught final weeks documented in the extraordinary Granada TV documentary *City!* The comparisons here with Kendall are obvious, extending even to employing their immediate predecessor as a coach (in Allison's case, Tony Book).[110] 'If you've been successful first time people expect nothing less than a repeat,' Andy Gray said about Kendall Mk 2. 'It was a case of his heart ruling his head and I felt it was never going to have a happy ending.'

Kendall had ignored the advice of friends and, like Allison, the rule of never returning

---

[110] In the documentary Allison talks about his relationship with Peter Swales: 'He wouldn't have had to tell me [about it not working out] I'd have told him if I couldn't see any light and I couldn't see any progress.' Compare to Kendall's statement from earlier: 'If my judgement proves to be faulty and things do not go well, no-one will need to tell me when it is time to go, because I will know.'

to former glories. The choice was made even worse because the decline was already too advanced even for someone with his gifts to reverse. 'His decision to go back to Everton struck me as quirkish, even hazardous,' John Giles wrote in the *Daily Express* in November 1992. 'Now it is confirmed as a seriously wrong turning. And the directors assumed Kendall would fish out the old magic wand. Such an object does not exist in football.' But James Lawton in the same newspaper had a more prosaic explanation: 'His story is a classic guide for any younger manager. It is an overwhelming lesson – don't fall in love with a football club…Kendall and Everton were a marriage. At least in his mind. For the club they were just another working arrangement.' But at the time of his departure the club had other business matters to contend with.

34

SHARES AND
SHARES ALIKE

JOHN MOORES DIED ON SATURDAY, 25 SEPTEMBER 1993. THE MAN, whose vision and demanding values – plus, it must be said, cold, hard cash – helped lift the club from the moribund 1950s to a decade of success, had been in poor health for some time. However, the fact that he died hours before the Toffees were trounced 5-1 at Goodison by Norwich City – a club who were two divisions below Everton when he joined the board in 1960 – was a poignant reminder of how those standards had dropped.

The Moores family owned 1,000 of the club's 2,498 shares when he died, an overall total that had remained unchanged since their original issue in 1892. Reports indicated that his instructions were that any successor should be a 'safe pair of hands' with 'Everton's interests at heart'. The ownership, he made clear, should not be used for 'speculative purposes'. But with the holding certain to be passed on to his children, who had little interest in moving the club on, then clearly anybody subsequently acquiring his shares would be the majority shareholder and hold enormous sway. Typically, in death as in his life, Moores still held huge influence in the direction of the club.

Across the Park Foods

Born in Birkenhead in 1940, Peter Johnson entered the family's butcher's business at the age of sixteen. A decade later when a local business contact told him about the flourishing Christmas food hamper trade in Liverpool, Johnson wanted a piece of the action and was such a success that he became a multi-millionaire following the floating of the company, Park Foods, on the stock exchange in 1983.

Four years later, after three decades of watching Liverpool, Johnson was asked to take over an ailing Tranmere Rovers, who had just escaped demotion from the Football

League. He developed Prenton Park and financed a team that, by the time Kendall was struggling in his second spell, was remarkably knocking on the door of the top flight. But Johnson had bigger ambitions. 'I still find it astonishing that a winning Tranmere Rovers team can't attract crowds of over 10,000 every week,' he said in May 1993. Looking across the River Mersey, he noted that Everton still drew average crowds of 20,000 despite struggling in the bottom half of the top flight. 'If anyone got hold of that club imagine the 30,000-35,000 which they could attract to Goodison,' he concluded. Ironically, two weeks before Moores' death, there was speculation that Johnson had met his nominees to discuss buying their shares. Although the Everton board had recommended a capital injection at the recent AGM, naturally Jim Greenwood played down talk of a takeover. Johnson, however, confirmed he had spoken with club representatives.

If the Park Foods magnate, with a personal fortune of £100 million, believed he had a clear run he was wrong. With the Littlewoods founder's death viewed as an opportunity for a potential power grab, during November stories emerged that Everton director Bill Kenwright had been speaking with Moores' children about a deal to take over the club, talks which pre-dated the death of their father. The theatre impresario was the public figurehead of a group which also included Tom Cannon, the former head of the Manchester Business School, advertising executives Michael Dyble (also based in Manchester) and Tony Tighe, plus Arthur Abercromby, a Cheshire builder. The financial clout came from Kenwright and Abercromby. With their presence largely at the other end of the M62, they were dubbed the 'Manchester Consortium' by the *Liverpool Echo*. This opportunity to land a low blow was taken by Johnson. 'I don't think he [John Moores] would have wanted to see Everton become another outpost of Manchester,' he provocatively said. However, to reinforce their credentials, Kenwright's allies were pictured holding their Goodison season tickets.

Having said that, nothing could legally progress until December when Moores' will left the shareholding to his sons, John and Peter. With his self-proclaimed blue blood plus boardroom connections, Kenwright attracted the initial support of the brothers, who were also willing to cede controlling interest without giving up their shares – meaning any investment could be used for the good of the club. The consensus was any investor would have to put in upwards of £10 million, initially via a further rights issue. The consortium's initial offer was believed to be a further issue of 2,500 shares, priced at £2,000 apiece, with each shareholder entitled to buy an extra share for every one owned. The Moores family would take up their rights to 1,000 additional shares, therefore adding £2 million to the club's coffers. With small shareholders unlikely to take up their option, the consortium had underwritten the remainder, meaning another £3 million.

Three days before Christmas, Johnson made his offer to the board (less Kenwright, who was excluded). He argued that an individual, and not a consortium, at the top would be less bureaucratic, plus he had experience of turning round the fortunes of an ailing club. Not unreasonably, the Tranmere chairman claimed the board was too inward-looking and required outside expertise. However, Kenwright remained in the driving seat, still enjoying the backing of the Moores brothers who were reportedly uninterested in any other options. 'I must say I was annoyed,' Johnson said on hearing that news. 'I appreciate that the Moores family own a majority shareholding, but surely they should at least have listened to all the alternatives before making their final decision.' However, there was hope for Johnson in that the board were obliged to consider which offer was best for the club. Should they side with Johnson, they were duty bound to go back to the brothers and ask them to reconsider their position.

Kenwright spoke about the takeover bid for the first time on Christmas Eve. 'I have always been confident that my offer, which is based on a group of committed Evertonians getting right behind the club, would be accepted [by the brothers],' he claimed. With the board discussing the consortium's offer two days after Christmas, he refused to be drawn on the opposition: 'I can't talk about any rival bid. All I know is I am an Evertonian who understands this club and what it needs.' Johnson however countered by explaining to *The Sunday Times*: 'There are five factors in my favour. I'm rich enough to handle it. I live on Merseyside. I love football. I've got the experience of running a big business. And I know what it takes to restore the fortunes of a football club.'

But with all parties holding their breath, there was anti-climax when the board gave both men another three days to provide further information on their bids. Afterwards the Wirral businessman aired his frustrations while making public his bid – he was offering £7.5 million against the £5 million of the consortium. 'Both bids were on the table,' he revealed, 'They [the board] should have made their minds up and my offer is so much ahead of theirs financially. My offer would be £3,000 a share. That works out at £7.5m. I understand the consortium's bid is two-thirds of mine… you have to consider the other shareholders and whether their shares would be devalued if someone offered only £2,000 for each of them.' The subsequent problem for the board was whether they should go with their heart or head: the former pointed towards the Everton-supporting consortium, the latter to a cash-rich former Anfield season-ticket holder. Although Kenwright said that 'I think it is important Everton fans know they are talking about a Liverpool supporter in Peter Johnson,' it was his rival who had the strongest support of fans who took part in local radio and newspaper polls.

After six board meetings in less than a fortnight there was still deadlock: with several aspects of their financial packages still requiring clarification the takeover decision was delayed. But as the saga stumbled into the new year the club had bigger priorities: a permanent manager was needed to ensure the new owners were not taking over a relegated side.

Playing the field

The usual suspects were trotted out as replacement for Kendall: Joe Royle, Ron Atkinson and Peter Reid were all in the frame. Elsewhere there were a couple of left-field potential candidates. David Marsh admitted that the club were willing to scour the continent for a new boss and Switzerland national-team manager Roy Hodgson was linked with a return to England, but he rejected any move to Goodison until after the following summer's World Cup. Intriguingly, Ric George in the *Liverpool Echo* also reported French sources claiming that Gerard Houllier – recently sacked as national coach after failing to qualify for the same tournament – would willingly offer his services, especially having been a teacher in the city 25 years before.

Elsewhere, any search for a new manager would not be complete without the name of Bobby Robson cropping up and this occasion was no exception, due to his recent departure from Sporting Lisbon. For many supporters, the arrival of the former England boss in the Goodison dug-out was long overdue and those hopes were enhanced when Robson left the door open. 'If a top job like Everton was offered, of course I would consider it,' he admitted. But there was another former national-team supremo in contention: Graham Taylor, who like Houllier had fallen on his sword after failure to qualify for the World Cup. 'Former England bosses Bobby Robson and Graham Taylor were last night set for a sensational battle to land the vacant Everton hot-seat,' Richard Tanner reported in the *Daily Mirror* in mid-December. 'I certainly wouldn't rule out either of them,' David Marsh announced. 'We're looking for an experienced, big-name manager.' Remarkably, in Robson's case at least, there was a feeling in the Goodison boardroom that a lack of recent domestic top-flight experience counted against him. Consequently, with first-choice Ron Atkinson chained to Villa Park, the club was operating off an initial shortlist of Joe Royle, Norwich City's Mike Walker plus Sheffield United's Dave Bassett. Notwithstanding Royle's true-blue connections, it was hardly one featuring the 'big-name manager' Marsh had promised.

Taking the Michael

There was a good reason for filling the role as soon as possible. With boardroom bandwidth filled by the takeover saga, Jimmy Gabriel took the caretaker role when Kendall departed but, by his own admission, the Scot struggled. Sheffield Wednesday inflicted a 2-0 defeat at Goodison two days after Christmas, in a game broadcast live on Sky in front of just 16,471 frozen spectators. 'I just looked at the four midfielder players and two front men and they were just clones of each other – all 5ft 8in tall doing the same thing,' Andy Gray said on commentary at full time, 'The way they just collapsed and threw in the towel at 1-0 down was a sad reflection of the mess they're in.'[111] The post-Kendall era had brought a paltry point from four matches. 'Everton's plight with only one goal in their previous five games and only one win in the last eight is beginning to look worrying,' Peter Ball pointed out in *The Times*. A 2-0 loss at Blackburn followed two days later and when a fifth-minute Tim Breaker goal secured three points for West Ham at Goodison on New Year's Day, the side passed nine hours without a goal. 'We need a new manager appointed as soon as possible,' former Hammer Tony Cottee admitted. 'We are like a ship floating in mid-Atlantic without a captain at the moment.'

James Lawton was an interested spectator from the press box and, with the game taking place when the directors spent most of the day discussing the takeover bids, the *Daily Express* man clearly spelt out who was to blame for the demise. 'The truth is Billy Bonds' revived side did more than take three points in Saturday's 1-0 win at Goodison. They exposed a classic case of near-terminal neglect,' he wrote, 'Just an old story of directors fiddling while Rome burned.' With the board still procrastinating over the two bids the club was heading towards the drop zone at an unhealthy rate. When Chelsea inflicted a 4-2 defeat at Stamford Bridge 48 hours later, there was some consolation when Tony Cottee ended the goal drought which had lasted ten hours forty minutes. The club had taken one point from seven games – their worst run since the relegation campaign of 1950/51.

However, by then, following an emergency meeting after the West Ham defeat, the board had sanctioned an approach to Norwich City for Mike Walker's services. Helping their cause was that he was in the final year of his contract and chairman Robert Chase had only promised a short-term extension. A reported basic salary of £45,000 was also the lowest in the top flight. But extracting the coveted Walker from Carrow Road proved difficult: Chase refused him permission to speak to Everton and made some indiscreet

[111] One supporter's letter to the *Liverpool Echo* carried much more sarcasm about the height of the Everton forward line: 'Is it true he's in the market for Snow White, now he's successfully signed up the Seven Dwarfs?'

333

comments on the potential salary on offer. Although the two clubs spoke – Bill Kenwright ironically leading the Everton negotiations – Chase rejected a second request for talks and Walker was effectively backed into a corner. 'Obviously I would like to speak with them [Everton]. I believe you should be able to speak with anyone you want about a job,' the frustrated Norwich boss groaned.

Faced with waiting for an enhanced offer or resigning from Carrow Road, Walker unsurprisingly took the latter option and handed in his notice on the Friday morning, immediately faxing his availability to now chief executive Jim Greenwood. By the evening the 48-year-old was the club's tenth permanent manager. But Norwich chairman Robert Chase was apoplectic and accused Everton of making an illegal approach: 'We feel Everton have effectively induced Mike Walker to take this action, and we will be sending an official written complaint to the FA and the Premiership.' The Blues vehemently denied this, insisting they had acted correctly.[112] Nevertheless, Walker's actions were probably influenced by his experience at Colchester United seven years before, where he was sacked with the team joint-top, after a clash of personalities with the chairman. Questioned over his integrity, Walker provided a robust response. 'Loyalty? That annoys me. People who are that can end up with nothing,' he told the *Daily Mirror's* Nigel Clarke. 'I've earned what I've got. Loyalty goes both ways.' He was probably referring to the Norwich chairman, who was showing a distinct lack of appreciation of his manager's abilities.

So why was Walker suddenly hot property? 'If you shout a bit you get noticed more. But that's not my style,' he said when in East Anglia. 'I prefer to let my team do my talking with me and let people judge me on my buying and selling and on my results.' By January 1994 that judgement could be nothing less than positive. After becoming manager during the summer of 1992, Walker crafted an attractive passing side from players previously classed as journeymen and saw his team eight points ahead at the top in early December. Although that run could not last, the Canaries remained in title contention until the final weeks of the 1992/93 campaign and a third-place finish was a well-deserved reward. Ominously perhaps, that was despite a negative goal difference, with the 65 goals conceded double the tally of champions Manchester United.

---

[112] Everton were eventually fined £75,000, plus £50,000 compensation and costs, after a Premier League inquiry found them guilty of enticing Walker to Goodison but cleared the club of approaching him directly.

Eighteen months of
spectacular progress at
Carrow Road left Mike
Walker a wanted man.

If anything, the current season was more impressive: seventh at the turn of the year, Norwich had games in hand on the European contenders and a significantly reduced goals-against column. Moreover, their UEFA Cup campaign had fired the imagination, Walker's outfit becoming the first from England to win at Bayern Munich and, following a 3-2 aggregate victory over the German giants, they took eventual winners Inter Milan to two hard-fought games in the next round, before bravely bowing out 2-0 on aggregate. During those encounters, Walker displayed both a cool head and tactical acumen. Off the pitch his sharp suits – and a nickname of 'Dessie' after the famous grey horse because of his distinguished looks – were part of a media-friendly image. Combined with two impressive victories at Goodison in the previous twelve months, the Toffees hierarchy found those attributes irresistible. For all that, the former goalkeeper was still unproven, having operated in the rarified air of English football for only eighteen months. 'I get tarred with the same brush as my team,' Walker had previously claimed. 'People think I'm just a flash in the pan.' Everton were about to find out.

Walker's crisp start

Parachuted into the club less than 24 hours before a tricky FA Cup third-round tie at second-tier Bolton Wanderers, the new incumbent at least made the trip to Burnden Park. Bruce Rioch – himself strongly linked with the role Kendall vacated – had fashioned a fine team and had removed Liverpool at the same stage twelve months before, following a 2-0 win at Anfield. They proved testing opponents but, despite playing with ten men for the final half-hour after Barry Horne's dismissal, the visitors showed the necessary resilience to escape with a 1-1 draw. But Walker had seen enough to realise there were problems. 'You don't get offered a job if everything is rosy. Not at this level,' he said. 'I went in [the dressing room] on Saturday and it gave it a lift. I'm not being big-headed because Mickey Mouse could have come in and given it a lift.'

During the following week Walker spoke about future transfer plans. 'I won't sign somebody just because he has pace or can head a ball,' he explained. 'I want a good all-round player. That's important to me and it's important to the club.' Like his predecessor, Walker recognised the need for a big striker, which accelerated when Paul Rideout was injured at Burnden Park. Before his first league game, at home to Swindon Town, the new manager consequently retraced Kendall's steps and returned to Southend to sign Brett Angell for £500,000. On the basis that a manager's first signing can set the tone for what follows, in retrospect the move for a player rejected by his predecessor was ominously unimaginative. That said, Walker did show some optimism. 'There is a bit of work to do here,' he said after joining, 'and you have got to be realistic, you are not going to turn it round straightaway, but I think we can get to the top six.'

Walker was earning a reputation as a lucky manager[113] and more evidence was gathered when his first league opponents were bottom-of-the-table newcomers – without an away win all season – who possessed little defensive know-how. Nevertheless, the subsequent encounter was a strange ninety minutes. After strolling to a 2-0 lead and seeing one-time Everton apprentice Andy Mutch sent off for poking John Ebbrell in the face, Everton let the ten-man visitors back in the game. Defensive errors allowed John Moncur to head home unchallenged and when Ian Snodin gave the ball away to Paul Bodin, the Wales international netted a deserved equaliser. But after Gary Ablett forced the ball over the line on 71 minutes, a tiring Swindon collapsed and Cottee completed a hat-trick as the home team ran out unlikely and illusory 6-2 victors – Walker's second win

---

[113]   Norwich only secured a UEFA Cup berth because Arsenal completed the domestic cup double, their FA Cup victory meaning qualification for the European Cup Winners' Cup. The now vacant UEFA Cup space, which the Gunners would have filled because of their League Cup win, was allocated to Norwich on account of their third-place finish in the Premier League.

by a four-goal margin at Goodison during the campaign. The new boss had mixed emotions after the game. 'At times we played some great stuff but at other times we played like schoolboys,' he said. 'I don't underestimate what needs to be done.'

Four days later on the same ground Walker was given further proof of the work required to turn fortunes around, during the FA Cup replay against Bolton. Like the preceding game, Everton were leading 2-0 shortly after the break, thanks to two goals from Stuart Barlow, before Bolton pulled a goal back through a volley from Scottish striker John McGinley. When Kirkby-born Alan Stubbs saw a header cleared off the line, the home team believed they had done enough to secure a fourth-round trip to Arsenal but five minutes from the end Walker's – and Everton's – luck ran out. Neville Southall stepped out to comfortably collect Tony Kelly's cross but only succeeded in colliding with the crouching Ablett. The Welsh goalkeeper spilled the ball and boyhood Evertonian Stubbs took great delight in stroking it over the line, in front of the large away following within the 34,642 crowd, the third-largest Goodison gate of the campaign.

For the second time in four days Everton had thrown away a two-goal lead but on this occasion there was no redemption. With the replay now in the throes of extra time, they were increasingly vulnerable to speedy counter-attacks and, on 100 minutes, the ball reached Owen Coyle on the edge of the Everton box and the Scot curled a beautiful left-footed shot past Southall. With their fragile confidence broken, the home team were unable to grab an equaliser and for the second successive campaign their FA Cup quest was strangled at birth. 'In an odious extra-time period all the deficiencies Walker will have to attend to in the weeks ahead grimly emerged,' David Prentice pointed out in the *Liverpool Echo*. 'That frailty in defence, a lack of focus up front and a midfield that knitted together only fitfully.' Walker for his part knew where the main problem lay. 'If you don't defend properly you will lose games,' he complained. 'If we can't handle it I will have to get players in who can handle it.'

Walker's return

Strange as it seems now, Walker's first two months were largely seen as positive. Following a 1-0 defeat at Old Trafford – when Everton supporters were widely lauded for their flawless behaviour during the minute's silence for the recently departed Matt Busby – the new manager took advantage of an unusual run of four successive home games to rack up eight points. That left Everton in the comparative safety of fourteenth place and nine points above the drop zone, with just eleven games remaining. 'It is a long time since I can recall a newcomer to the Merseyside sporting scene making as much impact as Mike

Walker has done since his arrival from Norwich,' Ian Hargraves optimistically proclaimed in the *Liverpool Echo*. 'It is not just a matter of optimism by fans starved of success, or even an instinctive reaction to a series of sensible and restrained comments accompanied by an immediate improvement in team performance. Walker has genuine presence.' The new manager's belief in quick passing football was acquiring many converts. 'The arrival of the new boss has given everyone a lift,' John Ebbrell said after an impressive 4-2 home win over Chelsea. 'Whether it's a few more ideas coming in I don't know. But we're playing attractive football and creating chances.'

Nevertheless, the glut of Goodison of homes games meant the run-in contained a disproportionate number of away trips: seven out of eleven matches. The first was at Anfield in mid-March where, like Walker, Roy Evans was a new incumbent to the manager's role. Whereas Evans had taken just four points from his first five games, Walker's eleven from six was seen as sparking a revival and there was genuine optimism that the Toffees could wrap up a first derby double in a decade. That said, a glance at the Liverpool team-sheet was a sad reminder of Everton's failing youth development policy. After training with both clubs since an early age, the eighteen-year-old Robbie Fowler had made his Liverpool debut early in the campaign and already had fifteen goals to his name. On the advice of his father the youngster always refused to make a commitment as a child but, entering his teenage years, he was spending more and more time at Melwood. 'It was always a contest between the two clubs who would get my signature, but it was Liverpool who always seemed to show the most interest,' he wrote in his 2005 autobiography. Although Everton still tried to lure him on two more occasions, he signed a first professional contract at Anfield. 'After being courted by both clubs I always felt more at home at Liverpool,' he explained, 'just felt a certain loyalty to them because they had looked after me since I was eleven, had instilled certain ideas and values into me.' Steve McManaman was three years older than Fowler and was developing into a skilful, hard-working winger with a goalscoring touch. Like his fellow Scouser, he had trained with both clubs with the same outcome: offered a one-year schoolboy contract at Everton, he moved to Liverpool because they offered the same plus, crucially, a two-year apprentice deal. 'Liverpool's scouting system was just a hundred times better,' he told Steve Tongue of the *Independent* in 2009. 'They made that extra effort, wheeled out Kenny Dalglish to meet you and made you feel as if this was the greatest club in the world.' The sad irony, of course, with all of this was both players were rabid Evertonians, as were their families.

With the demands of live television meaning the game started at the unusual time of 5 p.m. on a Sunday evening, the tea-time viewers were treated to typical derby-match fare in blustery conditions and before a standing Kop for the final time. Although McManaman was a constant source of danger on the right, the visitors' controlled and patient play ensured they held the early initiative and on 21 minutes Walker's side were rewarded for their enlightened start by a goal through Dave Watson's header from a Preki free-kick. But with the television cameras still showing replays of the strike, 37 seconds later the still-celebrating Everton defence was caught napping by a long ball straight from the kick-off and Ian Rush nipped in to volley past Southall.[114] Just before the break Fowler raced on to a John Barnes pass and drilled a powerful left-footed shot past the Welshman into the far corner. Although Everton continued to enjoy the bulk of possession, their goalkeeper had to be at his magnificent best and a brilliant save from McManaman followed by a full-length dive to take the ball off Fowler's toes was one of the finest of his career. After Watson blasted over when well-placed with twenty minutes left, the visitors thought they had earned a deserved point in added time. Peter Beagrie's deflected shot looked set for the top corner before David James dramatically tipped the ball around the post and secured the three points. 'Even the losing Evertonians should be able to hold up their heads in the city next week after yesterday's sizzling game,' Cynthia Bateman wrote in the *Guardian*. Walker, however, had little time for sentiment. 'The players generally did well and I haven't any complaints about their commitment,' he remarked. 'It's just a shame that it was three points down the drain.'

However, with teams below picking up points, the defeat was a salutary reminder that Everton were not out of danger, a fear reinforced after Walker returned to Carrow Road eight days later for a game transmitted live on a Monday evening. Any anger felt by those in East Anglia following his acrimonious departure had only been heightened by a winless run of nine league games since, as a once promising season was tailing off. After Walker entered the arena to a mixture of jeers and cheers, his former charges bit the hand that used feed them. Following a goal-line clearance and three saves from Southall had stopped the home team from opening the scoring, typically Norwich went ahead through Ian Culverhouse, a 100-1 shot for the first goal after just one in 360 appearances. Further strikes from Chris Sutton and Mark Bowen wrapped up a comfortable 3-0 home win. The paucity of the attacking threat was exemplified by only one corner and no shots on target from striking duo Cottee and Rideout. After the game Walker was asked whether his side was in relegation danger. 'I don't choose to be negative, I choose to be positive,' was his glib response. For Everton fans the worrying aspect about a troubling performance was

---

[114] Not for the last time a derby goal was not seen live by the watching television audience.

the lack of fight after conceding a second just after the break, which pointed to the problems of days gone by. 'I had heard that was something which had happened earlier in the season but I wasn't familiar with it,' Walker commented.

If the new boss did not have the finger on the panic button yet, that was certainly not the case after a damaging Saturday afternoon at Goodison five days later. Like Everton, Tottenham were a former powerhouse on the decline and Osvaldo Ardiles' outfit started the day three points behind the Toffees after a run of ten games without a win. But like their East Anglian counterparts, the London club found Everton easy meat. A feeble display by the home team – the players strolling around as if safety had already been secured – deserved nothing in an embarrassingly poor game. And that is what they got, the visitors sealing three points through a Steve Sedgley header twenty minutes from time, one that Southall really should have saved. A third successive defeat left Everton five points above the relegation trapdoor.

Aside from the attitude of the players, Walker was also having issues implementing his preferred style. Building from the back requires forward players to move into deeper positions and link play but that was not the forte of either Cottee or Rideout, who remained isolated with little service. Noticeably the most dangerous Everton player was John Ebbrell, who was proving more of a goal threat than either striker. Walker had also been hampered by Gary Ablett's toe injury, which meant playing Ian Snodin at centre-back, a position in which the versatile Yorkshireman struggled. Without adequate cover in midfield, the defence was becoming porous and, after only one clean sheet in his first eleven games, Everton were heading towards the precipice.

35

THE ART OF
FALLING APART

FORTY-EIGHT HOURS AFTER THE SPURS DEFEAT, AN UNMISTAKABLY angry Walker raised the spectre of relegation for the first time. 'We seem to think we are too good to go down,' he said. 'If our players are not going to respond to that then we have a problem, a real problem.' The situation was about to get worse, much worse.

That sinking feeling

Keen to shore up a shaky backline, four days later Walker played a three-man central defence at Villa Park and dragged out a point in a dour contest played in a howling wind. On Easter Saturday the Everton manager was not so lucky at Hillsborough. Bafflingly, Walker continued with three centre-backs but filled two of the roles with the inexperienced David Unsworth and Neil Moore. Walker – with eyes only on a point – insisted both full-backs stayed deep, thus inviting constant Wednesday pressure over ninety minutes. Before the match, he referred to the point at Villa and claimed: 'If we keep playing like that we won't lose too many of our remaining games.' But the not unexpected consequence of the defensive line-up was a total mismatch. Two goals ahead at the break, Trevor Francis' side added another before Tony Cottee ended a goal drought lasting six hours and forty minutes with a delightful chip. But two goals from Mark Bright in the final ten minutes completed a 5-1 drubbing before the large travelling army journeyed back over the Pennines fearing the worst, especially as fellow strugglers Oldham, Manchester City and Sheffield United (at Anfield of all places) had won. The soulless performance left Everton sixth from bottom, now only three points from the relegation places. However, the manager's relaxed insistence that matters remained in their own hands baffled some. 'Mike Walker sounded like a bandsman on the Titanic as he said: "Crisis, what crisis?" after this disastrous capsize,' Matt Dickinson wrote in the *Daily Express*. 'It may not be long for the lifeboats,' Ian Snodin added to continue that sinking feeling.

There was certainly no rescue attempt at Goodison 48 hours later, when 27,427 spectators witnessed title-chasing Blackburn Rovers ease to a comprehensive 3-0 victory on an afternoon when Dalglish's side barely had to move out of first gear. To make matters worse, returning striker Mike Newell stuck the knife into his former employers, the local-born striker scoring twice. 'We certainly didn't look like a bottom club today. Blackburn scored against the run of play. And in the first half we made them look ordinary,' Walker said afterwards. That view was not necessarily shared by the watching press. 'That is akin to Nero fiddling while Rome burned. And the relegation flames are threatening to consume Everton,' opined John Keith in the *Daily Express*, as the newspaper's disaster analogies moved to dry land.

Having abandoned the sweeper system, Walker appeared to be running out of options. Several striking partnerships had been utilised, with no luck. There had been any number of midfield combinations and various full-back pairings. 'Yesterday saw switches to the middle for Jackson and Stuart, and to the right flank for Snodin and Ebbrell but the end result was pretty much the same,' David Prentice wrote. 'No goals scored, more goals conceded and an increasingly agitated home support.' That support included booing Brett Angell after his substitution for a returning Stuart Barlow against Rovers, a reflection of one goal in eleven games. The reaction of the Goodison crowd irked the manager. 'The fans were frustrated,' he commented, 'but the time to kick us is not when we are down. What we need now is support.'

The fading Merseyside giants certainly needed that backing, as they now stood fifth from bottom, two points above the relegation zone and level with Oldham Athletic, who had played two games less. Walker was the third Everton manager to have a disagreement with Tony Cottee and he had left out the striker for two of the previous three games. But before the trip to the striker's former hunting ground at Upton Park he held out an olive branch: 'He needs a break but I am sure he can score the goals that keep us in the Premier League.' For once, the manager's hunch proved correct. However, for all his later claims that he gave a 'this is it' speech before the game, the visitors entered the Boleyn Ground like condemned men. 'Everton started with one point from their past six games, no away victories since October,' Mihir Bose wrote in *The Sunday Times*, 'and for most of the match had the look of a team that did not believe it was going anywhere but down.' With West Ham profligate in front of goal and, having barely ventured out of their own half, twenty minutes from time the visitors grabbed a lifeline. Ian Snodin broke up a West Ham attack and fed Graham Stuart down the Everton right, his cross found the unmarked Cottee, who turned and shot just inside goalkeeper Ludek Miklosko's far post: the forward's first goal on the ground since leaving six years before.

Cottee's eighteenth goal of the season took Everton four points clear of the drop zone and, although the five clubs below all had at least one game in hand, many had to face each other while Walker's side had four games against teams with little to play for. 'It's up to us,' he said after the game. 'I knew this was the big one.' Walker's relief was not necessarily shared by his squad. With significantly less dependence on TV money in the early years of the Premier League, relegation was not as financially disastrous as today, although an estimate of £2 million per season is not unreasonable. That said, Cottee understood the realities. 'It would be an absolute disaster if we were relegated,' the striker declared. 'It's totally unthinkable. We have to get our finger out and prevent it. Everton are a Premiership club and there's no way they could afford to go down.'

Tightrope Walker

Now more than three months into the job, Walker's honeymoon period was well and truly over. The lack of management experience counted against him and the early days at Goodison were merely a mirage. 'Walker was duped into thinking he had a side that would finish in the top ten – all on the evidence of wins against lowly placed opposition,' one letter to the *Liverpool Echo* concluded. 'Perhaps if most of those fixtures had been away from home he'd have got a truer impression.'

Walker's transfer dealings before the end of the deadline did not inspire confidence either. Brett Angell was clearly not of Premier League quality. For all his obvious shortcomings, Peter Beagrie had been one of the club's most consistent performers over the campaign yet he was allowed to go to Manchester City – a relegation rival – for £1 million when there were others who were more expendable. Beagrie's replacement was Swedish international winger Anders Limpar, a boyhood Blue who spent a trial period at Liverpool in 1987 before joining Arsenal three years later, where he enjoyed an outstanding first season as the Gunners lifted the title. The subsequent years were frustrating due to a combination of injuries and a breakdown of the relationship with manager George Graham, with his contract not going to be renewed in the summer.

So instead of the experienced, dominant midfielder they desperately needed, Walker bought a player who, although hugely gifted, had earned a reputation as not being the most trustworthy under pressure – 'not a player you would buy to get you out of a hole,' Steve Curry once claimed in the *Daily Express*. Walker had also failed to strengthen an increasingly shaky central defence, with a £3 million offer for Wimbledon's John Scales rejected.

Needing two wins from four games to secure survival, travelling to QPR's Loftus Road, Everton used the same template which had been so effective seven days before. And to be fair to the visitors, when Cottee raced clear on 64 minutes to fire them ahead that seemed justifiable. But Gerry Francis' side had a more potent forward line and, like at Anfield, the visitors conceded an equaliser straightaway. On this occasion though, Walker had reason to be aggrieved as Devon White appeared, to most observers, to punch the ball over the line after Southall had missed Ian Holloway's cross. 'White fisted the ball into the net,' Walker insisted afterwards. 'Everyone saw it except the officials.' But the Everton manager could have pointed a finger at his goalkeeper, who should never have allowed the ball to reach the Rangers scorer. The visiting players were clearly shaken by the controversial equaliser and, following several scares, two minutes from time David Bardsley's long ball wrong-footed Matt Jackson and the powerful Les Ferdinand drilled the ball past Southall.

With television evidence supporting Walker's view that White's goal was handball, there was no doubt where his ire was directed at full time. 'Whether other people like it or not, I thought the officials were scandalous,' he angrily complained. 'I tried to speak to the referee [Martin Bodenham] afterwards but he did not want to talk to me.' The damaging loss left the Toffees three points above Oldham Athletic, who were in the final relegation place but had *three* games in hand. Nevertheless, the out-of-luck Walker remained bullish after the game. 'I have said all along we will stay up,' he claimed, not for the first time. Yet such an utterance was increasingly sounding like somebody trying to sound convincing while hiding an unthinkable truth. 'With only three matches left to play, he must feel that Everton are doomed,' Mihir Bose wrote in *The Sunday Times*.

Get down to Goodison

The bookmakers took a different view: at 9-4 the Toffees were sixth in the betting to go down. One of the reasons was their next opponents were a moderate Coventry side, with little to play for, although Walker did not exactly endear himself to the Sky Blues by claiming this would be the easiest of the remaining matches. The *Liverpool Echo* was under no illusions about the significance of the game, urging 'all Everton fans to get down to Goodison on Saturday – and get behind the team for potentially the most important match in the club's recent history.' The Everton manager also joined in the cheerleading although whether his statement that 'Some of the fans are panicking, but we need them behind us,' provided reassurance is debatable.

In fact, just 23,217 fans turned up as, suitably motivated by the Everton manager's comments, Phil Neal's outfit put up a defensive wall, with the home team taking 89 minutes to engineer a shot on target. The resulting goalless stalemate and five points from 27 told a sorry story. 'Some people suggested Everton were too good to go down,' Richard Tanner wrote in the *Daily Mirror*. 'The harsh reality is they are not.' Like Walker, on his 600th career appearance Dave Watson hardly appeased supporters: 'At the end of the day we didn't create anything to go out and win the game…We're making things hard for ourselves. Looking at our last three matches, on paper this one appeared our easiest.' Even though three teams around them lost, the two points dropped looked damaging. Everton were still three points above the drop zone but the teams below all had games in hand. With the odds on the Toffees going down narrowing slightly to 6-4, Neville Southall defended his manager. 'Blame the players for our failings,' he pointed out. 'It is our fault. It is all very well people blaming managers and coaches but we are the ones out on the pitch.'

The major issue had been the lack of firepower, with Tony Cottee the only name on the scoresheet over the previous eight games. However, that was as much down to inadequacies elsewhere. Even with the addition of Limpar, any midfield with Horne, Ebbrell and Stuart possessed little or no creativity, or width. The only real imagination was derived from Andy Hinchcliffe's delivery from the left flank but even that had been below par. 'We needed a goal, but you can't blame Brett Angell or Tony Cottee because our strikers weren't given any chances to miss,' Walker complained after the Coventry game. 'The service was poor, and what we needed was somebody who could give us a goal out of nothing.' Sadly for Walker, they were in short supply.

Helland Road

Due to those inadequacies, on the final Saturday of April an apprehensive Everton squad travelled across the Pennines to Elland Road, where they had enjoyed no top-flight victory for 56 years. In the morning the *Independent* ran an interview with Walker during which he firmly laid the blame at the door of his predecessor. Walker scoffed when journalist Joe Lovejoy informed him that, a year before, Kendall had said Everton were a couple of players away from being a competitive team. 'Last season they survived relegation by just four points, so they've not been going anywhere for quite a while now,' he responded. 'To talk in terms of being not far away – two players off – is a bit of a statement, isn't it?' The Everton boss then made an inferred criticism of Kendall:

Standards are not as high as they should be. They've been allowed to slip. People talk about resurrecting Everton and winning things again, but we've got to raise our levels of performance everywhere before we can do it. I don't think the players train hard enough. They think a little running session is hard work, but we're only talking about what was normal at Norwich. The Everton lads hadn't been used to doing any running. Their training routine was a few five-a-sides and a bit of head tennis. That was it. It shows. That's why they can't do certain things I want. They're not fit enough.

Walker's critique of Kendall's methods may have been valid in early January but there had been ample time for the former Norwich boss to at least have made some difference. But only one win in nine league games since mid-March suggested that his methods had not been effective either. One complaint was that his team was too laboured in possession. 'That might be because the players are not good enough,' he explained – a comment hardly expected to lift morale. Elsewhere there was a feeling that Walker may not have been the sophisticated saviour supporters initially thought. 'Everton have shelled out left right and centre for Walker,' Simon Barnes wrote in *The Times*, 'and so far, all they have bought is trouble.'

On the pitch Neville Southall celebrated his 600th appearance for the club but, with Leeds looking more like a relegation-threatened side, the great Welshman enjoyed as quiet an opening period as any during his career. Meanwhile, the dominant visitors, backed by a large and vocal travelling army, wasted several opportunities before eventually pressing the self-destruct button. As one press-box cynic commented on the toothless Everton forward line: 'Three times out of ten they would have scored.'

The catalyst was the introduction of the former Manchester City striker David White midway through the second half. Immediately his cross was headed against the post by Rod Wallace but eighteen minutes from time came the killer blow: Ablett tackled White at the edge of the box but the ball fell to Gary McAllister whose shot beat Southall. Shortly after, Stuart failed to equalise when sent clear, the miss emblematic of a forward line which had lost all confidence. Then eight minutes from time referee Vic Callow chose not to stop play for handball by David O'Leary and within seconds White's cross-shot was deflected into the net by the unfortunate Watson. A White goal in the final minute summed up a miserable second half for Walker's side. Earlier in the season, Norwich had triumphed 4-0 on the ground but the dispiriting 3-0 defeat symbolised the extremes of his campaign. 'We should have been three-nil up but if we don't score, we won't win,' he admitted after the game. 'There was nothing in our performance to suggest that we can't stay up.' But with fellow strugglers Southampton and Sheffield United victorious on the same afternoon, Everton now fell into the bottom three. 'The future looks black now,' David Prentice wrote in the *Liverpool Echo*. The only consolation for Everton was the relegation battle was congested, with six clubs capable of filling the two remaining places:

Tottenham Hotspur	P 40	Pts 42
Southampton	P 40	Pts 42
Ipswich Town	P 41	Pts 42
Sheffield United	P 40	Pts 41

Everton	P 41	Pts 41
Oldham Athletic	P 39	Pts 38
Swindon Town	P 41	Pts 30

With the final games of the season on the following Saturday, there were several fixtures in midweek and results favoured the Toffees. Firstly, Oldham and Sheffield United drew their crucial clash 1-1 on Bank Holiday Monday, meaning the Yorkshire team (with a better goal difference) were still in the mix. Then 24 hours later Southampton, unsurprisingly, lost 2-0 at Old Trafford. On the Wednesday, Spurs won 2-0 at Oldham which took them out of relegation contention but left Joe Royle's side two points below Everton.

That left one game remaining for Everton, at home to Wimbledon. 'I like a bet and I will be betting on us beating Wimbledon next week,' Ian Snodin said defiantly after the defeat by his former club. But as Snodin subsequently conceded, even beating Wimbledon might not prove enough.

34
ABYSS

'WHEN IT COMES TO FIVE O'CLOCK NEXT SATURDAY, SOMEONE WILL need a large quantity of toilet paper.' Menacing words indeed from that well-known thespian Vincent Peter Jones. Significantly for Everton fans, an idle threat not made while holding a double-barrelled shotgun during a Guy Ritchie crime caper, but in the corridor outside the Selhurst Park home dressing room after word reached south London of his side's upcoming role in Everton's immediate future. 'It's not the case of a small club like Wimbledon taking satisfaction from sending down a big one like Everton,' he said. 'We want to go to Goodison, have a couple of light ales and do the business.'

One foot in the grave

'What Everton need to show is a lot more guts,' Jones added, 'Too many clubs think they are too good to go down.' Some home truths perhaps but given his abrasive reputation the comments at Selhurst Park landed him trouble. So the build-up to one of Everton's biggest games of the post-war era started unusually with an apology from the opposition chairman. 'I am rather concerned at the suggestion my side can hardly wait to rub Everton's noses in the mud,' Wimbledon owner Sam Hammam explained. 'That is completely untrue. We have the greatest respect for both the club and the players, and hope the game will be played in a good spirit.' There was no greater symbol of Everton's decline than attracting such comments from a club who had only been in the Football League for seventeen years.

Yet midfield-destroyer Jones was rapidly becoming an anachronism in the Wimbledon dressing room. In his place was a team of talented players. Full-back Warren Barton, classy centre-half John Scales and coveted striker Dean Holdsworth were all on the brink of the England squad. Robbie Earle was one of the best goal-scoring midfielders in the top flight. Marcus Gayle and Peter Fear were clever wingers. Indeed, it was entirely possible to claim that the only Everton player guaranteed a place in the Wimbledon line-up was Neville Southall. Sixth in the table, they were unbeaten in nine games – Joe Kinnear having just won successive manager-of-the-month awards – and, ominously, the run included victories over title-chasing duo Manchester United and Blackburn Rovers. 'The Dons, hunting a best-ever fifth finish and a Sam Hammam-sponsored jolly to Las Vegas, are the worst doomsday opponents,' Henry Winter pointed out in the *Independent*. With Swindon already down, the midweek results meant the final two relegation places were a shoot-out between five clubs with one game left:

Southampton	Pts 42	GD -17	8-1 odds to go down
Sheffield United	Pts 42	GD -17	5-1
Ipswich Town	Pts 42	GD -23	4-6

Everton	Pts 41	GD -22	11-10
Oldham Athletic	Pts 39	GD -26	1-10
Swindon Town	Pts 30	GD -48	

Although there were a multitude of scenarios, the bookmakers read it as a straight fight between Ipswich and Everton to avoid the drop, with Oldham almost certain to go down. A surefire way for Walker to escape was to secure victory while at least one of the three clubs above failed to win. A draw would suffice if Ipswich lost at Blackburn and Oldham did not win by four clear goals at Norwich City. A further, but unlikely, way of staying up was to draw while either Southampton or Sheffield United lost by six goals at West Ham and Chelsea respectively. Such was the interest in the game that fourteen countries worldwide were taking it live: Italy and Spain being obvious locations but Indonesia and Honduras less so.

For his part, Walker did not exactly play down the importance of the fixture. 'There's no doubt this is the biggest game in the club's history,' he claimed. 'It's got to be more pressure on you if you are talking down at the bottom…We've got one foot in the grave but not both of them yet.' But he was not short on confidence. 'I've got a gut feeling we'll stay up,' he said. However, interest in the game merely disguised the reality of Everton's situation, with one win and four goals in the previous ten matches. A predicament summed up by Peter Ball in *The Times*:

Champions seven years ago, and members of the "Big Five" who led the revolution against the Football League, they are now only 90 minutes away from finding themselves

*on the outside looking in at the rich man's club that they did so much to create. They
have only themselves to blame.*

Date with destiny

For all their 'crazy gang' subculture, there was some apprehension in the Wimbledon
camp before they arrived on Merseyside. 'It is not the nicest of places to go,' Warren
Barton admitted, 'especially with the situation as it is, that they could go down. That is
one thing that has crossed our minds. They are football fanatics up there.' Jim Greenwood
dismissed the fears as 'groundless'. However, any uneasiness the visitors felt was hardly
quelled when their team coach was set alight at 5 a.m. on the Saturday morning of the
game, outside their hotel in Warrington. However, Peter Reid, one of Goodison's
favourite sons, warned: 'They have no regard for reputations, and would revel in relegating
a club like Everton.'

Notwithstanding relegation after forty years in the top flight being in the offing, there
was a surreal feel to Goodison before the game, one played on a beautifully sunny
afternoon. In contrast to the visitors' fears, the atmosphere outside beforehand was
muted. 'The silent, shuffling queues recalled the hushed hordes who used to wind around
Red Square in Moscow on their way to Lenin's tomb,' was David Lacey's brilliant analogy
in the *Guardian*. With the Park End demolished and a new stand in the process of being
constructed, one quarter of the ground was incongruously shut. The capacity was
consequently reduced to 31,000 but, with the stadium full, several hundred fans took
advantage of the open building site at the Park End to watch from trees in Stanley Park.
Two weeks before Crystal Palace boss Alan Smith described Goodison Park as 'a great
stadium but not exactly hostile.' It was up to those fans to prove him wrong.

3.03 p.m.

In 'an atmosphere raucously reminiscent of the night Bayern Munich were beaten in a
Cup Winners' Cup semi-final,' according to Patrick Barclay in the *Observer*, Everton
suffered a nightmare start. Anders Limpar, who was not universally popular with
supporters after a leak revealed the presence of a 'relegation' clause in his contract allowing
him to leave should the worst happen, fouled Barton on the halfway line and the free-kick
resulted in a corner. Gary Elkins swung the cross in from the left but, with no visiting
player nearby, for reasons best known to himself Limpar jumped and clearly handled the
ball. With the tortured Swede holding head in hands, referee Robbie Hart had no
hesitation in pointing to the spot. Dean Holdsworth put the kick to Southall's right and,

although the Welshman got a hand to the ball, it nestled in the corner of the Gwladys Street goal.

3.20 p.m.
Although Oldham were leading at Norwich, more relevantly Southampton had conceded at Upton Park. But those developments paled into comparison with more disaster at Goodison. Dave Watson and David Unsworth both jumped for the same high ball, which dropped to Wimbledon striker Andy Clarke whose mishit shot, which was going wide, dribbled into the net off the shins of a panicking Gary Ablett. 'The crowd were stunned,' Joe Lovejoy said in the *Independent*, 'They had done their bit, only to have the wind knocked out of them by some Fred Karno defending.'

3.24 p.m.
Thankfully a seemingly irretrievable situation only lasted four minutes. Limpar dribbled into the right of the opposition penalty area and, although Peter Fear stepped across to challenge, there was not much in it and the Swede's theatrical dive seemed purely for effect. Remarkably referee Robbie Hart was conned and awarded a penalty. 'There wasn't much contact from Peter Fear but Limpar is the type of player to take advantage of it,' Martin Tyler said on commentary. 'I must say that does not look a very justifiable decision.' The problem was who would take the penalty. Four weeks before Walker had asked for volunteers and, with only Gary Ablett and Neville Southall for competition, Graham Stuart bravely stepped forward. On the day, though, a different scenario initially played out, according to Walker after the game. He revealed that beforehand Southall had volunteered to take any penalty and the goalkeeper now stepped up the pitch, only for Stuart to grab the ball. 'I can just see it now. We'll get one in the last match against Wimbledon and I'll have to score to keep us up – and I'll be terrified,' he had told David Prentice before the game. Although the home crowd were probably not aware that Stuart, in his Chelsea days, had skied his only previous attempt over the bar, the midfielder took the vital kick like a seasoned professional and sent Hans Segers the wrong way. 'Our lads swear Limpar dived but it probably saved his life after he had given us the penalty,' Dons boss Joe Kinnear admitted after the game.

3.31 p.m.
A key moment in the contest. Vinnie Jones' long throw was nodded on at the near post but, with Southall out of position, an unmarked Holdsworth somehow contrived to put

his header over the bar six yards out. The let-off gained extra significance with the news that Sheffield United had gone 1-0 ahead at Chelsea.

3.43 p.m.

Holdsworth missed another opportunity to put the visitors ahead. Delightful work by Marcus Gayle on the touchline was followed by a cross to the far post, but he struck it with too much pace and the striker could only head over the bar.

3.46 p.m.

Referee Hart blew for half-time. As the players reached the dressing room, they learned Southampton had just equalised at Upton Park. With Sheffield United and Oldham also leading, the picture was bleak, with Everton now second-from-bottom:

Sheffield United	45 pts
Southampton	45 pts
Ipswich Town	43 pts

Oldham Athletic	42 pts
Everton	41 pts

4.01 p.m.

The players reemerged for the second half. 'The boss had a pop at us as half-time which we deserved because it was a ridiculous start,' goalscorer Stuart said later. 'He said if we played controlled football we would get something.' Within seconds of the restart the former Chelsea man nearly did that himself. Freed to the right of the area, he saw his fiercely struck shot parried away by Segers and kicked to safety.

4.21 p.m.

Early energy having dissipated, there was sense that supporters and players were losing belief. With news that early goals in London had left Sheffield United leading 2-1 and Southampton now drawing two apiece, there was another fortunate escape. The unmarked Holdsworth's header beat Southall before Stuart blocked the ball on the line with what appeared to be a shoulder, before it rolled down perilously close to his hand. Referee Hart waved away furious protests from the visitors and, although a penalty award would have been harsh possibly, there were signs Lady Luck was with Walker's side.

4.22 p.m.

Within ninety seconds the roof came off Goodison Park. The ball fell loose in the middle of the park and Barry Horne – who had not scored since the opening day of the previous campaign – strode forward and his thirty-yard shot screamed past the helpless Segers. 'I was playing well and in good form leading up to the game and having a good game,' he told the *Liverpool Echo* some 25 years later. 'When you're confident you just do things. If that ball had bounced up to me some 12-15 months previously I'd have taken another touch and then another touch…But as things stood it sat up and before I knew it, the ball had left my foot and it was on its way.' But with Southampton having just made it 3-2 at Upton Park, it now looked like two from three would go down, with even a victory not enough if Ipswich scored:

Southampton	45 pts
Sheffield United	45 pts
Ipswich Town	43 pts

Everton	42 pts
Oldham Athletic	42 pts

4.37 p.m.

With fans with radios hearing Chelsea had equalised against Sheffield United, the Blades were very much back in the relegation battle and a victory now for Everton looked sufficient for them to stay up. But that seemed increasingly unlikely, with the home team acting like headless chickens and the composed visitors very much in control. Then on 81 minutes came the momentous moment. Stuart received the ball ten yards outside the box, played it into Cottee and continued towards goal. Taking the return in his stride, the former Chelsea player's right-footed block-cum-shot squirmed past the diving Segers. 'I sort of half-tackled the bloke then I just heard the crowd roar. I don't know how it went in,' Stuart remarked after the game. The general view was that the soft goal showed how luck was favouring the home team but, infamously of course, subsequent events suggested other possibilities. Kinnear's jokey suggestion that Segers must have had relatives on Merseyside may have been closer to the truth than he realised.

In mounting excitement and collective hyper-ventilation, the home team clung on, and helped by the referee's sensible decision to play just twenty seconds of injury time, the final whistle was welcomed with enormous relief and celebration in equal measure.

Two-goal hero Stuart – holding the match-ball – was then engulfed by several hundred relieved spectators who invaded the playing area. Even then there was still uncertainty, with other games still going on. When the mist had cleared, the failure of any of the three teams, above Everton at the start of the day, to win ensured Walker's side finished sixth from bottom. 'Everton, it must be said, also enjoyed the rub of the green, in the shape of a couple of dodgy decisions by the referee,' Joe Lovejoy wrote, 'but no one was inclined to begrudge them on a day when crowd and players united in a common purpose that had the hairs misbehaving on the back of the neck.'

Everton	44 pts
Southampton	43 pts
Ipswich Town	43 pts

Sheff United	42 pts
Oldham Athletic	40 pts
Swindon Town	30 pts

Afterwards the champagne flowed in both the dressing room and executive lounges as Everton's forty-year stay in the top flight thankfully did not end in humiliation. Another person just as happy was Wimbledon owner Sam Hammam, who was a big friend of Bill Kenwright. 'I am delighted Everton stayed up,' he said. 'The Premier League would not be the same without a club of their standing.' The match-winner also explained the penalty situation. 'It was me, Gary Ablett or Neville Southall on the penalty,' Stuart said. 'When I saw Neville coming up, I thought, "This is ridiculous. You can't have your goalkeeper taking a penalty. It doesn't say much for the other ten players does it?" I hit it well and I was made up to see it go in.'

The general perception was that Walker himself, on face value, subsequently played down the victory. 'I don't feel too clever about celebrating,' he said. 'It's more a day of relief, but I shall never forget the fanaticism these people have shown for the club.' Yet Steve Curry of the *Daily Express* revealed the statement about thanking the supporters was teased out of him. 'He must learn that on Merseyside the people matter as much as the players,' he wrote. 'Walker's opening words were: "I have said all along to those who have bothered to listen that we wouldn't go down." Humility is a quality in short supply with the Everton manager.' Subsequent events showed that Curry, as well as being a fine journalist, was also in fact a decent judge of character.

Two-goal hero Graham Stuart leaves the pitch with a kiss from a fan as a reward.

In the shadows

The consensus was when the shot headed towards the Gwladys Street goal, Wimbledon goalkeeper Hans Segers quite clearly made no or little effort to stop the strike. Yet there was no outcry or accusations of malpractice. After saving Tony Cottee's penalty in a league game during November 1991, the referee deemed Segers had moved and awarded a retake. The visiting custodian was so disgusted he basically stood aside and watched Cottee's second effort pass him by.

That was soon forgotten but, given its significance, the encounter against Wimbledon was never going to be consigned to the cobwebbed pages of history. Hair-raising decisions by the referee, some odd goals, a burned-out coach, plus a demolished Park End, all added a sense of unreality to the event. Within 24 hours of the final whistle there were already rumours circulating that events at Goodison may not have been as they seemed. Significantly, they did not go away and remained very much in the shadows.

However, on Wednesday, 9 November 1994 when a *Sun* exposé claimed Liverpool goalkeeper Bruce Grobbelaar had received payment to throw matches, those stories gained more prominence. Indeed, when rumours first emerged of a breaking football bribery scandal, insiders anticipated it would be about the events at Goodison on the first Saturday in May.[115] In his absorbing book about the resulting proceedings, *Foul Play*, author David Thomas revealed that Sam Hammam was approached about the rumours by a reporter *24 hours* before the Grobbelaar story reached the news-stands. 'Everyone thinks I threw the game because I'm a friend of Bill Kenwright,' he pleaded, before adding that, given he had promised the whole squad and their partners an all-expenses trip to Las Vegas if they finished fifth, the defeat ultimately cost them a holiday. That said, there had certainly been no inkling of any wrongdoing on the Wimbledon team's behalf – after all Dean Holdsworth had scored, rather than deliberately miss, from the spot. But the focus of attention was Everton's third goal. Before the Grobbelaar story the *Daily Mirror* informed Segers that the *Sun* would also be mentioning him in despatches. They did not but the Segers also claimed that 'for a few crazy hours, people had been ringing my home, asking if it was me.'

However, in the following March there was a startling development: Grobbelaar, the now Aston Villa striker John Fashanu and Malaysian-born businessman Heng Suan (Richard) Lim were arrested in connection with match-fixing. And so was Segers. After being released on bail the Wimbledon goalkeeper claimed two games were mentioned by police, but the Everton defeat was not one of them. Segers may have pleaded his innocence but in July he was charged with conspiracy under Section One of the Criminal Act, 1977.

The case went to court in early 1997. The allegation against Segers was for placing £104,000, received from a Far East betting syndicate in return for throwing games, in a Swiss bank account after Wimbledon had lost a string of matches between October 1993 and October 1994. Included in the deposits was £19,000 six days after the trip to Goodison. 'It was a match of crucial importance to Everton because it enabled them to stay up in the Premier division,' the prosecution counsel, David Calvert-Smith, told the jury at Winchester Crown Court. In his opening statement, Calvert-Smith also laid out

---

[115] On the evening of the newspaper story, on radio even BBC football correspondent Mike Ingham admitted surprise that it did not relate to the Wimbledon game.

details of a series of phone calls between Segers, Fashanu and Lim on the day before the Everton game, plus calls between Lim and contacts in Indonesia both immediately before and after the match. The prosecution counsel then informed the court of further calls between the parties, including in the hour before Segers deposited the £19,000. 'All the crown can do,' Calvert-Smith admitted, 'is say, look, here are these payments, here are these telephone contacts about which Mr Segers has lied, here are the matches Wimbledon have lost and telephone contacts around the time of those matches: can you draw the inference that the money, the telephone calls and the matches are linked?'

When cross-examined Segers claimed the money came from a tie company he was involved in plus forecasting the results of Dutch football games for Lim. Of the infamous Stuart goal, the Wimbledon goalkeeper said: 'I'm not sure who scored. He hit a shot and I dived. I had it covered all the way, but it hit a divot, popped up and changed direction.' Calvert-Smith held a different theory. 'After the Everton game did Joe Kinnear suggest he could have saved the last goal, that it went through your hands, and that he didn't realise you had a favourite uncle up on Merseyside?' 'I can't remember,' Segers responded. Eventually, after almost two months of countless witnesses and speeches, the jury was deadlocked and a retrial was ordered. The replay took place during the summer. After 45 days, on 6 August 1997, a jury found Segers not guilty.

Bored room

While Everton were clinging onto Premier League survival, behind the scenes the battle for control between Peter Johnson and the Kenwright consortium was hanging around like a persistent toothache. If one incident typified the damaging internal conflict, it came on BBC Radio's *606* show after the disastrous 3-0 defeat at Leeds. An Evertonian named Phil called the show and provided an articulate summation of the hopelessness engulfing Goodison. Host David Mellor described his manner as 'statesmanlike'. Then another caller – identified as 'Tom from Bill Kenwright's consortium' – responded by saying: 'I'd like to correct your previous caller. Peter Johnson doesn't have control of Everton. Nothing has been decided yet. He doesn't even have the support of the majority shareholder.' It was a ridiculous response – the nearest anybody associated with the club came to points-scoring all afternoon. No wonder David Prentice was moved to comment: 'Even with the club on the brink of calamity, there is an element of in-fighting and uncertainty which is frustrating the fans.' So why was everything still up in the air?

Prentice's comment was merely reflecting four months of damaging boardroom inertia resulting from the failure to resolve the ownership matter at the end of 1993.

Indeed, the complete lack of confident leadership was there for all to see in Kendall's final days. They should have either backed or sacked their manager but did neither, leaving Kendall to make everybody's mind up. Such dragging of feet resulted in the ridiculous situation of Walker's appointment being an exercise in appeasement of the board, Kenwright's consortium and Johnson. Begging the question, of course, whether Walker would have been their choice if either of the latter two had been in control. When Kenwright was in pole position early on there were strong rumours that the consortium was keen to bring Kendall back. As future events indicated, Johnson may have been keen to recruit a big name like Bobby Robson. With Walker being a compromise appointment, the indirect message from the boardroom was effectively to maintain the playing side in a holding pattern while the off-the-pitch battle was concluded. Almost certainly this contributed to the complacency permeating the dressing room after an early flurry of victories bred a false sense of security. 'Walker appears to have made the fatal mistake of believing his job does not start until next season,' William Johnson wrote in the *Daily Telegraph* after the Elland Road defeat. 'It took him a long time to wake up to the present crisis.'

Mike Walker celebrates the victory over Wimbledon. With Everton in the midst of a takeover battle when he was appointed, there were doubts that he was the unanimous choice of all those with a vested interest in the immediate future of the club.

While matters on the pitch were taking a turn for the worse, in the first four months of the year the ownership question remained unanswered. One reason was existing board members were in danger of losing their posts. Although Peter Johnson had said they were safe if he took the reins, obviously Kenwright would be looking to give roles to his consortium members. 'So someone is going to be asked to jump ship,' Len Capeling asked in the *Liverpool Daily Post*. 'Any volunteers? No, of course there aren't, which is why there is gridlock.' Inconveniently for the chairman and directors, there was obviously a mole in the club who was feeding information of a split at boardroom level over the rival bids. That said, the board also had a responsibility to ensure any bid maximised the value of the company and, to be fair, chairman Marsh's turning of the screw was doing just that. 'When we consider an acceptable offer has been made, we will react with all haste to bring the matter to a speedy conclusion,' he told shareholders in early February.

The situation was complicated even further by the apathy of John Moores' two sons who inherited the forty per cent shareholding. Peter Moores gifted one half to his two sisters, Lady Grantchester and Janatha Stubbs. This left the other brother, John Moores Jr., as effectively the largest single shareholder. Kenwright had signed an agreement with the Moores family securing their support in the previous December but John – impressed by Johnson's business and footballing credentials – had his head turned by the Rovers chief. He subsequently denied brother Peter's previous claims about his father's wishes. 'My father left no instructions at all in his will about his Everton shares. They were simply left to my brother and me,' he revealed, 'At no stage did he mention to me "a safe pair of hands" or a "true Blue."' On that basis John switched horses to the Tranmere chairman. However, Kenwright's agreement with Lady Grantchester remained and this split in the Moores family was a further source of the delay. Complicating matters was while her ladyship was a keen football fan, sister Janatha lived abroad and had no such interest.

Nevertheless, when Johnson upped his offer to £4,000 per share – nearly twice the original proposal – with 2,500 new shares to be issued, an extra £10 million would have immediately have been generated. Consequently, at the end of February the board backed Johnson's deal and wrote to shareholders to that effect. To see off the opposition, Johnson took the now disunified consortium over to Prenton Park and showed them how he had reinvigorated the fortunes of Tranmere Rovers. The strategy worked. That evening, three members – Tony Tighe, Michael Dyble and Cannon – signed away their rights to the Moores family's agreement in Tighe's house. According to David Conn's *The Football Business*, the signatures were witnessed by a taxi driver who had arrived to take Cannon home.

However, Johnson's offer required the backing of those collectively owning 75 per cent of the share capital and six weeks later there was still no armistice to end the debilitating war, with Kenwright and Arthur Abercromby still retaining the support of Lady Grantchester – who as de facto owner of 21 per cent of the shares was effectively the blocker to any deal involving the Tranmere chief. However, there was a glimmer of light at the end of April when stories emerged that the remaining members of the consortium were prepared to form a 'dream team' with Johnson, who would become chairman. That was enough to persuade Lady Grantchester to change her stance. 'The Moores family announce that they are happy to support Mr Peter Johnson's proposals to underwrite a rights issue to raise £10m for Everton and are particularly grateful for the efforts of Mr Johnson, Mr Bill Kenwright and Mr Arthur Abercromby in taking this matter forward,' their statement read. After 34 years, the Moores era at Goodison was ending. His legacy was a complex one.

37

FAREWELL TO THE REAL PREMIER

WHEN JOHN MOORES ENTERED THE GOODISON BOARDROOM FOR the first time in an official capacity in March 1960 it was hardly to sample the hospitality and swap idle business gossip. The fact the press described Moores as an 'industrialist' – a term in football usually associated with the powerful and merciless owners of wealthy Italian giants – acted as a clue to his intentions. The aim was to take the club to the same level at any price. 'For twenty years I have been disappointed with the results at Everton,' he said. 'It's up to everyone connected with the club – directors, management and players – to get results in the next year or make way for those who can, and I include myself in this.' Over the next two decades he was as good as his word: exacting, ruthless, but fair when required. Horace Yates' view in the *Liverpool Echo* that 'he is unlikely to be a silent partner in his new enterprise' was one of the great understatements.

Entering the elite

The timing of Moores' entry into the domestic game was deliberately planned. Barcelona's 5-2 destruction of English champions Wolves at Molineux in the European Cup, in the same month he became a director, was followed by a familiar tale of navel-gazing from those involved in the English game. Although exposure to the continent's giants had shown up a familiar shortfall in technique and skill, equally significant were the archaic restrictions on the payment – the maximum wage was £20 per week – and movement of players which dated back to Victorian times. Both factors may have helped support a competitive top flight but they prevented the growth of elite clubs capable of competing with rich European counterparts. The restrictions on pay were particularly damaging to some. 'In other countries boys can say, "I want a car and a house like [Alfredo] Di Stefano's so I'll be a footballer,"' Wolves boss Stan Cullis declared after the Barcelona

John Moores – during the 1960s his modernism, naked ambition and money took English football into unchartered territory.

thrashing, 'In this country they can probably earn more in other jobs.' Those limitations acted as a deterrent to anybody with real wealth to invest like those big businesses who had bankrolled the Italian giants. But by the start of the decade the winds of change were beginning to circulate. 'English soccer needs that MILLIONAIRE,' proclaimed the *Daily Mirror* after the Wolves humiliation, 'Only a man with money to burn could create a club to meet Barcelona on level terms and ALSO be successful in our League and Cup competitions.' Less than three weeks later, Moores became an Everton director. Within three months he was chairman.

Moores' intuition over developments in the sport was unsurprisingly correct. Within twelve months the maximum wage was lifted and the High Court judgement in the George Eastham case two years later ended the infamous 'retain and transfer' system which had placed enormous restrictions on players' freedom of movement, the ruling also allowing for lengthier contracts beyond twelve-month deals. Surprisingly, Moores voted against the lifting of the maximum wage – fearing it would grant players more power. But inevitably bulkier pay packets would result in the best players migrating to the biggest and richest clubs. With Littlewoods enjoying an annual turnover 450 times greater than Everton, then Moores had the financial capability and wherewithal to take advantage.[116]

---

[116] In 2024 equivalent to a company the size of Tesco providing financial backing.

Aside to the changes in pay and employment rights, there were other matters pointing to a sport entering a different era. Football and television had already realised the mutual benefits accruing from being bedfellows, although ironically Everton's and Arsenal's opposition to plans for screening live football in 1960 eventually led to the project stalling. Thereafter, the club's difficult relationship with the small screen was a recurring theme. Elsewhere, with future monies inevitably heading towards the big clubs there was talk of something regarded as taboo in the present day. Exposure to European football and more accessible air travel made a continental super league very much a possibility although, like today, plans were vague. 'Even the Football League seems to be of the view the European Super League is coming,' the *Liverpool Echo* commented. 'Real Madrid want it, Barcelona want it…But how is it going to be achieved? What will be the structure? How will we decide who goes in – and who goes out?' Words written in June 1960, not in 2024.

With other suggestions that English football was heading towards a streamlined top flight for elite clubs, Moores knew exactly where football was heading and was prepared to grab the opportunity. 'If, and when, the so-called "Super League" comes, Everton will be ready,' *World Sports* magazine proclaimed in 1962. As John Roberts wrote in the *Official Centenary History* in 1978:

> The whole purpose of the game was intensifying into an uncompromising quest for honours. Winners and losers no longer side-by-side in the old definition of a sporting tableau. There was only room for Number One. Everton while insisting that their success be achieved with style, were highly ambitious. They were determined to step up the pace of their operation, seeking success sooner rather than later.

From Carey to Catterick

The big question was who would lead the club in that operation. Johnny Carey was not that man. In 2021 a recording emerged of Granada's *Kick Off* football magazine programme from January 1977, where Carey explained to Paul Doherty the bizarre circumstances of his sacking in a taxi in London during April 1961. 'I don't think it was planned to do it that way,' he explained. 'The news leaked out somehow and he [Moores] was confronted by a journalist on the pavement as we came out of the Cafe Royal. I think then of course he realised that he has got to tell me that the board had already made this decision. You know that I should be relieved from my duties.'

While Harry Catterick and Moores were not exactly kindred spirits, the chairman clearly saw something of himself in the former player not present with Carey. Neither sought popularity for a start. A Venn diagram would have shown an overlap between Moores, as a businessman with a feel for the game, and Catterick as a football man with a feel for business. 'Pure economics will decide the future of football. If you can't keep up with the times then you must fall out,' Catterick said early in his tenure. Consequently there was a mutual empathy not there with his predecessor. Moores was also employing a manager close to the peak of his powers – there was a strategic vision and hunger about Catterick in the early part of the decade which largely disappeared by the end, when he became more a manipulator of moving parts.

Although English football was a far more level playing field when Catterick took over, there was still a hierarchy of the original 'big five' clubs – Arsenal, Burnley, Manchester United, Spurs and Wolves – who had been the dominant forces in the post-war era. While Carey had already effectively utilised funding made available by Moores to leave Catterick with a strong outfit, the reason why the latter bridged the gap to become champions within two years was initially due to his patience.

The easy option was to get out the cheque-book as soon as Catterick was behind the desk at Bellefield. But wisely the Everton boss took close to twelve months assessing the squad. While replacing Albert Dunlop with Gordon West was in retrospect an obvious change, the defining transfer of his first five years was the decision to sell Bobby Collins to Leeds in March 1962. The Scot was a supporters' favourite but Catterick quickly realised that, in his early thirties, the number eight role – the 'fetcher and carrier' who linked defence and attack – was beyond him, especially on their travels, which left the side vulnerable to the counter-attack and contributed to a poor away record. Although many queried the sale as Collins excelled at Leeds United, that was in the number ten jersey as playmaker, a role he was never going to perform while Roy Vernon was around. Replacement Dennis Stevens was younger, possessed greater mobility and was more defensively minded.

Thereafter, Catterick cleverly made incremental, not wholesale, changes which added extra quality and durability without affecting the equilibrium of the side: Alex Scott for Billy Bingham plus Tony Kay for Brian Harris. Catterick also improved the squad he inherited as individuals. Brian Labone was a talented but under-performing centre-half; nevertheless after his manager instructed him to lose a stone in weight during the summer of 1962, he returned a more mobile, speedier presence. On the pitch, the manager's view of Collins proved well-founded. The change in away form was startling: three victories in 1961/62, eleven in the following campaign.

By the time the freezing winter of 1962/63 had begun to thaw, Catterick's team were now perfectly balanced. A very good goalkeeper in West; a sound defence led by Labone; Kay's domineering presence in the middle plus the slickness and goals of Roy Vernon and Alex Young. Not only that but they showed the resilience of true champions by seeing off the challenge of Bill Nicholson's Spurs, one of the great English club sides. But then the title victory opened a whole load of questions.

The unwanted champions?

Accusations that Everton bought the title were never far away when the dust settled. More than £350,000 had been laid out on the squad, a huge figure, but other clubs had spent big too. The difference was Tottenham and Manchester United had done so from a position of strength, whereas in the space of three years Everton had gone from a footballing backwater to the summit of the game. The backdrop to that progress was without precedent. 'Yet, there are ways, and ways of buying, and Everton's, inspired and made possible by Mr John Moores, has been alarming in its cold systematic manner,' Brian Glanville claimed in *The Sunday Times*, 'Players seem to have been bought, less to remove a weakness than as an earnest of ruthless ambition.' At a time when most clubs still possessed a corps of local-born players Glanville noted that only Labone fell into this category, with Brian Harris having been jettisoned to make space for Kay.

The title victory may have felt like something new but both inside and outside grounds there was the growing spectre of hooliganism. Everton was a focal point, with Goodison widely viewed as a hostile environment while on the road there had been incidents involving supporters at several grounds. With the club increasingly newsworthy, some linked their ruthless desire for success on the pitch with bad behaviour off it. 'This is the club with a lunatic fringe of fans who have been involved in stoning, bottle throwing, train-wrecking riots,' Brian James wrote in the *Daily Mail*. 'West Ham and Burnley have tasted their savagery this season. Everton have the title now they must grow into champions. But I believe a club gets the crowd it deserves and the clean-up must start on the pitch – and Moores must make sure he does it.' But did Moores do that?

Beating the press

'Everton are a famous team and we don't want a bad press,' John Moores admitted in 1964. But the Everton chairman also used to say about being in the spotlight: 'If you live on high hills, you must expect high winds.' Marry those two quotes together and you arrive at the position Everton found themselves in at the time. By that stage not only had they been accused of 'buying' the title in some quarters but their supporters were regarded as hooligans. 'Visiting players say the Everton crowd projects viciousness, which, in turn, evokes ruthless, violent tackling,' *The Sunday Times* proclaimed after the notorious November 1963 incident when Spurs goalkeeper Bill Brown alleged he was struck by a dart at Goodison, which forced the club to put the notorious arcs behind the goals.

Yet a fair proportion of bad press – as Moores would call it – was of the club's own making. The 1964 *Report on Inquiry into Supporters' Behaviour*, a work commissioned by the chairman and the product of two Liverpool University academics, attempted to find out the reasons why. The answer was straightforward. 'The attitude of the club's officials in their press dealings leaves something to be desired. Sportswriters do not find Everton Club Officials very co-operative,' the report concluded, 'There is a strong opinion amongst press representatives that information is difficult to obtain from Everton Football Club Officials.'

What the report did not attempt to explain was the background to the board's attitude. This goes back in history and Everton's place as one of the forefathers and original giants of English football. That in turn bred a certain amount of haughtiness which was conservative in nature. Consequently, the club did not welcome change and this manifested itself several times during the decade, from failing to deal with the growing requirements of the popular press[117] to misjudging the rapidly changing demands of television. The strange thing about this stance was, given Moores' big business background, the new chairman did not make changes in recognition of the importance of good publicity and sound media relations to any organisation in the public eye. The Liverpool University report recommended the employment of a full-time press officer but the club sat on it for five years until David Exall was recruited. Playing contracts forbid players from talking to the press without permission. In addition, allegations in the *People* during 1964 over drug use and bribery during the title-winning season also inflicted reputational damage and exposed the club to the salacious tabloid tales which affected all aspects of British life over the next fifty years. The club's refusal to release players for international duty also brought press criticism. A certain amount of paranoia within the Goodison boardroom would have been no surprise.

Mistrust of outsiders extended to the small screen in the second half of the decade. While the club and Moores were originally open-minded about television – the attempt

---

[117] An example being the day Fred Pickering signed for a record fee of £85,000 in March 1964. Having invited the press to Bellefield, club officials then banned the taking of pictures of the new striker. Such pedantry was endemic and extended to not granting press passes to journalists and making them queue for tickets on matchdays.

to block the ITV deal in 1960 was in protest over the Football League's lack of consultation – by the middle of the decade the cameras were on occasions excluded from Goodison for fear of over-exposure or affecting the attendance. However, the most infamous instance of 'banning' coverage came when Everton were fighting at the top in early 1970, with chairman Jack Sharp suggesting it was due to Catterick feeling television analysis could give additional insight into team tactics – although his manager's silence spoke volumes. The wariness of television extended to not providing a vantage point for cameras on the halfway line until the 1970/71 campaign. That season Everton also led calls to stop Saturday lunchtime preview shows, feeling they gave clues to televised games that weekend, which in turn affected attendances.

Where did Harry Catterick fit into all of this? Commonly targeted for damaging the club's standing for not being 'media friendly' there are arguments for and against that theory. His admission in the 1964 report that 'the press is biased against Everton Football Club and [he] believes this is generally true of any Northern Club outside Manchester,' was hardly ground-breaking and a feeling that persisted for several decades among many. Consequently, he was certainly not alone during the 1960s in making life difficult for the fourth estate and, as mentioned in *Money Can't Buy Us Love*, some of Catterick's attitude resulted from being angry and embarrassed over players complaining about tactics to the Sunday newspapers in September 1961. Afterwards, when dealing with the press, it was a case of keeping your enemies close and players closer still.

There was an example of Catterick's business acumen with regards to his attitude to television. Unlike his club and peers elsewhere, who largely focused on the short-term impact on attendances, Catterick saw the bigger picture, believing the relatively new medium was a competitor for a similar customer base and providing football on the cheap was a bad business move. That said, if a better deal was available then his position would alter. 'My heart bleeds for television,' he said after Everton rejected coverage of the home victory over Chelsea in January 1971. However, asked if he would revise those objections if Everton received £4,000 per game, rather than the standard £750, his viewpoint changed completely. 'I certainly would,' he responded.

Even allowing for the fact that Catterick was not unique in his dismissive manner, by the end of the decade such a stance was outdated. In addition, the club's approach to the media continued to be insular and largely misguided. Nevertheless, while comparisons with the attitude across the park are held up as an example of Everton's weaknesses in this area, they too are unfair. Bill Shankly did not court the media; initially the media courted Shankly. Liverpool also shared a scepticism of television and banned the cameras for several months in 1966/67. 'TV is having a growing effect on cutting attendances throughout the country,' Shankly said in support of Everton's wish to stop Saturday lunchtime preview shows. That narrative, therefore, appears all too convenient in the same way as blaming Everton's decline on Heysel.

However, whereas Liverpool welcomed the cameras for the BBC *Panorama* documentary on the Kop, it is hard to imagine the stuffy Everton board doing likewise at Goodison. That said, the effect would not have been the same: Moores' ludicrous retention of the arcs – originally intended as a temporary measure – behind both goals for almost fifteen years undoubtedly did not add to the televisual spectacle.[118]

In *The Football Manager: A History* author Neil Carter claimed that by the mid-1960s 'Clubs became aware of the need to sell themselves and to promote the right image…The advertising of the club therefore, became a function of the manager, and he came to be seen as "the club."' Both the board and Catterick's failure to perform these tasks meant Everton were marginalised as football increasingly became a part of wider culture and the entertainment world in the years that followed. Consequently, even during the 1980s successes and up to the present day, supporters reasonably argue that the club remains on the outside and does not get the media coverage it deserves. The root cause is anchored in the first half of the 1960s, when the Everton board created a culture of insularity and suspicion which has proved difficult to shake off.

Pass the Dutchy

In his perceptive review of the Everton boardroom from the time of Moores ascension, for the *When Skies Are Grey* fanzine, Greg Murphy argued that the Littlewood supremo's departure as chairman in 1965, due to his wife's ill health, created an apathy which eventually hastened the club's decline. Moores' resignation certainly fashioned an ambiguity around decision-making within the club, as he remained on the board. His immediate successor was club solicitor and board member Edward Holland-Hughes – unsurprisingly nicknamed 'Dutchy' – but he resigned two years into the role and was succeeded by Jack Sharp.

But the arrival of Littlewoods director George Watts on the board at the same time regularised the relationship of the mail-order and pools giant with Everton. And that is the still unknown question: how did the relationship between the two parties work and what were the dependencies? It is undoubtedly true that the extent of Littlewoods'

---

[118] Bizarrely, the first game at Goodison with the arcs removed was Harry Catterick's testimonial in May 1978.

financial influence has largely been overstated over the years, given the money provided was largely in the form of short-term interest-free loans. From the start Moores made clear that the club should be self-funding. The first two payments – a loan of £56,000 in 1960 and £100,000 three years later – were both repaid inside five years. By the time Moores departed as chairman it was estimated that support had extended to £250,000. In addition, contrary to popular belief, their patronage was in the form of cash injections acting as working capital to fund the structural improvements at Goodison required for the World Cup plus the acquisition and redevelopment of Bellefield.

There was no requirement for Littlewoods to support day-to-day operations because, for all their big acquisitions, during Moores' first decade at the helm the club showed a profit in eight out of ten seasons.[119] The excellent financial numbers were largely because gate receipts more than trebled (from £125,000 in 1960) via increased prices, more cup matches and bigger home attendances throughout the following decade. With players' wages not increasing by anything like the same rate there was more scope to pay inflated transfer fees.[120]

Consequently, in the second half of the decade there was no requirement for Littlewoods' financial support. Everton's parsimony in the transfer market from 1967-70 was not due a lack of funds but, as Harry Catterick was keen to stress, the absence of available top-quality players plus the production-line of young talent at Bellefield. That said, during that period there were still big offers for players like Dave Connor, Colin Stein, potentially Jimmy Greenhoff and, before he eventually signed in 1970, Henry Newton.

However, the club clearly did overstretch itself with the building of the new Main Stand, which opened in 1970 and brought a certain amount of financial instability. Beforehand, the estimated costs were £620,000 although the final bill was reported to be £700,000. Initially funded through cash reserves, by the end of construction the club had to sell investments for £56,000 and go into the red to meet the final payments. Indeed by 1972 the bank overdraft was more than £150,000 and the club was loaned £250,000 at 'a very favourable rate of interest' from an unnamed source. It did not require a genius to establish who that was.

---

[119] The two seasons with losses were 1962/63, £20,000 due to fees paid for Alex Scott and Tony Kay, and £45,000 in 1966/67 because of the purchases of Alan Ball and Howard Kendall.

[120] Although the club spent more than £900,000 during the decade, £600,000 was recouped in sales meaning net spend – a much-loved recent addition to the footballing lexicon – was 'only' £330,000.

A Sharp intake of breath to Watts

While there were ambiguities over Littlewoods' financial support in the early part of the decade, the same can be said about their influence in the boardroom, especially when George Watts – then managing director of their mail order stores – became chairman in 1970. At Everton, there was the ridiculous situation where Watts was (nominally) the supremo and Moores a director, compared to Littlewoods where the opposite was true. Understandably this raised concerns over the governance of the club: how could the Everton chairman retain his authority while his de facto boss was on the board as well?

Such dysfunction at Goodison led to flawed decision-making. This was apparent even under Jack Sharp's reign, for example the ridiculous award of a nine-year contract to Harry Catterick in 1969. The Everton boss may have been successful but effectively gifting a deal that provided financial security for the rest of his managerial career – as well as generating a significant financial commitment – was hardly an incentive.

Indeed, the effect on Catterick was the opposite: with financial security assured, after a decade in one of football's most demanding roles he retained no appetite to rebuild yet again after 1970. Moreover, with doubts over his health even before the heart attack in early January 1972, his long-term contract certainly informed the decision to welcome him back to Bellefield that summer. Without that long-term deal, the board probably would have asked him to step down and started again with a new, younger boss. But Catterick stayed on and a decline dating back two years gathered further momentum.

By then Moores was chairman for a second time. While he did not hide his reasons for returning – 'the directors may have been too complacent about the way things were going' was his rationale – the issue was the Littlewoods supremo was now seen by supporters as part of the problem, not the solution. There was a lack of self-awareness in his statement that the club had to do 'a hell of a lot more to overcome this apparent bad image that we have' while failing to acknowledge that the snooty culture, which he had done little to banish a decade before, still lingered. 'I believe that the Everton administration has reached a position of aloofness where it has no place in a city such as ours,' one correspondent wrote in the *Football Echo* three months after Moores returned.

Also, whether it was the increased Littlewoods presence on the board or falling home support, but in the early 1970s the club made great efforts to raise revenues off the pitch. 'In business, if things go wrong, you have to come up with solutions, or go bust,' Moores commented on returning, with commercial manager David Exall visiting the United States in the summer of 1972 to gain ideas from box office and entertainment. The result was the controversial concept of what supporters jokingly called 'Eversell' or the ramping up of commercial activities at the club. The extensive provision of corporate facilities at Goodison was seen as the board prioritising off-the-pitch activities over actual football. It is taken for granted now but supporters claimed pre-match and half-time adverts in the ground, plus pitch-side hoardings, were an assault on the senses and diminished their matchday experience. Consequently, there was a feeling, rightly or wrongly, that Everton was no longer a football club but now just another outpost of the Littlewoods business empire. At the start of the 1972/73 season, even though both teams were top of the table, gates across the park were 15,000 greater than at Goodison. 'All he [Exall] had to do was visit Anfield,' one supporter wrote in the *Football Echo*. 'No gimmicks, no adverts, just loyalty, effort and good attacking football – the result a full house every home game.'

Although Exall made the very relevant point that modern football clubs needed to maximise income and corporate facilities were meeting the changing demands of supporters, in essence timing was everything. Had Everton been successful on the pitch, then the approach would have been viewed in a more positive way. As it stood, the commercial drive was just another stick to beat the club with. As one supporter claimed: 'It seems obvious that the Everton board are more interested in making money than building a team.'

Succession panning

A comparison between the departures of Johnny Carey and Harry Catterick is telling. In 1961 Moores was ruthless and decisive – notwithstanding his original choice for Carey's replacement, Stan Cullis, turned down the job. Twelve years later the Everton chairman was anything but. Although Catterick's departure had seemed on the cards for some time, there was clearly no succession planning. Sacking the manager in early April made no sense in any case. Carey left at the same time of the season but Catterick – who had all but been tapped up – was in situ within 72 hours. In 1973, with the club in no danger of relegation with six games left, and no obvious replacement in place, the decision would have best been parked until the end of the campaign when there were more options. Embarrassingly, when Bobby Robson and Jimmy Armfield both turned down the job, Catterick effectively remained in the post until the end of the season in any case. The unedifying spectacle followed of Moores' ultimately failed pursuit of Don Revie across Greece and, as revealed in *Money Can't Buy Us Love*, questions in the House of Commons.

Moores was clearly losing his touch as the historical demands from fifty or so years in business had taken a toll. Also, whether a big club should have as its major powerbroker somebody close to being an octogenarian is a moot point. When you have all the money and all the power the one resource you run out of is time and his was a case in point.

Moores may then have vacated the chairman's role in the summer but there was still no doubt who was in charge. There was one final decision in the role and, in typical fashion, he followed the strategy of so many at Goodison when faced with an appointment choice: when in doubt withdraw inwards and go with a tried and trusted Evertonian. On this occasion it was the selection of their former winger Billy Bingham as manager. Again, one of a series of poor decisions made by Moores and the board over a lengthy period. Bingham was probably, at best, sixth choice for the role and had no track record of successful club management. From chasing the best manager in the country, Moores ended up appointing somebody, with the club keen to repair a damaged reputation, whose only real qualification for the job was a flair for public relations.

The appointment of Alan Waterworth as chairman hardly changed matters. Although not a Littlewoods employee – he made his fortune via the family fruit-and-vegetable company – he was very much Moores' man. The patrician values continued: as inflation sky-rocketed, the club's refusal to increase the salaries of their players reinforced the board's reputation as a group who were businessmen not attuned to modern football. This led to unrest between the squad and Bingham which manifested itself in poor results while driving the departure of several players and causing a damaging lengthy contractual dispute with Bob Latchford.

The other issue, at the time, was of course the club across the park. 'When Liverpool are above us in the table, there will always be supporters who will criticise. It's a fact of life we have to live with in the city of Liverpool,' Moores said in 1972. A vast chasm lies between the two clubs in the 21st century but when did that begin to take effect? The answer is simple: when Liverpool started to win European trophies in the middle of the 1970s. Those triumphs ultimately proved self-propelling: increased revenues allowed the purchasing of the best players which drove even more success. Not only that but it created a nation- and world-wide fanbase which, when later monetised in a globalised sport, made that gap even wider. Everton found out in the years that followed it was not enough to be a big club within your own city. Consistent and prolonged success would increasingly require wider appeal.

For all that, Liverpool's success still required great management, which was sadly lacking at Goodison during the decade. Everything wrong with the running of the club was summed up in the sacking of Billy Bingham in January 1977, on the eve of a League Cup semi-final and having just signed two players for £400,000. Two months before, Moores had threatened to resign because of poor performances plus falling gates and

such a public display of egocentric impatience only undermined new chairman Bill Scott
and the manager. To make matters worse, the now vice-chairman was simultaneously,
and covertly, attempting to recruit Bobby Robson while Bingham was still in the role.
Tellingly, Moores and not Scott, told the Ulsterman he was surplus to requirements.
Interestingly, the future England manager claimed his meetings were with Moores and
then director Philip Carter and not the chairman.[121] Such blatant dysfunction, plus
Moores' reputation for being a difficult and overbearing boss, was off-putting for any
ambitious and accomplished manager. Bingham's later claim that he bought Latchford
merely because the board told him to get 'somebody big' shows where the ultimate
decision-making authority resided.

So instead of Don Revie, Brian Clough, Ron Saunders or Bobby Robson, Moores
ended up handing the poisoned goblet to the limited Billy Bingham and Gordon Lee.
Consequently, it is not an exaggeration to claim Everton effectively lost the hundred-year
war for Merseyside footballing supremacy by 1977 – afterwards it was a case of damage
limitation via less frequent instances of resistance both on and off the pitch.

Carter cashes out eventually

Gordon Lee took Everton to a pair of top-four finishes at the end of the decade but
where the club stood in the elite of English football was open to debate. Moores retired
in 1977 and a year later Philip Carter became chairman when the club was falling behind
the big guns of English football, as the lack of success and inferior attendances meant
Everton's annual income was broadly half (or £1 million) that of Liverpool and
Manchester United and £500,000 below Arsenal's.

Consequently, whether the club still retained the appetite – and the cash – to compete
at the top came into focus when Trevor Francis was put up for sale in early 1979. Carter
made it clear that the club would not be competing for the first £1 million domestic
footballer, revealing to Charles Lambert in the *Liverpool Echo*:

> *Francis may have made a difference to us, but weighing that against the price asked I
> have got to say that Everton considered this carefully and decided in the overall interests
> of the club that we would not participate in this particular auction…Paying ridiculous
> figures means that in one way we will unsettle the stability of the club, and therefore
> would have long-term consequences.*

[121] To complicate matters further, in a 1993 *Liverpool Echo* interview the departing Jim Greenwood revealed the only person Robson spoke to was director George Watts.

These words acted as a watershed. For the first time an Everton chairman was admitting the club no longer had the financial wherewithal to buy the best players. Consequently, apart from some big signings in the second half of the 1980s using the extra income derived from Howard Kendall's success, the club have since engaged in their own lengthy Retreat from Moscow, largely purchasing mid-ranking players, at best, while the elite have gone elsewhere. At the start of the decade, the Big Five did not include Everton – the membership being Manchester United, Liverpool, Arsenal, Nottingham Forest and Ipswich Town. The latter duo had approximately the same income as Everton, but won trophies.

One of the by-products of such a self-imposed strategy was that, unless investing in promising youngsters whose ceiling was unknown, the players purchased were largely no better than those they replaced. The consequence is stasis. That happened to Gordon Lee during the two years after Carter's admission and would have applied to his successor had Kendall not been gifted a troop of promising players and made some inspired signings from 1982-84. That applies even today.

Elsewhere during this period, the changing demographics due to the rapidly deteriorating economic climate in the city began to affect attendances and club finances. In the twenty years to 1980, the population of the city fell by 180,000 with many others dispersed to the outskirts following the notorious slum-clearance exercises. The economic decline of the 1970s witnessed a three-fold increase in unemployment. With traditional Everton fanbase strongholds in the north of the city disproportionally affected by these damaging developments, there was unsurprisingly a drastic drop in Goodison gates. After averaging close to 50,000 in the championship season of 1969/70, a decade later it was 28,000, slightly less than the break-even figure.

Yet for all the talk about board dysfunction and finances, the most important decision any club makes is the manager: get that correct and other issues can be papered over or removed. The Everton board, of course, did just that when they appointed Howard Kendall in 1981. To be fair, the move was brave but inherently risky. Although a distinguished former player, Kendall was hugely inexperienced, with just two years in management and, on face value, there were better options. However, in retrospect, the attractiveness of the appointment was that Kendall's managerial ceiling was unknown. Thankfully for Evertonians everywhere, it proved to be extraordinarily high. The adverse impact of Heysel has been vastly overstated but also true is that the European ban did not necessarily bring his team's journey to an end but froze it forever on the brink of greatness.

Five into four won't go

If the correct managerial appointment can lead to success, getting it wrong can lead to regression. And that occurred at Everton in the years after 1987. In retrospect Philip Carter was too hasty appointing Colin Harvey and should have given himself time. But with one eye looking across at Anfield, the Everton chairman was seduced by the cult of continuity when he should have acknowledged that the two clubs were at different stages of development. Liverpool were employing managers and backroom staff with a quarter-of-a-century's experience of success. Everton had Harvey only, now manager after just four years of working at first-team level. With Harvey's backroom staff featuring three former players plus a former youth coach, the appointments smacked of another example of the club, in times of change, distrusting outsiders who will challenge and instead looking inwards for a solution. Even when things were going wrong in 1990, Harvey appointed former player Jimmy Gabriel as coach. That insularity and damaging culture of narcissism has existed well into the 21st century.

That managerial appointment was the first mistake Carter made. The second was becoming president of the Football League during a time when the enervating demands of the role made it a full-time job, as various parties jockeyed for position to best take advantage of promised riches. Not only was the role a constant conflict of interest but he took his eye off the ball in the day job while Harvey and the side were struggling. His statement after being sacked as president that 'I shall now sit back and concentrate on the much more enjoyable task of supporting Everton' was not made in jest. Carter offered Kendall a guiding hand in their early years together at Goodison but with Harvey – who probably needed one more – that does not appear to have been the case.

As Carter's influence grew and Everton possessed riches from their new-found success, by the middle of the 1980s they were now included in a new Big Five with Manchester United, Liverpool, Arsenal and Spurs. A cadre of clubs with designs on mapping out their own future by dictating how the top flight should be structured and governed. Yet Everton were very much an outlier and included as a matter of happenstance. The club did not have the traditional large-scale support and appeal – and, with it, the associated commercial opportunities[122] – of Manchester United and Liverpool that, even in relatively poor seasons, afforded the kind of revenue protection which still made the best players affordable. As the decade ended and clubs were required to expand

---

[122]   Reflected in shirt sponsors. Whereas Manchester United, Arsenal and Liverpool had linked up with companies associated with the growing demand for home entertainment like Japanese technology giants Hitachi, Everton remained with Hafnia, a food company, until 1985. Only then, having increased their profile, were they able to gravitate to NEC.

commercially, cultivate a new type of wealthier fan while attracting outside investment, Everton – with a bedrock of support contained in some of the poorest areas of the country and located in a city described several years before as 'the Bermuda triangle of capitalism' – did not have the geographical, fiscal and demographic advantages of the north London rivals. The apathy of John Moores' family, who were still the major shareholders, hardly helped when strong leadership and a business vision were needed.

Those drawbacks increasingly came into play as the Premier League appeared on the horizon. With clubs enjoying extra revenues as top-flight gates increased by close to twenty per cent from their mid-1980s nadir, Everton's attendances were travelling in the opposite direction. A reduction of thirty per cent in the five years before 1992 left them very much mid-table in spectator appeal. By that time, with the mid-80s success that temporarily elevated them into the elite now a distant memory, annual revenue was returning to the norm more akin to Aston Villa, Leeds United and Manchester City. Consequently, having been a key player in the formation of the Premier League, by the time of the opening fixtures in August 1992 they were, ironically, a member of the Big Five in name only. Even now supporters talk of their natural peer group being Manchester United et al, but that myth is fifty years old.

Falling between the flawed boards

Of course, a return to the elite may have been possible with more success but the reappointment of Howard Kendall in 1990, three years after telling Patrick Barclay he would never return, undoubtedly hindered that. Understandably welcomed by supporters – and to be fair the press – the adage of never going back has never been more applicable. The warning signs were also there when Kendall selected Colin Harvey as coach in an inexplicable development.

A deeply flawed piece of recruitment was exacerbated by the equally bizarre appointment of Dr David Marsh as chairman in the summer of 1991, when a rapidly changing game dictated there was a prerequisite for considerable business acumen within any boardroom. Earlier in the year, Marsh's predecessor had hosted a meeting of the English game's powerbrokers which rubber-stamped the formation of the Premier League. Now Everton's leader was a full-time GP probably more interested in golf. Marsh may have recalled the sepia-tinted days of watching Joe Mercer and Alex Stevenson as a young man but the small point of saying 'they [Everton] are a wonderful club' rather than 'we' in his first interview as chairman spoke volumes.

On occasions too, the Everton hierarchy over the years has been in thrall to their manager. That was certainly true of the relationship between Marsh and Kendall. Even though finances were tight, considering the club was underperforming for long periods there was never a sense that their most successful manager was ever under pressure. Whether Marsh possessed the gravitas and personality to form a meaningful relationship with his manager is doubtful. Although there is an argument that Kendall's previous history had bought time, Marsh's attempts to defend his manager by citing the turnaround in fortunes a decade before always seemed unconvincing. The world of football in 1993 was vastly different to 1983. On the pitch, then there was only Liverpool to overcome, now there were probably four or five clubs. The financial gap to the elite was a chasm. The ridiculous decision of the board – if they even made one – allowing Kendall to travel to Bilbao 24 hours before the crucial FA Cup tie at Chelsea in January 1992 is in keeping with the theory he was indulged.

To be fair to Kendall, the departure of Jim Greenwood in the summer of 1993 meant his two allies from the glory years had gone. With the club drifting, his story about the attempt to sign Dion Dublin was significantly embellished to make it look like the motive for his resignation, when there were several other more compelling reasons. But the manner of the announcement of his departure, in the pressroom after the home game against Southampton in December 1993, reflected the drop in standards: a thirty-word statement scribbled on the back of a used white envelope.

By the time Kendall departed, the club was in the midst of a takeover battle which almost proved fatal. If he had stayed then there was still enough in the tank to provide stability while the ownership issue was resolved. However, Jimmy Gabriel's obvious discomfort in the caretaker role meant a replacement was required. The issue was who exactly appointed Mike Walker? Was it the passive board? Or one or both of Peter Johnson and Bill Kenwright? The likelihood is that it was all three parties and Walker was the compromise candidate. Either way the mistake was thinking the club was safe. Combined with the indifference of the Moores family and boardroom inertia over the takeover then it was no surprise performances on the pitch atrophied with the final-day escape more a case of luck than judgement.

The End

John Moores died in September 1993. Although the Premier League had started twelve months before, there was not an immediate sense of revolution in the English top flight. Only the trophy and means of viewing changed. The narrative since that football was born in 1992 is not strictly true. The first indication of a new identity was during the

1994/95 campaign when Blackburn pipped Manchester United to the title on the final day – when for the first time two league matches were broadcast live simultaneously – and a series of scandals crossed over to the news pages in the manner of today. An original and exciting narrative was beginning.

Poignantly, Moores therefore passed away during the final season of domestic football as it had existed for more than a century – a history that he had done so much to shape since entering the Everton boardroom three decades before and creating the first modern English football club. The irony, of course, is that the Premier League subsequently reflected the free-market values which Moores wanted to embrace in the early 1960s but was prevented from doing so thanks to the Football League's archaic voting structures.

After his death, a new and different history immediately played out to an audience that had been largely indifferent to the sport a decade before. Jurgen Klinsmann was followed by Dennis Bergkamp. *Fever Pitch*. Cantona went kung-fu fighting. *606* and *Fantasy Football*. Kevin Keegan said he would love it. Football came home. The cover of *Total Sport* magazine proclaimed the 'Golden age of English football is right now!' Then Beckham tried a shot from the halfway line and Arsene Wenger walked into Highbury. Three years after Moores' death, the Premier League was laying down the money-laden foundations for becoming the worldwide sporting, commercial and cultural colossus it is today.

But where did Everton fit into the brave new world of English football? Well, that question is for another time, another place.

BIBLIOGRAPHY

Everton v Liverpool: A Celebration of the Merseyside Derby, Brian Barwick/Gerald Sinstadt (BBC Books, 1988)

My Life Story, Peter Beardsley, (HarperCollinsWillow 1996)

Race, Ethnicity and Football, Daniel Burdsey (Editor) (Routledge, 2011)

The Football Business, David Conn (Mainstream Publishing 2002)

Everton: The School of Science, James Corbett (Macmillan, 2003)

Faith of our Families, James Corbett (deCoubertin, 2017)

The Everton Encyclopedia, James Corbett (deCoubertin, 2012)

Claret and Blues, Tony Cottee (Independent UK Sports Publications, 1995)

First Voice You Will Hear is, Ted Croker (Collins, 1987)

Out of Time: Why Football isn't Working! Alex Fynn, Lynton Guest (Simon & Schuster Ltd, 1994)

Shades of Gray, Andy Gray (Queen Anne Press, 1986)

Here We Go: Everton in the 1980s, Simon Hart (deCoubertin, 2016)

Out of His Skin: The John Barnes Phenomenon, Dave Hill (Faber & Faber, 1989)

Everton, The Official Complete Record, Steve Johnson (deCoubertin, 2010)

2008 Reasons Why Merseyside Is the Capital of Football, John Keith/Gavin Buckland (Robson Books, 2007)

Colin Harvey's Everton Secrets, John Keith/Colin Harvey (Trinity Mirror Sport Media 2005)

Love Affairs and Marriage, My Life in Football, Howard Kendall (deCoubertin, 2013)

Only the Best is Good Enough, Howard Kendall/Ian Ross (Mainstream Publishing, 1991)

Glory, Goals and Greed: Twenty Years of the Premier League, Joe Lovejoy (Mainstream Publishing, 2011)

Gary Lineker: Strikingly Different - A Biography, Colin Malam (Stanley Paul, 1993)

The Real McCall: Stuart McCall's Own Story, Stuart McCall with Alan Nixon (Mainstream Publishing, 1998)

The Forgotten Champions: Everton's Last Title, Paul McParlan (Pitch Publishing Ltd, 2021)

The Accidental Footballer, Pat Nevin (Monoray, 2021)

Everton Player by Player, Ivan Ponting (Hamlyn, 1998)

The Blues and I, Kevin Ratcliffe (Arthur Barker, 1988)

Cheer Up Peter Reid: My Autobiography, Peter Reid (Trinity Mirror Sport Media, 2017)

An Everton Diary, Peter Reid with Peter Ball (Futura Publications, 1988)

Everton, The Official Centenary History, John Roberts (Granada Publishing/Mayflower Books, 1978)

Everton's Z-Stars: The Men Who Made History 1984-1987, Ken Rogers/Howard Kendall (Trinity Mirror Sport Media, 2004)

The Immortals, Arrigo Sacchi, (BackPage Press, 2021)

Sharpy: My Story, Graeme Sharp (Mainstream Publishing, 2006)

So Good I Did it Twice, Kevin Sheedy (Trinity Mirror Sport Media, 2014)

The Binman Chronicles, Neville Southall (deCoubertin, 2012)

With Clough, By Taylor, Peter Taylor (Sidgwick & Jackson, 1980)

Foul Play, David Thomas (Corgi Books, 2004)

Hammered, Mark Ward (John Blake, 2010)

Determined: The Autobiography, Norman Whiteside (Headline 2007)

Rothmans Football Yearbooks, various (Queen Anne Press, 1985-94)

ACKNOWLEDGEMENTS

A BIG THANKS TO MY FELLOW TOFFEEOPOLIS COLLEAGUES –
James Corbett for copy-editing and direction, Simon Hart for proof-reading (and idea for
the title) plus Rob Sawyer for his advice and support. The websites evertonresults.com
(Steve Johnson) and efcstatto.com (Bradley Cates) were priceless resources. Also the
assistance of staff at the Liverpool, Manchester and British libraries.

INDEX

THE
END